www.wadsworth.com

wadsworth.com is the World Wide Web site for Wadsworth and is your direct source to dozens of online resources.

At wadsworth.com you can find out about supplements, demonstration software, and student resources. You can also send email to many of our authors and preview new publications and exciting new technologies.

wadsworth.com
Changing the way the world learns®

FROM THE WADSWORTH SERIES IN SPEECH COMMUNICATION

THEATRE
A Way of Seeing

Fifth Edition

Milly S. Barranger

University of North Carolina, Chapel Hill

WADSWORTH

THOMSON LEARNING

Australia • Canada • Mexico • Singapore • Spain
United Kingdom • United States

WADSWORTH
✳ ™
THOMSON LEARNING

Theatre Editor: Karen Austin
Assistant Editor: Nicole George
Executive Editor: Deirdre Cavanaugh
Publisher: Clark Baxter
Editorial Assistant: Mele Alusa
Technology Project Manager: Jeanette Wiseman
Executive Marketing Manager: Stacey Purviance
Marketing Assistant: Neena Chandra
Senior Project Manager: Cathy Linberg
Print/Media Buyer: Barbara Britton
Permissions Editor: Joohee Lee

Production Service: Electronic Publishing Services Inc., NYC
Designer: William Seabright and Associates
Photo Researcher: ImageQuest
Copy Editor: Electronic Publishing Services Inc., NYC
Cover Image: © P. Switzer/Alyssa Bresnahan as Thetis in the Denver Center Theatre Company/Royal Shakespeare Company production of *Tantalus* by John Barton, adapted by Sir Peter Hall.
Cover Printer: Phoenix Color Corporation
Compositor: Electronic Publishing Services Inc., NYC
Printer: Quebecor/World, Taunton, MA

For permission to use material from this text, contact us by
Web: http://www.thomsonrights.com **Fax:** 1-800-730-2215
Phone: 1-800-730-2214

Library of Congress Cataloging-in-Publication Data
Barranger, Milly S.
Theatre: a way of seeing / Milly S. Barranger.–5th ed.
p. cm.
Includes bibliographical references and index.
ISBN 0-534-51482-0 (pbk)
1. Theatre I. Title.
PN2037 .B32 2002
792--dc21   00-068619

Wadsworth/Thomson Learning
10 Davis Drive
Belmont, CA 94002-3098
USA

For more information about our products, contact us:
Thomson Learning Academic Resource Center
1-800-423-0563
http://www.wadsworth.com

International Headquarters
Thomson Learning
International Division
290 Harbor Drive, 2nd Floor
Stamford, CT 06902-7477
USA

UK/Europe/Middle East/South Africa
Thomson Learning
Berkshire House
168-173 High Holborn
London WC1V 7AA
United Kingdom

Asia
Thomson Learning
60 Albert Street, #15-01
Albert Complex
Singapore 189969

Canada
Nelson Thomson Learning
1120 Birchmount Road
Toronto, Ontario M1K 5G4
Canada

To Heather

CONTENTS

Part Three Theatre's Practitioners

Part Four Theatre's Modern Diversity

Part Five Theatre's Critics

PREFACE

Theatre as a way of seeing is the subject of this book. The experience of *theatre*—who sees, what is seen, and where and how it is seen—is a multifaceted subject dealing with a complex, living art. It takes a number of people engaged in the creative process to craft this living form of artistic expression. Many individuals—writers, actors, directors, designers, technicians, craftspeople, managers, producers—contribute to what is truly a collective performing art.

In the creation of a theatrical event, people make art out of themselves for others to watch, experience, think, feel, and understand. Chiefly through the actor's presence, theatre becomes humanness, aliveness, and experience. Nor does theatre exist in any book. Books only *describe* the passion, wisdom, and excitement that derives from experiencing theatre—in its motion, color, sounds, and stories.

This edition of *Theatre: A Way of Seeing* discusses theatre as a composite experience of art, life, and the human imagination. The discussions include artists, spaces, plays, designs, staging, styles, technology, productions, and performances. There are fourteen chapters, divided into five parts. Eight of the fourteen chapters deal with the complex answer to the question: What is theatre? And who are the "makers" of this collaborative form of expression? There are discussions of aesthetics, theatrical spaces, audiences, artists, creative processes, dramatic writing, forms, and conventions. Four chapters discuss playwriting, writing styles, stage language, and adaptations.

The cultural diversity and intercultural expressions of world theatre are threads woven throughout the fourteen chapters. Eastern and Western cultural and theatrical traditions, playhouses, and stages are presented in their historical and present-day contexts. Given the fact that so much has taken place in the theatre of the United States since mid-century that mirrors our multiracial and multicultural society, we have devoted a chapter to emerging companies, performers, bold texts, and intercultural artistic expression. These new companies and artists highlight contemporary responses to cultural and ethnic diversity in the American theatre of the late twentieth century (and the early twenty-first century). Finally, professional critics and their influences on productions and audiences are described, with samples of the writing styles of today's finest theatre critics.

In addition, sections of plays and theatre reviews, diagrams, definitions, and quotations are included to amplify discussion and to share artists talking about their work with readers. Eighteen photo essays also illustrate theatre's variety, its artists, architecture, critics, technology, performance styles, and notable productions.

None of these discussions, of course, takes the place of sitting with others in a theatre and experiencing the actors, text, scenery, costumes, lights, music, and sound effects in a carefully crafted event demonstrating the human imagination in its theatrical form.

Written as an introduction to the theatrical experience, *Theatre: A Way of Seeing* introduces readers to theatre as a way of seeing women and men in action: what they do and why they do it in the creation of an onstage reality. After all, Shakespeare said that "All the world's a stage,/And all the men and women merely players…" (*As You Like It*). To assist readers discovering theatre for the first time and perhaps even attending their first performances, there are "model" or representative plays used as examples of trends, styles, and forms of theatrical production. Ranging from the Greeks to the moderns, these representative plays are *Oedipus the King, The Trojan Women, Medea, Macbeth, Hamlet, Tartuffe, A Doll's House, Ghosts, The Cherry Orchard, The Little Foxes, The Caucasian Chalk Circle, A Streetcar Named Desire, The Glass Menagerie, The Bald Soprano, Waiting for Godot, Rockaby, The Zoo Story, Buried Child, Noises Off, Fences, Angels in America*, and *Glengarry Glen Ross*. Each play has a special place in the ongoing history of theatrical writing and performance. These model plays also represent, in combination, the extraordinary range and magnitude of human expression and theatrical achievement.

In addition, the complete text of Samuel Beckett's *Rockaby* is included for the reader's convenience along with excerpts from William Shakespeare's *Hamlet* and *Macbeth*, Euripides' *The Trojan Women* and *Medea*, Anton Chekhov's *The Cherry Orchard*, Luigi Pirandello's *Six Characters in Search of an Author*, Eugène Ionesco's *The Bald Soprano*, Tennessee Williams' *A Streetcar Named Desire* and *The Glass Menagerie*, Arthur Miller's *Death of a Salesman*, August Wilson's *Fences*, David Mamet's *Glengarry Glen Ross*, and Spalding Gray's *Monster in a Box*.

In this new edition, there are discussions of stage directors, such as Jerzy Grotowski, Elia Kazan, Alan Schneider, Peter Brook, Ariane Mnouchkine, Andrei Serban, Peter Schumann, Robert Wilson, Julie Taymor, Martha Clarke, and Anne Bogart; women playwrights and solo performers; producers and artistic directors; dramaturgs and literary managers, actor-voice-and-movement training; theatrical designers and production teams; and current stage and computer technologies. The photo essays illustrate contemporary stages, theatrical designs, international productions, and celebrated performances.

There are also tools to clarify questions of theatrical history, biography, definition, and example. Synopses of the model plays along with short biographies of playwrights, actors, directors, designers, producers, and critics parallel the central discussions. Other features include: a *glossary* of theatrical terms; *web sites* for research and entertainment; related *readings* and *video* sources. The "Video Library" guides the reader to recorded performances by Laurence Olivier, Jessica Tandy, Marlon Brando, James Earl Jones, Spalding Gray, Billie Whitelaw, Ruby Dee, Sidney Poitier, Kenneth Branagh, Laurence Fishburne, Spalding Gray, Anna Deavere Smith, Eric Bogosian, Laurie Anderson, Guillermo Gómez-Peña, and John Leguizamo. Many of these recordings illustrate the directing styles of Peter Brook, Elia Kazan, Jerzy Grotowski, Alan Schneider, Ariane Mnouchkine, Robert Wilson, and Julie Taymor.

Finally, this book is in no way a definitive treatment of theatre practice, history, or literature. It attempts to put readers in touch with theatre *as a performing art and humanistic event*. Most important, it introduces theatre as an *immediate* experience, engaging actors and audiences for a brief time in a special place. The Greeks called that special place—where audiences sat to watch performances—a *theatron*, or "seeing place." The idea of the "seeing place" has been our guide to understanding and enjoying theatrical writing and performance.

My thanks are due to colleagues for their encouragement and assistance in the preparation of the several revisions of this book. Those who assisted and advised on this fifth edition are artistic directors Gregory Boyd (Alley Theatre, Houston, Tex.) and Michael Wilson (Hartford Stage, Conn.); administrative director Donna Heins (PlayMakers Repertory Company, N.C.); *Fosse* production stage manager Mary Porter Hall; New York casting director Liz Woodman; Professor Emeritus at Hunter College and The Graduate School of the City University of New York Dr.

Vera Mowry Roberts; Dean of the College of Fine Arts at Webster University Peter Sargent; Marian Goldberg and Tanya Anthony of the Japan National Tourist Organization, New York; Alley Theatre Director of Public Relations Jennifer R. Garza and Resident Dramaturg Travis Marder; and colleagues at The University of North Carolina at Chapel Hill Judy Adamson, Bobbi Owen, Adam Versenyí, and Gregory Kable. Those who read an early version of the manuscript were Gayle Austin, Georgia State University; David H. Fennema, Cameron University; Kent G. Gallagher, Northern Illinois University; William Grange, University of Nebraska; Joe Karioth, Florida State University; Eric W. Margerum, Carthage College; Jared Saltzman, Bergen Community College; and E. J. Westlake, Auburn University.

Also, special thanks to my colleague Minda D. Brooks at the University of North Carolina at Chapel Hill for her invaluable assistance. Finally, editor Karen Austin of Wadsworth Publishing Company receives my appreciation for her guidance and encouragement.

Milly S. Barranger
Alumni Distinguished Professor
The University of North Carolina
Chapel Hill

*I can take any empty space
and call it a bare stage. A
man walks across this
empty space whilst some-
one else is watching him,
and this is all that is
needed for an act of
theatre to be engaged.*

PETER BROOK

The Empty Space[1]

Discovering Theatre

*While we are watching,
men and women make the-
atre happen before us. In
the theatre we see human
beings in action—what
they do and why they do
it—and we discover things
about ourselves and our
world.*

THE IMMEDIATE ART

Theatre is a performance art that places human experience before a group of people—an audience—in the present moment. For theatre to happen, two groups of people, actors and audience, must come together at a certain time and in a certain place. There, on a stage or in a special place, actors present themselves to an audience in a story usually involving some aspect of being human. The audience shares in the story and the occasion. We listen, gather information, feel emotions, and interact with the actors and their events that define in some way what it means to be a human being in circumstances both familiar and unfamiliar.

Theatre is a way of seeing men and women in action, of observing what they do and why they do it. Human beings are both theatre's subject and its means of expression. Because of its twofold connection to our humanity, theatre becomes one of the most immediate ways of experiencing another's concept of what it means to be human.

Let us ask the questions: What is theatre? How is theatre *a way of seeing*? What makes theatre different from other arts, particularly the mass media? How do we, as audiences, respond to, interact with, and experience theatre? Let us also define theatre and describe our experience of theatre. Let us consider theatre's special qualities that set it apart as a form of art: its immediacy, aliveness, doubleness, fictions, spaces, and audiences. Theatre's *immediacy* is our first concern.

THEATRE'S IMMEDIACY

Theatre always involves two groups of people, actors and audiences, and takes place in the present moment. Unlike video, television, and film, theatre is not a "canned" product to be mailed about the country, marketed in moviehouses and video stores, and broadcast to millions of people. It is a limited art because it requires that artists and audiences come together in a designated place for the few hours of the performance. That performance may, of course, be taped for television, but the theatre's special immediacy and aliveness is lost when transposed to another medium.

Theatre is most often *contrasted* with the mass media and technical arts: film, television, radio, and music videos. Certainly, there are shared influences among these arts, and artists participate in them in varying degrees. Here the comparison ends, for the mass media is the sum of its current technology, which produces, transmits, and receives an artistic product. In addition, the electronic media is forever expanding its number of spectators in various corners of the world, recording images of human experience from Kosovo, Moscow, and Beijing to beam into our living rooms in Chicago, Los Angeles, and Fargo. Theatre, on the other hand, is limited in all respects: size of auditoriums, number of spectators, technology, reproducibility, and outreach.

For theatre to happen, there must be a direct exchange between actor and spectator in the present time of the performance. Whereas we respond to the theatre event from moment to moment over a period of an hour or more, radio, film, and television require no immediate feedback from viewers. Unless we are watching television with friends, we are essentially alone with the medium.

It is undeniable that media arts have a large and significant place in our daily lives. Radio is often background music to driving a car or studying for an exam. The television set is part of our household furniture, the Internet is part of our daily lives, and the video recorder makes possible films of our own choosing in our homes. Our favorite moviehouses are numerous and widely located. In contrast, theatre is found in a comparatively small number of locations, takes place at unique hours (theatregoers say that the "curtain is at eight," meaning that the performance begins at eight o'clock), and engages us in an *active* construction of meaning in regard to human experience: Shakespeare's *Hamlet* engages us in untimely revenge and its deadly consequences; David Mamet's *Oleanna* presents us with the use and abuse of power in the classroom; María Irene Fornés' *Conduct of Life* confronts us with the family as mirror of totalitarian societies; and so on.

One vital difference between theatre and media arts is developing technology. Music videos by Britney Spears and Ricky Martin, for example, produce effects of a theatrical event, but technologies for reproducing sound, images, and permanent records on tape for worldwide dissemination are not, firstly, a part of the theatre experience. For one thing, the theatre's technology has changed little over 2,500 years. For another, theatre, unlike music video, is ephemeral. Once the theatrical performance concludes, it is gone forever. What is unique (and even disheartening) about the theatrical event is that, even as it is taking place, it is being lost to future generations. We can read about the early performances of Shakespeare's plays, but we can never fully know what it was to experience *Hamlet* on stage in the Elizabethan period. We can have our own first experience of Shakespeare's play, but we cannot make permanent our experience except in memory, photographs, or film. What is it, then, that makes this ancient art so elusive? It is the centrality of human beings—actors and spectators—to the art.

As director Peter Brook says about making theatre, "A man walks across this empty space whilst someone else is watching him, and this is all that is needed for an act of theater to be engaged." It is theatre's *immediacy* that makes it different from other arts. Theatre presents human beings playing fictional characters who move, speak, and "live" *before* us, creating recognizable people, events, and places. For a short time we share an experience with actors that is imitative, provocative, entertaining, and magical. Theatre's *living quality* sets it apart.

THEATRE'S ALIVENESS

In many ways, theatre parallels life. On stage, actors represent our humanness (our bodies, voices, minds, and souls) in an imitation of certain human truths and realities. In *Tartuffe,* for example, Molière presents the perils to a family of a phony religious person's greed; in *The Caucasian Chalk Circle,* Bertolt Brecht demonstrates the selfless act of a young woman saving a child in time of war. As we sit in the audience, we constitute a human community—a collective presence—as we laugh, cry, enjoy, and applaud.

Theatre is thus "alive" as actors tell a story in immediate communion with its audience. Film is a means of recording and preserving that "aliveness" for all time. The television program "Live from Lincoln Center" is one highly successful effort to record on videotape a stage performance with its audience. From our homes we can watch opera stars Luciano Pavarotti and Jessye Norman and hear the audience's enthusiastic response, but we are removed from the original event. We know that both theatre and film/video are equally convincing in their storytelling powers, but their modes of presentation are vastly different.

For example, the great performances of Marlon Brando and Vivien Leigh as Stanley Kowalski and Blanche DuBois in *A Streetcar Named Desire* are captured in the 1951 film. But the wonderful theatrical performances of Laurette Taylor, Jessica Tandy, Vanessa Redgrave, Natasha Richardson, and others in plays by Tennessee Williams are lost to us as the performance ends. Theatre is an evanescent art, lasting only those two or three hours it takes to see the play. The experience can be repeated night after night as long as the show is running, but once the play closes and the cast disperses, that performance is lost.

The Museum of Modern Art/Film Stills Archive

The 1951 film version of Tennessee Williams' play *A Streetcar Named Desire* captures for all time a moment between Vivien Leigh (as Blanche DuBois) and Marlon Brando (as Stanley Kowalski). Each time the film is shown (and it may be many times), film audiences experience this interaction between these two actors. A similar moment in the theatre is lost to audiences even as it takes place on stage.

Although admittedly frustrating, this intriguing quality of theatre, which critic Brooks Atkinson calls the "bright enigma," is the source of its vitality and our pleasure.

Theatre, then, is a *living* art form, continually before us in present time until that final moment when Shakespeare's Hamlet is lifted from the stage to Fortinbras' command, "Take up the bodies," or when Samuel Beckett's tramps "do not move" from the appointed place for their meeting with Godot, who never comes. Theatre also bears a unique relationship to the aliveness (and humanity) it mirrors. What are these parallels between theatre and life? There are five essential ones:

actors ⟷ humanity
simulation ⟷ reality
rehearsal ⟷ learning
improvisation ⟷ spontaneity
audiences ⟷ society

At all times in the theatre there is a doubleness. The actors are human beings playing at being other human beings; the stage is a platform that convinces us it is another world. Shakespeare said it best in *As You Like It:* "All the world's a stage/And all the men and women merely players." Theatre's doubleness—art mirroring life, life mirroring art—is another special quality of this complex art.

Jessica Tandy as Blanche DuBois with Marlon Brando as Stanley Kowalski in the original New York production of *A Streetcar Named Desire* (1947), directed by Elia Kazan.

THEATRE'S DOUBLENESS

Shakespeare and others have said that there is a doubleness about the theatrical experience that reflects a sense of life lived on stage. For instance, the audience experiences the actor both as actor—the living presence of another human being—and as fictional character. Audiences experience Ralph Fiennes as Hamlet and Laurence Fishburne as Othello. Likewise, the performing space is a stage and at the same time an imaginary world created by playwrights, designers, directors, and actors. Sometimes this world is as familiar to us as a New Orleans tenement or a Midwestern farmhouse. The stage might resemble a modern living room or a hotel room or a front yard. Sometimes it is unfamiliar, like Macbeth's blighted castle at Dunsinane, Oedipus' plague-ridden city of Thebes, or Othello's storm-tossed island of Cyprus.

The Elizabethans thought the theatre mirrored life. Shakespeare's Hamlet describes the purpose of acting, or "playing," in this way:

> … the purpose of playing, whose end, both at the first and
> now, was and is to hold as 'twere the mirror up to Nature, to
> show Virtue her own feature, scorn her own image, and the very
> age and body of the time his form and pressure. (3, ii)

Types of Contemporary Theatres

Today's theatres are found in large cities as well as in small towns. Just as their locations are diverse, so theatre buildings and stages differ in size and shape.

London's ROYAL NATIONAL THEATRE, located on the South Bank of the Thames River, was completed in 1976. The huge complex contains three theatres (the Lyttelton, the Cottesloe, and the Olivier), rehearsal rooms, workshops, offices, restaurants, and foyers. Named for English actor Sir Laurence Olivier, the Olivier Theatre has an open stage and 1,150 seats. The fan-shaped auditorium encircles the stage on three sides.

©Mike Smallcombe/Courtesy Royal National Theatre

Interior of the 400-seat COTTESLOE THEATRE, part of the Royal National Theatre complex. Modeled on an Elizabethan courtyard with balcony above and flexible seating below, it is used for all types of plays ranging from Shakespeare's *Othello* to small contemporary plays.

©Mike Smallcombe/Courtesy Royal National Theatre

The GUTHRIE THEATER, Minneapolis, built in 1963, houses a large auditorium (1,441 seats) encircling the unique seven-sided thrust stage. No seat is more than fifty-two feet from the center of the stage. The photo shows the audience's relationship to the actors and stage.

Courtesy Guthrie Theatre

The OREGON SHAKESPEAREAN FESTIVAL THEATRE in Ashland (founded in 1935) is an open-air theatre. The audience sits in front of a platform stage. A multilevel building serves as a permanent background for plays by Shakespeare and other playwrights.

Photo by Jennifer Donahoe/Courtesy Oregon Shakespeare Theatre

In the ARENA STAGE, built in 1960 in Washington, D.C., the audience surrounds the stage action. Lighting instruments are visible above the stage, and scenery and furniture are minimal. Actors enter and exit through entrances, called *voms,* for the Roman *vomitorium* or entranceways into the seating and arena in the early amphitheatres.

The EISENHOWER THEATRE, located in the John F. Kennedy Center for the Performing Arts in Washington, D.C., is a proscenium theatre or picture-frame stage. The curtain is closed, awaiting the arrival of the audience who will "discover" the play's world when the curtain rises.

The NEW AMSTERDAM THEATRE, called the "Jewel of Forty-Second Street," was built in 1903 in New York City. Its epic history includes such names as producer Florenz Ziegfield and performers Marilyn Miller, Will Rogers, Fanny Brice, Bert Williams, Jack Benny, Fred and Adele Astaire, and Bob Hope. The theatre fell into disuse and disrepair, but in 1997, the Walt Disney Company renovated the theatre and installed *The Lion King* on stage, reclaiming once again the "Jewel of Forty-Second Street."

©Whitney Cox

AMERICAN AIRLINES THEATRE, the Roundabout Theatre Company's new 740-seat flagship theatre on Forty-Second Street, New York City. Formerly the Selwyn Theatre, then a neglected B-movie house, it was transformed in 2000 to its gilded 1918 neo-Renaissance origins and renamed. The proscenium stage is seventy-five feet wide and fifty feet deep with an orchestra pit.

©Z Jedrus

Theatre and Life

Michael Cumpsty (center) as Jaques in the 1999 Williamstown Theatre Festival production of *As You Like It*.

Courtesy of Williamstown Theatre Festival/Richard Feldman

Jaques' speech from Shakespeare's *As You Like* It provides us with one of the most famous discussions on the similarities between theatre and life:

All the world's a stage,
And all the men and women merely players.
They have their exits and their entrances,
And one man in his time plays many parts,
His acts being seven ages. At first the infant,
Mewling and puking in the nurse's arms.
And then the whining school-boy, with his satchel
And shining morning face, creeping like snail
Unwillingly to school. And then the lover,
Sighing like furnace, with a woeful ballad
Made to his mistress' eyebrow. Then a soldier,
Full of strange oaths, and bearded like the pard,
Jealous in honor, sudden and quick in quarrel,
Seeking the bubble reputation
Even in the cannon's mouth. And then the justice,

In fair round belly with good capon lined,
With eyes severe and beard of formal cut,
Full of wise saws and modern instances,
And so he plays his part. The sixth age shifts
Into the lean and slippered Pantaloon,
With spectacles on nose and pouch on side,
His youthful hose, well saved, a world too wide
For his shrunk shank, and his big manly voice,
Turning again toward childish treble, pipes
And whistles in his sound. Last scene of all,
That ends this strange eventful history,
Is second childishness and mere oblivion,
Sans teeth, sans eyes, sans taste, sans everything.

(2, vii)

Chapter One

Hamlet speaks here of the Elizabethan idea that the stage, like a mirror, shows audiences both their good and bad qualities along with an accurate reflection of the times.

The Elizabethan idea of the stage as a mirror, related as it is to the act of seeing, can help us understand the dynamics of theatre and its aesthetics. Looking into a mirror is, in a sense, like going to the theatre. When we look into a mirror we see our double—an image of ourselves and possibly a background and anyone standing around the reflection. The image can be made to move; we make certain judgments about it; it communicates to us certain attitudes and concerns about our humanness. As reflected in the mirror, our humanity has shape, color, texture, form, attitude, and emotion; it is even capable of limited movement within the mirror's frame. Onstage the actor's living presence as a fictional character—as Oedipus, Othello, Hamlet, or Blanche DuBois—creates the doubleness that is theatre's special quality. It is both a stage world and an illusion of a real world.

Theatre is life's double, but it is also something more than a reflection of life. As a form of art it is *a selected reflection*. It is life's reflection *organized meaningfully* into stories and fictions about events and people.

THEATRE'S FICTIONS

Theatre presents itself as a fiction—the performance of stories about events and people. We are emotionally and intellectually pulled into the lives and feelings of the characters before us. We would like Blanche DuBois to find that handsome mythical gentle-man who will make life kind and tolerable for her, but we are made aware of her destructive tendencies with alcohol and sex, and cringe before the inevitable ending to her life.

In contrast, radio and television programming make extraordinary efforts to separate fact from fiction. Anchor people and television journalists, like Jane Pauley and Dan Rather, assure us that we are being told the facts of the day's news from Tokyo to Los Angeles; program credits on prime time television shows tell us that we are watching a fiction of Ally McBeal's law practice.

In the case of such films as *Henry V* and *Much Ado About Nothing*, Kenneth Branagh did not stage Shakespeare's plays prior to capturing the stories on film. The cutting, editing, framing, and camera movements rearranged Shakespeare's text while retaining the language pertinent to telling the story on film. The theatrical dimension is concentrated in certain scenes of *Henry V*, for example, when the comic rogue Falstaff exhorts his friend in the tavern, or when King Henry proposes marriage to Katherine of France. These are concentrated scenes like those found in a play, but in the film as a whole the rapid editing from place to place, the contrasts of faces and images, the realistic scenes of horses falling in battle and men dying, and the rearranging of the old text into useful fragments create the film.

In film, we are transported by images into new worlds of discovery. Theatre uses other means to persuade us that we are sharing in new experiences. As the proverbial curtain goes up, we enter into a form of artistic illusion that is now 2,500 years old.

THEATRE'S ILLUSION

Theatre creates the *illusion,* as we watch, that we are sharing an experience with others *for the first time.* As members of the audience we tacitly agree with the actors that, for the time of the performance, the play is a living reality. We know that theatre is not life, but we suspend this knowledge for the few hours we watch the play. We share with the actors the illusion that life is being lived on stage as we observe their actions, which can be repeated night after night. As we watch and listen, we share their experiences—both spontaneous and rehearsed. Moreover, actors contribute further to the illusion, for they are both actors and characters. We are simultaneously aware that Oedipus, the central figure in *Oedipus the King,* is Sophocles' central character and that he is being played by an actor named Sir John Gielgud. Theatre's grand fiction is twofold: that the actors are other than who they are in the present moment, and that life is taking shape before us for the first time.

In the theatre we both believe in what is happening before us ("suspend our disbelief," as the poet Coleridge said) and disbelieve in the pretense. We give way to theatre's magic and fiction as our minds and emotions are involved, yet we exist apart.

THEATRE'S SPACES

At the heart of the theatre experience, as Peter Brook suggests, is the act of seeing and being seen. That requires a special place. The word *theatre* comes from the Greek word *theatron,* meaning "seeing place." At one time or another during the history of Western culture, this place for seeing has been a primitive dancing circle, an amphitheatre, a church, an Elizabethan platform stage, a marketplace, a garage, a street, or a proscenium theatre. Today, it may be a Broadway theatre, a university playhouse, or a renovated warehouse. But neither the stage's shape nor the building's architecture makes a theatre. Rather, the use of space to imitate human experience for an audience to see makes that space special—*a seeing place.* This seeing place or theatre is where we are entertained and learn about ourselves and others. It is the place where we perceive the how, the what, and the why of our humanness in the company of others.

The three basic components of theatre are, as we shall discover, the actor, the space, and the audience. The history of theatre has been, in one sense, the record of the changing physical relationships of actor and audience. This changing relationship mirrored the changing status of audiences and the social, economic, and

(continued on page 18)

Stage Actors Perform Shakespeare in Film

In the 1990 film of *HAMLET*, starring Mel Gibson as the Prince of Denmark, Glenn Close (Gertrude), Alan Bates (Claudius), and Ian Holm (Polonius) stare in disbelief at Hamlet's antics. Directed by Franco Zeffirelli.

Gertrude (Eileen Herlie) and Claudius (Basil Sydney) try to persuade Hamlet (Laurence Olivier) to join in their festivities in the 1948 film of *HAMLET*, which Olivier also directed.

The Museum of Modern Art/Film Stills Archive

Kenneth Branagh (who also directed) as King Henry V comforts an English soldier and exhorts his troops on the battlefield of Agincourt in the 1989 film of Shakespeare's *HENRY V.*

Actor/director Sir Laurence Olivier in the title role of *RICHARD III* with Claire Bloom in the 1954 film of Shakespeare's chronicle history play.

Marlon Brando, as Mark Antony in the 1953 film of Shakespeare's *JULIUS CAESAR*, addresses the Roman mob in the famous speech that begins, "Friends, Romans, countrymen, lend me your ears ..."

Anthony Hopkins as Titus Andronicus in *TITUS*, the 1999 film directed by Julie Taymor.

Laurence Fishburne as Othello, Irene Jacob as Desdemona, and Kenneth Branagh as Iago in the 1996 film of *OTHELLO*.

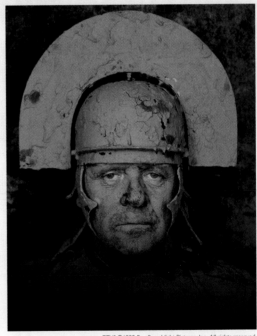

political importance of theatre to society. The audience has moved from the hillside of the Greek open-air theatre to a place before the Christian altar, to standing room around the Elizabethan theatre's platform stage, to seats in a darkened hall before a curtained proscenium stage, to the floor or scaffolds of a modern environmental production.

In the same historical sequence, the actor has moved from the dancing circle of the Greek theatre to the church, to the open stage of the Elizabethan theatre, to the picture-frame stage of the proscenium theatre, to contemporary environmental spaces. The effects of historical trends and social institutions on theatre are important. What is crucial is an understanding of the common denominators, unchanged since, as unsubstantiated legend has it, the sixth-century B.C. tragic poet Thespis introduced the first actor (himself) to converse with the chorus and created dialogue. It is no accident that the Greek word for actor is *hypokrites,* meaning "answerer." That first actor literally stepped apart and answered questions asked by the chorus.

Whether the physical space becomes more elaborate or less so, whether the performance occurs indoors or out, the actor–audience relationship is theatre's vital ingredient. In one sense, the formula for theatre is simple: *A man or woman stands in front of an audience in a special (or prepared) place, and performs an action that leads to interactions with other performers and audiences.* For some theorists, theatrical communication begins and ends with the audience.

THEATRE'S AUDIENCES

A modern audience enters a theatre lobby with an air of excitement and a sense of anticipation. There is usually a last-minute crush at the box office to pick up tickets, then to get programs and find seats. An audience is not an unruly crowd but a very special group assembling for a special occasion; it is the final, essential participant in the creation of the theatre event. The audience is the assembled group for which all has been written, designed, rehearsed, and produced.

What, then, are the audience's expectations as they wait for the house lights to dim and the curtain to rise? We find that expectations are essentially the same whether theatregoers are in the Shubert Theatre on Broadway or the Guthrie Theater in Minneapolis.

1. *Audiences expect plays to be related to life experiences.* (It goes without saying that audiences expect plays and performances to hold their attention and to be entertaining.) Audiences do not actually expect to have experienced the events taking place on stage. None of us would willingly exchange places with Oedipus or Blanche DuBois. Instead, we expect the play's events (and also the actor's performances) to be *authentic,* to "ring true," in feelings and experiences. We are moved by *A Streetcar*

Named Desire because it rings true in terms of what we know about ourselves and others. It confirms what we have studied, read, and heard about human behavior. Williams' characters and situation may not be literally a part of our lives; yet, we all recognize the need for fantasies, self-delusion, and refuge from life's harsh realities. In short, we go to the theatre expecting the performance to be an authentic representation of some aspect of life as we know it or can imagine it.

2. *Most audiences go to the theatre expecting the familiar.* These expectations are based largely on plays we have already seen or on our experiences with movies and television. Audiences enjoy the familiar in plots, characters, and situations. For this reason, daily television soap operas, like "The Young and the Restless" and "As the World Turns," are popular with all ages. Also, audiences frequently have difficulty understanding and enjoying plays from the older classical repertory or from the contemporary avant-garde. We are not as comfortable with the concerns of Oedipus or Estragon as we are with the domestic affairs of Frasier or Drew Carey.

All audiences come to the theatre with certain expectations that have been shaped by their previous theatregoing experiences. If those experiences have been limited to musicals, summer stock, or local community theatre, then they may find the first experience of a play by Anton Chekhov or Samuel Beckett a jarring, puzzling, or even boring experience. But masterpieces somehow ring true! In them we find authentic life experiences, even if the language is difficult, the situations strange, or the production techniques unfamiliar.

The response to the first American production of *Waiting for Godot* is a good example of audiences being confronted with the unfamiliar and having their expectations disappointed on their first experience with the play. Audiences in Miami and New York were baffled by it. But in 1957, Jules Irving and Herbert Blau's San Francisco Actor's Workshop presented *Waiting for Godot* to the inmates of San Quentin Prison. No play had been performed at San Quentin since the French actress Sarah Bernhardt had appeared there in 1913, and the director and actors were apprehensive.

Of the 1,400 convicts assembled to see the play, possibly not one had ever been to the theatre. Moreover, they were gathered in the prison dining room to see a highly experimental play that had bewildered sophisticated audiences in Paris, Miami, and New York. What would be the response? It was simply overwhelming. The prisoners understood the hopelessness and frustration of waiting for something or for someone that never arrives. They recognized the meaninglessness of waiting and were aware that if Godot finally came, he would probably be a disappointment.

By now, *Waiting for Godot* is no longer considered experimental, and most audiences are no longer baffled by it. It has become a classic of the modern theatre, exemplifying how initial audience expectations can change over a period of years in response to an unusual, but profound play.

Waiting For Godot

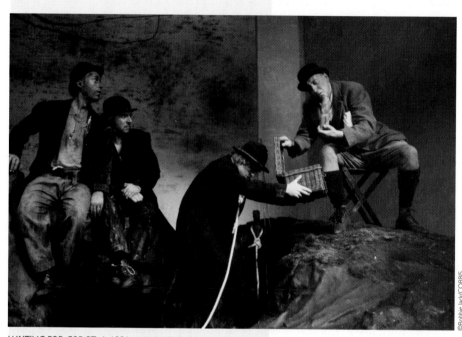

WAITING FOR GODOT A 1991 revival of *Waiting for Godot* by Samuel Beckett at the Queen's Theatre, London.

Waiting for Godot, by the Irish playwright Samuel Beckett, was first produced at the Théâtre de Babylone, Paris, in 1953. On a country road in a deserted landscape marked by a single leafless tree, Estragon and Vladimir are waiting for someone named Godot. To pass the time, they play games, quarrel, make up, fall asleep. In comes Pozzo, the master, leading Lucky by a rope tied around his neck. Pozzo demonstrates that Lucky is his obedient servant, and Lucky entertains them with a monologue that is a jumble of politics and theology. They disappear into the darkness, and Godot's messenger (a boy) announces that Mr. Godot will not come today.

In Act II, a leaf has sprouted on the tree, suggesting that time has passed, but the two tramps are occupied in the same way. They play master-and-slave games, trade hats, argue about everything. Pozzo and Lucky return, but they are not the same: The master is blind and the slave is mute. Godot again sends word that he will not come today, but perhaps tomorrow. As the play ends, Vladimir and Estragon continue waiting, alone but together. In this play Beckett demonstrates how each of us waits for a Godot—for whatever it is that we hope for—and how, so occupied, we wait out a lifetime.

Even though audiences desire to see the familiar—this is probably the reason there are so many revivals of *Arsenic and Old Lace* and *Charley's Aunt*—they also appreciate and look forward to novel experiences in the theatre. Imagine the surprise of audiences in 1970 when director Peter Brook reinterpreted Shakespeare's *A Midsummer Night's Dream,* exploring the complications of young love in a white boxlike setting with actors in circus-like clothing on trapezes. Most audiences around the world were delighted with the new concept for staging a very old play, although a few were dissatisfied by not having their expectations fulfilled.

Like all great art forms, the theatre gives us a heightened sense of life and self-awareness. Great theatre also provides a sense of *new possibilities.* We go to plays (whether consciously aware of our reasons) to realize a fuller, deeper understanding of our lives, our society, and our universe. When we are satisfied, we no longer cling to our need for the familiar.

3. *Another facet of the audience experience is the collective response.* We experience a performance as a group—as a collective thinking and feeling presence. Psychologists tell us that being in an audience satisfies a deeply felt human need: the need to participate in a collective response, whether with laughter, tears, appreciative silence, or thundering applause. As part of an audience, we become very much aware of group dynamics at the conclusion of a powerful and moving play. Sometimes when audiences are deeply moved, there are moments of silence before the beginning of applause. At other times applause is instantaneous, with audiences leaping to their feet clapping and shouting "bravo." The response to a great performance, as it was to Brian Dennehy's Willie Loman in *Death of a Salesman,* is immediate and unrestrained.

Even though applause is a theatre-going convention, it is also a genuine expression of the audience's appreciation and approval. One major element of the experience of live theatre is this sharing of feelings with others around us. Sometimes

Courtesy Shakespeare Centre Library, Stratford-Upon-Avon

A radical adaptation of Shakespeare's *A Midsummer Night's Dream* directed by Peter Brook in 1970 for Britain's Royal Shakespeare Company. Oberon (Alan Howard) and Puck (John Kane) speak Shakespeare's lines while perched like acrobats on trapezes.

Brian Dennehy (center) as Willy with Kevin Anderson and Ted Koch as Biff and Happy Loman in the 1998 revival of Arthur Miller's *Death of a Salesman* at the Goodman Theatre, Chicago. Directed by Robert Falls.

©Eric Y. Exit/The Goodman Theatre (pictured are: Kevin Anderson, Brian Dennehy & Ted Koch.)

this even happens in moviehouses, especially in horror films, but rarely does it happen when we sit before the television set at home—because we are often watching alone, or we are distracted by movements and sounds around us. An audience by definition is a sharing with others—of laughter and tears, expectations and delight.

4. *The audience or spectator is central to the theatrical event.* In recent investigations, the role of the audience as a "co-creator" has received attention. In this view, the audience comes into the performance area as an active participant sharing in the cultural, social, and political issues set forth by the production. These groups are usually not mainstream audiences. They are likely to be found today in public parks, union halls, warehouses, and community centers. In these nontraditional areas, audiences compare and contrast social and cultural experiences during and after the theatrical occasion and broaden their understanding of different cultures. As an active participant in the theatrical occasion, audiences share in defining the "global village."

TRANSITION

Theatre takes place as we watch actors present themselves before audiences in stories usually about human beings. The heart of the theatrical experience is the act of seeing and being seen; hence, theatre is "a way of seeing."

Theatre, like life, happens within the present moment and has an immediacy that most other art forms do not have, or require. For theatre to happen, two groups of people—actors and audience—must come together in a certain space. There, the actors present themselves to the audience. The space, the actor, and the audience are the three essential ingredients of the theatre event.

Contrasting theatre with film and other forms of entertainment helps clarify theatre's special qualities. Theatre's *immediacy* and *aliveness*—living actors presenting themselves before a live audience—are the most notable differences between theatre and film. Film's rapidly evolving technology also provides another significant difference.

Theatre is also an act of discovery. When the curtain goes up, we discover new worlds and share in unlooked for experiences. We also learn about ourselves, our society, and our world. While great plays raise questions about what it means to be a human being, great performances communicate this knowledge to us in fresh, entertaining, and challenging ways.

As audiences, we first experience the theatrical space as we enter a theatre, and that space influences the way we see and experience theatre.

WEB SITES

The best mega Web sites on theatre are the following:

Art and Culture/Performing Arts—Brief Introduction to Theatre as a Performing Art; Information and Links to Theatre Artists and Movements

> http://www.artandculture.com/cgi-bin/WebObjects/
> Aclive.woa/wa/movement?id=906&sel=res

Artslynx International Theatre Resources—Comprehensive, Well-Maintained, and Easy-To-Use Library of Online Theatre Resources

> http://www.artslynx.org/theatre/

Complete Guide to All Aspects of Theatre on the Net

> http://www.theatre-link.com/

A brief guide to Internet resources in theatre and performance studies:

McCoy's Guide

> http://www.Stetson.edu/departments/csata/
> thr_guid.html

Theatre Central—A First Stop for Theatre Links, Theatre News, and Theatre Information, Plus Listings of Plays in New York, London, and Regional Theatres

> http://www.playbill.com/cgi-bin/plb/
> central?cmd=start

World Wide Web Virtual Library of Theatre and Drama

> http://www.vl-theatre.com

Yahoo!'s Directory of Theatre Sites (and a search engine)

> http://www.yahoo.com/Arts/Performing_Arts/
> Theater/

International theatre sites:

Greek National Theatre

> http://www.culture.gr

Royal National Theatre, London

> http://www.nt-online.org

The Seeing Place

There are, for example, privileged places, qualitatively different from all others—a man's birthplace, or the scenes of his first love ... as if it were in such spots that he had received the revelation of a reality other than that in which he participates through his ordinary daily life.[1]

MIRCEA ELIADE

The Sacred and the Profane: The Nature of Religion

Since its beginnings, theatre has been a place for seeing—for viewing, presenting, perceiving, understanding. Places for theatre to happen are found in all societies, ancient and modern. Throughout history the theatre space has been arranged so that audiences can see and performers can be seen.

L et us begin the discovery of theatre with the places, stages, and auditoriums where it all happens. All cultures, from early to modern times, have theatrical performances and places for seeing these events. The earliest theatrical spaces were areas for performance of rituals dealing with life and death.

Ritual and Theatre

When we examine the origins of ritual and theatre, we find that both are concerned with "the things done," with emphasis on the action rather than the agent, on the concrete and actual rather than the metaphysical or spiritual. They both deal with social relationships through the enactment of those relationships by living people. The difference between them is also distinctive. The theatre confines itself to showing and saying things about social relationships; ritual does things with them to reinforce or bring about change. For example, the marriage ritual where a young woman's status is forever changed in the community and the rite of passage, or puberty rite, where a young man is initiated into adulthood are familiar rituals. But the young woman who dresses in ceremonial wedding clothes to play Rosalind in *As You Like It* is clearly an actress representing a bride, and she will do so repeatedly during the play's run. The ritual has defined social change; the theatre has shown why and how Rosalind "got her man."

First Performance Spaces

Ritual and theatre also share special places of enactment. The earliest agent or "actor" performs in a special or privileged place. The priest, the guru, the dancer, or the actor performs in a threshing circle, or in a hut, a building,

A SHAMAN PERFORMS A CEREMONIAL DANCE A Dayak shaman performs a cermonial dance-ritual for villagers in Borneo, Indonesia.

or an enclosure that is shared with the onlooker or audience. In some ritual spaces, a circular area is surrounded by spectators in much the same way that the semicircular Greek theatre is configured. In others, special buildings are constructed for the occasion and often destroyed at the end of the rite in the same sense that a modern production is "struck," or removed from the stage at the end of the play's run. Some groups moved from place to place in early societies, like today's touring companies.

For many years, theatre historians have connected the origins of theatre with agrarian and fertility rites and with *special places* for enactment of these rites. Early societies staged mock battles between death and life in which the king of the old year, representing death, perished in a duel with the champion of the new year. In these rituals we can see the beginnings of today's theatrical experience—*enactment, imitation,* and *seasonal performances*—all held in special or privileged spaces designated by the community.

Dramatic overtones were added to early ceremonies designed to win favor from supernatural powers. The rain dance ceremonies of the Native Americans of the Southwest were meant to ensure that the tribal gods would send rain to make crops grow. Early societies acted out seasonal changes—patterns of life, death, and rebirth—until their ceremonies became formalized dramatic rituals. Harvest rituals, for example, celebrated abundant food supplies. Imitation, costumes, makeup, masks, gestures, and pantomime were theatrical elements in these early rituals.

Whereas rituals of early societies were concerned with the protection of the community, theatre's most common objective is to please and entertain rather than to pacify, protect, or heal. And its audiences are not secondary to what is going on onstage, as they may very well be in the practice of ritual traditions. Theatre's audiences are central and indispensable to the theatrical experience.

Theatre deals with the mystery, history, and ambiguity of human behavior and events. Plays speak to us of individuals, as well as of groups. They hold the mirror up to our joys and our sorrows, to our questions and our tentative answers about life. Theatre aims to provoke thought while entertaining us, rather than provide concrete answers or solutions. Since the beginning of the Greek festivals, playwrights have expressed concern for the human condition. Shakespeare demonstrates the sensitivity of a supreme dramatic artist in this speech by Hamlet:

> What a piece of work is a man, how noble in reason, how
>   infinite in faculties; in form and moving how express and
>   admirable, in action how like an angel, in apprehension how
>   like a god: the beauty of the world, the paragon of animals! And
>   yet to me what is this quintessence of dust? (2, ii)

Hamlet speaks about himself, but he also speaks in universal terms about all of us. He raises questions about human nature; insights are there for those who want them. But even so, the play's essential function is to entertain. For without diversion, all else in the theatre must inevitably fail and audiences become bored, restless, "turned off." Although ritual performances are often entertaining, their objective is largely practical: crops will grow, the hunt will succeed, illness will be cured, warring tribes will be placated or defeated. In ritual, entertainment is a bonus for the onlooker; in theatre, we share in a complex experience that is simultaneously entertaining, imitative, provocative, subversive, and even magical.

Although theatre's origins share kinship with early rituals and those special places reserved for enactment of communal rites, theatre differs from ritual in several essential ways. Unlike participants in a ritual, actors create fictional characters. Actors also present themselves on a stage, or in a special place, using the playwright's words to create a sense of place and life.

What is certain in these early beginnings is that theatre, as we know it now, is a kind of ritual act performed not in a hut or other temporary structure that will be dismantled after the ceremony, but in a permanent building that will be used again and again. Theatrical space as we know it in modern terms has two components: the *stage* and the *auditorium*. And the first such permanent theatre building we know of in Western culture stands in the curve of a hillside in Greece.

WESTERN THEATRE

The Greek Theatre

Orchestra and Skene

The most celebrated theatre of fifth-century B.C. Athens, called the Theatre of Dionysus in honor of the fertility god, was an open-air structure located on the slope of the hill below the Acropolis.

In time, there were two performance areas cradled within the curve of the hillside: the dancing circle (or *orchestra*), and the area backed by the scene building (or *skene*). The chorus, usually portraying ordinary human society, performed in the dancing area. One speaking actor (later three) portrayed mythical and historical characters, first in an "empty space" and later in front of a rectangular, wooden scene building, which formed a neutral background easily representing many places—a palace, temple, house, cave, or whatever was needed. A late addition to the theatre was the wooden scene building erected on a stone foundation. The actors may also have performed in the *orchestra*, or on a raised stage, although no one knows for sure. The chorus, actors, and audience all entered the theatre through passageways called *parodoi*, and the audience stood, or were seated on the ground and later on wooden or stone benches, on the hillside "auditorium."

In the ancient Greek theatre there were no barriers between the performing area and the auditorium. The audience on the hillside had an unbroken view of actor and chorus as they do in the photo of the Theatre at Delphi. The spectators in the lower tiers near the orchestra, in fact, were so near the chorus that they were practically an extension of it.

The Chorus as Spectator

The Greek chorus, which was eventually reduced from fifty people to fifteen or twelve by the time Aeschylus, Sophocles, and Euripides were writing for the festivals, shared the audience's reactions to events and characters, and sometimes interacted with the actors. Functioning as the spokesman for the play's community or society, the chorus gave advice, expressed opinions, asked questions, and generally set the ethical framework by which events were judged. They frequently served as the "ideal spectator," reacting to characters and events as the playwrights hoped audiences would. With their costumes and masks, the chorus added spectacle, movement, song, dance, and visual interest to the occasion, and their moods heightened the story's dramatic effectiveness.

Unlike the chorus, the actor, representing a heroic figure like Oedipus or Medea, stood apart in the performance space, just as he stood apart from ordinary mortals in life. Thus, the dancing circle and the chorus formed a kind of bridge between actor and audience, serving as both commentator about and spectator for the deeds it witnessed.

The arrangement of spaces in the Greek theatre indicates how the Greeks saw their world: Classes separated by convention and social status found themselves on common ground when faced with spectacles of terror and misfortune. Individuals could measure their own experiences against the great human misfortunes enacted before them. Sophocles' *Oedipus the King* speaks to master and slave when the chorus concludes: "Count no man happy until he has passed the final limit of his life secure from pain."

THE THEATRE AT DELPHI The Theatre at Delphi, an ancient Greek theatre, is built on a hillside with seating on three sides surrounding the dancing circle, or *orchestra*. The photo shows the stone benches placed on the hillside for the audience, the flat dancing circle for the chorus (and possibly actors) at the foot of the hill, and the remains of the stone foundation of the scene building.

THE EPIDAURUS FESTIVAL THEATRE, GREECE The modern audience looks down upon the ancient *orchestra*, or dancing circle.

Aeschylus and the Athenian Festivals

Aeschylus (525/4–456 B.C.), Sophocles, Euripides, and Aristophanes are four Greek playwrights whose work has survived. Aeschylus began at an early age to write tragedies for the annual festivals in the Theatre of Dionysus, Athens, winning thirteen first prizes during his lifetime.

Sometime before or during Aeschylus' career, the features of Greek tragedy became fixed: At an Athenian festival, three groups of male players, each consisting of a chorus and two (later three) actors, competed in acting four sets of plays. Each set contained three tragedies and a satyr play, a burlesque of Greek myth, for comic relief. The plays were based on Greek legend, epic poems, or history. Costumes were formal, masks elaborate, physical action restrained; violent scenes occurred offstage. The playwright expanded and interpreted the characters and stories of legend or history.

Although Aeschylus wrote more than seventy plays, we have inherited scripts for only seven: *The Suppliants, The Persians, The Seven Against Thebes, Prometheus Bound, Agamemnon, The Libation Bearers,* and *The Eumenides.* These last three make up the *Oresteia* (458 B.C.), the only surviving Greek trilogy, or sequence of three tragedies. Its satyr play is missing.

We know little about Aeschylus as a person except that he fought at Marathon (490 B.C.) and probably at Salamis (480 B.C.) during the Persian Wars. His epitaph, which he wrote himself, shows that he was most proud of his military record:

Under this monument lies Aeschylus the Athenian, Euphorion's son, who died in the wheatlands of Gela. The grove of Marathon with its glories can speak of his valor in battle. The long-haired Persian remembers and can speak of it too.

From the classical to the Hellenistic period (c. 990–30 B.C.), the Greek theatre underwent changes: wooden seats were replaced by stone; the addition of the scene building made the actors' area more complex, providing a scenic background and dressing area; a low raised stage was probably added sometime after the fifth century B.C. for the actors to perform on. But the theatres remained in the open air, with well-defined places for the audience to sit and for the actors and chorus to perform. As we shall discover in a later chapter, the division of space and other conventions such as the formal entrances, choral odes, and two to three speaking actors dictated the structure of the plays performed there. The plays of Aeschylus, Sophocles, Euripides, and Aristophanes were shaped as much by the theatre's conventions as by the world view of the playwrights.

Tropes

The **trope,** made up of chanted dialogue, was the beginning of medieval church drama and the first step toward creating plays after the Dark Ages. The tenth-century *Quem Quaeritis,* from a Benedictine abbey in Switzerland, consisted of questions and answers sung by the two halves of the choir during an Easter Mass. The Angels and the Marys were not actually impersonated, but the seeds of character and dialogue were there. Ultimately, the trope expanded into a little play or opera. It is significant that a question and answer, so familiar to us in theatrical dialogue today, was used so long ago to introduce the Easter Mass.

QUESTION (BY THE ANGELS):	Whom do ye seek in the sepulcher, O followers of Christ?
ANSWER (BY THE MARYS):	Jesus of Nazareth, who was crucified, just as he foretold.
ANGELS:	He is not here: He is risen, just as he foretold. Go, announce that he is risen from the sepulcher.

Medieval Theatre

The medieval theatre (c. 950–1500) began in churches with Latin playlets performed by priests to teach Christian doctrine and encourage good moral behavior. (An early example is the *Quem Quaeritis* trope.) Gradually, as performances became more concerned with entertainment and spectacle, they moved out of the churches into the marketplaces. Lay performers replaced priests, and scripts grew longer and more complex, mixing the serious with the boisterous and farcical.

Like Greek and Roman practice, the medieval European theatre was an open-air festival theatre. There were few permanent structures. The plays, grouped in cycles, dealt with Biblical events and ranged from the creation to the destruction of the world. One cycle contained as many as forty-two plays. They were performed in spring and summer months on religious holidays such as Corpus Christi, Easter, and Whitsuntide. Productions were sponsored by town councils, often with the help of local priests. Religious confraternities or secular trade guilds usually produced them; they hired a director or stage manager and recruited actors from the local population, who turned out en masse to be part of the event.

Types of Medieval Staging

The variety of theatrical activity in the Middle Ages is reflected in the staging. Every place was potentially a site for theatre: streets, churches, guild halls, private manor

©Giraudon/Art Resource, NY

houses, open fields, marketplaces, and innyards. In general, there were two approaches: fixed (or linear) stages, and movable (or single-focus) stages.

FIXED STAGES   Precursors of medieval *fixed stages* are to be found in the permanent Greek and Roman theatres and in the Christian churches with their aisles, naves, and raised altars. The movable stage had its beginnings in the medieval processions that celebrated religious and state occasions. We can see the influence of the medieval theatre on our own fixed and movable stages, including open-air theatre buildings, amphitheatres, street and festival stages, and holiday parades with floats.

VALENCIENNES, FRANCE   One of the best-known fixed stages was constructed in 1547 for the Valenciennes Passion Play, in northern France. Other important medieval fixed stages include the Roman amphitheatres, the "rounds" in Cornwall, England, and the stages, like the Valenciennes stage, set up in public squares in France.

The fixed stage at Valenciennes was a rectangular platform with two chief areas. One contained the "mansions," or huts, which depicted specific locales; the other was the *platea,* an open playing space. There were no scene changes as we know them in our theatre. The actor merely went from hut to hut to indicate change in

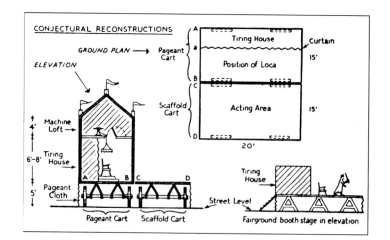

Courtesy Columbia University Press

A CORNISH CIRCULAR AMPHITHEATRE (FIXED STAGE)

A typical permanent open-air theatre in Cornwall (also called a *round*) was made out of earth with circular turf benches surrounding a level area 130 feet in diameter. Openings on two sides of the earthen mound provided entrances and exits. This diagram (of the fourteenth-century theatre at Perranzabulo) shows the staging for a Biblical cycle called *The Resurrection of Our Lord Jesus Christ*. There are eight scaffolds located in the round's center. Action requiring a specific locale took place on the scaffolds; actors progressed from one scaffold to another around the circle. The audience, seated on the earthen tiers of seats, could follow the scenes with ease.

locale. Heaven and hell were usually represented on each end of the stage, with earthly scenes of humor, travail, and so on occurring between them. The fixed stage made it possible to present numerous scenes and actors, along with the required costumes, properties, and special effects.

In Cornish amphitheatres, the audience probably viewed the action from two or more sides. When the stage was the platform type, viewers might be grouped around three sides of the playing areas, or they might gather at the front only. Whichever way, the stage was always in the open air; there was a definite performing space for the actors and a definite audience area. Actors were close to the audience, and performances sometimes continued from dawn to dusk.

PROCESSIONAL OR MOVABLE STAGES   Although fixed stages were common in many parts of Europe, theatrical space sometimes took on entirely different forms. In England and Spain, for example, the pageant wagon or processional, or portable, staging was used. The pageant wagon (in Spain called a *carro*) was a platform on wheels, something like our modern parade float. It was a portable playing area with a hut on top for the actors, which could also serve as a scenic background or acting area. No one is certain of the wagons' dimensions, but they had to move through the

AN ENGLISH PAGEANT WAGON

Glynne Wickham's drawing is a conjectural reconstruction of an English pageant wagon and ground plan of the overall playing arrangement. The drawing shows the essential features of an Elizabethan playhouse: a platform acting area, a tiring-house with a recessed area (the *loca*) for interior scenes, a space for costume changes, and an area above the cart for machinery.

Glynne Wickham, Early English Stages

narrow streets of medieval towns. The wagons stopped for performances at a number of places and may have been used individually or in groups.

The audience stood around the wagons to watch, so the actors were very close to the audience, just as they were on the fixed stage. The flexible playing space encouraged vigorous action (especially by the Devil, who was energetically booed and hissed); episodic, loose-knit plot structure; and some sort of scenic element to fix locale. *The Crucifixion Play,* one of thirty-two surviving plays of the English Wakefield cycle (c. 1375), is based on Biblical scenes of Christ's torture at the hands of soldiers, followed by his death on the cross. The cycle requires continuous action from the scourging of Christ to raising him on the cross to his death.

The Elizabethan Theatre

By the late sixteenth century, permanent structures were being built in England and Europe to house a new kind of theatrical entertainment, one that was losing its ceremonial and festive qualities and focusing more on plays with commercial appeal performed by acting companies. In 1576, James Burbage built London's first theatre, naming it simply "The Theatre." It was an open-air structure that adopted features from various places of entertainment: innyards, pageant wagons, banquet halls, fixed platforms, and portable booth-stages.

Shakespeare's Globe

In 1599, Richard Burbage, James's son and leading actor for The Lord Chamberlain's Men (Shakespeare's company), and associates built the Globe Theatre, which became a showcase for Shakespeare's talents as actor and playwright. The most famous of all Elizabethan theatres, the Globe was an open-air building with a platform stage in the middle surrounded on three sides by open standing room. This space was surrounded in turn by a large enclosed balcony topped by one or two smaller roofed galleries. The stage was backed by a multilevel facade as part of the superstructure, called the tiring-house. On the stage level were places for hiding and discovering people and objects, highly influenced by the variety of medieval stages with their many huts or mansions. A roof jutting out above the stage platform was supported by two columns; the underside of the roof, called "the heavens," was painted with moons, stars, and planets. After paying an admission fee, the audience stood around the stage or, for an additional charge, sat in the galleries or private boxes. Like the medieval audience, they were never far removed from the performers.

With little scenery and few properties by today's standards, the Elizabethan theatre encouraged both playwright and actor to create unlimited illusions, transporting the audience from Juliet's tomb in one play to a raging storm at sea in another.

THE GLOBE THEATRE An enlargement of a theatre labeled "The Globe" from the engraving by J. C. Visscher, c. 1616.

By permission of the Folger Shakespeare Library

William Shakespeare

Courtesy Shakespeare Centre Library,
Stratford-Upon-Avon

William Shakespeare (1564–1616) was an Elizabethan playwright of unsurpassed achievement. Born in Stratford-upon-Avon, he received a grammar-school education and married a twenty-six-year-old woman when he was eighteen. He became the father of three children, Susanna and twins Judith and Hamnet.

Few other facts about Shakespeare's life have been established. By 1587–1588 he had moved to London, where he remained until 1611, except for occasional visits to his Stratford home. He appears to have found work almost at once in the London theatre as an actor and a writer. By 1592 he was regarded as a promising playwright; by 1594 he had won the patronage of the Earl of Southampton for two poems, *Venus and Adonis* and *The Rape of Lucrece*.

In 1594–1595 he joined James Burbage's theatrical company, The Lord Chamberlain's Men, as an actor and a playwright; later he became a company shareholder and part owner of the Globe and Blackfriars theatres. He wrote some thirty-seven plays for this company, suiting them to the talents of the great tragic actor Richard Burbage and other members of the troupe. Near the end of his life he retired to Stratford as a well-to-do country gentleman.

Shakespeare wrote sonnets, tragedies, comedies, history plays, and tragicomedies, including some of the greatest plays written in English: *Hamlet, King Lear, The Tempest, Macbeth,* and *Othello*.

Theatrical Influences

The Elizabethan theatre, like that of Greece and medieval Europe, was a festive theatre depicting cosmic drama that touched all people: peasant, artist, merchant, and noble. Its architecture, as we shall see, affected the structure of the plays written for it. Yet it all happened so long ago. What is our interest in these ancient modes of theatre, whose traditions are often so hard to trace? Do they really tell us anything about our own theatre buildings and stages? Are they related to the buildings and performance spaces that we think of as being so modern?

The answer is yes, and you will agree the next time you see a Mardi Gras, a mummers' float, or an open-air theatre designed for summer productions of Shakespeare. In large parks, plays with historical themes are performed outdoors for audiences looking for family entertainment; touring groups travel widely to college campuses with portable stages, costumes, and properties to present plays about current themes. And street theatre performers aided by puppets, mimes, musicians, loudspeakers,

(continued on page 36)

Elizabethan Theatres and Modern Reconstructions

The De Witt drawing of the SWAN THEATRE (left) in London dates from about 1596; it is the first sketch we have of the interior of an Elizabethan theatre. In *The Globe Restored* (1968), C. Walter Hodges describes the Elizabethan theatre as self-contained, adjustable, and independent of any surroundings other than its audience.

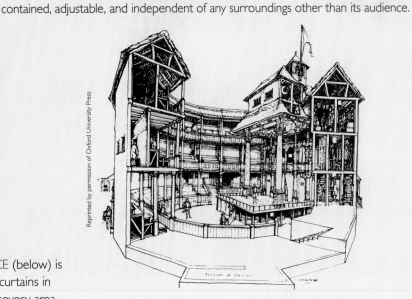

The INNER STAGE or DISCOVERY SPACE (below) is thought to be a small, recessed area with curtains in the tiring-house wall. Hodges shows a discovery area surrounded by curtains. The permanent upper level or upper stage is a characteristic feature of the Elizabethan stage; it was used for scenes such as the balcony scene in *Romeo and Juliet*. Hodges' reconstruction of the inner and upper stages brings them forward into the main acting area.

The Hodges' detailed reconstruction (above) of the GLOBE PLAYHOUSE (1599–1613) shows the building's superstructure, with galleries, yard, and railed stage. Notice the trapdoor in the stage, stage doors, curtained inner and upper stages, tiring-house (as backstage area with workrooms and storage areas), hut with machines, "the heavens," and playhouse flag.

It is generally agreed that the TIRING-HOUSE (right) (the area around and within the house wall at the back of the stage as shown in Hodges' drawing) was divided from the stage by hangings of some sort, usually curtains opening in the middle.

A MODERN FESTIVAL THEATRE
The "Elizabethan Theatre" at the Oregon Shakespeare Festival in Ashland is a modern reconstruction similar to the Fortune Theatre in Shakespeare's London. The stage and seating areas were renovated in 1992. The theatre, seating 1200, remains open to the sky.

and colorful displays trumpet political and social messages with the spectacle and passion of a medieval pageant.

The Proscenium Theatre

The proscenium theatre dates from the Italian Renaissance of the early seventeenth century. The Farnese Theatre built in 1618 at Parma was one of the early proscenium theatres. An ornamental facade framed the stage and separated the audience from the actors and scene.

The development of the proscenium arch, framing the stage and masking its inner workings, brought innovative scenery and painting techniques. Renaissance architects painted perspective scenery on large canvas pieces placed on a raked, or slanted, stage. In the seventeenth century, an architect named Giambattista Aleotti created a new system for changing scenery with movable, two-dimensional wings painted in perspective. This method, now called a wing-in-groove system (because grooves were placed in the stage floor to hold the scenery), replaced the raked stage.

SHAKESPEARE'S "NEW" GLOBE The theatre is a modern reconstruction on Bankside, Southwark, London, seats 1,401 (including standing room for 500 in an uncovered yard). It opened in 1996.

©Churchill & Klehr

AN EARLY PROSCENIUM THEATRE The Farnese Theatre in Parma, Italy, was one of the earliest to have a permanent proscenium arch. Our modern proscenium theatre with perspective scenery had its origins in Italy. Between 1500 and 1650, a typical theatre eventually developed with an auditorium, painted scenery, proscenium, curtain, and musicians' pit. Spectacle, illusion, and entertainment were its primary purpose.

PAINTED SCENERY The principles of perspective painting were introduced to theatrical scene design in the sixteenth century. Perspective scenery was painted to create the illusion of large streets or town squares, with houses, churches, roofs, doorways, arches, and balconies, all designed to appear exactly as they would seem to a person at a single point. This kind of painted background was intended to give a sense of depth to the scene. In his book *Architettura*, Sebastiano Serlio (1475–1554) explained the construction and painting of scenery for comedy, including the houses, tavern, and church shown in the drawing.

Most of the theatres built in the Western world over the last 350 years are proscenium theatres. The concern of scenic designers working within this *picture-frame stage* was to create *illusion,* that is, to use perspective scenery and mobile scenic pieces to achieve the effect of life being lived within the picture frame. The result was literally to frame the actors so that an audience, sitting in an enclosed, darkened space, could observe the actors in their setting. Playgoers were confined to the tiered galleries and to the orchestra or pit, as the ground-level seats were called.

The Proscenium, or Picture-Frame, Stage

THE EISENHOWER THEATRE This is a proscenium theatre at the John F. Kennedy Center for the Performing Arts in Washington, D.C. The audience is seated before the Eisenhower Theatre's closed curtain.

As audiences grew larger and playhouses became more profitable in the eighteenth century, the auditoriums of public theatres increased steadily in size. As auditoriums expanded, theatre architects added boxes for the affluent and cheap seats in the galleries for the less well-off. In the nineteenth century the proscenium opening was enlarged to exploit the pictorial possibilities of the stage space. The auditorium was made shallower so that the audience was drawn closer to the stage, where spectators could see the actors' expressions and the details of their environment.

Today our proscenium theatres (many built in the early 1900s) contain a framed stage with scenery, machines, lighting, and sound equipment; an auditorium (possibly with balconies and orchestra pit) seating 500 to 600 or more; and auxiliary rooms, including foyers, box offices, workrooms, dressing rooms, and storage space.

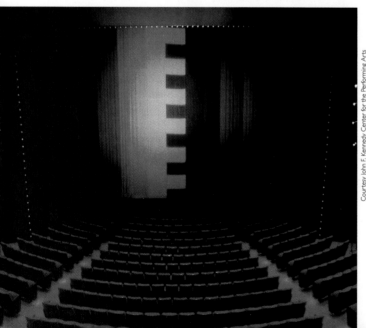

Courtesy John F. Kennedy Center for the Performing Arts

THE BOX SET FOR *THE CHERRY ORCHARD* The setting for the 1904 Moscow Art Theatre production of *The Cherry Orchard* includes box set (with ceiling), details of a recognizable room (notice the doors, windows, curtains, furniture, dog), and morning light coming through the windows as essential details.

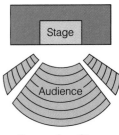

Proscenium Stage

The function of the proscenium theatre is to create illusion. In this complex, technicians, designers, directors, playwrights, and actors collaborate to create recognizable worlds. For instance, the box set of Anton Chekhov's *The Cherry Orchard* (1904) contains the world of the play—Madame Ranevskaya's drawing room on her bankrupt estate in rural Russia at the turn of the century.

In the proscenium theatre, the stage is usually hidden by a curtain until it is time for the play's world to be "discovered" by the audience. Staging, scenery, lighting, sound, and production style all work together to suggest that inside the proscenium arch is a self-contained world. The room may look like a typical living room. The street, barroom, garden, factory, or railway station may resemble places audiences know. But in the proscenium theatre, audiences are intentionally kept at a distance. They are primarily onlookers or witnesses to an event.

The Thrust, or Open, Stage

Variations of the proscenium theatre often display features from Elizabethan inn-theatres and open stages. Today's thrust or open stage is an example. Thrust stages were largely designed to minimize the separation of actor and audience

THE THRUST STAGE AT THE STRATFORD (ONTARIO) FESTIVAL THEATRE The stage has a permanent facade or background resembling the Elizabethan tiring-house.

created by the proscenium arch and the recessed stage. The actor literally performs on a platform that thrusts into the audience, and audiences have a keen sense of the actor's presence in direct communication with them, sharing the spoken word and the world of the play.

EASTERN THEATRE

The theatrical traditions of Eastern cultures comprising dozens of countries have been curiously removed from the West for centuries by geography, politics, and culture. The drama of India is first known to Westerners in the form of Sanskrit drama-theatre. Popular for more than a thousand years, Sanskrit drama was succeeded by regional dance-drama, named *Kathakali* ("story play"), based on the many stories found in the two great Indian epics, *Ramayana* and *Mahabharata*. The music-drama (*xiqu*) of China flourished in the thirteenth century during the Yuan Dynasty, with the Chinese opera becoming the dominant theatrical form by the mid-nineteenth century. The Japanese Noh theatre, developed in the late fourteenth century and unchanged since the seventeenth century, has only recently influenced Western directors and designers. The same is true of Kabuki performances, despite their popularity in Japan since 1600.

The Chinese Theatre

The Classical Theatre

China enjoyed one of the theatre's golden ages during the Yuan Dynasty (1279–1368), the period during which the Italian explorer Marco Polo visited China and returned to tell Europeans of the wonders of this civilization. Yuan dramatists created the classical drama (*zaju*) of China with stories drawn from history, legend, epics, and contemporary events that advocated the virtues of loyalty to family and friends, and devotion to work and duty. The staging traditions in this period required a bare stage, with one door on either side at the rear for exits and entrances, and an embroidered, decorative tapestry hanging between the two doors. Performers (both men and women) wore makeup, colorful clothes of the period with long wide sleeves, and beards for the men.

Each play consisted of four acts with ten to twenty songs or arias, all sung by the main character. If the dramatic action was too complicated to be represented in four acts, a wedge (*chieh tze*), one or two short arias, provided a prologue or interlude. Simple, unadorned musical accompaniment using a seven-tone scale was played onstage by an orchestra consisting of gong, drums, clapper, flute, and *p'ip'a* (a plucked instrument similar to a lute).

The "New" Drama: Kunqu

During the Ming Dynasty (1368–1644), a new drama (*kunqu*) emerged in the southern province of Hangchow, where Tang Xianzu (or T'ang Hsien-tsu) perfected plays with five or more acts accompanied by five-tone scale music. The performance style did not differ remarkably from earlier staging. The great texts of the Chinese classical theatre were written by Kuan Han-ch'ing (called the father of Chinese drama), Tang Xianzu or T'ang Hsien-tsu, Wang Shih-fu, Kao Ming, Shen Ching, Kung Shang-len, and Li Yu.

The Opera, or Jingxi

By the mid-nineteenth century, the dominant theatrical form of the Chinese capital Beijing (earlier Peking) was *Jingxi*, or Beijing Opera. Primarily a theatrical rather than a literary form, its emphasis is upon rigidly controlled conventions of acting, dancing, and singing rather than upon a text.

Many conventions of Beijing Opera, like theatrical conventions the world over, are related to the architectural features of the playhouse. The earliest stages were probably the porches of temples, or other temporary outdoor stages. The traditional stage is an open platform, often square and raised a few feet above the ground, covered by a roof supported by lacquered columns. It is equipped with a carpet, two doors in the rear wall (the one on stage right is used for all entrances and that on stage left for all exits), and hanging between the doors, a large embroidered curtain. The only permanent properties are a wooden table and several chairs.

Many of the early public theatres were temporary. In the seventeenth century actors began to perform in *teahouses* where customers were seated at tables. When permanent theatres were built, this arrangement was retained and the ground floor was fitted out with tables and stools at which spectators were served tea while watching the play. The permanent theatres also included a raised platform around the sides and back of the auditorium where poorer spectators sat on benches. A balcony, divided into sections much like the boxes of the Western theatre, was also added. In some periods the balcony was occupied by the wealthy class; in others, entirely by women. After the Chinese Republic was formed in 1912, the auditoriums were changed to include Western-style seating, but audience behavior changed very little. Spectators still carry on conversations, eat and drink, and come and go freely, usually remaining for their favorite passages while ignoring others.

The performance conditions for the music drama are rigid: rapid changes of place are possible through speech, action, or properties. To circle the stage indicates a lengthy journey. The table and chairs are transformed by a prescribed formula into a law court, banqueting hall, or interior scene. For example, an incense tripod on the table indicates a palace; paper and an official seal indicate an office; an embroidered divided curtain hung from a bamboo pole indicates an emperor's chamber, and so on. Throughout the performance, assistants dressed in ordinary street clothes help the actors with their costumes and bring on or remove the properties as needed.

From the Chinese in Modern Times (1975), Colin Mackerras

EARLY CHINESE STAGE A performance of a drama during the Yuan period (1280–1368). The five men in the foreground are the actors. Behind them are the musicians. The bearded musician on the left is playing a drum; behind him, to his left, a musician is playing a *ti-tzu*; the second musician from the right is playing a clapper. Behind the stage there is a curtain. From a wall painting in a temple in Shansi province, 1324.

$\mathcal{P}$laywright

Tang Xianzu

©Liu Liquin/ChinaStock

Tang Xianzu, also Tang Hsien-tsu, (1550–1616) was one of the finest Ming dynasty dramatists whose four plays—called the "Four Dreams"—develop the theme that life is an illusion. The most admired of the four, *The Peony Pavilion,* tells the story with poetry and music (adapted from tunes of the time) of a girl who pines away for a lover that she has seen only in a dream. The lover appears at her grave, and she is resurrected. Romantic love, dreams, and the supernatural provide the emotional impact of the famous play.

THE PEONY PAVILION This 400 year-old *kunqu* drama, directed by Chen Shi-Zheng, was performed in its complete 19-hour form as part of the 1999 Lincoln Center Festival in New York City. Written in 1598 by Tang Xianzu (a contemporary of William Shakespeare), *Peony* is based on the most universal myths: resurrection from the dead in which a devoted savior descends to the netherworld to restore a loved one to life. But there is always a price to be paid: natural law is rarely overturned without penalty and pain. The struggles against human limitations is one of the great recurring themes of Eastern and Western art.

©Stephanie Berger Photography

©Liu Liqun/ChinaStock

Music is an integral part of every opera performance. It provides atmospheric background, accompanies the many sung passages, controls the timing of movements, and welds the performance into a rhythmical whole. The string, wind, and percussion instruments of the Chinese orchestra have no counterparts in the West. Much of the onstage action is performed to a musical background, and entrances and exits are signaled by brass gongs and symbols.

BEIJING OPERA PRODUCTION   The heart of the Beijing Opera is the actor. On a bare stage furnished with only a few properties, the colorful and lavishly dressed actors speak, sing, and move according to prescribed conventions. The male bearded roles (*sheng*) include scholars, statesmen, patriots, and similar types. Actors playing these roles wear simple makeup and, except for the young heroes, beards. The female roles (*dan*) are subdivided into six types: the good and virtuous wives and lovers, coquettish types, warrior maidens, young unmarried girls, evil women, and old women. Originally, all *dan* roles were played by women, but in the late eighteenth century actresses were forbidden to appear. After 1911, actresses returned to the stage and have now largely supplanted the male *dan* actors. The *ching* roles include warriors, courtiers, gods, and supernatural beings and are characterized by painted faces in brilliant patterns. The comic actor (*chou*), who combines the skills of a mime and an acrobat, speaks in an everyday dialect and is the most realistic of the characters.

The actors' heavily patterned and colorful costumes likewise signify the wearers' ages, social status, and types. Color is always used symbolically: yellow for royalty, red for loyalty and high position, and dark crimson for barbarians or military advisors. Designs also have symbolic significance: the dragon is the emblem of the emperor; the tiger stands for power and masculine strength; the plum blossom for long life and feminine charm. The actors' visual appearance is completed with makeup and beards for the *sheng* actors. The female roles, with the exception of old women who wear very little makeup, require white painted faces with the eyes surrounded by a deep red,

Actor

Mei Lanfang in *The Peony Pavilion* (1959).

Mei Lanfang

Mei Lanfang (1894–1961), one of the greatest of all Asian actors, was born in Beijing of an old theatrical family and trained at the Fuliancheng school there. He made his professional debut at the age of ten and became noted in *dan* (female) roles. He acted chiefly in Beijing until the Japanese occupied Manchuria in 1931; he moved to Shanghai and then to Hong Kong during the war years. He returned to Beijing in 1949 and remained there until his death in 1961.

Tours to the United States, Europe, and Russia in the 1930s established his fame and popularity as the foremost Chinese performer and brought the traditions of Beijing Opera to the West. He excelled in the female roles and in the aristocratic *kunqu* drama. His appearances in theatres in Moscow, Berlin, London, and Paris made lasting impressions on the leading theatre people of the day, including Bertolt Brecht, Vsevolod Meyerhold, and Sergei Eisenstein.

shading into pink. The clown's distinguishing feature is the white patch around the eyes with distinctive black markings.

The actor's delivery of lines is controlled by convention: each role has a required vocal timbre and pitch; spoken passages are governed by strict rhythms and tempos; each word is accompanied by hand and arm gestures that have codified meanings.

Once the communist government assumed control over mainland China in 1949, a number of changes were made in Beijing Opera to make subjects and ideas conform to communist goals. In its traditional form, Beijing Opera is now most fully preserved on Taiwan and to a lesser extent in Hong Kong and Singapore. Although Western influences have brought about changes in Chinese theatre and spoken drama, the Beijing Opera and its symbolic conventions continue to fascinate Westerners and influence modern productions.

Japanese Theatre

Theatre in Japan is a popular cultural activity for millions of modern Japanese. The major theatrical centers are located in Tokyo, Osaka, and Kyoto, but there are performances by a variety of companies throughout Japan. The origins of present-day Japanese theatre are found in written accounts dating from the eighth century A.D., but rituals predate these writings. Since the late fourteenth century, the range of

(continued on page 48)

Eastern Influences on Western Theatre

The Caucasian Chalk Circle . Pacific Overtures . Richard II .

The King Stag . Les Atrides . Drums on the Dike

Courtesy of Berliner Ensemble

Bertolt Brecht's production of *THE CAUCASIAN CHALK CIRCLE* at the Theater am Schiffbauerdamm, in (formerly East) Berlin, in 1954 shows the influence of Eastern theatre. In the photo, Grusha journeys with the child to the mountains. On a bare stage she mimes her long journey before a simple white curtain with pine trees in the center.

Martha Swope/TimePix

Kabuki costumes, like the one worn by this principal actor in *PACIFIC OVERTURES,* are made of layers of richly embroidered, hand-painted kimonos. This elaborate 1975 Broadway musical was directed by Harold Prince, with lyrics by Stephen Sondheim and dazzling costumes by Florence Klotz.

Shakespeare's *RICHARD II,* as directed in 1981 by Ariane Mnouchkine for her celebrated company, the Théâtre du Soleil (Paris), was visually modeled on the grand theatrical styles of the Kabuki and Noh theatres. Designer Jean-Claude Barriera's costumes are a mix of Japanese and English period dress. Here, actors stand in classical Japanese poses, clad in layered clothing, cutaway kimonos, belted sashes, and heavily lined makeup.

THE KING STAG by Carlo Gozzi in the 1991 American Repertory Theatre (Cambridge, Mass.) production, directed by Andrei Serban, designed by Julie Taymor and Michael Yeargan with Eastern costumes, masks, and puppetry influences.

©Martine Franck/Magnum Photos, Inc.

LES ATRIDES A scene from *THE LIBATION BEARERS* in Théâtre du Soleil's production of the story of the House of Atreus from the plays by Euripides and Aeschylus, staged by Ariane Mnouchkine in 1992.

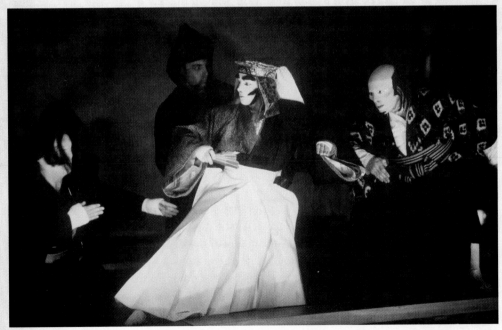

©Martine Franck/Magnum Photos, Inc.

DRUMS ON THE DIKE (TAMBOURS SUR LA DIGUE), a 1999 production of the Théâtre du Soleil with text by Hélène Cixous based on an ancient marionette play using actors as puppets. Staged by Ariane Mnouchkine in the style of Japanese Bunraku.

Courtesy Japan National Tourist Organization, New York

THE NOH STAGE The stage is a square, polished cedar platform open on three sides; it has a temple roof and a back wall with a painted pine tree. In this photo the National Theatre of Japan performs for a modern audience. The musicians and chorus surround the principal actor (*shite*) on two sides; the audience is seated in front and to the left of the stage.

performance genres and styles has proliferated from early performances (labeled *kagura*) at Shinto festivals to the serious Noh plays and comic Kyogen forms favored by the imperial courts and shogunates, to the latter-day Kabuki and Bunraku plays. Noh and Kabuki are the best-known Japanese performance styles in the West today.

Noh Theatre

The Japanese Noh theatre was established in the fourteenth century and has maintained its present form since the seventeenth century. Unlike Western drama, it is highly stylized and depends heavily on music and mime.

THE NOH STAGE   The Noh stage is situated in a corner of a building at the audience's right hand. A temple roof rises above the stage floor, which is divided into two areas: the stage proper (*butai*) and the bridge (*hashigakari*). All elements on this stage, including the four columns supporting the roof, have names and significance during performances.

The stage proper is divided into three areas: The largest is about eighteen feet square and marked off by four pillars and roof; at the rear of the stage are the musicians—a flute player and two or three drummers; and to the left of the main area sits the six- to ten-member chorus. The stage's two entrances are the bridge, a railed gangway that leads from the dressing room to the stage that is used for all important entrances, and the "hurry door." Only three feet high, the hurry door is used by minor characters, musicians, chorus, and stage assistants. Three small pine trees in front of the bridge symbolize heaven, earth, and humanity. Another pine tree, symbolizing the play's earthly setting, is painted on the center wall behind the musicians. This wall forms the scenic background for all Noh performances.

NOH ACTORS   Like the stage, all features of a Noh performance are carefully controlled and fixed by tradition. The principal character (*shite*) is usually an aristocrat, lady, or supernatural being. The actor playing this character performs facing the column at the downstage (nearest the audience) right corner. The downstage left column is associated with the secondary character (*waki*).

The conventions of performance are handed down from one generation of actors (all male) to the next. Every movement of the hands and feet and every vocal intona-

MASK-MAKING The ancient craft of *mask-making* for the Noh theatre has been handed down from one generation of artists to the next. The masks are made of wood and painted. The purity and simplicity of the Noh mask reflect the highly formal theatrical tradition of which it is a part.

tion follow a set rule. The orchestra supplies a musical setting and controls the timing of the action. The chorus sings the actor's lines while he is dancing, and narrates many of the play's events. Song and dialogue outline circumstances.

Some Noh actors wear painted wooden masks that designate basic types: men, women, elderly persons, deities, monsters, spirits. The silk costumes and headdresses are rich in color and design.

Kabuki Theatre

By about 1600 the Noh theatre was replaced in popular taste, first by the Bunraku puppet theatre and then by Kabuki. Whereas Noh largely remained the theatre of the court and nobility, Kabuki—which originated in Edo, Kyoto, and Osaka, and was less formal and restrained—had more popular appeal. The modern Kabuki stage is a rare combination of the old and the new, of thrust- and proscenium-type stages.

THE KABUKI STAGE   The Kabuki stage covers the entire front of the theatre and is approached by a ramp, called a *hanamichi,* or "flower way," which is a raised narrow platform connecting the rear of the auditorium with the stage proper. The

performers (all male) make dramatic entrances and exits on this runway. Occasionally, they perform short scenes on the *hanamichi* as well, literally in the middle of the audience.

The proscenium stage is long (some as long as ninety feet) but has a relatively low opening. Visible musicians (usually seated stage left) generally accompany the stage action. Kabuki plays originally required a full day in performance but today are about five hours long. They deal with vendettas, revenge, adventure, and romance, and feature elaborate and beautiful scenic effects, including a revolving stage that was developed in Japan before it was used in the West.

MODERN KABUKI The theatrical excitement and commercialism of modern Kabuki are illustrated by the painted scenery, elaborate costumes, musicians, and the *onnagata* in a climactic pose atop a giant bell.

Courtesy Japan National Tourist Organization, New York

KABUKI ACTORS   Like Noh actors, Kabuki actors are trained from childhood in singing, dancing, acting, and feats of physical dexterity. Kabuki roles are divided into such basic types as brave and loyal men, villains, comic roles, children, and women's roles. Male actors who play women's parts are called *onnagata*. They are

The Théâtre du Soleil production of *Drums on the Dike* uses actor as puppets in the style of Bunraku theatre to tell a universal story of greed and environmental catastrophe.

© Martine Franck/Magnum Photos, Inc.

$\mathcal{P}$laywright

Chikamatsu Monzaemon

From Naniwa Miyage (souvenir from Naniwa, 1738.)

Born into a provincial samurai (warrior) family in the seventeenth century, **Chikamatsu Monzaemon** (1653–1724) became the most important Japanese playwright since the great period of Noh drama 300 years earlier. When he was thirty, Chikamatsu began writing for the Bunraku puppet theatre; he also wrote for the Kabuki theatre, and many of his puppet plays were later adapted for Kabuki.

Chikamatsu wrote both history and domestic plays—loosely constructed stories about the nobility featuring military pageantry, supernatural beings, battles, suicides, beheadings, and many kinds of violent deeds, all rendered through choreographed movements. His domestic plays featured unhappy lovers driven to suicide. Every play was characterized by the beauty of Chikamatsu's poetry.

A prolific writer, Chikamatsu has been compared by Western critics to William Shakespeare and Christopher Marlowe for the power of his verse and the sweep of his social canvas. His best-known plays in the West are *The Battles of Coxinga* (1715) (his most popular work); *The Love Suicides at Sonezaki* (1703); *The Battle of Kokusenya* (1715); and *The Love Suicides at Amijima* (1721).

---

particularly skillful in their ability to imitate feminine sensibilities through stylized gestures and attitudes.

The Kabuki actor does not use a mask but instead wears boldly patterned makeup—a white base with designs of red, black, brown, or blue. The makeup symbolizes the character and describes the role. *Onnagata* use only white makeup, along with false eyebrows and rouging to shape the mouth and the corners of the eyes. Each role has its conventional costume, based on historical dress and often weighing as much as fifty pounds.

The Kabuki actor's performance is always highly theatrical, colorful, and larger than life. Since he does not sing, he is often assisted by a narrator and chorus. The narrator may set the scene, speak dialogue, recite passages, and even comment on the action.

In recent years, Western directors, actors, and scholars have become interested in Eastern theatrical practices: minimal staging; revolving stages; fixed conventions

$\mathcal{D}$oll $\mathcal{P}$uppets

Bunraku

The Japanese doll-puppet theatre, dating from the mid-seventeenth century, is a sophisticated and commercial entertainment for adults. It is named Bunraku for a nineteenth-century theatre manager, Uemura Bunrakuen (or Bunrakuken), who moved from Awaji Island to Osaka, where he staged puppet plays at shrines and professional theatres with an all-male troupe of professional performers.

The complex style of Bunraku consists of a domestic or history play in five acts written in alternating sections of spoken dialogue (prose) and sung narrative (verse) accompanied by music. The chanter or narrator, who reads from the text (actually it is memorized), which rests on a lacquered stand before him, and a *samisen* player sit on a revolving dais to stage left of the proscenium in view of the audience. Some fifty puppet heads provide the variety of characters. The wooden puppets have movable parts, and each puppet is controlled traditionally by three puppeteers, or handlers. Bunraku is performed on a small proscenium stage that is divided into three levels (front to rear) with low partitions between the levels where the handlers sit.

With the touring in the West of modern Bunraku troupes, many of their performing techniques are now borrowed by Western puppeteers and stage directors. Today, Bunraku is under the sponsorship of the Japan National Commission for the Protection of Cultural Properties and performs both in Osaka and in a small theatre created for it within the National Theatre, Tokyo.

of movement, style, and dress; symbolic properties, dress, and masks; musical interludes; visible musicians and stage assistants. In addition, the main forms of Eastern theatre—the Beijing Opera (China); Noh theatre, Bunraku or puppet theatre, and Kabuki theatre (Japan); shadow puppets (Malaysia); Balinese dance theatre (Bali); and Kathakali dancers (India)—have influenced Western producer-directors and playwrights, such as Edward Gordon Craig, William Butler Yeats, Vsevolod Meyerhold, Antonin Artaud, Bertolt Brecht, Jerzy Grotowski, Peter Brook, Ariane Mnouchkine, Harold Prince, Peter Schumann, and Julie Taymor.

TRANSITION

Both Western and Eastern theatres are divided into stage and auditorium. Beginning with ritual performances in early societies, the theatrical space has always been a special, "privileged" place where spectators share in the revelation of a reality separate from that of their daily lives but related to it. Those creating theatre have traditionally sought out a variety of places—hillsides, streets, marketplaces, buildings—to engage audiences in the experience of seeing life imitated by performers to entertain and often to teach. In all cases, conventions developed regarding the relation of spectator to performer, and vice versa.

A number of modern theatre practitioners have played with these conventions, violated them, even turned them upside down, as they attempted to engage audiences by breaking the established molds of actor–audience relationships. The names *alternative* (and even *environmental*) are given to theatrical performances found in nontraditional spaces. In the modern theatre, most have been products of the theatrical avant-garde.

WEB SITES

Medieval Drama Links
http://www.leeds.ac.uk/theatre/emd/links.htm

Shakespeare and the Globe: Then and Now
http://www.Shakespeare.eb.com/Shakespeare/index2.html

Skenotheke: Images of the Ancient Stage
http://www.usask.ca/antharch/cnea/skenotheke.html#theaters

Theatre History Sites
http://www.win.net/~kudzu/history.html

Theatron Limited/Projects (Virtual Models of Historical Theatres)
http://www.theatron.co.uk/

Virtual Site—Non-intrusive Archaeological Reconstructions and Historical Recreations of Theatres and Other Architecture
http://hometown.aol.com/virtusite/virtual_site.htm

International Theatre Web sites

Théâtre du Soleil, Paris, France—"Tambours Sur La Digue"
www.theatre-du-soleil.fr/tambour/resentation.html

Japanese Theatre
www.Japantravelinfo.com

National Theatre of Tokyo
www.nntt.jac.go.jp/english/teatre/t2.html

New Amsterdam Theatre, New York City
http://disney.go.com/disneyonbroadway/newamsterdam/nat.htm

These search terms are provided to assist you in exploring the topics introduced in this chapter at:

http//www.infotrac-college.com

ritual, shaman, trope, pageant wagon, the Globe theatre, the New Globe Theatre, proscenium theatre, thrust stage, arena stage, Kathakali, Beijing Opera, Noh theatre, Bunraku puppet theatre, Kabuki theatre.

Alternative Theatrical Spaces

Modern efforts to find new kinds of theatrical space have created different ways of experiencing theatre. In recent decades Jerzy Grotowski in Poland, Ariane Mnouchkine in Paris, Peter Schumann in Vermont, and Peter Brook in France have rearranged theatrical space to bring audiences and actors closer together. As audiences, we become part of the staged action, seeing both as spectators and as participants.

All theatre people who have performed singly or in groups wherever an audience could be gathered around them are background to the modern avant-garde creation of alternative performance spaces. These alternative forms are associated in particular with the Vietnam War era in the United States, although they are international in practice.

Much of the work of Julian Beck and Judith Malina (the Living Theatre), Jerzy Grotowski (the Polish Laboratory Theatre), Peter Brook (the International Centre for Theatre Research), Ariane Mnouchkine (Théâtre du Soleil), and Peter Schumann (the Bread and Puppet Theatre) within the last four decades has been labeled alternative and/or environmental theatre. This is a type of theatrical performance that rejects conventional seating and arranges the audience as part of the playing space.

Writing about environmental production as a particular way of creating and experiencing theatre, American director Richard Schechner says: "The thing about environmental theatre space is not just a matter of how you end up using space. It is an attitude. *Start with all the space there is and then decide what to use, what not to use, and how to use what you use.*"[2] Polish director Jerzy Grotowski describes the essential concern as "finding the proper spectator–actor relationship for each type of performance and embodying the decision in physical arrangements."[3]

By definition, environmental theatre rejects conventional seating and includes audiences as part of the performance space. Like the actors, the spectators become part of what is seen and done. They are both seeing and seen.

FORERUNNERS OF ALTERNATIVE APPROACHES

In modern Russia and Germany, such leaders as the inventive Vsevolod Meyerhold (1874–c. 1940) and Max Reinhardt (1873–1943) developed unorthodox production methods and uses of theatrical space. They are the chief forerunners of today's many experiments in nontraditional performance styles and alternative spaces. In the 1930s in Moscow, the Russian director Meyerhold, rejecting the proscenium arch as too confining for his actors, removed the front curtain, footlights, *and* proscenium. Stage-hands changed properties and scenery in full view of audiences, and actors performed on trapezes, slides, and ramps to arouse exhilarating feelings in both performers and audiences.

Max Reinhardt explored vast acting areas, such as circus arenas to stage *Oedipus the King* (1910) in Berlin's Circus Schumann, which he thought of as a people's the-atre—his "theatre of the five thousand." He dreamed of a theatre on the scale of classical Greek and Roman theatres to be used for spectacles and mass audiences. In 1920, he created his most famous spectacle (*Everyman*) in the square before the Salzburg Cathedral.

During the last forty years, especially in the United States, many theatre directors and designers also looked for new theatrical spaces in warehouses, garages, lofts, and town halls. They reshaped *all* of the space available to audience and actor, bringing the audience into direct contact with the actor, thereby making the audience a more essential part of the theatrical event.

This chapter discusses three alternative approaches to the use of theatrical space in modern times: the Polish Laboratory Theatre, the Théâtre du Soleil, and the Bread and Puppet Theatre.

THE POLISH LABORATORY THEATRE

Grotowski's "Poor" Theatre

When Jerzy Grotowski founded the Polish Laboratory Theatre in Opole in 1959, he set out to answer the question: What is theatre? Grotowski first evolved a concept that he called "poor theatre." For him, theatre's essentials were the actor and the audience in a bare space. He found that theatre could happen without costumes, scenery, makeup, stage lighting, and sound effects; all it needed was the actor and audience in communion in a special place. Grotowski wrote:

> I propose poverty in theatre. We have resigned from the stage-and-auditorium plant: for each production, a new space is designed for the actors and spectators…. The essential concern is finding the proper spectator–actor relationship….[4]

"[Grotowski] was, with Stanislavky, Meyerhold, and Brecht, one of the West's four great 20th century theatre theorist-practitioners."

RICHARD SCHECHNER
Environmental Theatre Theorist

*D*irector

Jerzy Grotowski

©Max Waldman

Jerzy Grotowski (1933–1999) was founder and director of the Polish Laboratory Theatre, an experimental company located in Opole and then in Wroclaw (Breslau). Not a theatre in the usual sense, the company became an institute for research into theatre art in general and the actor's art in particular. In addition, the laboratory also undertook performances for audiences as well as instruction of actors, producers, students (many of them foreigners), and people from other fields. The plays performed were based on Polish and international classics. In the 1960s and 1970s, Grotowski's productions of Stanislaw Wyspianski's *Akropolis,* Shakespeare's *Hamlet,* Marlowe's *Dr. Faustus,* and Calderón's *The Constant Prince* attracted worldwide attention. His closest collaborators were actor Ryszard Cieslak and literary adviser Ludwik Flaszen. He wrote about his methods in *Towards a Poor Theatre* (1968)—a theatre that eliminates everything not truly required by the actor and the audience.

After 1970, Grotowski reorganized his company to explore human creativity outside the theatre and called this period *Holiday.* He intended to lead participants back to elemental connections between themselves and the natural world by exposing them to basic myths, dancing, playing, bathing, and the elements of fire, earth, air, and water. In 1975 the event called *Holiday* took place in a forest, where participants were encouraged to rediscover the roots of theatre and their true being.

In 1983 at the University of California–Irvine, Grotowski began a third phase called "objective drama" to combine source materials with precise tools of actor-training that he had developed in earlier years. In 1986, he established a Workcenter (*Centro di Lavoro*) in Pontedera, Italy, where he began the last phase of his work, called "art as vehicle," to explore how theatre differentiates and relates performance "truths" in many cultures.

The 1999–2000 season was declared the "Year of Jerzy Grotowski" in Wroclaw, Poland, where his Theatre Laboratory began in 1965. Year-long festivities, exhibits, symposia, and publications took place.

Within the whole space, Grotowski created what he called "holy theatre": The performance was a semireligious act in which the actor, prepared by years of training and discipline, undergoes a psychospiritual experience. Grotowski set about to engage the audience in this act, and thus to engage both actor and audience in a deeper understanding of personal and social truths.

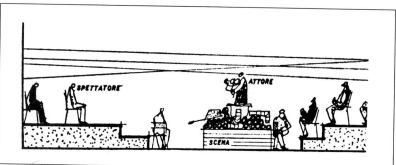

THE THEATRICAL SPACE AT THE BEGINNING OF THE PERFORMANCE OF *AKROPOLIS* (1962) Note that the wire struts above the audience are empty.

THE THEATRICAL SPACE AT THE END OF *AKROPOLIS* The actors have disappeared, leaving the stovepipes hanging from the wire struts as gruesome reminders of the events in the concentration camps.

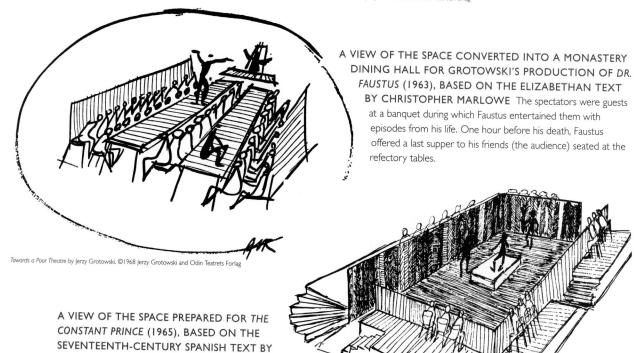

A VIEW OF THE SPACE CONVERTED INTO A MONASTERY DINING HALL FOR GROTOWSKI'S PRODUCTION OF *DR. FAUSTUS* (1963), BASED ON THE ELIZABETHAN TEXT BY CHRISTOPHER MARLOWE The spectators were guests at a banquet during which Faustus entertained them with episodes from his life. One hour before his death, Faustus offered a last supper to his friends (the audience) seated at the refectory tables.

A VIEW OF THE SPACE PREPARED FOR *THE CONSTANT PRINCE* (1965), BASED ON THE SEVENTEENTH-CENTURY SPANISH TEXT BY PEDRO CALDERÓN DE LA BARCA The audience, seated behind a barrier, looked down on the actors like medical students watching a surgical operation, or spectators observing contestants in a bullring.

Chapter Three

Akropolis (1962)

In *Akropolis*, Grotowski adapted a text written by Polish playwright Stanislaw Wyspianski in 1904. In the original, statues and paintings in Cracow Cathedral come to life on the eve of Easter Sunday. The statues re-enact scenes from the Old Testament and antiquity. But Grotowski shifted the action to a modern extermination camp, Auschwitz, in wartime Poland. In the new setting he contrasted the Western ideal of human dignity with the degradation of a death camp.

Akropolis takes place in a large room. Spectators are seated on platforms; passageways for the actors are created between the platforms. Wire struts are strung across the ceiling. In the middle of the room is a large, boxlike platform for the actors. Rusty pieces of metal are heaped on top of the box: stovepipes, a wheelbarrow, a bathtub, nails, hammers. With these objects the actors build a civilization of gas chambers. They wear a version of a camp uniform—ragged shirts and trousers, heavy wooden shoes, and anonymous berets.

Grotowski juxtaposes Biblical and Homeric scenes and heroes against the grotesque reality of the modern death camp. The love of Paris and Helen, for instance, is played out between two men to the accompaniment of the laughter of the assembled prisoners; Jacob's bride is a stovepipe with a rag for a veil. *Akropolis* ends with a procession around the box in the center of the room led by a Singer carrying the headless corpse of the Savior. As Grotowski describes it:

> The procession evokes the religious crowds of the Middle Ages, the flagellants, the haunting beggars.... The procession reaches the end of its peregrination. The Singer lets out a pious yell, opens a hole in the box, and crawls into it, dragging after him the corpse of the Savior. The inmates follow him one by one, singing fanatically.... When the last of the condemned men has disappeared, the lid of the box slams shut. The silence is very

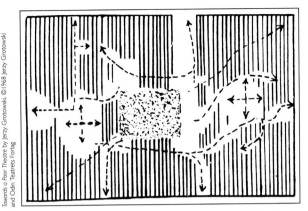

Towards a Poor Theatre by Jerzy Grotowski. © 1968 Jerzy Grotowski and Odin Teatrets Forlag

GROTOWSKI'S USE OF SPACE FOR *AKROPOLIS* The lines with arrows indicate the actors' movements and areas of action; the straight lines show audience areas. The central playing space is a boxlike "mansion" where pipes are assembled and into which the actors disappear at the end of the performance.

Towards a Poor Theatre by Jerzy Grotowski. © 1968 Jerzy Grotowski and Odin Teatrets Forlag

This photo depicts a "dialogue between two monuments." The metal stovepipe and human legs with boots make a visual statement about the way human beings can be treated as objects. This is one of many statements in the performance about the effects of inhumanity throughout our history. The actor is Zbigniew Cynkutis.

sudden; then after a while a calm, matter-of-fact voice is heard. It says simply, "They are gone, and the smoke rises in spirals." The joyful delirium has found its fulfillment in the crematorium. The end.[5]

Grotowski's poor theatre returns us to the essentials of theatre: actor, audience, space.

THE LIVING THEATRE

The oldest of the collective groups in the United States began in 1948 in a basement on New York City's Wooster Street. The zeal and talents of Julian Beck and Judith Malina were directed toward productions that encouraged a nonviolent revolution to overhaul society and created a performance style to confront that society, namely, the United States of America.

Attention was fully paid to their work in 1958 with the production of Jack Gelber's *The Connection,* a disturbing play about heroin addicts, produced in a converted space on Fourteenth Street in New York City. The audience shared the addicts' naturalistic environment as spectators to the making of a documentary film about "real" addicts and their lifestyle. *The Brig* in 1963 recreated the senseless routine of a day in a Marine Corps prison camp.

Following an encounter in 1963 with the U.S. Internal Revenue Service over a failure to pay taxes, the company lost its theatre and went abroad where they developed works in Rome, Berlin, and Paris. They performed in streets, prisons, even bars, provoking audience riots and confrontations with civil authorities. The Living Theatre returned to the United States in 1968 with significant works of their own creation advocating freedom from all restraints: *Mysteries and Smaller Pieces, Frankenstein,* and *Paradise Now.*

The Brig

A dazzling act of rebellion against the political and theatrical establishments, *The Brig,* written by Kenneth Brown, who had served in the Marine Corps, opened on May 15, 1963. As part of the World Wide General Strike for Peace organized by the Becks a week earlier, *The Brig* represented civil disobedience.

Directed by Judith Malina, who drew on interviews with Marines, material from the "Guidebook for Marines" issued to recruits, and the desire to mold a genuine community among the company, *The Brig* was, first, an *environment* of intimidation, and, second, a *plea* for nonviolence.

Kenneth Brown's script covers a single day (from reveille to bedtime) in a brig for United States military offenders on Okinawa. The eleven prisoners are drawn

(continued on page 62)

The Living Theatre's Gurus:
Julian Beck and Judith Malina

©Fred W. McDarrah

©Fred W. McDarrah

Julian Beck (1925–1985) and **Judith Malina** (b. 1926) were the foremost gurus of the sixties' **Off Off Broadway** groups. Julian Beck's father was from Alsace and his mother was a first-generation German American; he grew up on New York City's Upper West Side. Judith Malina was born in Kiel, Germany; her father, a rabbi, brought the family to America in 1929. The two artists met in 1943 and married in 1948.

Beck began as a painter and writer, while Malina studied theatre under Erwin Piscator at the New School Dramatic Workshop. Finding that the Broadway theatre was closed to them, they made an unsuccessful attempt in 1948 to start a theatre in a basement on Wooster Street and eventually relocated to their own living room on West End Avenue. The first performance of the Living Theatre occurred in the Becks' apartment in 1951 with four short plays by Paul Goodman, Gertrude Stein, Bertolt Brecht, and García Lorca. These modest beginnings contained the abiding concerns of their future work: anarchism, poetry, Asian-inspired theatre, didacticism (via Bertolt Brecht), improvisation, and experimentation with language. The Living Theatre came of age with productions of *The Connection* (1958) and *The Brig* (1963).

Asked to give a quick assessment of the work of the Living Theatre, Julian Beck once said: "… our aim was to increase conscious awareness, to stress the sacredness of life, to break down walls."[6]

THE BRIG The Living Theatre's 1963 production of Kenneth Brown's play recreated the repetition and senseless routine of a day in a Marine prison camp. The audience sat outside the fence as observers.

from a cross section of society. The atmosphere was one of isolation, intimidation, and brutality, by victims and tormentors. In Beck's and Malina's view, *The Brig* aimed at destroying violence by representing it. The actor became a "sacrificial" presence in the demonstration of mindless evil where no freedoms of the most basic kind exist.

The production replicated the caged wire, the dormitory of bunk beds, and floor sectioned off by painted white lines. A blackboard listed offenses committed by the prisoners. Spectators sat before the barbed wire cage as witnesses to the dehumanizing of the soldiers and as participants in society's responsibility for permitting such abuse of human beings.

The Living Theatre on Tour

The Living Theatre toured the United States in the late sixties, arousing bitter controversy and debate over the nature of theatre and the role of art in society. In 1970, the company returned to Europe and split into four groups, or "cells." The Becks' contingent went to Brazil for purposes of developing a new way of doing performance, one that was less didactic and more responsive to the needs of specific communities. In 1984, the company returned to the United States and presented four works of "collective creation" in New York City, which critics found largely lacking in significant content. With Julian Beck's death in 1985, the future of the Living Theatre passed into the hands of Judith Malina, who continues to produce upon occasion but without the same impact of the earlier company.

The significance of the Living Theatre rests on its naturalistic environmental productions and later techniques that included altering texts to argue for anarchy and social change; nudity and athleticism in performance; use of human voices and cacophonous sounds to assault the audiences' sensibilities, and confrontations with audiences with calls for revolution.

Julian Beck once said that "art opens perception and changes our vision. I think without art we would all remain blind to reality. We go to the theatre to study ourselves. The theatre excites the imagination, and it also enters into the spirit...."[7]

THÉÂTRE DU SOLEIL

Ariane Mnouchkine's Environmental Space

Théâtre du Soleil ("Theatre of the Sun") is another group having impact on environmental production styles, especially in Europe. Founded in Paris in 1964 by Ariane Mnouchkine and a group of politically committed individuals, the Théâtre du Soleil modeled itself on an egalitarian commune, dividing the theatre's profits equally among the company. The ensemble works on the notion of collaborative creation and democratic participation at all levels of decision-making. Productions grow out of improvisations, discussions, and group study; all members share the various responsibilities of research, writing, interpretation, design, and construction in an effort to abolish the theatrical hierarchy that reaches upward from the ticket takers to the director of the production.

The company has challenged traditional modes of theatrical presentation in its attempts to create a populist theatre, using improvisation as well as techniques from mime, *commedia*, Chinese opera, Japanese Noh and Kabuki, and circus clowning. Audiences move from platform to platform to keep up with the play's action or sit around the edge or even in the center of a large pit for many productions.

Beginning with productions in the late sixties, the company attracted considerable international attention and was acclaimed for its radical environmental staging techniques and

THE ENVIRONMENTAL PRODUCTION OF *THE AGE OF GOLD (L'AGE D'OR)*, IN 1975, BY THÉÂTRE DU SOLEIL Here a character declaims while standing in the middle of the audience.

©Martine Franck/Magnum Photos, Inc.

*D*irector

©Martine Franck/Magnum Photos, Inc.

Ariane Mnouchkine

©Martine Franck/Magnum Photos, Inc.

**THÉÂTRE DU SOLEIL'S *1793*
PRODUCED IN VINCENNES IN
1972 AT THE CARTOUCHERIE (A
FORMER MUNITIONS FACTORY)**
This view of the performance shows
actors on raised platforms and scaffolds
with the audience seated in a center pit.

its explosive politicizing of dramatic materials. Their commitment to left-wing political beliefs and to creating vibrant "performance texts" out of the whole cloth of French history resulted in *1789,* then *1793,* and *The Age of Gold.* In the 1980s, the company's Kathakali- and Kabuki-inspired productions of Shakespeare's plays blended Eastern and Western traditions. In the environmental space of the former munitions factory that directly engaged audiences, these performances dealt with theatre as revolution, historical data, contemporary social and political facts; improvised stage action and audience participation; and emphasized spectacle and ritual.

As political fervor waned worldwide in the late 1970s, along with the winding down of the Vietnam War, many groups either went out of existence or, like Théâtre du Soleil, turned to other artistic expressions, which overshadowed any "environmental" trendiness or political and social messages contained in their works. Théâtre du Soleil's Asian-inspired Shakespearean productions and *Les Atrides,* the four-part cycle of Greek

Of the French directors who have come to prominence since 1965, **Ariane Mnouchkine** (b. 1939) is one of the most important. She founded the Théâtre du Soleil, a workers' cooperative composed of ten initial members, in 1964. Until 1970 they performed around Paris, creating a considerable stir with productions of Shakespeare's *A Midsummer Night's Dream* and Arnold Wesker's *The Kitchen*.

In 1970 the company moved to an abandoned munitions factory just outside Paris (the Cartoucherie de Vincennes), where they have since produced internationally celebrated environmental and intercultural productions of *1789* (in 1970) and *1793* (in 1972), treatments of the early years of the French Revolution that argued that the revolution was more concerned with property than with social injustice. *The Age of Gold* (*L'Age d'Or*, in 1975) dealt with various aspects of materialism; *The Terrible but Unfinished History of Norodom Sihanouk, King of Cambodia* (in 1985) and *The Indiade* (*L'Indiade*, in 1987), with modern political history. The group traveled with their Asian-inspired productions of Shakespeare's *Richard II, Henry IV, Part 1*, and *Twelfth Night* to the 1984 Olympic Arts Festival of Los Angeles, and in 1992 they returned to North America with the ten-hour, four-part cycle of Greek tragedy called *Les Atrides*. In 1998–99, *Suddenly, Nights of Awakening* (*Et Soudain, Des Nuits D'Éveil*) and *Drums on the Dike* (*Tambours Sur La Digue*) were staged in Paris.

Théâtre du Soleil is one of France's finest theatre companies, inspired by its director Ariane Mnouchkine for forty years. "Theatre is doubtless the most fragile of arts," she has said, "the theatre public is now really a very small group, but the theatre keeps reminding us of the possibility to collectively seek the histories of people and to tell them…. The contradictions, the battles of power, and the split in ourselves will always exist. I think the theatre best tells us of the enemy in ourselves. Yes, theatre is a grain of sand in the works."[8]

tragedy based on Euripides' *Iphigeneia at Aulis* and Aeschylus' three plays of *The Oresteia*, have further challenged contemporary notions of theatrical presentation.

More recently, Mnouchkine and her company turned their attention to other Asian traditions. In 1998, the company created *Suddenly, Nights of Awakening* (*Et Soudain Des Nuits D'Éveil*), which took the form of a touring Tibetan acting troupe putting on a play; in mid-performance the actors step out of the play to seek political asylum from the audience. As is now a familiar practice of Théâtre du Soleil, the production grew out of improvisations (shaped into a text by author-critic Hélène Cixous) and performed with a mix of Tibetan dance, Buddhist ritual, *commedia dell'arte lazzi* (clowning), political discourse, and actors wandering freely among audiences, speaking and passing out faxes as they argued their need for political asylum. *Drums on the Pier* (*Tambours Sur La Digue*) is an ancient marionette play adapted for the company in a Bunraku performance style.

Environmental Theatre: A Forty-Year Perspective

**The Polish Laboratory Theatre . The Living Theatre . The Performance Group .
New York Theatre Strategy . Théâtre du Soleil**

THE POLISH LABORATORY THEATRE, WROCLAW,
POLAND *Akropolis*, directed by Jerzy Grotowski, with
actor Ryszard Cieslak as the character Esau, who sings of
the freedom of a hunter's life while enmeshed in the
wire struts of the concentration camp.

Towards a Poor Theatre by Jerzy Grotowski. ©1968 Jerzy Grotowski and Odin
Teatrets Forlag.

THE LIVING THEATRE, NEW YORK CITY Actors
in one of many theatrical rites that composed *Paradise Now: The Revolution of Cultures* (1968). The
piece was one of the first to incorporate nudity (of
the actors and—sometimes—the audience) as an
integral part of the performance.

©Max Waldman

THE PERFORMANCE GROUP, NEW YORK CITY *Dionysus in 69,* a 1969 environmental production by the Performance Group whose leader was Richard Schechner. The theatre on Wooster Street in New York City was a converted garage with towers and platforms scattered about to be used by both actors and spectators. The company's first production, *Dionysus in 69,* was a reworking of Euripides' *The Bacchae* into a series of rituals, including the "Birth Ritual," relating to the freedoms of sexual and spiritual expression..

©Max Waldman

THÉÂTRE DU SOLEIL, VINCENNES, FRANCE The production of the Asian-inspired Shakespeare's *Richard II* staged in a munitions factory in Paris in 1981.

©Martine Franck/Magnum Photos, Inc.

*P*uppeteer

Peter Schumann

©Fred W. McDarrah

The Bread and Puppet Theatre performed *The Same Boat: The Passion of Chico Mendes* in an open town space as part of the 1990 "Earth Day" celebration. The masked actors, the band, and the larger-than-life-size puppets are traditional features of a Bread and Puppet production.

Dan Charlson/Durham Herald-Sun

THE BREAD AND PUPPET THEATRE

Peter Schumann's Open-Air Performances

Peter Schumann founded the Bread and Puppet Theatre in New York City in 1961. Today, the group makes its home on a farm in Glover, Vermont. Unlike many radical theatres that grew out of the social and political unrest of the 1960s in America, the Bread and Puppet Theatre flourishes today. Schumann's group does not attempt to create an environment but performs in almost any setting: streets, fields, gravel pits, gyms, churches, and sometimes theatres. Developed from Biblical and legendary

Peter Schumann (b. 1934 in Silesia) moved from Germany to the United States in 1961 and two years later founded the Bread and Puppet Theatre in New York City.

Until he was ten, the Schumann family lived in a village near Breslau, renamed Wroclaw at the end of the Second World War when this part of Germany was incorporated into Poland. In late 1944, the family fled barely ahead of the Soviet army and survived on his mother's baked rye sourdough bread until they reached Schleswig-Holstein. The twin themes of family and survival in Schumann's work stem from this period. In 1956, he met American Elka Scott in Munich; they married and emigrated to the United States in 1961, where their artistic collaboration began with the creation and performances of street pageants, anti–Vietnam War parades, productions based on religious themes, and summer workshops with giant puppets.

In 1970, Schumann was invited to take up residency at Goddard College in Plainfield, Vermont, and "practice puppetry." Living now in Glover, Vermont, Schumann has assembled a small troupe of puppeteers, designers, musicians, and volunteers. Each August at harvest time, the troupe performs in a grassed-over gravel pit with actors walking on five- or six-foot stilts, strolling jazz bands, rope walkers, and fire jugglers. Sourdough rye bread that Schumann baked himself is passed among audiences. All is free, having been donated and prepared by volunteers.

Schumann's pageants are always about life and death, good and evil. His work with puppets reflects a traditionalism that harks back to Indian effigies, Japanese Bunraku and Noh theatre, and to the masks of African and Alaskan shamans. Mistrusting the power of words, Schumann uses puppets to simplify and caricature the horror of modern living in a time of potential global annihilation. His aim is to bring the spiritual into the lives of ordinary spectators.

In a Bread and Puppet performance the stories are simple, the giant puppets riveting, and the tempo majestically slow. Schumann is best known for his antiwar and nuclear disarmament pieces dating from 1965: *Fire, The Gray Lady Cantata, The Stations of the Cross,* and *A Man Says Goodbye to His Mother.*

sources and using actors, stilt-walkers, and larger-than-life-size puppets, Bread and Puppet plays advocate the virtues of love, charity, and humility.

The group takes its name from two constant elements of their work: puppets and bread. Peter Schumann believes that "the theatre should be as basic as bread." At the start of a Bread and Puppet performance, loaves of bread are passed among the spectators. Each person breaks off a piece and hands the rest to the next person, who does the same. When everyone has tasted bread, in an act of social and spiritual communion, the performance begins. Thus the audience participates in an instantly recognizable ritual: sharing the staff of life, a symbol of humanity's most basic need.

Domestic Resurrection Circus

The Nineteenth Annual Domestic Resurrection Circus (each is labeled number nineteen) is performed each August on a farm in Glover, Vermont, in a grassed-over gravel pit with sloping sides as large as a football field. Free to the six or eight thousand people who attend this harvest weekend, the ten-hour extravaganza features gods, demons, angels, peasants, dragons, birds, along with a mélange of morris dancers, fire jugglers, rope walkers, and strolling jazz musicians. People enjoy the corn and potato roast and the sourdough rye bread, which Schumann has himself prepared each morning for six weeks.

The *Circus* begins around four in the afternoon with a prayer for peace spoken in eight languages. The twenty-foot effigies and head-sized masks of the monstrous red figure of Yama, the King of Hell; the Nature God that resembles a Bigfoot dressed in cedar boughs; and a tall, careworn Madonna Godface with a cryptic smile and hair woven of milkweed and goldenrod are central figures in the story that sweeps across millennia. Toward the end, white birds with wingspans of fifteen feet (flown by three puppeteers holding long poles) travel fast, making sounds of seagulls crying and finally bringing peace to the kingdoms of animals and humans, as the Moon on an ox-drawn wagon appears. On the horizon the real moon rises above a pinewoods, opposite the last rays of a real sunset. The pattern of events reinforces the "death and resurrection" theme that Schumann repeats in all of his Bread and Puppet events.

Of his unique work with puppets, Peter Schumann has said, "Puppet theatre, the employment of and dance of dolls, effigies, and puppets ... is an anarchic art, subversive and untamable by nature ... an art which does not aspire to represent governments or civilizations but prefers its own secret demeaning stature in society, representing, more or less, the demons of that society and definitely not its institutions."[9]

TRANSITION

Many theatrical groups in recent decades set about to rethink, reshape, and re-create the theatrical experience for actors *and* audiences. Jerzy Grotowski worked in large rooms and forests, Ariane Mnouchkine in a munitions factory, Peter Brook in an abandoned theatre and rock quarries, and Peter Schumann in streets and fields.

Environmental or alternative theatre, as this type of nontraditional performance has been called since the 1960s, rejects conventional seating and arranges the audience as part of the playing space. Like the actors, spectators become part of what is seen and performed; they are both seeing and seen. In contrast, traditional theatre arranges the audience *before* a stage, where they see and hear at a distance.

Throughout the ages, the theatre's *space* has influenced those who work within it: playwrights, actors, directors, and designers. These artists are the theatre's "image makers," for they create the world of the production as theatrical metaphor for audiences to experience. The playwright, who creates the text, most often provides the blueprint for the production.

WEB SITES

Blue Man Group—Multi-sensory Theatre Group Combining Theatre, Percussive Music, Art, Science, and Vaudeville

http://www.blueman.com/home.shtml

Center of Studies on Jerzy Grotowski, Wroclaw, Poland

http://www.grotcenter@mikrozet.wroc.pl

Peter Schumann's Bread and Puppet Theatre

http://www.scenesofvermont.com/bread&puppet/bread.htm

Polish Laboratory Theatre—Source Material on Jerzy Grotowski's Work

http://www.owendaly.com/jeff/grotows3.htm

Théâtre du Soleil, Paris, France

http://www.theatre-du-soleil.fr

These search terms are provided to assist you in exploring the topics introduced in this chapter at:

http//www.infotrac-college.com

avant-garde, environmental theatre, political theatre, street theatre, experimental theatre, puppetry.

The Image Makers: The Playwright

The playwright envisions the play's world, its people, environment, objects, relationships, emotions, attitudes, and events. Playwriting is a creative act that enlarges our understanding of human experience and enriches our appreciation of life.

Who fills the theatrical space? Who is seen in the space? What methods and materials are used to create the stage environment, what a famous designer called "the machine for acting"? In theatre we continually encounter the idea of building. Actors speak of building a character. Technicians build the set and costumers build costumes. The director often "blocks" the play. The word *playwright* is formed in the same way as *wheelwright* and *shipwright:* It means "playbuilder." Theatre is the creative collaborative effort of many builders. A number of creative artists using various methods and materials builds an imaginary world, but the initial builder is most often the playwright.

The working methods of playwrights—their tools, perspectives, conventions, and styles of writing—are discussed in the next several chapters.

THE PLAYWRIGHT

The Play: A Blueprint Not Yet Built

The playwright writes a play—crafts words on paper—to express some aspect of reality, some emotions and feelings connected with all of humanity, some measure of experience, some vision or conviction about the world. Like any artist, the playwright shapes a personal vision into an organized, meaningful whole.

A playwright's script is more than words on a page—it is the playwright's *blueprint* of a special kind of experience, created to appeal as much to the

TENNESSEE WILLIAMS' *CAMINO REAL* The 1999 revival, with Rip Torn as Casanova and Betty Buckley as Marguerite Gautier, directed by artistic director Michael Wilson, Hartford Stage Company (Conn.).

eye as to the ear. As Tennessee Williams said, "The printed script of a play is hardly more than an architect's blueprint of a house not yet built…." All in all, playwriting is the search for the truth of human experience as the playwright perceives it. Playwrights such as Henrik Ibsen write plays to expose truths about the realities of social injustice. Others, like Bertolt Brecht and Caryl Churchill, make political statements about people, economies, and political systems. These writers use the theatre as a vehicle for a message or ideology. Most writers turn their personal experiences, wishes, and dreams into drama. For Adrienne Kennedy writing is an outlet for psychological confusion and questions stemming from childhood. Other writers, like Eugène Ionesco, ridicule the conventions of the theatre and certain kinds of human behavior to persuade us to see the world differently.

THE PLAYWRIGHT'S BEGINNINGS

The playwright creates on paper a sense of life being lived before us, and the script is of major importance because it is the usual starting point for the theatrical production.

Playwrights start with an idea, theme, dream, image, or notes and work out an action; or they begin with an unusual character or a real person and develop an action around that character; or they start with a situation based on a personal experience, their reading, or an anecdote. Writers working within groups evolve scenarios with actors and arrange a final script from the group's improvisations, situations, dialogue, and movement. Some write from scenarios or plot summaries; others write from outline, crisis scene, images, dreams, myth, or imagined environment.

Bertolt Brecht usually worked from a story outline, which he called the draft plan. Next, he summarized the story's social and political ideas before developing scenes based on the outline. Sam Shepard writes by hand in a notebook first. He wrote literally a dozen different versions of *Fool for Love* (1982), but the first five pages remained the same in each version. After spending a long evening in the theatre making script revisions with the director, Marsha Norman, author of *'Night, Mother* (1983), returns home and types the changes into her computer in the early morning hours. Some

(continued on page 76)

$\mathcal{P}$laywright

Coutesy of Edward Albee/William Morris Agency

Edward Albee

EDWARD ALBEE'S *THE AMERICAN DREAM*
Directed by the playwright for the Alley Theatre, Houston, in 1999. Bettye Fitzpatrick as Grandma and Jason Westley as the Young Man.

© Bruce Bennett/Alley Theatre

With the passing of Eugene O'Neill and Tennessee Williams, Arthur Miller and Edward Albee are today's reigning American playwrights. Albee's (b. 1928) career has interestingly mirrored his private life. Adopted by Frances and Reed Albee, he was beloved as an infant, rejected as a youth, and finally driven from home when he was twenty. When he first exploded on the New York theatre scene in the early 1960s with *The Zoo Story* and *Who's Afraid of Virginia Woolf?*, he was celebrated by the critics,

(continued)

Edward Albee (continued)

but they turned against his increasingly cryptic and abstract plays that followed: *Tiny Alice* (1964), *A Delicate Balance* (1966), *All Over* (1971), *Seascape* (1974), *The Lady from Dubuque* (1979), and *Marriage Play* (1987). His war with the critics ended on a happier note with *Three Tall Women* (1991), which reinstated him as the country's top playwright with three Pulitzer Prizes and forced a new appraisal of his earlier work. *The Play About the Baby* followed, with its world premiere in London (1998) and its favorable critical reception Off Broadway in 2001.

> "...when I write a play, I write one draft of it because as I'm writing it, I see it and I hear it as a performed piece on stage. I know exactly what it looks like, I know exactly what it sounds like, and I have some accuracy about what the play does to me as an audience...."[2]
>
> EDWARD ALBEE
> Playwright

playwrights claim their characters talk to them and develop themselves; others claim they hear the play's voices and dialogue in their heads. Some playwrights speak lines out loud before writing them down, or work from mental images of their characters moving and talking.

THE PLAYWRIGHT'S ROLE

In the theatre the playwright is an anomaly. Although playwrights win Pulitzer Prizes and Nobel awards, they are both central and peripheral to the production. In the privacy of the home, studio, or hotel room, the playwright turns on the computer and constructs an imaginary world. As the creative imagination takes over, people, events, conflicts, words, and whole speeches resound in the writer's inner eye and ear. The script belongs to the playwright, but once this original creative act—this blueprint for performance—is completed and handed over to director, designers, actors, and producers, the playwright in one sense becomes peripheral to the final process. In the harrowing process of transforming the manuscript into a living performance, the writer takes a backseat in the rehearsal hall only to emerge a success or a failure on opening night. One exception is the playwright who also directs his or her own work, such as Bertolt Brecht, Samuel Beckett, Edward Albee, María Irene Fornés, or David Mamet. They remain central to the production process. Others, like Shakespeare and Molière, were not only part owners of their companies but were also actors in their plays. To prolong the New York run of *Small Craft Warnings* in 1972, Tennessee Williams, by no means a professional actor, took the role of narrator in his play; his performance was critically acclaimed.

In rehearsals, playwrights usually take a backseat to their collaborators. Huddled in a back row with a legal pad in hand, their job is to note awkward lines and words that don't ring true, to rewrite speeches and even whole scenes when directors or actors find difficulties in making sense of the action, or need a few more seconds for an actor to make a costume change or an entrance.

$\mathcal{P}$laywright

© 1996 Susan Johann

Marsha Norman

Marsha Norman (b. 1940), grew up in Louisville, Kentucky, of fundamentalist parents and was encouraged in her writing by Jon Jory, then artistic director of Actors Theatre of Louisville. *Getting Out,* about a young woman being released from prison, was first produced there and became an Off Broadway success in 1979. In 1983, she won the Pulitzer Prize for *'Night, Mother,* about a determined young woman's suicide. In 1991, she wrote the book and lyrics for the musical *The Secret Garden,* winning an Antoinette Perry "Tony" Award for Best Book of a Musical. *Trudy Blue* received its Off Broadway premiere in 1999.

The playwright's independence also makes him or her an anomaly in the theatre. Like novelists, playwrights usually create alone, though there are exceptions. Their material, even for a political writer like Bertolt Brecht, is highly personal. For example, Grusha in *The Caucasian Chalk Circle* is both a personal creation and a political statement on the human instinct for survival. We look to playwrights to give us insights into the world around us—to provide fresh perspectives and new visions. To do this, they reach inside themselves, in a private act, and pull forth intensely personal feelings, perceptions, and situations to construct the public world of the play.

Where do playwrights come from? What are their origins? Their backgrounds? Though drama departments offer courses in playwriting, no mastery of technique has ever made a writer. Playwrights have come from every conceivable background: acting, literary, gag-writing, teaching, housewifery, politics, medicine, and so on. Lillian Hellman worked as a reader for a literary agent before writing her first play, *The Children's Hour.* Tennessee Williams worked in a shoe factory and wandered the United States writing poems, short stories, one-acts, and his first full-length play, *Battle of Angels.* Aeschylus was a soldier, Terence a slave, Shakespeare an actor, Luigi Pirandello a teacher, Anton Chekhov a doctor, Caryl Churchill a housewife, and Margaret Edson a kindergarten teacher. Among playwrights, there is no common denominator other than the exercise of the creative imagination in dialogue form—the conversion of dreams, fears, thoughts, and inner voices into a concrete, visible world that expands our horizons and our understanding of society and the universe.

(continued on page 83)

WIT Winner of the 1999 Pulitzer Prize, *Wit* is Margaret Edson's first play. Between earning degrees in history and literature, she worked on the cancer inpatient unit of a research hospital. The material for the play grew out of these experiences with literature and cancer research.

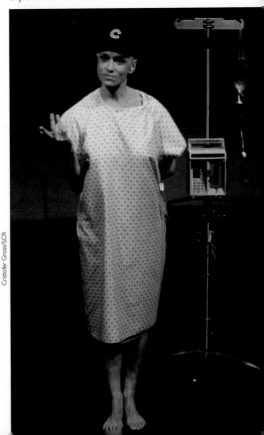

Cristofer Gross/SCR

Women Playwrights: Emerging Voices and New Perspectives

Lillian Hellman . Lorraine Hansberry . María Irene Fornés . Tina Howe

Caryl Churchill . Wendy Wasserstein . Paula Vogel . Suzan-Lori Parks

Women writers are emerging in growing numbers to make significant contributions to the contemporary theatre as playwrights. In trying to explain the increasing number of women playwrights in the American theatre, Marsha Norman says, "Plays require active central characters. Until women could see themselves as active, they could not really write for the theater. We are the central characters in our lives. That awareness had to come to a whole group before women could write about it...."[3]

Whereas Lillian Hellman and Lorraine Hansberry were singular voices for many years, the feminist movement, Off Broadway producers, and regional theatres now provide new avenues for women writers both here and abroad.

National Archives

LILLIAN HELLMAN (1905–1984) was produced successfully on Broadway for almost thirty years. Best known for *The Children's Hour, The Little Foxes,* and *Toys in the Attic,* Hellman pioneered as a woman in the tough commercialism of the Broadway theatre. She said of the theatre: "The manuscript, the words on the page, was what you started with and what you have left. The production is of great importance, has given the play the only life it will know, but it is gone, in the end, and the pages are the only wall against which to throw the future or measure the past."[4]

LORRAINE HANSBERRY (1930–1965) is best known for *A Raisin in the Sun* (1959), which ran on Broadway for 530 performances and then was made into a film. She was the youngest American playwright, the first African American writer, and only the fifth woman to win the New York Drama Critics' Award for the Best Play of the Year. Of playwriting, Hansberry said: "Plays are better written because one must, even if people think that you are being either artsy-craftsy or a plain liar if you say so. One result of this is that I usually don't say it any more, I just write—at my own dismally slow (and, yes, heartbreaking and maddening) commercially disinterested pace and choice of subject matter…."[5]

Cuban-born MARÍA IRENE FORNÉS (b. 1930) emigrated to the United States in 1945. She emerged in the mid-sixties with New York City's Judson Poets' Theater and the Open Theater as a writer, director, and designer. She is legendary both as a playwright of ruthless self-exposure and disjunctive action and as a teacher with New York University, the Intar Hispanic American Arts Center, and the Padua Hills (Calif.) Playwrights Festival, where she has influenced Eduardo Machado, Tony Kushner, and Paula Vogel, among many writers. Her more than thirty plays, produced largely Off Broadway, include *Promenade* (1965), *Fefu and Her Friends* (1977), *Evelyn Brown* (1980), *Mud* (1983), *The Conflict of Life* (1985), *Abington Square* (1987), *And What of the Night?* (1990), *Enter the Night* (1993), *Drowning* (1999), and *Letters from Cuba* (2000). The Signature Theatre Company (New York City) produced a *"Fornés Retrospective"* in the 1999–2000 season.

Of women playwrights she says: "… We have to reconcile ourselves to the idea that the protagonist of a play can be a woman and that it is natural for a woman to write a play where the protagonist is a woman. Man is not the center of life. And it is natural when this fact reflects itself in the work of women."[6]

TINA HOWE (b. 1937) born in New York City and educated at Sarah Lawrence College (Bronxville, N.Y.) writes comedies about women as artists and survivors that reveal a sensitivity to the terrors of existence, including aging and death. Her best known plays are the early *Nest* (1969), followed by *Museum* (1976), *Birth and After Birth* (1977), *The Art of Dining* (1979), *Painting Churches* (1983), *Coastal Disturbances* (1986), *Approaching Zanzibar* (1989), and *Pride's Crossing* (1998). Tina Howe talks about putting her "antic vision" of what it means to be a woman on stage: "My plays have been wildly female.... Plays about women artists don't seem to fall under the heading [of feminist]. Or perhaps—this is a dicey thing to say, though it's been true in my case—the only way a woman can have a career in the theatre at this time is to cover her scent a bit."[7]

©Cori Wells Braun/Courtesy of Tina Howe

CARYL CHURCHILL (b. 1938) (right) is a British writer associated with the joint Stock Theatre Company, the Royal Court Theatre, and the Royal Shakespeare Company. She is best known for *Cloud 9* (1979), *Top Girls* (1980), *Fen* (1983), *Serious Money* (1987), *Mad Forest* (1991), and *Blue Heart* (1997), produced Off Broadway to critical acclaim. Churchill says, "I believe in the magic of theater, but I think it's important to realize that there is nothing magical about the work process behind it. I spend ages researching my plays and sitting alone writing them."[8]

Courtesy: Subuskey & Associates

WENDY WASSERSTEIN (b. 1950) was born in Brooklyn, grew up in New York City, and studied playwriting at the Yale School of Drama. Early in her career, she was associated with Playwrights Horizons (New York City). Her plays deal with the contemporary woman's hopes, dilemmas, ambitions, and personal conflicts. *Uncommon Women and Others* (1977) was followed by *Isn't It Romantic* (1981), *The Heidi Chronicles* (1989), *The Sisters Rosensweig* (1992), *The American Daughter* (1997), and *Old Money* (2000). *The Heidi Chronicles* won the Pulitzer Prize for Drama and the "Tony" Award for Best New Play of the season. On the difficulties women face as writers and directors in theatre and film, she says, "There are many, many more women playwrights now, and many, many more plays by women being produced. I don't think a play does not get produced because it's by a woman."[9]

PAULA VOGEL (b. 1951) grew up in suburban Maryland and arrived on the national scene by writing on such highly charged issues as pornography, domestic violence, gay parenthood, AIDS, feminism, pedophilia, and incest. Unlike most writers on political issues, she is not interested in persuading audiences to adopt political or moral positions but rather to understand that there are no easy answers. *The Baltimore Waltz* (1992), her first success, grew out of her brother's dying of AIDS. It was followed by *Hot 'n' Throbbing* (1994), *The Mineola Twins* (1996), *How I Learned to Drive* (1997), and *The Mammary Plays* (1998). *How I Learned to Drive* won the 1998 Pulitzer Prize for Drama; in 1999, she accepted a three-year playwriting residency at Arena Stage in Washington, D.C.

Paula Vogel insists that her writing is not guided by political issues. "When I write," she says, "there's a pain that I have to reach, and a release I have to work toward for myself. So it's really a question of the particular emotional circumstance that I want to express, a character that appears, a moment in time, and then I write the play backwards."[10]

Courtesy of Paula Vogel/William Morris Agency

© 2001, Susan Johann

SUZAN-LORI PARKS (b. 1963) became interested in theatre during a writing course at Mount Holyoke College (Mass.) taught by novelist James Baldwin. Inspired by the works of Adrienne Kennedy and Ntozake Shange, Parks is one of the notable African American women writing for today's theatre. *Imperceptible Mutabilities in the Third Kingdom* (1986), her first full-length play to be produced, was followed by *What of the Night* (1989), *The Death of the Last Black Man in the Whole Entire World* (1990), *The America Play* (1993), *Venus* (1995), *In the Blood* (1999), and *Top Dog/Under Dog* (2000). She established the Harlem Kids Internet Playwriting Workshop and produced a video called "Alive from Off Center."

Of her writing Suzan-Lori Parks says: "… As a playwright I try to do many things: explore the form, ask questions, make a good show, tell a story, ask more questions, take nothing for granted…. I don't explode the form because I find traditional plays 'boring.' … It's just those structures never could accommodate the figures which take up residence inside me."[11]

Sam Shepard

Allen Nomura

CURSE OF THE STARVING CLASS The play deals with a family—father Weston (Will Marchetti), son Wesley holding the lamb (Paul Richard Connell), and daughter Ella (Kathy Baker)—starved, not for class status but for belonging and distinctiveness as individuals. Performed by the Magic Theatre, San Francisco, in 1982, and directed by John Lion, who called Sam Shepard "the inkblot of the 80s."[12]

QUESTION: So, why are you writing plays?

ANSWER: I have to. I have a mission (*Shepard laughs*). No, I don't know why I do it. Why not?[13]

Sam Shepard (b. 1943) began his theatrical career as a bit actor. Since 1964 he has explored contemporary American myths among the refuse of our junk culture. His characters are Americans we all know, but his situations are often unfamiliar and jarring. Eight-time recipient of the Off Off Broadway Obie Award for distinguished playwriting, Shepard received the Pulitzer Prize in 1979 for *Buried Child*. Among his other well-known plays are *Cowboys* (1964); *Chicago* (1965); *Red Cross* and *La Turista* (1967); *Operation Sidewinder* (1970); *The Tooth of Crime* (1972); *Angel City* and *Curse of the Starving Class* (1976); *True West* (1980); *Fool for Love* (1982); *A Lie of the Mind* (1987); *States of Shock* (1991); *Simpatico* (1994); and *The Late Henry Moss* (2000).

Shepard also acted in such films as *Days of Heaven, The Right Stuff, Country, Crimes of the Heart, Steel Magnolias, Thunderheart, The Pelican Brief,* and *Hamlet* with Ethan Hawke; and wrote screenplays for *Far North* and *Paris, Texas*.

THE PLAYWRIGHT'S TOOLS

The essential tools of the playwright's craft are plot, character, and language. These are also familiar to us as the novelist's tools, and like novels, plays are studied as literature and read for pleasure. Although plays are an arrangement of words on a page (as dialogue), the play-as-text is incomplete. It attains its finished form only in performance on the stage. That is why we call the text of the play a blueprint for performance. To look at several lines of dialogue without actors, scenic space, lights, sound, and costumes is to be convinced of the "incompleteness" of a script. The following lines of *Waiting for Godot* strike us as wholly incomplete without the production elements:

ESTRAGON:	He should be here.
VLADIMIR:	He didn't say for sure he'd come.
ESTRAGON:	And if he doesn't come?
VLADIMIR:	We'll come back to-morrow.
ESTRAGON:	And then the day after to-morrow.
VLADIMIR:	Possibly.
ESTRAGON:	And so on. (Act 1)

Despite the dialogue's bare bones quality, the play script is most often the basis for the production that becomes the play's complete realization.

The playwright "builds" that foundation with plot, character, and language. A story is told with characters, physical action, and dialogue. But the building does not begin until the playwright conceives a whole event with *conflict* (the clashing of personal, moral, and social forces) and then develops a series of related events to resolve that conflict in new and unusual ways. The conflict and events must be compelling. Some are bold and unusual—such as Sophocles' Oedipus unwittingly chasing his own identity through a plague-ridden city, or Shakespeare's Hamlet avenging his father's murder at the invitation of a ghost. Some are seemingly ordinary, like many domestic situations depicted in modern realistic plays. But, Blanche DuBois' encounter with her brother-in-law in a New Orleans tenement becomes life-threatening in Tennessee Williams' *A Streetcar Named Desire* (1947), and Troy Maxon destroys his domestic tranquility

> "I feel like there are territories within us that are totally unknown. Huge, mysterious, and dangerous territories. We think we know ourselves, when we really know only this little bitty part. We have this social person that we present to each other. We have all these galaxies inside of us. And if we don't enter those in art ... whether it's playwriting, or painting, or music, or whatever, then I don't understand the point in doing anything."[14]
>
> SAM SHEPARD
> *Playwright*

TENNESSEE WILLIAMS' *A STREETCAR NAMED DESIRE*
The 1998 revival, with Annalee Jefferies as Blanche DuBois, by the Hartford Stage Company (Conn.), directed by artistic director Michael Wilson.

© T. Charles Erikson/Hartford Stage

𝒫laywright

David Mamet

As David Mamet's Hollywood types, Madonna, Joe Mantegna, and Ron Silver act out movie-biz pathology in *Speed the Plow*, first presented at Lincoln Center Theater (New York City) in 1988. Directed by Gregory Mosher.

Bridgette Lacombe

Courtesy Bridgette Lacombe/Billy Rose Theatre Collection, The New York Public Library for the Performing Arts, Astor, Lenox and Tilden Foundations

through his need to control his son and assert his own manhood in August Wilson's *Fences* (1987).

> *"I think that people are generally more happy with a mystery than with an explanation. So the less that you say about a character the more interesting he becomes."*[15]
>
> DAVID MAMET
> *Playwright*

Playwrights conceptualize events—hear and see them in the mind's eye—for they are to be enacted and must hold the audience's attention. *Performability* is the key to the success of the playwright's story and dialogue. Whether the story is told in a straightforward manner (linear, point-to-point storytelling) or arranged as a series of nonlinear or discontinuous scenes, audiences respond to powerful and sustained dramatic impact. But that impact must be based on the dramatization of events with believable persons brought together in some sort of meaningful and satisfying fashion for audiences.

In the playwright's so-called bag of tools, plot—what Aristotle called the "soul" of drama—requires compression, economy, and intensity. Romeo and Juliet meet, marry, and die within a "two-hour traffic upon the stage." Although plots may

David Mamet (b. 1947), born in Chicago, worked as a bit player with Hull House Theatre, attended the Neighborhood Playhouse School of Theatre (New York City) in the sixties, and graduated from Goddard College in 1969. He returned to Chicago and became a founding member of the Nicholas Theatre Company, where he began writing and directing plays. His early plays, *Sexual Perversity in Chicago* (1975), *American Buffalo* (1975), and *A Life in the Theatre* (1977), established his style, language, and subjects.

Mamet is known as a playwright of the panic and poetry of the working class in America. He writes of the spiritual failure of entrepreneurial capitalism in the junkyards, real estate offices, and Hollywood agencies of America. Noted for his distinctive language, Mamet's beleaguered characters demonstrate their frustration, rage, laughter, and incomprehension in undeleted expletives—what one critic called the "sludge in American language."

More recently, Mamet has written *Glengarry Glen Ross* (1983), which received the Pulitzer Prize for Drama, *Speed the Plow* (1988), *Oleanna* (1992), *The Cryptogram* (1995), *The Old Neighborhood* (1997), and *Boston Marriage* (1999); and film scripts for *The Postman Always Rings Twice, The Verdict, House of Games, Glengarry Glen Ross, The Edge, Wag the Dog, The Spanish Prisoner,* and *State and Main.*

DAVID MAMET'S *GLENGARRY GLEN ROSS* The 2000 revival at the McCarter Theatre, Princeton, New Jersey, with Charles Durning and directed by Scott Zigler.

©T. Charles Erickson

encompass many years, the events are compressed so that the story is introduced, told, and resolved within a reasonable amount of time. The intensity of emotions, changed fortunes, and unexpected happenings account for our interest in the story and its outcome.

To sustain our interest, the playwright's characters must be believable, multifaceted, and psychologically complex. We may never meet a Hamlet, but his dilemma and responses are credible and far more complex and intriguing than events in our daily lives. Characters, according to Tennessee Williams, add the mystery and confusion of living to plays:

> My chief aim in playwriting is the creation of character. I have always had a deep feeling for the mystery in life, and essentially my plays have been an effort to explore the beauty and meaning in the confusion of living.[16]

AUGUST WILSON'S *FENCES*
The Yale Repertory Theatre's production, New Haven (Conn.) with James Earl Jones.

William B. Carter

Plot and character are only two of the playwright's means of conveying the confusion and mystery of life. Language is the playwright's third essential tool. As dialogue, it must be speakable as words filled with potential for gesture and revelation of meanings—both obvious and hidden. As justification for the pain he causes his family, Troy Maxson talks of his plight as an African American in a predominantly white society:

> … you born with two strikes on you before you come to the plate. You got to guard it closely … always looking for the curve-ball on the inside corner. You can't afford to let none get past you. You can't afford a call strike. If you going down … you going down swinging. (2, i)[17]

Wilson's language is graphic, active, filled with gesture, emotion, and metaphor that convey the essence of Troy's plight and personal understanding of his situation in life. He has been born "with two strikes" against him before he steps up to the "plate" in the game of life.

In *Fences,* Troy Maxson speaks in language highly charged with feelings, gestures, and baseball images. Wilson's character swings his favorite baseball bat against a rag ball and delivers pronouncements on life in a manner that is at once believable and actable. No baseball diamond is required to convey Troy's philosophy of life as he stands in his front yard in reduced circumstances and swings the bat against defensive thoughts and lost dreams.

THE PLAYWRIGHT AND THE INDUSTRY

Since the Greek festivals in ancient Athens, producers have clamored for new and better plays from playwrights. Today, hundreds of producers and literary agents are anxious to discover new authors and new scripts. To do so, they employ a cadre of "readers" to find the exceptional manuscript: a play by a "new" David Mamet, or an "undiscovered" Wendy Wasserstein. International Creative Management (ICM) and the William Morris Agency are the largest literary agencies in New York City, representing Arthur Miller, Edward Albee, Paula Vogel, and others. For years Tennessee Williams was represented by Audrey Wood, who guided him through the most successful part of his career. The agent and the producer are two essential connections for the playwright's success. Moreover, some writers dev-elop working relationships with directors; for example, Arthur Miller and Tennessee Williams with Elia Kazan, August Wilson with Lloyd Richards and Marion McClinton, Neil Simon with Mike Nichols and Jerry Zaks, Wendy Wasserstein with Daniel Sullivan, and Paula Vogel with

(continued on page 88)

𝒫laywright

William B. Carter

August Wilson

© Jim Caldwell/The Alley Theatre

AUGUST WILSON'S *MA RAINEY'S BLACK BOTTOM*
Ma Rainey (Theresa Merritt) in the recording studio. Produced at the Alley Theatre, Houston, in 1994.

August Wilson (b. 1945), born in Pittsburgh, has had five plays produced on Broadway: *Ma Rainey's Black Bottom* (1984), *Fences* (1987), *Joe Turner's Come and Gone* (1988), *The Piano Lesson* (1990), *Two Trains Running* (1990), and *King Hedley II* (2001). He has won two Pulitzer Prizes (for *Fences* and *The Piano Lesson*). At nineteen, Wilson left home to become a writer; he supported himself as a cook and stock clerk; in his spare time he read voraciously in the public library. Writing became his means of responding to changing race relations in America and to the violence erupting within African American families and communities. In 1968, he co-founded Pittsburgh's Black Horizons Theatre and secured a production of his first play, *Black Bart and the Sacred Hills*, in St. Paul, Minnesota, where he has lived since 1977. In St. Paul, Wilson was hired as a scriptwriter for the Science Museum of Minnesota, which had a theatre company attached to the museum. In 1981, after several rejections of other scripts, a draft of *Ma Rainey's Black Bottom* was accepted by the Eugene O'Neill Theatre Center's National Playwrights Conference in Waterford, Connecticut, and Wilson's career was launched.

(continued)

August Wilson (continued)

Wilson's major plays, set in different decades of twentieth-century America, are a series in progress, including the recent *Jitney* and *King Hedley II.* He is writing a history of black America, probing what he perceives to be crucial oppositions in African American culture between those who celebrate black Americans' African roots and those who deny that historical reality.

AUGUST WILSON'S *KING HEDLEY II* First produced in 2000 by the Pittsburgh Public Theater and directed by Marion Isaac McClinton, with Tony Todd as Hedley and Russell Andrews as Mister.

Molly Smith. Others, like David Mamet and Edward Albee, frequently direct their own plays but establish relationships with producers and regional theatres.

For the successful Broadway playwright, the rewards are staggering, including television, film, recording, and publishing contracts and interviews in glamorous magazines. Prestigious awards are also forthcoming as indicators of success: the Pulitzer Prize, the Drama Critics' Circle Award, the Antoinette Perry "Tony" Award, and for some, even Nobel Prizes for Literature. Luigi Pirandello, Eugene O'Neill, and Samuel Beckett received Nobel awards.

In many respects, playwrights are the most celebrated of the theatre's artists, because audiences are aware that they sit in the presence of the writer's world. We listen to and experience a personal vision that makes us laugh and cry. The public may revere the actor—an Al Pacino or a Jessica Lange—but the actor's creativity usually begins with the playwright's creation: the characters, situations, environment, and original world of conflicts, feelings, and choices.

In one sense, playwriting is only one facet of the theatre profession and the theatrical machine—the industry. In another sense, it transcends both because when the curtain comes down on a production, there still remain the playwright's words, shaping characters, conflicts, ideas, and fictions. As Lillian Hellman, creator of *The Little Foxes,*

(continued on page 90)

$\mathcal{P}$laywright

Tennessee Williams

Martha Swope/Timepix

©Eileen Darby/Billy Rose Theatre Collection, The New York Public Library for the Performing Arts, Astor, Lenox and Tilden Foundations

TENNESSEE WILLIAMS'
SWEET BIRD OF YOUTH
Paul Newman as Chance
Wayne (left) and Madeleine
Sherwood as Miss Lucy con-
front their personal histories.
Directed by Elia Kazan and
designed by Jo Mielziner for the
1959 Broadway production.

Born Thomas Lanier Williams in Columbus, Mississippi, **Tennessee Williams** (1911–1983) was the son of a traveling salesman and an Episcopalian minister's daughter. The family moved to St. Louis in 1918. He was educated at Missouri University, Washington University in St. Louis, and later the University of Iowa, where he received his bachelor's degree.

In 1939, *Story* magazine published his short story "A Field of Blue Children," the first work to appear under his nickname "Tennessee," which was given to him because of his Southern accent. That same year he compiled four one-act plays under the title *American Blues,* and won a prize in the Group Theatre's American play contest. This aroused the interest of New York agent Audrey Wood, who asked to represent him.

The Glass Menagerie in 1944–45 marked Williams' first major success and established him as an important American playwright. It was followed by his major plays: *A Streetcar Named Desire* (1947), *The Rose Tattoo* (1951), *Cat on a Hot Tin Roof* (1955), *Sweet Bird of Youth* (1959), and *The Night of the Iguana* (1961). Although his later plays failed to please critics, he continued to write until his death.

𝒫laywright

Arthur Miller

Inge Morath/Magnum Photos, Inc.

© Jim Caldwell/Alley Theatre

ARTHUR MILLER'S
A VIEW FROM THE BRIDGE
The 1999 revival, with James
Black and Annalee Jeffries (right)
and Kevin Waldron (left),
directed by Stephen Rayne and
produced by the Alley Theatre,
Houston.

Arthur Miller and Tennessee Williams were the most influential American playwrights following the Second World War. **Arthur Miller** (b. 1916) had his first success
with *All My Sons* (1947), a realistic play about a wartime manufacturer of airplane
engines who put profit above the safety of fighter pilots. He wrote the now classic
Death of a Salesman (1949), followed by *The Crucible* (1953), *A View from the Bridge*
(1955), and *The Price* (1968). His reputation rests largely on these five plays. His more
recent works received mixed critical reviews: *The Creation of the World and Other
Business* (1972), *The American Clock* (1980), *The Archbishop's Ceiling* (1986), *The Ride
Down Mount Morgan* (1991), *Broken Glass* (1994), and *Mr. Peters' Connections* (1999).

Arthur Miller is often thought of as a moralist and social dramatist. His plays deal
with the individual's responsibility in the face of society's emphasis on such false values as material success and personal happiness at any price.

said: "The manuscript, the words on the page, was what you started with and what you have
left" after the production is over. Whereas we might not have an opportunity to see a production of *A Streetcar Named Desire* or *Fences,* we can read the playwright's published script
and partake of the writer's creative act, incomplete though it may be without production.

NEW AMERICAN WRITING: ALTERNATIVE VOICES

In the late 1980s and through the 1990s, an underrepresented, and often invisible, America emerged on stages throughout the country. The new writers were gay and lesbian, African American, Asian American, Latino/a, Hispanic, and Chicano. The central issues of their lives became the material of their plays: oppression, racism, sexism, classism, homophobia. America's stages came to mirror ethnic, social, and political diversity among the many cultures that make up our society. Gender, ethnicity, and sexual orientation have become the defining subjects of the new writing.

PAULA VOGEL'S *HOW I LEARNED TO DRIVE,* directed by Mark Brokaw, was produced Off Broadway at the Vineyard Theatre (1997) with Mary-Louise Parker as Li'l Bit and David Morse as Peck

Gay and Lesbian Writing

In the late 1960s gay and lesbian issues came to be treated as serious dramatic subjects in the American theatre. In his groundbreaking play, *Boys in the Band* (1968), Mart Crowley introduced sexual orientation as a permissible romantic topic. What followed were mainstream Broadway musicals (*La Cage aux Folles, Falsettos, Kiss of the Spider Woman*) and serious dramas (*Bent, M. Butterfly, The Normal Heart, Angels in America, Baltimore Waltz, Love! Valour! Compassion!, Gross Indecency: The Three Trials of Oscar Wilde, Stop Kiss, The Laramie Project*). That new and terrible illness whose early victims in the United States and Europe were predominantly gay produced writing in the 1980s that addressed

"I'm interested in the dust that settles when worlds collide. Sometimes these worlds are cultural, as in my explorations of a Chinese past meeting an American present.... I am fascinated by America as a land of dreams— people pursue them and hope some day to own one."[18]

DAVID HENRY HWANG
Playwright

KISS OF THE SPIDER WOMAN This musical is by John Kander and Fred Ebb with book by Terrence McNally based on the novel by Manuel Puig. Directed by Harold Prince with Brent Carver and Chita Rivera, Broadway, 1993.

THE LARAMIE PROJECT This play was written by Moisés Kaufmann and the members of Tectonic Theater Project from interviews with the townspeople of Laramie, Wyoming, about the murder of Matthew Shepard. First presented in 2000 by the Denver Center Theatre Company.

political, medical, and personal issues in the age of AIDS. Larry Kramer, Terence McNally, Tony Kushner, Paula Vogel, Paul Rudnick, and Diana Son have examined the political, cultural, and aesthetic implications of gay and lesbian issues in their plays.

African American Writing

African Americans writing for the theatre made inroads in the early years of the twentieth century with Langston Hughes's *Mulatto* in the 1930s and Lorraine Hansberry's *A Raisin the Sun* in the late 1950s. Paralleling the civil rights movement in the 1960s, Amiri Baraka's (then LeRoi Jones) writing became a revolutionary force. *Dutchman* and *Slave Ship* confronted American racism head on.

Beginning in the sixties, a growing number of African American playwrights emerged on the national scene, among them Charles Gordone (*No Place to Be Somebody*), Lonne Elder III (*Ceremonies in Dark Old Men*), Adrienne Kennedy (*Funnyhouse of a Negro*), Ntozake Shange (*for colored girls who have considered suicide/when the rainbow is enuf*), Suzan-Lori Parks (*The America Play*), John Henry Redwood (*The Old Settler*), Pearl Cleage (*Blues for an Alabama Sky*), Cheryl L. West (*Jar the Floor*), and George C. Wolfe (*The Colored Museum*). Lavishly produced musicals about the black experience with predominantly black casts found their way to Broadway: *Purlie, Bubbling Brown Sugar, The Wiz, Ain't Misbehavin', Sophisticated Ladies, Dreamgirls, Five Guys Named Moe, Jelly's Last Jam, Bring in 'da Noise, Bring in 'da Funk,* and *Ain't Nothing but the Blues.* August Wilson in his explorations of the twentieth-century history of black America in powerful and provocative plays from *Ma Rainey's Black Bottom* to *King Hedley II* has become the leading African American playwright of his time.

AMIRI BARAKA'S DUTCHMAN The 2000 revival, with Chris McKinney and Vivienne Benesch, directed by Jonathan Wilson, and produced by Hartford Stage Company (Conn.).

DIANA SON'S *STOP KISS* Directed by Sharon Ott at the Seattle Repertory Theatre, Wash., 2000, with Jodi Somers (left) and Amy Cronise.

Asian American Writing

Asian theatre and opera traditions were imported by laborers from China as early as the 1850s and by Japanese and Filipinos settling in the United States at the turn of the century. As interest in traditional Eastern performance styles diminished, Asian stereotypes and stock characters dominated plays and films with Asian themes until the civil rights era. Beginning in the sixties, new Asian American writers found it necessary to establish their own theatres to showcase their writing, which exploded narrow stereotypes and misperceptions about Asian culture, people, and traditions. Such playwrights as Philip Kan Gotanda (*Sisters Matsumoto*), Han Ong (*L.A. Stories*), and Diana Son (*Stop Kiss*) introduced complex issues of race, prejudice, family, compromise, and struggles for self-fulfillment into writing for the theatre. It was David Henry Hwang's *M. Butterfly* in 1988 that effectively introduced the Asian American voice into mainstream American theatre.

U.S. Latino/a Writing

A Spanish-speaking theatre has existed in North America since the late sixteenth century whose purpose was to preserve Hispanic traditions and language for the minority culture. In 1965, a Latino theatre under the wing of the United Farm Workers burst on the political scene to address the plight of migrant farm workers in California. Led by Mexican-American theatre artist Luis Valdez and his bilingual Chicano company El Teatro Campesino (The Farm Workers' Theatre), Hispanic-American writing found a contemporary voice. By 1967, El Teatro Campesino moved away from union involvement, expanding its subjects to address working-class and urban issues. A growing number of writers followed: Cuban-born María Irene Fornés (*The Conduct of Life*) and Eduardo Machado (*The Floating Island Plays*); Puerto Rican–born José Rivera (*Marisol*); Latina dramatist Milcha Sanchez-Scott (*Roosters*), and Chicano authors Josefina Lopez (*Real Women Have Curves*) and Carlos Morton (*The Miser of Mexico*).

JOSÉ RIVERA'S *REFERENCES TO SALVADOR DALI MAKE ME HOT* Directed by Julieete Carrillo, at the South Coast Repertory (Costa Mesa, Calif.) in 2000.

*A*lternate Voices

Barry Forbus/Courtesy of Goodman Theatre

Pearl Cleage: An Atlanta-based writer whose recent plays had their premieres at the Alliance Theatre Company (Atlanta) with subsequent productions throughout the country. These include *Flying West* (1992), *Blues for an Alabama Sky* (1995), and *Bourbon at the Border* (1997). Cleage is a columnist for the *Atlanta Tribune* and a contributor to *Essence* and *Ms.* magazine. Her first novel, *What Looks Like Crazy on an Ordinary Day* (1999), was an Oprah Winfrey Book Club selection. She has said that as a black artist what informs her writing is her cultural heritage which is a "rich legacy of protest and resistance."

Rebecca Gilman: The Alabama-born graduate of the University of Iowa's playwriting program settled in Chicago, where she worked as a temporary employee in an accounting firm and wrote plays by night. Her work attracted the attention of Chicago's Goodman Theatre, where *Boy Gets Girl* and *Spinning into Butter* were first produced. Her plays avoid easy categorization. *The Glory of Living* is about child abuse and serial murder; *Spinning into Butter* deals with racial objectification; and *Boy Gets Girl* is about a woman and her stalker. Gilman's work has been produced in London and New York. She has received major awards, including the American Theatre Critics Association's Osborn Award and London's *Evening Standard* Award for Most Promising Playwright.

Courtesy of Goodman Theatre

© Carol Rosegg

Philip Kan Gotanda: A third-generation Japanese American grew up in Stockton (Calif.), played in a rock band, studied ceramics in Japan, and went to law school. He got his first exposure as a playwright in 1979 with Mako at the East West Players in Los Angeles with his rock musical *The Avocado Kid*. His next plays were presented at the Asian American Theatre Company in San Francisco. *The Wash* was produced in 1985 at the Mark Taper Forum's New Theatre for Now Festival in Los Angeles, followed by *A Song for a Nisei Fisherman*. Gotanda's recent plays, *The Dream of Kitamura, Yankee Dawg You Die*, and *Sisters Matsumoto*, have been produced at regional theatres in Berkeley, Seattle, Chicago, and New York City. He serves with David Henry Hwang as co-dramaturg for the Asian American Theatre Company in San Francisco.

Courtesy of David henry Hwang

David Henry Hwang: A second-generation Chinese American, he grew up in Los Angeles and studied at Stanford University. His playwriting career began in 1979 following a writing workshop with Sam Shepard at Padua Hills Playwrights Festival. *FOB, Family Devotions,* and *The Dance and the Railroad* were written as a Chinese American trilogy. He became the first Asian American to win Broadway's "Tony" Award for Best Play with *M. Butterfly* in 1988. *Face Value, Golden Child* ("Tony" Award nomination for Best Play in 1998), and librettos for *1,000 Airplanes on the Roof, The Voyage* with Philip Glass, and *The Silver River for Bright Sheng* followed. He was appointed by President Bill Clinton to the President's Committee on the Arts and Humanities.

Eduardo Machado: Born in 1953 in Havana, Cuba, he was sent from his homeland as a child to the United States. The family settled in Canoga Park, California, where in the summer of 1978 Machado was introduced to the Padua Hills Playwrights' Festival and to María Irene Fornés. He became her assistant on *Fefu and Her Friends* and began writing and acting. Later, in New York City as part of INTAR (Hispanic American Arts Center), he wrote *The Floating Island Plays* (*The Modern Ladies of Guanabacoa, Fabiola, Broken Eggs, In the Eye of the Hurricane*) between 1983 and 1991. Since then he has written *Rosario and the Gypsies, Why to Refuse, Once Removed,* and *Related Retreats.* In all of his writing Machado seeks the meaning of his people's history.

©Jonathan Cramer

Gary Bonasorte/Courtesy of William Morris Agency

Terrence McNally: He grew up in Corpus Christi, Texas, attended Columbia University in New York City, and began his theatre career as a stage manager for the Actors' Studio. He wrote *As Things that Go Bump in the Night* in 1962 followed by *Where Has Tommy Flowers Gone?, Bad Habits, The Lisbon Traviata, Frankie and Johnny in the Claire de Lune, Lips Together, Teeth Apart, Master Class, Love! Valour! Compassion!,* and *Corpus Christi.* With an abiding interest in music and opera, he wrote or adapted the musical books for *The Rink, Kiss of the Spider Woman, Ragtime,* and *The Full Monty* (based on the film).

(continued)

Diana Son: A graduate of New York University, she is a member of the Playwright's Unit and an Associate Artist at The Joseph Papp Public Theater. Her early plays *Stealing Fire, The R.A.W. Plays: Short Plays for Raunchy Asian Women,* and *2000 Miles* were produced Off Off Broadway. Her fiction has been published by *Asian Pacific American Journal.* Her best known work, *Stop Kiss,* was first produced in 1998 at The Joseph Papp Public Theater/New York Shakespeare Festival and received the 1999 Media Award from GLAAD (Gay and Lesbian Alliance Against Defamation) for Outstanding New York Theatre Production on Broadway and Off Broadway. Talking about the play's context of "gay-bashing," she said: "I would never personally say, 'This is a play about homophobia. This is a play about gay-bashing. This is a play about the civil rights of gays and lesbians in America.' I would describe the play as a love story."[19]

© Lia Chang Gallery Collection

Cheryl L. West: Originally from Chicago, she lives in Seattle and has written a number of plays, including *Before It Hits Home* (1991), *Jar the Floor* (1992, revised 1999), *Puddin' Pete: Fable of a Marriage* (1992), *Holiday Heart* (1994), and the book for the musical *Play On!* (1997). She writes both musical books and serious plays that deal with family and race in America.

© Joan Marcus

George C. Wolfe: Kentucky-born, he studied musical theatre at New York University and found champions in Stephen Sondheim, Arthur Laurents, and Richard Maltby Jr. His big break came with *The Colored Museum* (1986), which opened at the Crossroads Theatre (N.J.) and moved to The Joseph Papp Public Theater. He wrote *Spunk* (1990), based on the stories of Harlem Renaissance writer Zora Neale Hurston; wrote the book for *Jelly's Last Jam* (1992) and directed the musical for Broadway; staged Tony Kushner's *Angels in America: Millennium Approaches* and Anna Deavere Smith's *Twilight: Los Angeles* for Broadway; collaborated as writer and director with choreographer Savion Glover on the long-running *Bring in da' Noise, Bring in 'da Funk* (1996); directed the Broadway revival of *On the Town* (1998) and the musical *The Wild Party* (2000). Named a resident director at The Public Theater, he succeeded Joseph Papp in 1993 as producer for The Public Theater/New York Shakespeare Festival with the goal of making the theatre "inclusive and healthy in a non-token way."

AP/Wide World Photos

TRANSITION

When the theatrical process begins with the script, the playwright becomes the theatre's most essential collaborative artist. The playwright creates the play's world—its events, people, and meanings—on paper. The playwright's tools, conventions, forms, and styles of writing are endlessly fascinating and the subject of the next three chapters.

WEB SITES

Alex Catalogue of Electronic Texts: A Collection of Digital Documents
   http://www.sunsite.berkeley.edu/alex/

Association of Hispanic Art
   http://latinoarts.org

Dramatic Exchange (Web Resource for Playwrights, Producers, and Others Interested in Plays)
   http://www.dramex.org/

The Dramatists Guild of America, Inc.
   http://www.dramaguild.com

National Endowment for the Arts
   http://arts.endow.gov

National Playwrights Conference (at the Eugene O'Neill Theater Center, Waterford, Conn.)
   http://www.oneilltheatercenter.org

Women in Theatre
   http://www.geocities.com/Broadway/Alley/5379/

The United States Copyright Office
   http://www.lcweb.loc.gov/copyright/

These search terms are provided to assist you in exploring the topics introduced in this chapter at:

http//www.infotrac-college.com

playwriting, playwright's agent, copyright, National Playwright's Conference, commercial theatre, non-profit theatre, performance texts, stage directions, divisions into acts and scenes, one-act plays.

CHAPTER 5

If art reflects life it does so with special mirrors.[1]

BERTOLT BRECHT

A Short Organum for the Theatre

Perspectives and Forms of Theatrical Writing

Playwrights use different dramatic forms to express their understanding of human experience. Tragedy and comedy are the forms most familiar to us, but there are many other ways to classify plays and to label the playwright's vision—the way he or she perceives life in theatrical terms. A study of drama's changing forms is also a study of the playwright's changing perception of the world.

DRAMA'S PERSPECTIVES

Over the centuries, playwrights developed ways of imitating behavior in different dramatic forms and styles. Drama's forms change as societies and perceptions of the world change. This is what Peter Brook means when he says that every theatrical form, once born, is mortal.[2] Dramatic forms, what Bertolt Brecht called "special mirrors," fall into many categories. The main ones are *tragedy, comedy, tragicomedy, melodrama,* and *farce.* In the twentieth century, two more significant forms have been devised: *epic* and *absurd.*

Drama's essential forms are ways of seeing human experience. The words *tragedy, comedy,* and *tragicomedy* are not so much ways of classifying plays by their endings as ways of talking about the playwright's vision of experience—of the way he or she perceives life. They furnish clues about how the play is to be taken or understood by audiences. Is the play a serious statement about, say, the relationship between men and women? Does it explore issues of gender and sexual orientation? Does it despair at the possibilities of mutual understanding? Or does it hold such attempts up to ridicule? Or does it explore humanity's unchanging existential situation?

TRAGEDY

It is not altogether simpleminded to say that a tragedy is a play with an unhappy ending. Tragedy, the first of the great dramatic forms in Western drama, makes a special statement about human fallibility.

The Tragic Vision

The writer's tragic vision of experience conceives of people as both vulnerable and invincible, as capable of abject defeat and transcendent greatness. Tragedies like *Oedipus the King, Medea, Hamlet, Ghosts, Death of a Salesman,* and *A Streetcar Named Desire* show the world's injustice, evil, and pain. Tragic heroes, in an exercise of free will, pit themselves against forces represented by other characters, by their own inner drives, or by their physical environment. We witness their suffering, their inevitable defeat, and sometimes, their personal triumph in the face of defeat. The trials of the hero give meaning to the pain and paradox of our humanity.

Some tragedies are concerned with seeking meaning and justice in an ordered world, others with humanity's helpless protest against an irrational one. In both kinds, the hero, alone and willful, asserts his or her intellect and energy against the ultimate mysteries of an imperfect world.

Tragic Realization

The realization (a *recognition* or *anagnorisis*) that follows the hero's efforts usually takes one of two directions: that, despite suffering and calamity, a world order and eternal laws exist and people can learn from suffering; or that human acts and suffering in an indifferent, capricious, or mechanical universe are futile, but at the same time the hero's protests against the nature of existence are to be celebrated. In *Oedipus the King* and *A Streetcar Named Desire,* we find examples of these two kinds of tragic realization.

Aristotle on Tragedy

In the first writing on drama in the West, called *The Poetics* (c. 335–323 B.C.), the Greek philosopher Aristotle spoke of tragedy as "an imitation of an action ... concerning the fall of a man whose character is good (though not pre-eminently just or virtuous) ... whose misfortune is brought about not by vice or depravity but by some error or frailty ... with incidents arousing pity and fear, wherewith to accomplish the catharsis of these emotions."[3]

Aristotle emphasized the pre-eminence of plot over character and defined tragedy's action as an imitation of a noble hero experiencing a downfall and tragedy's subjects as suffering and death. The heroes of ancient tragedies, as depicted by the playwrights, were usually aristocrats, to show that even the great among us are subject to the fate of the human condition. In modern plays, the hero's averageness speaks to us of kinship in adversity. Whether the hero is aristocratic or ordinary, his or her actions are shaped by the writer's tragic view of life, which centers on the need to give meaning to our fate even though we are doomed to failure and defeat.

Euripides' *Medea* as Tragedy

Produced in the City Dionysia festival (Athens) in 431 B.C., Euripides' *Medea* tells the story of Jason's betrayal of his wife, Medea, to further his fortunes (and those of his

Sophocles' Oedipus the King

One of several Greek playwrights whose work survives today, Sophocles wrote three plays about Oedipus. *Oedipus the King* (427 B.C.) is generally considered the greatest of Greek tragedies. (*Antigone*, 441 B.C., and *Oedipus at Colonus*, 406 B.C., are the other two.)

Oedipus the King tells the story of a man who flees from Corinth, to avoid fulfilling a prophecy that he will kill his father and marry his mother. On his journey, at a place where three roads meet, he kills an old man (an apparent stranger but actually his real father, the king of Thebes). He then proceeds to Thebes and solves the riddle of the sphinx. As a reward, he is made king and married to the widowed queen, who is actually his mother, Jocasta. He rules well and has four children.

The play opens with Thebes stricken by a plague. Declaring that he will rid the city of this infection, Oedipus sends his brother-in-law Creon to consult the Delphic oracle about the cause of the plague. As he pursues the plague's source, Oedipus comes face to face with himself as his father's killer, as his mother's son and husband, and as his children's father and brother. When the truth is learned, Jocasta kills herself and he puts out his eyes. By his own decree, Oedipus is exiled from Thebes and wanders blind into the countryside.

Oedipus the King explores human guilt and innocence, knowledge and ignorance, power and helplessness. Its fundamental idea is that wisdom comes to us only through suffering.

---

two small sons) by marriage to the Princess of Corinth. The Athenian audience would have known the story of Medea, the barbarian princess and sorceress, related to the gods, who helped Jason and the Argonauts steal the Golden Fleece from her father. To help them escape, she murdered her brother and threw pieces of the body into the sea so that her father's pursuing fleet would be slowed in order to collect the fragments for burial.

With a background of violence, passion, and sorcery, Euripides' play begins in Corinth, where Jason and Medea have taken refuge. Whether to strengthen his economic and social position, or because he has grown tired of his dangerous foreign wife, Jason decides to put her aside and marry the daughter of Creon, King of Corinth. At this point the action begins. Medea's jealous rage and desperate sense of betrayal by a husband for whom she sacrificed all spurs her revenge. She uses her magical powers to destroy both Creon and his daughter by means of a poisoned robe that clings to their flesh and melts them in a fiery death. Despairing of her children's safety and wishing to injure Jason totally, she kills her sons and escapes with their bodies in a supernatural chariot drawn by dragons to take refuge with the elderly

$\mathcal{P}$laywright

©Gianni Dagli Orti/CORBIS

Diana Rigg played Medea in the 1994 revival of Euripides' tragedy at the Almeida Theatre, London, and on Broadway.

Euripides

©Joan Marcus

Euripides (c. 480–406 B.C.), one of the three great fifth-century B.C. writers of tragedy, won only five contests during his lifetime. Scholars attribute his relative unpopularity to his innovations with play structure and to the characters and subjects of his plays.

The son of aristocrats, Euripides held political office in Athens, where he became a member of the unpopular peace party during the Peloponnesian War and an opponent of Athenian imperialism. Toward the end of his life he sought exile at the court of Macedonia and died there, rumored to have been killed by the Macedonian king's hunting dogs.

He is credited with writing eighty-eight plays (twenty-two sets of four), of which nineteen plays have survived. His best known are *Medea, Hippolytus, Electra, The Trojan Women,* and *The Bacchae. The Cyclops,* also by Euripides, is the only complete satyr play that now exists.

Aristotle, surveying Greek drama decades later, called Euripides the "most tragic of poets," presumably because of Euripides' dark materials: sexual repression, irrational violence, human madness and savagery. Twentieth-century critics consider him the most modern and innovative of the Greek tragic writers, for he speaks to audiences of the hero's demoralization and savagery and of the barbarity of armies at war.

Aegeus, King of Athens, who has promised asylum in exchange for her powers to restore his manhood.

Euripides uses the *Medea* story of unrequited love, unreasonable passion, and catastrophic revenge to depict a world where order is ever tenuous and where human beings are subject to the irrationality of gods and other humans. As the chorus says at the end in ironic explanation:

... What we thought
Is not confirmed and what we thought not God
Contrives. And so it happens in this story.

COMEDY

In the eighteenth century, Horace Walpole said: "The world is a comedy to those that think, a tragedy to those that feel." In comedy the playwright examines the social world, social values, and people as social beings. Frequently, comic action shows the social disorder created by an eccentric character who deviates from reasonable values like sensibility, good nature, flexibility, moderation, tolerance, and social intelligence. Deviation is sharply ridiculed in comedy because it threatens to destroy revered social structures such as marriage and family.

Differences Between Tragedy and Comedy

Tragedy	Comedy	Tragedy	Comedy
Individual	Society	Terror	Euphoria
Metaphysical	Social	Unhappiness	Happiness
Death	Endurance	Irremediable	Remediable
Error	Folly	Decay	Growth
Suffering	Joy	Destruction	Continuation
Pain	Pleasure	Defeat	Survival
Life-denying	Procreative	Extreme	Moderation
Separation	Union/Reunion	Inflexible	Flexible

The Comic Vision

The writer of comedy calls for sanity, reason, and moderation in human behavior so that society can function for the well-being and happiness of its members. In comedy, society survives the threat posed by inflexible or antisocial behavior. In Molière's *Tartuffe* the title character's greed is revealed and Orgon's family is returned to a normal, domestic existence at the play's end. For the seventeenth-century French playwright, as for some of his English contemporaries, the well-being of the family unit is a measure of the health of the society as a whole.

Playwright

Molière

Courtesy French Press and Information Office

©Jim Caldwell

Tartuffe (Jeffrey Bean) attempts to seduce Elmire (Annalee Jefferies) in the 1994 revival of Molière's play at the Alley Theatre, Houston. Directed by Gregory Boyd in collaboration with the California-based Dell'Arte Players.

At the end of almost any comedy, the life force is ordinarily celebrated in a wedding, a dance, or a banquet symbolizing the harmony and reconciliation of opposing forces: young and old, flexible and inflexible, reasonable and unreasonable. These social ceremonies allow us to see that good sense wins the day in comedy and that humanity endures in the vital, the flexible, and the reasonable.

TRAGICOMEDY

Definitions

Tragicomedy, as its name implies, is a mixed dramatic form. Up to the end of the seventeenth century in Europe, it was defined as a mixture of tragedy, which went from good fortune to bad, and comedy, which reversed the order from bad fortune to good.

Molière (Jean-Baptiste Poquelin, 1622–1673), French playwright-actor-manager, was the son of Louis XIV's upholsterer. Poquelin spent his early years close to the court and received a gentleman's education. He joined a theatrical troupe in 1643 and became a professional actor with the stage name Molière. Molière helped to found the Illustre Théâtre Company in Paris, which soon failed, and spent twelve years touring the French provinces as an itinerant actor and company playwright. He returned to Paris to become the foremost writer and comedian of his time. Within thirteen years (1659–1673), he wrote and acted in *Tartuffe, The Misanthrope, The Doctor in Spite of Himself, The Miser,* and *The Imaginary Invalid.* Written during France's golden age, Molière's comedies balance follies of eccentric and devious humanity against society's reasonable good sense.

Tartuffe (1664) is Molière's comedy about a hypocrite. Tartuffe disguises himself as a cleric, and his apparent piety ingratiates him with the credulous merchant Orgon and his mother, Madame Pernelle. As the play begins, Tartuffe has taken over Orgon's house. Both Orgon and his mother believe that Tartuffe's pious example will be good for the family. But everyone else in the family, including the outspoken servant Dorine, is perceptive enough to see through Tartuffe.

Despite the protests of his brother-in-law Cléante and his son Damis, Orgon determines that his daughter Marianne, who is in love with Valère, will marry Tartuffe. When Orgon's wife Elmire begs Tartuffe to refuse Marianne's hand, he tries to seduce her. Damis, who has overheard, denounces Tartuffe. Orgon banishes his son rather than his guest and signs over his property to Tartuffe.

Elmire then plots to expose the hypocrite. She persuades Orgon to conceal himself under a table while she encourages Tartuffe's advances. Orgon's eyes are opened, but it is too late. The impostor realizes he has been discovered and turns Orgon's family out of the house. Then he reports to the authorities that Orgon has a strongbox containing seditious papers and contrives to have Orgon arrested. But, by the king's order, the arresting officer takes Tartuffe to prison instead.

The play ends with Damis reconciled to his father, Orgon reconciled with his family, and Valère and Marianne engaged.

Tragicomedy combined serious and comic incidents as well as the styles, subject matter, and language proper to tragedy and to comedy, and it also mixed characters from all stations of life. The *ending* (up until the nineteenth century) was its principal feature: Tragicomedies were serious and potentially tragic plays with happy endings, or at least with averted catastrophes. Shakespeare's *All's Well That Ends Well* and *The Winter's Tale* are considered tragicomedies.

The term *modern tragicomedy* is used to designate plays with mixed moods in which the endings are neither exclusively tragic nor comic, happy nor unhappy. The great Russian playwright Anton Chekhov wrote plays of mixed moods in which he described the lives of "quiet desperation" of ordinary people in rural Russia around the turn of the last century: provincial gentry, writers, professors, doctors, farmers, servants, teachers, government officials, and garrisoned military. What they had in common, finally, was their survival.

$\mathcal{A}$nton *Chekhov's* The Three Sisters

THE THREE SISTERS With Kim Stanley as Masha, Shirley Knight as Irina, and Geraldine Page as Olga in the 1964 Actors Studio Theatre production, directed by Lee Strasberg, at Broadway's Morosco Theatre.

Chekhov's most frequently revived play, *The Three Sisters* (1901), tells of the provincial lives of the Prozorov family: three sisters (Olga, Masha, and Irina), their brother (Andrey), his wife (Natasha), their lovers, a brother-in-law, and military friends. The play's only action in the traditional sense is the departure of a military regiment from a small town after an interval of several years. For four acts the sisters dream of returning to Moscow to escape from the dull routine of their lives. But, unlike the regiment, they are unable to move on to new places and experiences.

As we scrutinize the seriocomic quality of Chekhov's play, a theme emerges: *the value of surviving in the face of social and economic change.* The three sisters are emotionally adrift in a society whose institutions supply avenues of change only for the soldier, the upstart, and the entrepreneur. The weak and ineffectual, like the three sisters (and these women are products of their time), are locked into a way of life that is neither emotionally nor intellectually rewarding. The most Chekhov's people can

Chekhov's most critically acclaimed work during his lifetime was first produced at the Moscow Art Theatre in 1901 with Olga Knipper as Masha, Constantin Stanislavski as Colonel Vershinin, and Vsevolod Meyerhold as Baron Tusenbach.

In a garrison town in rural Russia, the cultured Prozorov sisters think longingly of the excitement of Moscow, which they left eleven years earlier. Olga, the oldest, is constantly exhausted by her work as a schoolteacher; Masha, married at eighteen to a man she considered an intellectual giant, bitterly realizes that he is merely a pedant; Irina, the youngest, dreams of a romantic future and rejects the sincere love of Lieutenant Tusenbach and the advances of Captain Solyony. Their brother, Andrey, an unambitious man, courts Natasha, the daughter of a local family. Into this circle comes Lieutenant Colonel Vershinin. Like Masha, he is unhappily married. They are immediately attracted to one another.

The Prozorovs and their friends recognize the frustration of their lives, but hope in some vague future keeps their spirits high. For the sisters it is a dream of returning someday to Moscow. The situation changes when Andrey marries Natasha. The sisters' immediate prospects of returning to Moscow are dashed. Irina tries to find relief in her job in the telegraph office. Natasha takes control of the household, and as time goes on the sisters are moved into smaller quarters to make room for her two children. Andrey takes refuge in gambling and mortgages the house that is owned jointly by him and his sisters.

News that the garrison is to be transferred brings depressing prospects for the future. Irina decides to marry Tusenbach, an unattractive but gentle man, who resigns his army commission in the hope of finding more meaningful work. As Masha and Vershinin, who have become open lovers, bid each other goodbye, and the regiment prepares to leave, word comes that Tusenbach has been killed by Solyony in a duel over Irina. The sisters cling to one another for consolation. As the military band strikes up, the gaiety of the music inspires them to hope that there is a new life in store for them in another "millennium."

do is endure the stultifying marriage, the routine job, and the tyrannical sister-in-law. But they survive. With no prescription for the future, Masha says only that "We've got to live."

Modern Tragicomedy

Samuel Beckett subtitled *Waiting for Godot* a "tragicomedy," though it is also an enduring absurdist play of modern times. In this play, two tramps entertain themselves with comic routines while they wait in a sparse landscape adorned by a single tree for someone named Godot to arrive. But Godot never comes. As they react to this situation, humor and energy are mixed with anguish and despair. In the modern form of tragicomedy, playwrights show people laughing at their anxieties and life's contradictions with little effect on their situations. Beckett's Vladimir summarizes this type of writing when he says, "The essential doesn't change."

*P*laywright

Samuel Beckett

Samuel Beckett (1906–1989) was an expatriate Irishman who lived in France. Beckett grew up near Dublin and attended Trinity College, where he received two degrees in literature and began a teaching career. In the 1930s Beckett left his teaching position, traveled in Europe, published his first book (*More Pricks Than Kicks*), and wrote poetry in French. During the Second World War, he worked with the French Resistance and barely escaped capture by the Nazis.

Beginning in 1953, Beckett wrote some thirty theatrical pieces, including radio plays, mime sketches, monologues, and four full-length plays (*Waiting for Godot, Endgame, Krapp's Last Tape, Happy Days*), which have become modern classics.

Beckett's last plays were minimal. *Come and Go* (1965) is a three-minute play, *Breath* (1966) is a thirty-second play, *Rockaby* (1980) is a fifteen-minute play, and *Not I* (1973) consisted of eight pages of text. With these brief pieces Beckett constructed a theatrical image of how we come and go on this earth, briefly filling a void with our bodies and voices, and then disappear into darkness without a trace.

WAITING FOR GODOT A 1994 British revival of *Waiting for Godot* by Samuel Beckett at the Lyric Theatre, Hammersmith.

©Robbie Jack/CORBIS

Sam Shepard's *Buried Child* and August Wilson's *Fences* are more recent tragicomedies. Although principal characters die in both plays, the writers affirm humanity's endurance—despite anguish and loss and little potential for social and personal change.

MELODRAMA

Another mixed form, melodrama derives its name from the Greek word for music, *melos*. It is a combination of music and drama in which the spoken word is used against a musical background. Jean-Jacques Rousseau, who introduced the term's modern use in 1772, applied it to his *Pygmalion*, a *scène lyrique* in which words and music were linked in action.

The Mixed Form

Melodrama became widely used in the nineteenth century to describe a play without music but having a serious action usually caused by the villainy of an unsympathetic character. Melodrama's characters are clearly divided—either sympathetic or unsympathetic—and the villain's destruction brings about the happy resolution. Melodrama usually shows a main character in circumstances that threaten death or ruin from which he or she is rescued at the last possible moment. Like a film's musical score, incidental music heightens the mood of impending disaster. The term *melodrama* is most often applied to such nineteenth-century plays as *Uncle Tom's Cabin* (1852), based on Harriet Beecher Stowe's novel, and Dion Boucicault's *The Octoroon* (1859). Today, we apply the term to such diverse plays as Lillian Hellman's *The Little Foxes* (1938), Lorraine Hansberry's *A Raisin in the Sun* (1959), and such suspenseful thrillers as *Night Must Fall, Death Trap*, and *Sleuth*.

Melodrama's View of Life

The melodramatic view of life sees human beings as whole, not divided; enduring outer conflicts, not inner ones, in a generally hostile world; and sees these conflicts resulting in victory or defeat as they are pressed to extreme conclusions. Melodrama's characters win or lose in the conflict. The endings are clear-cut and extreme. There are no complex and ambiguous resolutions, as when Hamlet wins in the losing. Replying to critics complaining of her melodramatic plots, Lillian Hellman said: "If you believe, as the Greeks did, that man is at the mercy of the gods, then you write tragedy. The end is inevitable from the beginning. But if you believe that man can solve his own problems and is at nobody's mercy, then you will probably write melodrama."[4]

Melodrama oversimplifies, exaggerates, and contrives experience. In short, melodrama is the dramatic form that expresses the truth of the human condition as we perceive it most of the time. We have our victories, but our "accidents" or failures are attributable to external factors, or to the faults of others.

FARCE

Farce is best described as comedy of situation. In farce, pies in the face, beatings, mistaken identities, slips on the banana peel—exaggerated physical activities growing

Lillian Hellman's The Little Foxes

Regina Gibbons, played by Tallulah Bankhead (on sofa, center), and her brothers cultivate Mr. Marshall (Lee Baker) to secure the cotton mill and their fortunes while Birdie and Alexandra (right) talk of other matters in the 1939 Broadway production of Lillian Hellman's *The Little Foxes.*

The Little Foxes, written by Lillian Hellman in 1938–39, is a quintessential melodrama. The play takes place in the American South in 1900 and concerns the wealthy Hubbards, a prosperous family eager to parlay their success as merchants and bankers into vast industrial wealth. "To bring the machines to the cotton, and not the cotton to the machines," as Ben Hubbard says. Regina Hubbard Gibbons is the powerful villainess of

out of situations—are substituted for comedy's traditional concern for social values. Writers of farce present life as mechanical, aggressive, and coincidental and entertain us with seemingly endless variations on a single situation. A typical farce situation is the bedroom crowded with concealed lovers as the cuckolded husband or deceived wife arrives on the scene.

The "Psychology" of Farce

The "psychology of farce," as Eric Bentley calls it, is that special opportunity for the fulfillment of our unmentionable wishes without taking responsibility for our actions or suffering the guilt.[5] Farce as a dramatic form gives us a fantasy world of violence (without harm), adultery (without consequences), brutality (without reprisal), and aggression (without risk). Today, we enjoy farce in the films of Charlie Chaplin, W. C. Fields, the Marx Brothers, Woody Allen, Steve Martin, and Eddie Murphy; and in the

a play that demonstrates the corrosive consequences of money and lust.

To compete with her brothers, Oscar and Ben, Regina must persuade her dying husband, Horace Gibbons, to invest one-third interest in their get-rich-quick scheme. Because of a heart condition, Horace has been in a Baltimore hospital. Regina sends their daughter Alexandra to bring him home so that Regina can invest his Union Pacific bonds in the scheme. Horace arrives but refuses to advance the money. Her brothers tell Regina they will go elsewhere for another business partner, although they would prefer not to bring in an outsider. When the brothers learn from Leo—Ben's son who works in the bank that holds Horace's bonds—that the bonds could be "borrowed" from the bank strongbox without fear of discovery, they take the bonds and tell Regina she's out of the deal. When Horace discovers the bonds are missing and learns of his wife's manipulations, he says he will claim that he loaned the bonds to his brothers-in-law. Regina's scathing verbal attack on Horace brings on his fatal heart attack. Because his death will eliminate her problems and make her rich, she stands immobile while he pleads with her for his medicine. She watches his desperate but futile struggle to climb the stairs to reach his medicine.

With her husband's death, the bonds now belong to Regina and she is once again victorious. Regina blackmails her brothers into giving her 75 percent interest in the venture for her unauthorized "investment." Their alternative is jail. Alexandra, who suspects Regina's complicity in her father's death, voices her disgust and leaves home, but this is only a faint shadow on the bright horizon of Regina's future.

Hellman's scenes turn on theft, blackmail, sudden and unexpected shifts of fortune, unrelenting greed, and major changes in the balance of power in the Hubbard money game. The play's characters range from the genteel Birdie Hubbard and naive Alexandra to the "little foxes that spoil the vines"—the vicious and manipulative Regina, Ben, and Oscar Hubbard. Hellman does not attempt to deepen our understanding of society or of human values. Rather she shows evil in conflict with evil and the good and decent as merely impotent onlookers. The fascination with Regina's manipulations and her victory over her pernicious brothers stimulate audiences into applauding her resourcefulness and withholding moral judgment before her wit, glamour, and cunning.

plays of Georges Feydeau, Neil Simon, Alan Ayckbourn, Michael Frayn, Steve Martin, and Elaine May; and in the performance work of The Flying Karamazov Brothers, Penn & Teller, Bill Irwin, and Robin Williams. Farce has also been an element of the world's great comedies, including those of Shakespeare, Molière, and Chekhov.

ADAPTATIONS

The Life and Adventures of Nicholas Nickleby, Les Misérables, The Grapes of Wrath, Ragtime, Gross Indecency: The Three Trials of Oscar Wilde, Having Our Say: The Delany Sisters' First 100 Years, and *James Joyce's The Dead* are enormously successful examples of another play form: *the adaptation.* The current explosion of interest in adaptations in contemporary French, English, Russian, and American theatres is not

Michael Frayn's Noises Off

MICHAEL FRAYN'S *NOISES OFF,*
WHERE THE ACTORS ARE
PERFORMING "NOTHING
ON" A real-life sex farce backstage
parallels the fictional one in the play-
within-the-play in the 1983
Broadway production.

Noises Off (1982) by British playwright Michael Frayn is a farce about farce. It ridicules
the many clichés of the genre within the format of a play-within-the-play. Act 1 is the
final dress rehearsal by a provincial touring company of *Nothing On.* The typical con-
fusions of farce result from actors who can't remember their lines, their entrances, and
their stage business. Plates of sardines, multiple doors, and telephones add to the
actor's difficulties. Frayn heaps onto his play-within-the-play a melee of stock characters—cheery housekeeper, incompetent burglar, unexpected lovers, outraged wife,
harried husband—who stampede in and out of the many doors. The stage clichés of
the farce *Nothing On* (Act 1) are repeated in the backstage confusion of relationships
during a matinee performance. Act 2 repeats Act 1, only from behind the stage. Act 3
takes place again from the front of the theatre where a performance of *Nothing On* is
beginning as in Act 1; there are even further actorly mishaps and temper tantrums.

Frayn's farcical contrivances are further compounded by the *onstage* versus the
backstage view of life. The director of *Nothing On* summarizes the improbable con-
fusions of the farce: "… That's what it's all about. Doors and sardines. Getting on—
getting off. Getting the sardines on—getting the sardines off. That's farce. That's the
theatre. That's life."

related so much to the availability of new plays as to a desire of theatre companies to create their own texts.

The novels of Charles Dickens, with their wealth of dramatic incident and social detail, have been prime properties for adaptation. Many theatrical adaptations (not counting films and television shows) have been made of *A Christmas Carol, The Pickwick Papers, A Tale of Two Cities, David Copperfield, Great Expectations, Nicholas Nickleby,* and *Little Dorrit.*

THE LIFE AND ADVENTURES OF NICHOLAS NICKLEBY This Dickens novel, written in 1838–39, is one of the most popular stage adaptations of a novel in modern times. Adapted by David Edgar for the Royal Shakespeare Company and directed by Trevor Nunn and John Caird, the daring concept involved forty-two actors in a production that ran more than eight and a half hours. Even more so than Dickens novel, the RSC production conjured up the seaminess and violence of Victorian England, with its extremes of cruelty and compassion, wealth and poverty, corruption and innocence.

Adapting for the Stage

How is a dramatic adaptation created and how does it work theatrically? An adaptation is oftentimes the result of the director's concept and the actors' work. The Steppenwolf production of John Steinbeck's novel, *The Grapes of Wrath,* was a collaboration among director/writer Frank Galati and the acting company. Sometimes a theatre's artistic director, who is also a writer, is the primary creator, as in Emily Mann's adaptation of a popular memoir by Sadie and Bessie Delany called *Having Our Say: The Delany Sisters' First 100 Years.* As French director Antoine Vitez says: "The theatre is *someone* who takes his material wherever he finds it—even things not made for the stage—and puts them on stage. Or, rather, stages them."[6] In the process of adaptation, directors and actors most often emerge as primary creators of the new work.

One method of adapting novels to the stage is to retain the novel's narrative voice (with actors serving as narrators), substituting storytellers for characters. The aim is to blend narrative techniques (descriptions, comments, interior monologues) with dramatic ones (one character in dialogue with another). In some cases, social documents relevant to the action are read aloud; for example, trial transcripts and newspaper accounts are included in Moisés Kaufmann's *Gross Indecency: The Three Trials of Oscar Wilde.* Descriptions are sometimes included in what is spoken. Sometimes actions simply give voice to both descriptions and conversations, including the phrases "he said," or "she said."

Playwright Moisés Kaufmann said of his adaptation of *Gross Indecency* that he wanted to tell the story of Oscar Wilde's three trials and to explore how the theatre can reconstruct history. To achieve both goals, he included the many accounts of the three trials from historical documents and newspapers of the day.

(continued on page 118)

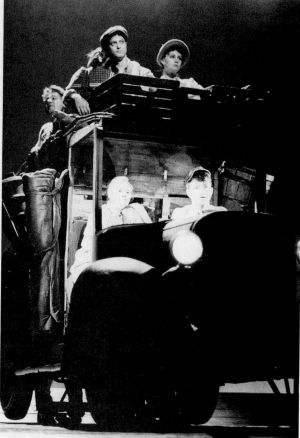
Recent Adaptations for the American Theatre

The Grapes of Wrath . Having Our Say: The Delany Sisters' First 100 Years .

Gross Indecency: The Three Trials of Oscar Wilde

The Grapes of Wrath

John Steinbeck's novel was first published in 1939 and was awarded the Pulitzer Prize in 1940. The stage adaptation was commissioned in 1988 by the Steppenwolf Theatre Company, Chicago, and adapted by writer-director Frank Galati for a thirty-five-member cast. The production came to Broadway in 1989, where Frank Galati was awarded a Antoinette Perry "Tony" Award for Best Play of the 1989 season.

THE HUDSON SUPER SIX TRUCK Concentrating on the place and time of John Steinbeck's novel, director Frank Galati creates a stage action that tells an epic story about dislocation as the Joads move across country (on a bare stage) in the play's most significant stage prop, the heavily laden Hudson Super Six truck. Driven by Tom Joad (Gary Sinise), the Joad family and friends ride through the night along Route 66 toward "the promised land" of California. The converted Hudson, made of authentic parts taken from 1930s vehicles, is the play's most important scenic element.

Galati shaped Steinbeck's epic story into a two-and-a-half hour production. He used Steinbeck's words to create the play's dialogue and to tell the story of an epic adventure in which adversity follows adversity but the human spirit endures.

M. Aginol/NYT Pictures

A BREAK IN THE JOURNEY Gary Sinise as Tom Joad and Terry Kinney as his friend Jim Casey discuss their future in California.

TOM JOAD LEAVES THE FAMILY AT THE PLAY'S END In their farewell scene, Ma Joad (Lois Smith) embraces her son Tom (Gary Sinise). After his struggle with police and camp guards, Tom must abandon the family for their well-being and to save his life.

The Grapes of Wrath (novel and stage adaptation) is a compelling, realistic treatise on the plight and nobility of ordinary laborers in the 1930s American West. It is also a bitter commentary on the human costs of industrial "progress" and on the way social injustice radicalizes individuals. Tom Joad promises his mother at the end: "Wherever they's a fight so hungry people can eat, I'll be there. Wherever they's a cop beating up a guy, I'll be there."

M. Agins/NYT Pictures

Having Our Say: The Delany Sisters' First 100 Years

At ages 104 and 102 the Delany sisters, Sarah L. Delany and A. Elizabeth Delany (known as Sadie and Bessie), told their story to the *New York Times:* "Two 'Maiden Ladies' with Century-Old Stories to Tell." Encouraged to write their autobiography, they published *Having Our Say: The Delany Sisters' First 100 Years* in 1993. It became a best-seller. Emily Mann, artistic director of Princeton's McCarter Theatre and author of *Execution of Justice, Still Life,* and *Greensboro,* adapted the Delany sisters' story for the stage. Following a successful run at the McCarter Theatre in 1995, the production transferred to Broadway for 308 performances.

HAVING OUR SAY AS ORAL HISTORY As acted by Saidah Ekulona (Bessie Delany) and Brenda Thomas (Sadie Delany, seated), the women observed over 100 years of American history, met Eleanor Roosevelt, and worked for black Americans' civil rights. Personal anecdotes are interspersed with reports of historical occasions. Directed by Tazewell Thompson for Play-Makers Repertory Company, Chapel Hill.

HAVING OUR SAY AT THE MCCARTER THEATRE, PRINCETON, NEW JERSEY Gloria Foster as Miss Sadie Delany (right) and Mary Alice as Dr. Bessie Delany (seated) bake in their kitchen and set their dining room table for a birthday dinner. The two actresses play Sadie and Bessie and dozens of characters as the sisters tell the story of six generations and nearly 200 years of black American life.

116   *Photo Essay*

©Joan Marcus

Michael Emerson was the original Oscar Wilde in the Off Broadway production of Moisés Kaufmann's *Gross Indecency: The Three Trials of Oscar Wilde*.

Gross Indecency: The Three Trials of Oscar Wilde

Gross Indecency: The Three Trials of Oscar Wilde, written and first directed by Moisés Kaufmann, combines biography and historical documents to tell the story of Oscar Wilde's descent from darling of London's theatre world with two plays (*An Ideal Husband* and *The Importance of Being Earnest*) running simultaneously on the West End to convicted felon imprisoned for two years at hard labor. Convicted on the third trial of having sexual relations with young men (called "gross indecency" in the legal language of Victorian England), the play uses the transcripts from the 1895 trials as the centerpieces of the adaptation.

As adapted by Moisés Kaufmann, the characters (Oscar Wilde, Marquess of Queensberry, Sir Edward Clarke, and Lord Alfred Douglas) who are central to the three trials of Oscar Wilde are present along with five actors who play the narrators, journalists, friends, and accusers. *Gross Indecency* opened for an Off Broadway run in 1997 and played for two years.

OSCAR WILDE'S FIRST TRIAL with Jamie Horton as Oscar Wilde in the Denver Theatre Company's 1999 production.

Jamie Horton, Denver Center Theatre Company photo by Terry Shapiro

𝒫laywright

Bertolt Brecht

BERTOLT BRECHT'S *THE GOOD PERSON OF SETZUAN* Directed by Andrei Serban with music by Elizabeth Swados, this production was staged by the American Repertory Theatre, Cambridge, Massachusetts, in their 1986–87 season. Like Brecht's *The Caucasian Chalk Circle,* this play combines a non-illusionistic performance style with the statement that it is hard for human beings to reconcile instincts for goodness with the necessity for economic survival.

©Richard Feldman

EPIC THEATRE

Bertolt Brecht, the director and playwright who has probably influenced our postwar theatre more than any other theatrical artist, reacted against Western traditions of the well-made play and pictorial illusion. Over a lifetime, he adapted methods from Erwin Piscator (who pioneered the docudrama for German working-class audiences in the twenties), films, Chinese opera, Japanese Noh staging, English chronicle history plays, and music-hall routines to create "epic" theatre.

The Epic Play

When Brecht spoke of *epic* theatre, he was thinking of plays as *episodic* and *narrative:* as a sequence of incidents or events narrated without artificial restrictions as to time, place, or formal plot. Play structure was more like that of a narrative poem than of a well-made play.

Because Brecht wanted to represent historical process in the theatre and have it judged critically by audiences, he departed from many theatrical traditions. First, he

Bertolt Brecht (1898–1956) was born in Augsburg, Germany, where he spent his early years. In 1918, while studying medicine at Munich University, he was called up for military service as a medical orderly. He began writing poems about the horrors of war. His first play, *Baal*, dates from this period.

After the First World War, Brecht drifted as a student into the bohemian world of theatre and literature, singing his poetry in Munich taverns and coffee-houses. By 1921, Brecht had seriously entered the German theatre as a reviewer and playwright. During the 1920s in Berlin, Brecht became a Marxist, wrote plays, and solidified his theories of epic theatre. *The Threepenny Opera* (1928)—produced in collaboration with the composer Kurt Weill—was an overnight success and made both Brecht and Weill famous.

With the rise of the Nazi movement, many German artists and intellectuals left Germany. Brecht and his family fled in 1933, first to Sweden and then to the United States, where he lived until 1947. In October of 1947, Brecht was subpoenaed to appear in Washington, D.C., before the House Committee on Un-American Activities to testify on the "Communist infiltration" of the motion-picture industry. He left the United States the day following his testimony, eventually settling in East Berlin, where he founded the Berliner Ensemble. This great theatre company continues to perform his works today at the Theater am Schiffbauerdamm, where he first produced *The Threepenny Opera*. Brecht's greatest plays date from his years of exile (1933–1948): *The Good Person of Setzuan, Mother Courage and Her Children, The Life of Galileo,* and *The Caucasian Chalk Circle.*

thought of the stage as a platform on which political and social issues could be debated. He rejected the idea that a play should be "well made," reminding us that history does not end but moves on from episode to episode. Why should plays do otherwise? Brecht's plays therefore were a series of loosely knit scenes, each complete in itself. The effect was achieved through the juxtaposition of contrasting *episodes.* The nonliterary elements of production—music, acting style, lighting, sound, and moving scenery—also retained their separate identities. His epic play is, therefore, *historical, narrative, episodic,* and highly *theatrical.* It treats humans as social beings in their economic, social, and political milieus.

Brecht's characters are both individuals and collective beings. This type of characterization dates to the morality plays of the late Middle Ages, where "Everyman" is both a recognizable individual and a representative of all human beings.

In Brecht's plays, character emerges from the individual's social function and changes with that function. In keeping with the idea that the theatre is a platform to discuss political and social issues, theatrical language is discursive and polemical.

Dramatic Theatre Versus Epic Theatre

Brecht's table, published in *The Modern Theatre Is the Epic Theatre* (1930), shows the differences between dramatic theatre (for example, the theatre of Henrik Ibsen and Arthur Miller) and epic theatre.[7]

Dramatic Theatre	Epic Theatre
Plot	Narrative
Implicates the spectator in a stage situation	Turns the spectator into an observer, but
Wears down his capacity for action	Arouses his capacity for action
Provides him with sensations	Forces him to make decisions
Experience	Picture of the world
The spectator is involved in something	He is made to face something
Suggestion	Argument
Instinctive feelings are preserved	Brought to the point of recognition
The spectator is in the thick of it, shares the experience	The spectator stands outside, studies
The human being is taken for granted	The human being is object of inquiry
He is unalterable	He is alterable and able to alter
Eyes on the finish	Eyes on the course
One scene makes another	Each scene for itself
Growth	Montage
Linear development	In curves
Evolutionary determinism	Jumps
Man as a fixed point	Man as a process
Thought determines being	Social being determines thought
Feeling	Reason

Epic Theatre as Eyewitness Account

Early in his career Brecht admonished actors not to regard themselves as impersonating or becoming characters so much as narrating the actions of people in a particular time, place, and situation. The model he used to demonstrate this approach was the behavior of an eyewitness to a traffic accident.

In retelling the event, eyewitnesses clearly differentiate between themselves and the victim, although they may reconstruct the victim's reactions and gestures. So, too,

Brecht argued, actors clearly differentiate between themselves as actors and the characters in the play. The eyewitness never *becomes* the victim. He further explained:

> It is comparatively easy to set up a basic model for epic theatre. For practical experiments I usually picked as my example of completely simple "natural" epic theatre an incident such as can be seen at any street corner; an eyewitness demonstrating to a collection of people how a traffic accident took place. The bystanders may not have observed what happened, or they may simply not agree with him, may "see things a different way": the point is that the demonstrator acts the behavior of driver or victim or both in such a way that the bystanders are able to form an opinion about the accident.[8]

©Ken Friedman/Berkeley Repertory Theatre

THE LIFE OF GALILEO BY BERTOLT BRECHT From the 1999 Berkeley Repertory Theatre production, directed by Mark Wing-Davey, with Michael Winters as Galileo.

In Brecht's theatre, the actor did not "become" the character as in the Stanislavski approach to acting; rather, actors "demonstrated" the characters' attitudes while retaining freedom to comment (with attitude and gesture) on the actions of the person whose behavior they were displaying. This device of the actor as eyewitness to the play's events was also part of Brecht's efforts to distance or "alienate" the audience emotionally from what was happening on stage.

The Alienation Effect

Brecht called this jarring of the audience out of its sympathetic feelings for what is happening on stage his alienation effect (sometimes called *A-effect* or *Verfremdungseffekt*). He wanted to prevent the audience's empathetic "willing suspension of disbelief," to force them to look at everything in a fresh light and, above all, to think. Brecht wanted audiences to absorb his social criticism and to carry new insights out of the theatre into their own lives.

Brecht was certainly aware of the entertainment value of theatre. For Brecht, pleasure in the theatre came from observing accounts of past situations, discovering new truths, and enlarging upon an understanding of the present. What he opposed was a theatre solely of catharsis (what he called "culinary" theatre), where the audience lost its critical detachment by identifying emotionally with the characters. All of the epic devices—music, loudspeakers, scenery, lighting, placards, projections, acting style—reminded audiences that they were in a theatre, that the stage was a stage and not someone's living room.

THE CHALK-CIRCLE TEST FROM THE 1954 BERLINER ENSEMBLE PRODUCTION OF BRECHT'S *THE CAUCASIAN CHALK CIRCLE*
The circle drawn in white chalk signifies the test of true motherliness and rightful ownership. Judge Azdak gives the child to Grusha who fails in the tug-of-war for fear of harming the boy.

ABSURDIST THEATRE

In 1961 Martin Esslin wrote a book called *The Theatre of the Absurd* about trends in theatre following the Second World War. He used the label to describe new theatrical ways of looking at existence devised by postwar European writers.

Absurdist writers, like Eugène Ionesco and Samuel Beckett, made their breakthrough in dramatic writing by *presenting,* without comment or moral judgment, situations showing life's irrationality. The common factors in the absurdist plays of Ionesco, Beckett, and others are unrecognizable plots, mechanical characters, situations resembling dreams and nightmares, and incoherent dialogue. The absurdist does not tell a story or discuss social problems. Instead, the writer presents in concrete stage images, such as two tramps waiting for a person who never shows up, *a sense of being* in an absurd universe.

The Absurd

Absurdist playwrights begin with the premise that our world is *absurd*, meaning irrational, incongruous, and senseless. Albert Camus (1913–1960)—a French philosopher, novelist, and playwright—diagnosed the human condition as absurd in a book of essays called *The Myth of Sisyphus:*

> A world that can be explained even with bad reasons is a familiar world. But, on the other hand, in a universe suddenly divested of illusions and lights, man feels an alien, a stranger. His exile is without remedy since he is deprived of the memory of a lost home or the hope of a promised land. This divorce between man and his life, the actor and his setting, is properly the feeling of absurdity.[9]

*P*laywright

Eugène Ionesco

Courtesy French Press and Information Office

Eugène Ionesco (1912–1994) was a Rumanian-born schoolteacher and refugee from Nazism who lived in France until his death. Fifty years ago he puzzled and outraged audiences with plays about bald sopranos, octogenarian suicides, homicidal professors, and human rhinoceroses as metaphors for the world's absurdity. Today, *The Bald Soprano, The Chairs, The Lesson,* and *Rhinoceros* are modern classics.

Since *The Bald Soprano* was first produced in Paris at the Théâtre de Noctambules in 1950, Ionesco wrote more than thirty plays in addition to journals, essays, and children's stories. Ionesco said that his theatre expressed the malaise of contemporary life, language's failure to bring people closer together, the strangeness of existence, and a parodic reflection of the world. Breaking with the theatre of psychological realism, Ionesco pioneered a form of theatre closer to our dreams and nightmares.

Ionesco defined *absurd* as "anything without a goal ... when man is cut off from his religious or metaphysical roots, he is lost; all his struggles become senseless, futile and oppressive."[10] The meaning of Ionesco's plays is simply what happens on stage. The old man and old woman in *The Chairs* gradually fill the stage with an increasing number of empty chairs and address absent people in the chairs. At the play's end, the two elderly people leave the message of their life's meaning to be delivered by an orator, and jump out of windows to their deaths. The orator comes forward to address the empty chairs, but he is a deaf-mute and cannot make a coherent statement. The subject of Ionesco's play—the emptiness and absurdity of the world—is conveyed by the presence of the empty chairs.

Ionesco subtitled his first play, *The Bald Soprano* (written in 1949), "the tragedy of language." In it, he became one of the first to confront the absurdity of the universe with new dramatic techniques. This farce, like many of his early plays, demonstrates the emptiness of middle-class life in a world devoid of significant problems.

In more recent plays, Ionesco's concerns about middle-class conformity have a more political cutting edge. In *Rhinoceros,* written in 1958, Ionesco's hero, Bérenger, is an individual in a world of conformists. Ionesco's political concern is with people who are brutalized by dogma (in this case, fascism) and changed by it into thick-skinned beasts. The rhinoceros, with its thick hide and small brain, is Ionesco's brilliant analogue for the herd mentality. Bérenger's emerges as a lonely

THE CHAIRS BY EUGÈNE IONESCO The 1998 Broadway production, with Geraldine McEwan and Richard Briers, and directed by Simon McBurney.

but authentic hero, for he resists the physical and moral conformity that overwhelms his world and his loved ones. Like other Ionesco heroes, he represents a genuine assertion of personal value in a world dominated by nationalism, bureaucracy, and "groupthink."

His later plays, such as *Exit the King* (1962), *Macbett* (1972), *Man With Bags* (1975), and *Scene* (1982), are parables on human evil, the will to power, and the inevitability of death.

The American "Absurd"

Edward Albee's The Zoo Story

The Zoo Story, written by Edward Albee in 1958, introduced the absurd into American playwriting. The play is a confrontation in New York City's Central Park between two men: Jerry, a carelessly dressed man in his late thirties, and Peter, a man in his early forties who wears tweeds and smokes a pipe. Peter is seated on a park bench reading a book when he is accosted by Jerry, who at once teases, taunts, and threatens him. Finally, Jerry forces Peter to take hold of a knife, provokes him, and then rushes toward him, impaling himself on the blade. In the shocking ending, Jerry dies.

*E*ugène *Ionesco's* The Bald Soprano

The maid dominates the scene with the Smiths, the Martins, and the fire chief. The photo is from the original Paris production of *The Bald Soprano* at Théâtre des Noctambules, 1950, directed by Nicholas Bataille.

Courtesy French Press and Information Office

The Bald Soprano (produced at the Théâtre des Noctambules, Paris, 1950) is Ionesco's "antiplay" that dramatizes the absurdity of human existence. In 1948, while taking a course in conversational English, Ionesco conceived the idea of using many of the practice sentences to create a theatre piece.

Mr. and Mrs. Smith talk in clichés about the trivia of everyday life. The mean-inglessness of their existence is caricatured in dialogue in which each member of a large family, living and dead, regardless of age or sex, is called Bobby Watson. Mr. and Mrs. Martin enter. They converse as strangers but gradually discover they are both from Manchester, that they arrived in London at the same time, that they live in the same house, sleep in the same bed, and are parents of the same child. The Martins and the Smiths exchange banalities, a clock strikes erratically, and the doorbell rings by itself. A fire chief arrives. Although in a hurry to extinguish all fires in the city, he launches into long-winded, pointless anecdotes. After he leaves, the two couples exchange clichés until language breaks down to basic sounds. The end of the play completes a circle: The Martins replace the Smiths and speak the same lines that opened the play.

THE ZOO STORY Directed by Edward Albee, with Curtis Billings as Jerry and James Belcher as Peter, produced at the Alley Theatre, Houston, in 1998.

The centerpiece of the confrontation between the two men is the story of "Jerry and the dog." Jerry tells Peter how he tried to communicate with his landlady's dog, who at first growls at him and then becomes his total enemy. Jerry decides to kill the dog with kindness and then just kill the dog if kindness does not work. One day, he poisons the dog, who becomes very ill but survives. Thereafter, man and dog regard each other with a mixture of sadness, suspicion, and feigned indifference. Jerry regards this as an understanding between them; that is, neither kindness nor cruelty by themselves have any effect on our lives, but the combination of the two can teach us emotion and a truce of understanding.

For Jerry, life is a zoo; people and animals are at war with one another. As he challenges Peter for possession of the park bench and intentionally provokes his own death, Jerry not only sacrifices his life but he passes on to Peter the suffering and truth of his experience.

Albee's *The Zoo Story* had its premiere in German at the Schiller Theater in Berlin on a double-bill with Samuel Beckett's *Krapp's Last Tape*. The American premiere took place in 1960 at New York City's Provincetown Playhouse. With this short play about a bench, two men, and their inability to communicate, Edward Albee launched the American absurd in which two disaffected and disconnected strangers contend for a park bench and mutual understanding.

TRANSITION

Drama's forms are the organization of the playwright's vision of and statement about the world. Tragedy, comedy, tragicomedy, melodrama, farce, epic, and absurd are ways of labeling the playwright's view of the world's substance, shape, and meaning. However, there is a larger pattern of writing that has the potential for becoming living words and actions. We call this pattern for "doing" or "becoming" *drama*. It all begins with the *imitation* of human events, speech, and behavior shaped into a structure or pattern of experience.

WEB SITES

The Ancient World: What Kind of World Did the Classic Tragedians Live In?

http://www.museum.upenn.edu/Greek_World/
   Index.html

August Wilson: Anthology of American Blues, Time-line for Plays, Reviews, and Other Information

http://www.humboldt.edu/~ah/Wilson/index.html

The Brecht Centennial

http://www.versuche.org/ie4/main.html

Broadway Theater Archive (contains about forty made-for-television productions available on videocassettes, including Irene Worth in Samuel Beckett's Happy Days *[1980] and James Earl Jones in* King Lear *[1974])*

http://www.broadwayarchive.com

The Samuel Beckett Endpage

http://beckett.English.ucsb.edu/

Theatre: Website Honoring the Prolific Greek Theatre Tradition (contains images of classic and contemporary theatres and historical information)

http://www.istos.net.gr/theatre/menu.htm

These search terms are provided to assist you in exploring the topics introduced in this chapter at:

http//www.infotrac-college.com

drama, genre, tragedy, Dionysus, comedy, farce, melodrama, tragicomedy, absurdist theatre, epic theatre.

The play is a quest for

a solution.[1]

DAVID MAMET

Writing in Restaurants

Structures of Seeing

To read the printed page of a script is to experience much of the playwright's art. Words on a page have the potential for becoming human speech, activity, movement, and sound. Playwrights use many kinds of play structures and dramatic conventions to aid in the telling of their stories about familiar and unfamiliar worlds.

DRAMA: THE PLAYWRIGHT'S ART

Drama, the playwright's art, takes its name from the Greek verb *dran,* meaning "to do" or "to act." Drama is most often defined as a pattern of words and actions having the potential for "doing" or "becoming" living words and actions.

On the printed page drama appears as *dialogue*—words arranged in sequence to be spoken by actors. Stage dialogue can be similar to the dialogue we speak in conversation with friends. In some cases, as with Shakespeare's blank verse or the complex verse forms of the Greek plays, dialogue is more formal. But, in all cases, stage dialogue differs from ordinary conversation in one important way: the playwright creates it and the actor speaks it. *Performability* is the link between the playwright's words and the actor's speech.

Let us begin the discussion of drama as a way of seeing by considering childhood *play,* with which it shares similar features.

Drama as Imitation

Children at play are a kind of amateur playwright as they imitate reality through playing such games as "space invaders," "school," and "dinosaurs." Children play to entertain themselves, to imitate adult behavior, and to help fit themselves into an unfamiliar world. In play, children try out and learn roles they will experience in their adult lives. In their imitations they develop what American psychiatrist Eric Berne called *life-scripts.*

What do we mean by imitation, especially imitation at the psychological level? In *Play, Dreams and Imitation in Childhood,* French psychologist Jean Piaget says that we tend to imitate through play those things that arouse ambivalent emotions within us. We do this to handle the fears those things evoke by their strangeness. We imitate the unknown as a way of mastering and gaining dominance over it. Children, adults of early societies, and artists all use imitation and for many of the same reasons.

So imitation is a process through which we confront and transform our fears of the strange and unknown by becoming one with them, even managing them. Every drama is an imitation that confronts the mystery of human behavior. It does so concretely through *the living presence* of the actor, who is both a real person and a fictional character. The great British actor Laurence Olivier once remarked, "Acting is an almost childish wish…. Pretend to be somebody else…. Let's pretend—I suppose that's the original impulse of acting…."[2]

Play and drama have much in common. The child playing an astronaut or the actor playing *Hamlet* must start with a scenario or script, or imagined situation, character, dialogue, and locale. Both play and drama entertain. They contribute to a sense of well-being and to an understanding of ourselves and others. They have their own fixed rules. Most important, they *imitate* human events.

In the fourth century B.C., Aristotle described drama as *mimesis*—the imitation of human beings in action. In his *Poetics* (written between 335 and 323 B.C.), he showed that the playwright used certain devices to turn written material into human action: plot, character, language, thought or ideas, music, and spectacle. From our modern perspective, we add time and space to Aristotle's list of dramatic elements.

DRAMA'S ELEMENTS The elements of drama make up a pattern for doing. Today the list is more extensive than it was in Aristotle's time. Modern elements of drama are words, symbols, signs, plot, action, character, gesture, conflict, time, visual effects, sounds, and meaning.

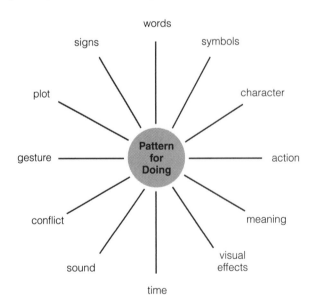

The Elements of Drama

Chapter Six

Drama's Elements

Plot, Character, Language, Spectacle

Drama's chief elements are still often modeled on Aristotle's criteria, beginning with plot, character, and language. *Plot* is an arranged sequence of events or incidents usually having a beginning, middle, and end. These incidents spring from an action or motive. *Character* includes the physiological and psychological makeup of the persons in the play.

Language is the spoken word, including symbols and signs. The play's *meaning* is its underlying idea—its general and particular truths about experience. Today we frequently use the word *theme* or message when we talk about a play's meaning. A play may have more than one basic theme. *Macbeth*, for example, is a play about crime and punishment, but it is also about the destructive effects of power and ambition on the human psyche.

Aristotle used the word *spectacle* to include all visual and aural elements: costumes, music, choral dancing and singing, properties, machines (wagons and cranes), lighting effects (torches and open flames). In the modern theatre, we add scenery, lighting, and sound effects to this list.

Time: Actual and Symbolic

The modern idea of a play's *time* refers not to *actual time*—the length of the performance—but to *symbolic time*, which is integral to the play's structure and may be spread out over hours, days, or years. *Hamlet* takes about four hours to perform, although the story covers many months. In Henrik Ibsen's *Ghosts* we are asked to believe that the incidents take place in a little more than twenty-four hours.

Action

Action is a crucial element of drama. Aristotle did not use *action* to refer to those external deeds, incidents, situations, and events we tend to associate with a play's plot. He likened the relationship of action and drama to that of the soul and the body. He saw action as the source of the play's inner meaning, the spiritual and psychological forces that move through the play, holding all its elements together in a meaningful way.

American scholar Francis Fergusson defined action as "the focus or aim of psychic life from which the events, in that situation, result."[3] The source of the play's outward deeds, action embodies all the physical, psychological, and spiritual gestures and motivations that result in the visible behavior of the characters. The action of Oedipus in Sophocles' play occurs on several levels. On one level, Oedipus' action is to find the killer of Laius, the former Theban king, and to purify the city of plague by punishing the guilty person. During his investigation of the plague's cause, Oedipus discovers that he is the guilty man, that he unwittingly killed his father and married his mother. On another, deeper level, the action of *Oedipus the King* is really a man's efforts *to know himself.* In short, action is the play's all-encompassing purpose.

Henrik Ibsen

Culver Pictures, Inc.

Henrik Ibsen (1828–1906), Norwegian playwright, is considered by many to be the most influential playwright since Shakespeare. Finding his early plays (celebrating his country's past glories) poorly received, Ibsen immigrated to Italy. There he wrote *Brand* (1865), a symbolic tragedy in verse, which brought him immediate fame. For twenty-seven years he remained with his family in self-imposed exile in Rome, Dresden, and Munich, writing such plays as *A Doll's House, Ghosts, An Enemy of the People, The Wild Duck,* and *Hedda Gabler.* These plays changed the direction of the nineteenth-century theatre. In 1891 Ibsen returned to Norway, and in 1899 he completed *When We Dead Awaken,* the play that novelist James Joyce considered his finest. He died there in 1906.

Called the father of modern drama, Ibsen wrote plays dealing with problems of contemporary life, particularly those of the individual caught in a repressive society. Although his social doctrines, radical and shocking in his own day, are no longer revolutionary, his portraits of humanity are timeless.

Over the centuries, playwrights developed different ways of using dramatic forms, structures, and styles to mirror the changing intellectual and emotional life of their cultures. The play's structure is the playwright's way of *organizing* the dramatic material into a coherent whole.

PLAY STRUCTURES

In Western drama, plot and action are based on a central *conflict* and organized usually in the following progression: exposition–confrontation–crisis–climax–resolution. This generalization is true for plays written by William Shakespeare, Henrik Ibsen, or Sam Shepard. The way the playwright varies this pattern determines the play's structure. In general, plays have been organized in three basic ways: *climactic, episodic,* and *situational.* Entirely new structures, such as *"talking pieces"* and *"synthetic fragments,"* have recently been devised.

Climactic Structure

Found in classical and modern plays, climactic structure confines the character's activities and intensifies the pressures on the characters until they are forced into irre-

Henrik Ibsen's Ghosts

Ghosts, written in 1881, is the story of the Alving family. Mrs. Alving, widow of the admired and respected Captain Alving, has been living alone on her husband's estate with her maid Regina, carrying on her husband's philanthropic projects. Her son, Oswald, has returned from Paris for the dedication of an orphanage she has built.

The play opens with a conversation between the carpenter Jacob Engstrand and Regina, his supposed daughter. He tries to convince the girl to do her duty to her father and become the "hostess" of a sailors' hostel, which he plans to open with his savings. Regina refuses; she hopes for a more genteel life. Pastor Manders, a long-time friend of the family, arrives to dedicate the orphanage. He and Oswald heatedly discuss new moral codes. Oswald goes into the dining room, where sounds of his amorous advances to Regina are heard. Mrs. Alving remarks that the "ghosts" of the past have risen to haunt her.

In Act 2, Mrs. Alving explains that Regina is actually Captain Alving's daughter by a serving girl, and that his upstanding reputation has been falsely derived from her own good works. At the end of Act 2 the orphanage burns to the ground as a result of Engstrand's carelessness.

In Act 3, it is revealed that Manders' fear of scandal has led him to bribe Engstrand. (Engstrand convinced Manders that the pastor started the fire himself.) Engstrand goes off with Regina to open the sailors' "home." Oswald confesses that he suffers from syphilis inherited from his father—another "ghost." Mrs. Alving promises to give him a deadly drug should he become insane as the disease progresses. As the play ends, Oswald's mind disintegrates under a final seizure, and Mrs. Alving must decide whether to administer the drug as she has promised or to let her son live as a helpless invalid. The curtain falls as she tries to decide.

---

versible acts—the climax. As the action develops, the characters' range of choices is reduced. In many cases, they are aware that their choices are being limited and that they are being moved toward a crisis and turning point. Climactic structure is a *cause-to-effect* arrangement of incidents ending in a climax and quick resolution.

Episodic Structure

Episodic play structure, found in medieval plays and the works of William Shakespeare, Bertolt Brecht, Edward Bond, and Tony Kushner, traces the characters through a *journey* of sorts to a final action and to an understanding of what the journey meant. It can always take a new turn. In Shakespeare's plays, people are not forced immediately into unmaneuverable positions. Possibilities of action are usually open to them until the very end. Events do not accumulate to confine the characters because the play encompasses large amounts of time and distance. *Hamlet*

(continued on page 136)

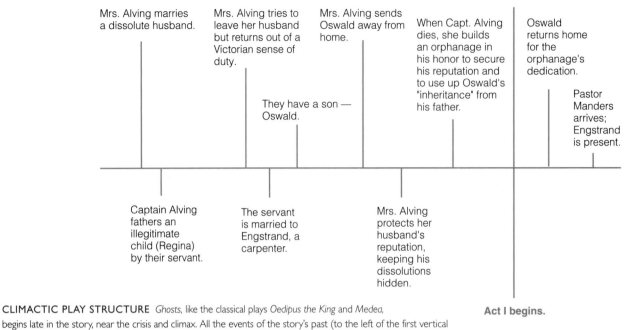

Mrs. Alving marries a dissolute husband.

Mrs. Alving tries to leave her husband but returns out of a Victorian sense of duty.

Mrs. Alving sends Oswald away from home.

When Capt. Alving dies, she builds an orphanage in his honor to secure his reputation and to use up Oswald's "inheritance" from his father.

Oswald returns home for the orphanage's dedication.

They have a son — Oswald.

Pastor Manders arrives; Engstrand is present.

Captain Alving fathers an illegitimate child (Regina) by their servant.

The servant is married to Engstrand, a carpenter.

Mrs. Alving protects her husband's reputation, keeping his dissolutions hidden.

Act I begins.

CLIMACTIC PLAY STRUCTURE *Ghosts*, like the classical plays *Oedipus the King* and *Medea*, begins late in the story, near the crisis and climax. All the events of the story's past (to the left of the first vertical line) occur before the play begins and are revealed in exposition. Each act of Ibsen's play ends with a climax, building to the highest point of tension: Oswald's collapse. Since a climactic plot begins late in the story, the period of time covered is usually limited. *Ghosts* begins in the afternoon and ends at sunrise the following day

EPISODIC PLAY STRUCTURE Episodic structure begins early in the story and involves many characters and events. Place and event do not confine the characters; instead, the plot expands to include a variety of events and activities. Brecht's *The Caucasian Chalk Circle* is made up chiefly of two stories, Grusha's and Azdak's. The expanding plot moves in a linear fashion, telling the seemingly unrelated stories until Brecht combines them in the chalk-circle test to make his point about decent people caught in the injustices of a corrupt political system.

Grusha's story

Prologue

1945— People from two valleys dispute the land's owner- ship.

Narrator tells the story of Grusha, a peasant girl, saving the governor's child in the midst of a revolution.

She flees with the child Michael to the mountains, leaving her fiancé behind.

She bargains to feed the child, escapes pursuing soldiers, and marries to provide food and shelter for Michael.

The soldiers capture Grusha and Michael; they are returned to the city.

Adzak's story

The rogue Adzak harbors a fugitive.

He turns himself in for sheltering the grand duke.

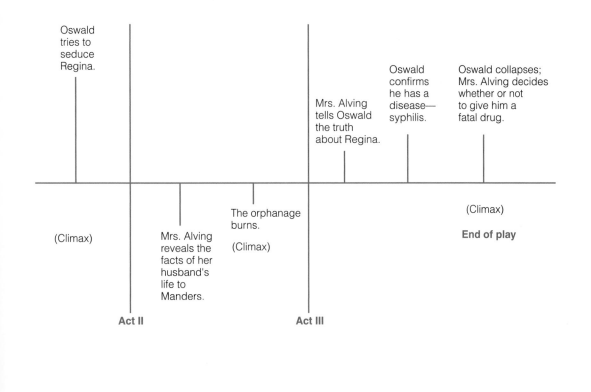

Oswald tries to seduce Regina.

Mrs. Alving tells Oswald the truth about Regina.

Oswald confirms he has a disease— syphilis.

Oswald collapses; Mrs. Alving decides whether or not to give him a fatal drug.

(Climax)

Mrs. Alving reveals the facts of her husband's life to Manders.

The orphanage burns.

(Climax)

(Climax)

End of play

Act II

Act III

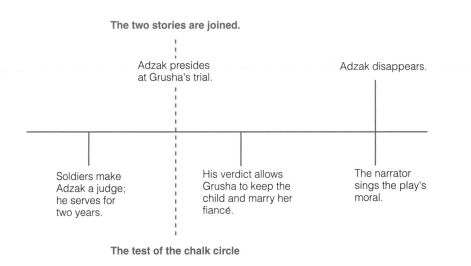

The two stories are joined.

Adzak presides at Grusha's trial.

Adzak disappears.

Soldiers make Adzak a judge; he serves for two years.

His verdict allows Grusha to keep the child and marry her fiancé.

The narrator sings the play's moral.

The test of the chalk circle

$\mathcal{H}$enrick *Ibsen's* A Doll's House

Ibsen's *A Doll's House* on Broadway in 1997 with Janet McTeer as Nora (right) and Jan Maxwell as Mrs. Elvsted, directed by Anthony Page.

A *Doll's House,* written two years before *Ghosts* in 1879, places climactic playwriting at the service of a social problem dealing with women's rights both legal and personal. The long story of the Helmer marriage (Nora's forgery, her hidden efforts to repay the debt, those little signs of Nora's concealed nature as she eats the forbidden macaroons) point to a compressed past that explodes into a complacent present with her girlhood friend's arrival. Mrs. Linde, like the Greek messenger, precipitates the revelations of Nora's past and ensures the catastrophe in the present. *A Doll's House* has a small cast (five principals), a short time span (several days at

takes place over several years and countries. And the expanding plot takes in a variety of events. In this loose structure, characters are not caught in circumstances but pass through them, as Grusha does in *The Caucasian Chalk Circle.*[4]

Brecht's The Caucasian Chalk Circle

In *The Caucasian Chalk Circle,* Brecht tells three stories. The setting is a meeting of two Soviet collective farms in 1945 to decide which group should own a certain valley. Before they vote, they are told the stories of Grusha and the child Michael, which make up the play proper, and of the disreputable career of Azdak, a village rogue whom rebellious soldiers make a judge. The three stories come together as Azdak tries the case of the child's ownership and settles it by reversing the old test of the chalk

Christmas), and a single setting (the Helmers' living room). Technical contrivances—a blackmail plot with reformed villain and fateful letter, the family crisis at Christmas time, the heroine's masquerade costume and frenzied dancing, the close friend's imminent death by inherited disease, the "debate" between husband and wife—are in the service of realistic writing that thrusts festering social and personal problems from the past into the present with unexpected and disastrous consequences.

One timeliness of Ibsen's play is that the ending is not clear-cut. Nora's forgery of her father's signature despite her worthy reasons (to get money to save her husband during his grave illness) was legally wrong—no less than a criminal act. At the same time, she had no legal means of borrowing money in the society of the day. Her discovery that her secret pride in preserving her husband's health is looked upon as a disgraceful felony in the eyes of her husband and the legal system shocks her into a larger understanding of herself and her situation.

The action of the play is the transformation of Nora Helmer from her father's, then husband's, doll and pet "squirrel" into a woman of unknown potential. At the end as Nora sets out in quest of her self in an uncertain world, we see her as the product of her social conditioning and a value system that stunted women's personal development, impoverished and trivialized their lives, and degraded them in their own eyes. Her story is the tragedy of wasted human potential and the unlikelihood that she can redeem that waste in the future. As she slams the door on family, husband, children, and friends and the curtain comes down on the bewildered husband who stays behind, Ibsen makes a statement to his late-nineteenth-century audiences: both men and women are victims of a society that condones inequities in social conventions and legal systems. A famous contemporary described the effect of the play on audiences of Ibsen's day: "The door Nora Helmer slammed shut on her marriage sent shock waves through thousands of homes."

NORA: I have other duties equally sacred.

HELMER: You do not. What duties would they be?

NORA: My duties to myself.

HELMER: You are a wife and a mother before you are anything else.

NORA: I don't believe that any more. I believe I am first of all a human being, just as much as you—or at any rate that I must try to become one. (Act 3)

circle. He awards the child to Grusha rather than to the biological mother (the governor's wife), who had abandoned him in wartime and now, to win custody of the child, pulls him roughly from the circle. Brecht's moral is that both child and valley should belong to those who will serve them best.

Situational Structure

In absurdist plays of the 1950s and later, *situation* shapes the play, not plot or arrangement of incidents. It takes the place of the journey or the pressurized events. For example, two tramps wait for a person named Godot, who never arrives (*Waiting for Godot*); a husband and wife talk in meaningless clichés as they go about their daily routines (*The Bald Soprano*).

(continued on page 139)

$\mathcal{B}$ertolt $\mathcal{B}$recht's The Caucasian Chalk Circle

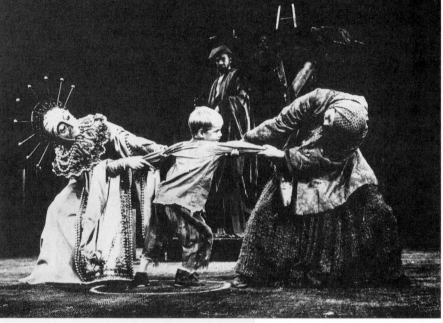

BRECHT'S GESTIC LANGUAGE
The circle drawn in white chalk on the stage signifies a test of true motherliness and rightful ownership based on mutual interests and well-being. The governor's wife (left) and Grusha (right) pull at the child as Judge Azdak looks on in the 1965 production of *The Caucasian Chalk Circle* at the Guthrie Theater. Grusha (Zoe Caldwell) releases the child before harming him.

Storytelling in ***The Caucasian Chalk Circle,*** written by German playwright Bertolt Brecht in 1944–45, begins in 1945 with two Soviet villages disputing the ownership of a fertile valley.

Before they decide the issue, a singer entertains them with a Chinese parable, the story of the chalk circle. The scene changes to a Georgian city being overthrown by a nobles' revolt. The governor is killed, and his wife abandons their son Michael in order to escape. Grusha, a peasant girl, rescues the child and flees to the mountains with him. In order to give the child a name and status, she marries a peasant whom she believes is near death. When the revolt ends, the governor's wife sends soldiers to get the child. The scene shifts again, to the story of Azdak, a rogue made village judge by the rebel soldiers. He is corrupt and prepares to judge the case of Grusha versus the governor's wife for possession of Michael. He uses the test of the chalk circle to identify the child's true mother, but reverses the outcome: The child is given to Grusha because she will not engage in the tug-of-war that is supposed to end in the child's being pulled out of the circle by maternal affection. He also decrees Grusha a divorce so that she can return to her soldier fiancé, Simon. Brecht's moral is that things—children, wagons, valleys—should go to those who serve them best.

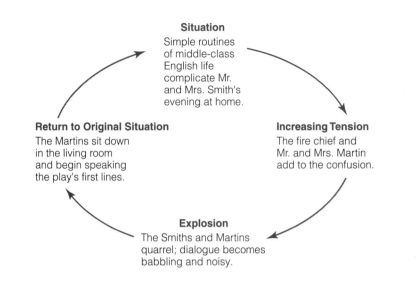

Situation
Simple routines
of middle-class
English life
complicate Mr.
and Mrs. Smith's
evening at home.

Return to Original Situation
The Martins sit down
in the living room
and begin speaking
the play's first lines.

Increasing Tension
The fire chief and
Mr. and Mrs. Martin
add to the confusion.

Explosion
The Smiths and Martins
quarrel; dialogue becomes
babbling and noisy.

SITUATIONAL PLAY STRUCTURE
IN IONESCO'S *THE BALD
SOPRANO* The "theatre of the absurd"
emerged in Europe following the Second
World War. Absurdist plays convey a
sense of alienation, of people having lost
their bearings in an illogical or ridiculous
world. Situational play structure mirrors
this worldview.

The situation has its own inner rhythms, which are like the basic rhythms of life: day, night, day; hunger, thirst, hunger; spring, summer, winter. Although the situation usually remains unchanged, these rhythms move in a continuing cycle.

Ionesco's The Bald Soprano

In *The Bald Soprano* (1949), Ionesco introduces a fire chief and the Martins into Mr. and Mrs. Smith's typical middle-class English living room. After a series of absurd events, the dialogue crescendos into nonsensical babbling. The words stop abruptly and the play begins again. This time Mr. and Mrs. Martin are seated as the Smiths were at the play's beginning, and they repeat the Smiths' lines from the first scene. With this repetition, Ionesco demonstrates the interchangeability of middle-class lives.

RECENT STRUCTURES

Solo Texts

Solo performances have a long stage history, beginning with medieval mimes and jugglers. Most recently in the mainstream of the American commercial theatre, solo performances staged biographies of famous people. We have seen actress Zoe Caldwell as Lillian Hellman, Julie Harris as Emily Dickinson, Hal Holbrooke as Mark Twain, Robert Morse as Truman Capote, and Barrie Humphries as Dame Edna.

Solo performances have also become a vital part of our contemporary avant-garde, as evidenced in the work of Sandra Bernhard, Eric Bogosian, Spalding Gray, Eve Ensler, John Leguizamo, Tim Miller, Anna Deavere Smith, Ellen DeGeneres, and others. In the

(continued on page 142)

Excerpt from The Bald Soprano

Ionesco's middle-class English couple, Mr. and Mrs. Smith, discuss dinner, the newspaper, and Bobby Watson in the original 1950 Paris production of *The Bald Soprano*.

The "Bobby Watson" exchange from Ionesco's *The Bald Soprano* (1950) presents aural and visual images showing the banality of middle-class suburban life. Mr. and Mrs. Smith, seated in their middle-class English living room discussing their middle-class English dinner, engage in conversation about Bobby Watson.

Another moment of silence. The clock strikes seven times. Silence. The clock strikes three times. Silence. The clock doesn't strike.

MR. SMITH [*still reading his paper*]: Tsk, it says here that Bobby Watson died.

MRS. SMITH: My God, the poor man! When did he die?

MR. SMITH: Why do you pretend to be astonished? You know very well that he's been dead these past two years. Surely you remember that we attended his funeral a year and a half ago.

MRS. SMITH: Oh yes, of course I do remember. I remembered it right away, but I don't understand why you yourself were so surprised to see it in the paper.

MR. SMITH: It wasn't in the paper. It's been three years since his death was announced. I remembered it through an association of ideas.

MRS. SMITH: What a pity! He was so well preserved.

MR. SMITH: He was the handsomest corpse in Great Britain. He didn't look his age. Poor Bobby, he'd been dead for four years and he was still warm. A veritable living corpse. And how cheerful he was!

MRS. SMITH: Poor Bobby.

MR. SMITH: Which poor Bobby do you mean?

MRS. SMITH: It is his wife that I mean. She is called Bobby too, Bobby Watson. Since they both had the same name, you could never tell one from the other when you saw them together. It was only after his death that you could really tell which was which. And there are still people today who confuse her with the deceased and offer their condolences to him. Do you know her?

MR. SMITH: I only met her once, by chance, at Bobby's burial.

MRS. SMITH: I've never seen her. Is she pretty?

MR. SMITH: She has regular features and yet one cannot say that she is pretty. She is too big and stout. Her features are not regular but still one can say that she is very pretty. She is a little too small and too thin. She's a voice teacher.

[The clock strikes five times. A long silence.]

MRS. SMITH: And when do they plan to be married, those two?

MR. SMITH: Next spring, at the latest.

MRS. SMITH: We shall have to go to their wedding, I suppose.

MR. SMITH: We shall have to give them a wedding present. I wonder what?

MRS. SMITH: Why don't we give them one of the seven silver salvers that were given us for our wedding and which have never been of any use to us?

[Silence]

MRS. SMITH: How sad for her to be left a widow so young.

MR. SMITH: Fortunately, they had no children.

MRS. SMITH: That was all they needed! Children! Poor woman, how could she have managed!

MR. SMITH: She's still young. She might very well remarry. She looks so well in mourning.

MRS. SMITH: But who would take care of the children? You know very well that they have a boy and a girl. What are their names?

MR. SMITH: Bobby and Bobby like their parents. Bobby Watson's uncle, old Bobby Watson, is a rich man and very fond of the boy. He might very well pay for Bobby's education.

MRS. SMITH: That would be proper. And Bobby Watson's aunt, old Bobby Watson, might very well, in her turn, pay for the education of Bobby Watson, Bobby Watson's daughter. That way Bobby, Bobby Watson's mother, could remarry. Has she anyone in mind?

MR. SMITH: Yes, a cousin of Bobby Watson's.

MRS. SMITH: Who? Bobby Watson?

MR. SMITH: Which Bobby Watson do you mean?

MRS. SMITH: Why, Bobby Watson, the son of old Bobby Watson, the late Bobby Watson's other uncle.

MR. SMITH: No, it's not that one, it's someone else. It's Bobby Watson, the son of old Bobby Watson, the late Bobby Watson's aunt.

MRS. SMITH: Are you referring to Bobby Watson the commercial traveler?

MR. SMITH: All the Bobby Watsons are commercial travelers.

MRS. SMITH: What a difficult trade! However, they do well at it.

MR. SMITH: Yes, when there's no competition.

MRS. SMITH: And when is there no competition?

MR. SMITH: On Tuesdays, Thursdays, and Tuesdays.

MRS. SMITH: Ah! Three days a week? And what does Bobby Watson do on those days?

MR. SMITH: He rests, he sleeps.

MRS. SMITH: But why doesn't he work those three days if there's no competition?

MR. SMITH: I don't know everything. I can't answer all your idiotic questions! ...[5]

*S*olo *Performer*

Spalding Gray

©Paula Court

Spalding Gray (b. 1941) is a writer, performer, and teacher. A graduate of Emerson College, he came to New York City in 1967, where he performed in Off Broadway plays. He worked for brief periods with the Alley Theatre in Houston and with Joseph Chaikin's Open Theatre before joining Richard Schechner's Performance Group in 1969. There he played in Sam Shepard's *The Tooth of Crime* and in Bertolt Brecht's *Mother Courage and Her Children*. In 1975, he and Elizabeth LeCompte, with other members of the Performance Group, formed the Wooster Group. Here, Gray composed and/or performed in his own work in *Sakonnet Point, Rumstick Road, Nayatt School, Point Judith,* and *Route 1 & 9.* The first three are known as *The Trilogy: Three Places in Rhode Island,* based on Gray's life. He also created a series of monologues, or talking pieces, including *Swimming to Cambodia* (1983), a monologue about that country, Thailand, Hollywood, and his participation as an actor in the film *The Killing Fields.* His more recent works are *Terrors of Pleasure* (1990), *Monster in a Box* (1992), *Gray's Anatomy* (1993), *Impossible Vacation* (a novel, 1993), *It's a Slippery Slope* (1996), and *Morning, Noon and Night* (1999).

Gray taught in the Experimental Theatre Wing of New York University's School of Drama and led many workshops there and in India and Europe. His workshops for both children and adults emphasize autobiography; participants are encouraged to develop material and theatrical metaphors from their own lives.

1990s, the solo performer provides a low-budget means of exploring (often with nudity and explicit language) such timely issues as censorship, pornography, AIDS, feminism, dysfunctional families, prostitution, racism, and alternative lifestyles.

The solo text is a highly personal response to today's social and political issues, and also a powerful means of speaking directly to America's collective conscience. Spalding Gray has worked within this minimalist form since the 1960s, and Anna Deavere Smith began her "search for American character" in the early 1980s.

Spalding Gray's "Talking Pieces"

In the late 1970s, the inflationary economy and the lack of large social and political issues resulted in the disbanding of many American theatrical collectives that had gathered momentum in the 1960s over issues like the Vietnam War. Many performers, such as Spalding Gray, who had worked for a time with Richard Schechner's Performance Group in New York City, turned to creating a new kind of theatre piece for the solo performer (and also for small casts). Gray's pieces have been called "talking pieces," even "epic monologues." They represent a new and interesting dramatic structure, as well as theatrical event.

(continued on page 144)

_E_xcerpt from _Spalding Gray's_
Monster in a Box

Monster in a Box is Gray's thirteenth autobiographical monologue, first performed in Washington, D.C., in 1990. Like his other monologues, it was not previously written down but evolved through performances. Gray works from an outline containing key words to guide him through his stories. The "Monster" is the novel he is writing called _Impossible Vacation_ that is kept in a "box."

In the following section from _Monster in a Box_, Spalding Gray receives an invitation to play the stage manager in the Lincoln Center Theater production of Thornton Wilder's _Our Town:_

… the phone rings and it's Gregory Mosher, the director of Lincoln Center Theater, saying, "Hi, Gregory here. Listen, Spalding, how would you like to be the stage manager of the eighties? How would you like to play the Stage Manager in Thornton Wilder's _Our Town_ on Broadway?"

I can't believe what I'm hearing and I say, "Gregory, listen, thank you very much. I am honored, but I can't. I have to finish my book."

And he says, "Write it in the morning. We'll rehearse in the afternoon."

I say, "Gregory, it's not just the book. I would come and see the play, I love the play. It's a favorite of mine, but I, I don't think I could do it. I simply don't think I could say those lines. They're too wholesome and folksy. Get Garrison Keillor."

"We don't want Garrison Keillor, we want you. This is a farewell to all the sentimental _Our Town_s. It's a farewell to the Hallmark card of _Our Town_. We want you. We want your dark, New England, ironic sensibility."

"Well, Gregory, you got me there. I'll tell you what. Give me a day to think about it."

I hang up, I think, my God! This is a chance of a lifetime. Here it is. It's a limited run. I could work on the Monster in my dressing room. The role is great. I could speak from my heart at last, provided I could memorize the lines—I could at last use my New England accent. So I think I'd better just call my Hollywood agent, see if she has any opinions on this before I say yes or no.

I call her up and she says, "Dear heart, dear heart! No way! Why, after all these years of acting, would you want to be a stage manager?"[6]

Spalding Gray performs _Monster in a Box_ at Lincoln Center Theatre, New York City, 1991.

Samuel $\mathcal{B}$eckett's Rockaby with $\mathcal{T}$ext

Billy Whitelaw as the woman in the rocking chair in Samuel Beckett's *Rockaby* at the Samuel Beckett Theater, New York City, 1984.

©Irene Haupt

Beckett's ***Rockaby,*** written in 1980, was interpreted for New York audiences by British actress Billie Whitelaw and directed by Alan Schneider. *Rockaby* is a fifteen-minute monodrama in which a woman, seated in a rocking chair, rocks herself into the grave. The actress speaks only one word ("more") four times. The single word is separated

Gray improvised his memories, free associations, and ideas of childhood, family relationships, and private emotions to create an open narrative of personal actions. He called these "talking pieces." Using properties bought at discount stores, a tape recorder, family photograph albums, slide projections, and phonograph records, he worked before small audiences and with director Elizabeth LeCompte of the Wooster Group in New York City, giving shape to his autobiographical sketches. The text as it developed was talked through with the director and audiences in what Gray calls "an act of public memory." Once satisfied with the final product, Gray "set" the text.

Because of these improvisational methods, Gray refers to his solo pieces as "poetic journalism" or as "talking pieces"—a series of simple actions using free associations as building blocks to turn a series of memories and everyday experience into art.

Gray's series of monologues, or talking pieces, include *Sex and Death to the Age 14; A Personal History of the American Theatre; Booze, Cars and College Girls; Ter-*

by a litany of words recorded on tape by the actress. The words on tape represent the final thrashings of the woman's consciousness. As death comes, she ceases rocking. A single light picks out the actress' face; her eyes close. Then, darkness is total.

With no scenery, one actor, few words, and scant movement, Beckett makes us feel the weight of the solitary, seemingly endless last night of a life. Death comes as a release—a happy ending.

W = Woman in chair.
V = Her recorded voice.

Fade up on W in rocking chair facing front downstage slightly off center audience left. Long pause.

W: More.

Pause. Rock and voice together.

V: till in the end
the day came
in the end came
close of a long day
when she said
to herself

whom else
time she stopped
time she stopped
going to and fro
all eyes
all sides
high and low
for another
another like herself
another creature like herself
a little like
going to and fro
all eyes
all sides
high and low
for another
till in the end
close of a long day
to herself
whom else
time she stopped
time she stopped
going to and fro
all eyes
all sides

(continued)

rors of Pleasure; Monster in a Box; Gray's Anatomy; It's a Slippery Slope; and Morning, Noon and Night. In Rumstick Road Gray discusses his acting career, his mother's psychiatric treatment, her Christian Science faith, her illness from cancer, and her eventual suicide. It's a Slippery Slope is a monologue about life after fifty and regaining one's personal equilibrium through the joys and terrors of learning to ski.

Monodrama

Samuel Beckett's Monodramas

Since the original production of *Waiting for Godot* in 1953, Samuel Beckett has been a major influence on experimentalists looking for ways to introduce into the theatre intuitive events, talking pieces, interior monologues, and minimal staging. To do so required new dramatic forms, conventions, and performance techniques. Cause-to-

(continued on page 148)

high and low
for another
another living soul
one other living soul
going to and fro
all eyes like herself
all sides
high and low
for another
another like herself
a little like
going to and fro
till in the end
close of a long day
to herself
whom else
time she stopped
going to and fro
time she stopped
time she stopped

Together: echo of "time she stopped,"
coming to rest of rock, faint fade of light.

Long pause.

W: More.

Pause. Rock and voice together.

V: so in the end
close of a long day
went back in
in the end went back in
saying to herself
whom else
time she stopped
time she stopped
going to and fro
time she went and sat
at her window
quiet at her window
facing other windows

so in the end
close of a long day
in the end went and sat
went back in and sat
at her window
let up the blind and sat
quiet at her window
only window
facing other windows
other only windows
all eyes
all sides
high and low
for another
at her window
another like herself
a little like
another living soul
one other living soul
at her window
gone in like herself
gone back in
in the end
close of a long day
saying to herself
whom else
time she stopped
time she stopped
going to and fro
time she went and sat
at her window
quiet at her window
only window
facing other windows
other only windows
all eyes
all sides
high and low
for another
another like herself
a little like

another living soul
one other living soul

Together: echo of "living soul,"
coming to rest of rock, faint fade
of light.

Long pause.

W: More.

  Pause. Rock and voice together.

V: till in the end
  the day came
  in the end came
  close of a long day
  sitting at her window
  quiet at her window
  only window
  facing other windows
  other only windows
  all blinds down
  never one up
  hers alone up
  till the day came
  in the end came
  close of a long day
  sitting at her window
  quiet at her window
  all eyes
  all sides
  high and low
  for a blind up
  one blind up
  no more
  never mind a face
  behind the pane
  famished eyes
  like hers
  to see
  be seen
  no

a blind up
like hers
a little like
one blind up no more
another creature there
somewhere there
behind the pane
another living soul
one other living soul
till the day came
in the end came
close of a long day
when she said
to herself
whom else
time she stopped
time she stopped
sitting at her window
quiet at her window
only window
facing other windows
other only windows
all eyes
all sides
high and low
time she stopped
time she stopped

Together: echo of "time she stopped,"
coming to rest of rock, faint fade
of light.

Long pause.

W: More.

  Pause. Rock and voice together.

V: so in the end
  close of a long day
  went down
  in the end went down
  down the steep stair

(continued)

Samuel Beckett (continued)

let down the blind and down
right down
into the old rocker
mother rocker
where mother sat
all the years
all in black
best black
sat and rocked
rocked
till her end came
in the end came
off her head they said
gone off her head
but harmless
no harm in her
dead one day
no
night
dead one night
in the rocker
in her best black
head fallen
and the rocker rocking
rocking away
so in the end
close of a long day
went down
in the end went down
down the steep stair
let down the blind and down
right down
into the old rocker

those arms at last
and rocked
rocked
with closed eyes
closing eyes
she so long all eyes
famished eyes
all sides
high and low
to and fro
at her window
to see
be seen
till in the end
close of a long day
to herself
whom else
time she stopped
let down the blind and stopped
time she went down
down the steep stair
time she went right down
was her own other
own other living soul
so in the end
close of a long day
went down
down the steep stair
let down the blind and down
right down
into the old rocker
and rocked
rocked

effect plots, soliloquies, and large theatrical moments were no longer adequate to express the mystery and pain of psychic distress.

Beckett's monologues and narrative voices together with his minimalist staging (an old man, a table, and a tape recorder; a woman buried in a mound of dirt; two lips speaking; a woman in a rocking chair surrounded by darkness) influenced the work of Harold Pinter, Lee Breuer, Spalding Gray, and others. The aim of the convention (let us call it *monodrama*) is the same as that of the stream-of-consciousness novel: to present the conscious and unconscious thought processes of the speaker. To take

saying to herself
no
done with that
the rocker
those arms at last
saying to the rocker
rock her off
stop her eyes
fuck life
stop her eyes
rock her off
rock her off

*Together: echo of "rock her off," coming
to rest of rock, slow fade out.*

NOTES

Light

Subdued on chair. Rest of stage dark. Subdued spot on face constant throughout, unaffected by successive fades. Either wide enough to include narrow limits of rock or concentrated on face when still or at mid-rock. Then throughout speech face slightly swaying in and out of light. Opening fade-up: first spot on face alone. Long pause. Then light on chair. Final fade-out: first chair. Long pause with spot on face alone. Head slowly sinks, comes to rest. Fade out spot.

W

Prematurely old. Unkempt grey hair. Huge eyes in white expressionless face. White hands holding ends of armrests.

Eyes

Now closed, now open in unblinking gaze. About equal proportions section 1, increasingly closed 2 and 3, closed for good halfway through 4.

Costume

Black lacy high-necked evening gown. Long sleeves. Jet sequins to glitter when rocking. Incongruous frivolous headdress set askew with extravagant trimmings to catch light when rocking.

Attitude

Completely still till fade-out of chair. Then in light of spot head slowly inclined.

Chair

Pale wood highly polished to gleam when rocking. Footrest. Vertical back. Rounded inward curving arms to suggest embrace.

Rock

Slight. Slow. Controlled mechanically without assistance from W.

Voice

Lines in italics spoken by W with V a little softer each time. W's "More" a little softer each time. Towards end of section 4, say from "saying to herself" on, voice gradually softer.[7]

---

us into the character's or speaker's consciousness, playwrights (following Beckett's lead) have added electronic amplification, sound tracks, holograms, and voice-overs.

POSTMODERN THEATRE

In the 1970s a movement in reaction against the "modern" emerged in architecture, painting, music, literature, and theatre. Called *postmodern,* the new movement most

HAMLETMACHINE. A postmodern theatre piece adapted from Heiner Müller's play is the work of El Periférico de Objectos from Buenos Aires (Argentina) in a Spanish-language production called *Máquina Hamlet* with Felictas Luna as Ophelia. Brooklyn Academy of Music, New York, 2000.

©Richard Termine

often called for *doubling; that is, placing contradictory experiences within the same frame of reference.* For example, the actor against the stenographic image in Philip Glass's opera *1,000 Airplanes on the Roof,* or Andrei Serban's postmodern *Hamlet* in which Polonius uses a microcassette recorder to tape his observations and the acting ensemble files on stage carrying posters of past *Hamlets.*

Artist Andy Warhol's repetitive screen prints of photographic images of Marilyn Monroe, Elizabeth Taylor, and Campbell soup cans are likewise typical of postmodern art. The paintings are both a collection of images reproduced by technological means from an "original image"—the photograph—and not from the real thing or person. This "reframing" of human experience with technology dispenses with realism and naturalism in art and celebrates the *fragmentation of experience.* When we talk today about "computer viruses," we are reframing experience to suggest that human biology is at work in computer networks. This kind of playful discourse (and even parody) is found in postmodern art.

In the theatre, postmodern works spring directly from the earlier antirealistic theatre of the symbolists and surrealists. Whereas symbolists and surrealists in the early part of the century set about to the reveal inner truth, postmodernists celebrate the randomness of truth where experience is improvised, parodic, haphazard, self-referential, and arbitrary. The brief texts (of German playwright Heiner Müller, for example) are composed of extended monologues, notations on stage images, notes on multiple and simultaneous sensory impressions, and paragraphs of word-fragments that explore the world's cultural history. These texts are often called "assemblages" or "collages." They make bold associations between old plays (*Medea* and *Hamlet,* for example) and current icons to refocus the audience's attention on present-day social issues and values. In Heiner Müller's theatre piece *Hamletmachine* examines the collapse of Western Civilization. Ophelia becomes a terrorist and Hamlet a demolisher of those "ideologues" Karl Marx, Lenin, and Mao Zedong to demonstrate modern Europe's political, intellectual, and social failures.

Theatre of Images

In 1976 critic Bonnie Marranca coined the term "Theatre of Images" to describe the postmodern work of American writer-director-designer-composers Robert Wilson, Philip Glass, and Lee Breuer. Revolting against words and "old-fashioned" verbal texts, these innovators created theatrical events dominated by visual and aural

images. Since the early 1970s, their avant-garde experiments have evolved to resemble *the painter's collage*. Absent are climactic drama's cause-to-effect relationships of action, plot, and character. In their place we find actors juxtaposed with holographic shapes, atonal sounds, and sculpted images that develop as large-scale performances requiring more than a few hours to complete. This new mixture of creative sources (sound, music, light, technology, scenarios) ultimately raises the same issues as more traditional theatre: questions of humanity's relationship to society, to the environment, and to itself.

©Richard Feldman

ROBERT WILSON'S *THE KNEE PLAYS* These short plays were originally intended as interludes between the fifteen scenes of *the CIVIL warS*, created by Robert Wilson in 1984. Nine dancers create a cascade of imagery—visual, aural, and choreographic—focusing on "a tree of life." Using square modules, puppets, and masks, *The Knee Plays* with words and music by David Byrne tell stories dealing with the life cycle through history.

Robert Wilson, a student of architecture and painting, creates living pictures on stage with sculptured forms, some text, sounds, music, and visual images that require many hours to experience. Wilson's *Ka Mountain* lasted seven days. *A Letter for Queen Victoria* is composed of bits and pieces of overheard conversations, clichés, newspaper blurbs, colors, spot announcements, television images, and film clips. One theme of the piece was American imperialism, but instead of discussing the topic, Wilson projected *images* of that imperialism: Pilots talk about faraway lands against a scenic background of sounds of gunfire and bomb blasts.

Robert Wilson's the CIVIL warS

One of Robert Wilson's boldest ventures is the opera *the CIVIL warS: a tree is best measured when it is down,* a collaborative work involving German playwright Heiner Müller, American composer Philip Glass, and others. Wilson first thought of the work as an exploration of the American Civil War and the Industrial Revolution. He expanded his vision to include all "civil struggles" that have existed throughout history, from ancient Greece to the distant future. With haunting, violent images of the American Civil War at its center, the recurrent theme is destruction and death contrasted with the importance of civilization and the value of life.

Wilson's postmodern theatre of *the CIVIL warS* combines architectural landscapes, striking verbal and musical images, long physical and verbal pauses that exaggerate our sense of time passing, and incongruous characters (including astronauts, Robert E. Lee, Dorothy and the Tin Man of Oz). Literally towering above them all is Abraham Lincoln, a sixteen-foot-tall figure formed by a singer suspended in a harness and wearing a long black coat—the startling image of the "tree" that is best measured when it has been cut down.

*P*laywright – *Director* – *Designer*
Robert Wilson

Ralph Brinkoff/Courtesy Byrd Hoffman
Foundation

*The Black Rider: The Casting of the Magic
Bullets* premiered in Hamburg, Germany,
in 1990, with direction and design by
Robert Wilson.

©Haremann & Clarchen Baus

Born in 1941, **Robert Wilson** created the Byrd Hoffman Foundation to work with
autistic children, as well as performers of all ages, on developing a new kind of theatre. The results were unusually long performances—five to seven hours—intended
to provoke contemplation rather than to tell a story.

Wilson's productions—usually in collaboration with composer Philip Glass—
"assemble" actors, sounds, music, sculptured scenic pieces, light, and shadow to
comment on American society and cultural myths. They are known as much for their
length and complexity as for their unique titles:

- *The Life and Times of Joseph Stalin*
- *Einstein on the Beach*
- *The Life and Times of Sigmund Freud*
- *A Letter for Queen Victoria*
- *Death, Destruction and Detroit*
- *I Was Sitting on My Patio This Guy
  Appeared I Thought I Was Hallucinating*
- *The Golden Windows*
- *The Knee Plays*
- *the CIVIL warS: a tree is best mea-
  sured when it is down*

- *The Forest*
- *Danton's Death* (based on Georg
  Büchner's play)
- *The Black Rider: The Casting of the
  Magic Bullets*
- *Time Rocker*
- *Monsters of Grace*
- *The Days Before: Death, Destruction &
  Detroit III*
- *A Dream Play* (based on August
  Strindberg's play)

His epic productions stretch the audience's attention in an attempt to alter per-
ceptual awareness of people, places, and things. Wilson says of his work: "Most theatre that we see today is thought about in terms of the word, the text.... And that's not
the case with my work. In my theatre, what we see is as important as what we hear.
What we see does not have to relate to what we hear. They can be independent."[8]

Theatre for a High-Tech World

Einstein on the Beach . The Forest . 1,000 Airplanes on the Roof . The Voyage .

The Days Before: Death, Destruction & Detroit III

In the late twentieth century, Robert Wilson and composer Philip Glass forged a new kind of theatre that manipulates technology, images, sound, light, music, and actors to create experiences that audiences cannot find in any other medium. Wilson says that "… the authentic experience in the theatre is the uncovering. Theatre is not something we can comprehend; it's something we can experience."[9]

©Paula Court

EINSTEIN ON THE BEACH (left) Originally produced in 1976 at the Metropolitan Opera House, New York City, Einstein on the Beach is a collaboration between Robert Wilson and composer Philip Glass. The five-hour production dealt with the contradictions implicit in the genius of Albert Einstein and his legacy to our world. Dancers Sheryl Sutton and Lucinda Childs move as sculpted forms against a background image of the young Einstein.

THE FOREST (below) Scene from the 1988 American premiere of Robert Wilson's The Forest (with music by David Byrne) based on The Epic of Gilgamesh and produced at the Brooklyn Academy of Music. Enkidu (right, actor Howie Seago), the story's hero, confronts images of civilization's history: hunter, whore, slave, priest, scholar, and godhead. Wilson's production takes Enkidu on a journey through the history of civilization from primitive times up through the nineteenth-century industrial revolution and the end of the "modern" world.

©Gerhard Kassner

1,000 AIRPLANES ON THE ROOF With music and direction by Philip Glass and libretto by David Henry Hwang, *1,000 Airplanes on the Roof* was produced at the Beacon Theatre, New York City, in 1988. The actor is diminished by the 3-D stenographic projection of a modern high-rise building. Design by Jerome Sirlin.

Tom Caravaglia

THE VOYAGE With music and story by Philip Glass (with libretto by David Henry Hwang), *The Voyage* was commissioned for the Metropolitan Opera Company's Christopher Columbus Quincentenary Celebration in 1992. Production design by Robert Israel tells the story visually of people who have the courage to follow where their vision leads.

Winnie Klotz/Courtesy Metropolitan Opera, Lincoln Center, New York.

©Stephanie Berger Photography

THE DAYS BEFORE: DEATH, DESTRUCTION & DETROIT III Robert Wilson's *The Days Before* opened the 1999 Lincoln Center Festival, New York City, with a two-hour exploration of the process of destruction and reconstruction interwoven with narrative, philosophy, and memory. Featuring actress Fiona Shaw as the narrator with music by Ryuichi Sakamoto and text based on a novel by Umberto Eco and "Tone Poems" by Christopher Knowles.

TRANSITION

Drama, the written text, is a special way of imitating human behavior and events. Depending upon the playwright's attitudes toward and interpretations of experience, that imitation can take many forms. For 2,500 years, Western writers have used climactic, episodic, and situational play structures and a fairly consistent set of dramatic conventions.

In a world today of high technology and ambivalent meanings, writers and directors try different methods and tools to create verbal and visual texts that speak to audiences in tune with computer graphics, sophisticated electronic sound systems, video equipment, and spectacular holographic effects. Almost in ironic juxtaposition with the elaborate technology found in a Robert Wilson production is the minimalist art of Samuel Beckett, Harold Pinter, and Spalding Gray.

Almost despite technology, drama's conventions and unique language continue to satisfy audiences as means of communicating the complexities of human experience.

WEB SITES

Essays on the Craft of Dramatic Writing
http://www.teleport.com/~bjscript/index.htm

Interview with Spalding Gray
http://www.altx.com/io/gray1.html

The Playwriting Seminars
http://www.vcu.edu/artweb/playwriting

Einstein on the Beach
http://www.robertwilson.com

http://www.philipglass.com/einstein.html

These search terms are provided to assist you in exploring the topics introduced in this chapter at:

http//www.infotrac-college.com

imitation, mimesis, plot, character, dramatic time, performance, dramatic action, dramatic conflict, episodic playwriting, climactic playwriting, postmodernism, minimalism.

Suellen Fitzsimmons/Pittsburgh Public Theater

CHAPTER 7

Drama's Conventions and Language

All that lives by the fact of living, has a form, and by the same token must die— except the work of art which lives forever in so far as it is form.[1]

LUIGI PIRANDELLO

Preface to Six Characters in Search of an Author

Playwrights have common strategies to develop plot, character, and action; to manipulate time; and to end plays. Taken all together, dramatic conventions are agreed-upon artistic means used to communicate information and experience to audiences. Drama's language— verbal and nonverbal—is a way of seeing that engages our eyes, ears, and minds.

DRAMA'S CONVENTIONS

Over the years, playwrights worked out various strategies, called dramatic conventions, to convey experience and activity to audiences. A convention is an agreed-upon method of quickly getting something across to audiences. Just as we have social conventions to help us meet strangers or answer telephones, so the playwright has conventions to solve problems, pass along information, develop plot and action, and create interest and suspense. These shortcuts make it possible for the playwright to give information and to present experiences that in life would require weeks or even years, to tell two or three stories at once, and to complicate the stage action. What follows is a discussion of nine dramatic conventions: stage directions, exposition, point of attack, complication, crisis, climax, resolution, simultaneous or double plots, and the play-within-the-play.

Stage Directions

Before the printing press made possible a general readership for plays, stage directions (if they existed at all) were used solely by theatre personnel. In modern editions of *Hamlet*, for example, we find such abbreviated directions as "A flourish," "Exeunt," "Aside," "Dies," and "Exit Ghost." We assume that these directions were added later to Shakespeare's original promptbook by players or printers. Nevertheless, by modern standards, these directions are sparse.

Modern stage directions are included at the beginning of each act to provide information about how the playwright imagines details of the three-dimensional stage space, such as the Kowalski apartment in *A*

Tennessee Williams' *A Streetcar Named Desire* (1947) with Jessica Tandy as Blanche DuBois.

Streetcar Named Desire. (Some stage directions are a result of the original director's and actors' contributions to the script during rehearsals and performance.) The playwright's "directions" include facts about geography, season of the year, time of day or night, weather conditions, furnishings, dress, mood, stage properties, music cues, and general impressions of place or environment. The opening stage direction in *A Streetcar Named Desire* is a full page in length. In it, Tennessee Williams provides atmosphere with graphic details of place, time, light, and sounds: New Orleans, Elysian Fields Avenue, a May twilight, blue sky, barroom piano music. The age, dress, and movements of Stanley Kowalski and his friend Mitch are also described.

Scene One

The exterior of a two-story corner building on a street in New Orleans which is named Elysian Fields and runs between the L & N tracks and the river. The section is poor but, unlike corresponding sections in other American cities, it has a raffish charm. The houses are mostly white frame, weathered grey, with rickety outside stairs and galleries and quaintly ornamented gables.

This building contains two flats, upstairs and down. Faded white stairs ascend to the entrances of both.

It is first dark of an evening early in May. The sky that shows around the dim white building is a peculiarly tender blue, almost a turquoise, which invests the scene with a kind of lyricism and gracefully attenuates the atmosphere of decay. You can almost feel the warm breath of the brown river beyond the river warehouses with their faint redolences of bananas and coffee. A corresponding air is evoked by the music of Negro entertainers at a barroom around the corner. In this part of New Orleans you are practically always just around the corner, or a few doors down the street, from a tinny piano being played with the infatuated fluency of brown fingers. This "Blue Piano" expresses the spirit of the life which goes on here.

Two women, one white and one colored, are taking the air on the steps of the building. The white woman is Eunice, who occupies the upstairs flat; the colored woman a neighbor, for New Orleans is a cosmopolitan city

(continued on page 160)

Tennessee Williams' A Streetcar Named Desire

Tennessee Williams' *A Streetcar Named Desire* was first produced at the Barrymore Theatre, New York, in 1947. Her family's Mississippi estate sold, Blanche DuBois arrives at the New Orleans tenement home of Stella and Stanley Kowalski, her pregnant sister and her brother-in-law. Blanche's faded gentility clashes with Stanley's brutish masculinity. As she seeks protection from the world, she competes with Stanley for Stella's affections but finds herself no match for his sexual hold over her sister. She tries to charm Mitch, Stanley's poker-playing friend, into marrying her. However, Stanley destroys Blanche's hopes for marriage by telling Mitch about her past drunkenness and promiscuity. As Stella reproaches Stanley for his cruelty, her labor pains begin and Stanley rushes her to the hospital.

Blanche is visited by a drunken Mitch, who accuses her of lying to him and makes an effort to seduce her. Stanley returns to find Blanche dressed for a party, fantasizing about an invitation to go on a cruise with a wealthy male friend. Angered by her pretensions, Stanley starts a fight with her that ends in rape. In a final scene some weeks later, Blanche, her tenuous hold on reality shattered, is taken to a mental hospital.

The tragedy of *Streetcar* reveals human duplicity and desperation in Williams' modern South, where fragile people are overcome by violence and vulgarity.

A tender moment between actors Jessica Tandy as Blanche DuBois and Karl Malden as Mitch in the original New York production of *A Streetcar Named Desire* (1947), directed by Elia Kazan.

where there is a relatively warm and easy intermingling of races in the old part of town.

Above the music of the "Blue Piano" the voices of people on the street can be heard overlapping.

[Two men come around the corner, Stanley Kowalski and Mitch. They are about twenty-eight or thirty years old, roughly dressed in blue denim work clothes. Stanley carries his bowling jacket and a red-stained package from a butcher's. They stop at the foot of the steps.]²

Blanche, Stella's sister—dressed for a garden party in white suit, hat, gloves—comes unexpectedly into this setting. Williams describes her appearance:

She is about five years older than Stella. Her delicate beauty must avoid a strong light. There is something about her uncertain manner, as well as her white clothes, that suggest a moth.

In contrast, Shakespeare and his contemporaries did not have the advantage of sophisticated print technology. Nor were they interested in the specifics of environment as a factor that shapes human events. Their writing tradition placed all indications of time, place, weather, and mood in the dialogue of minor characters in the play's beginning moments. They provided the background information and also captured the audience's attention preparatory to the entrance of the principals. In the jargon of the theatre, these are "weather lines." Within eleven lines at the beginning of *Hamlet*, the two guards give us a sense of place ("castle battlements"), time ("'Tis now struck twelve"), weather ("'Tis bitter cold"), mood ("I am sick at heart"), and what's happening ("not a mouse stirring").

Stage directions are an important part of writing conventions, especially in the modern theatre. They provide crucial information for the reader, describing how the playwright has imagined the play's environment and the characters' ages and appearances. As a result of a recent legal ruling in the United States, only the playwright's stage directions, not the contributions of the original director, may be printed or otherwise used in subsequent stagings without permission.

Exposition

Classical Exposition

In a play's opening scene we are frequently given certain information about what is going on, what has happened in the past, and who is to be seen. In Euripides' *The Trojan Women*, a formal prologue is spoken by the gods Poseidon and Athene. The sea god Poseidon describes the treachery of the Greeks' use of the Trojan horse to gain entry into the city of Troy, the city's collapse, and the fate of its defenders. Athene, the goddess defender of Troy, describes how the Greeks defiled her altars. Then, Troy's Queen Hecuba tells of the physical and mental suffering of the Trojan people. Fol-

"Stage Directions" in Shakespeare's Hamlet

BERNARDO:	Who's there?
FRANCISCO:	Nay, answer me; stand, and unfold yourself.
BERNARDO:	Long live the King!
FRANCISCO:	Bernardo?
BERNARDO:	Here.
FRANCISCO:	You come most carefully upon your hour.
BERNARDO:	'Tis now struck twelve; get thee to bed, Francisco.
FRANCISCO:	For this relief, much thanks; 'tis bitter cold. And I am sick at heart.
BERNARDO:	Have you had quiet guard?
FRANCISCO:	Not a mouse stirring.
BERNARDO:	Well, good-night. If you do meet Horatio and Marcellus, The rivals of my watch, bid them make haste.
FRANCISCO:	I think I hear them. Stand, ho! Who's there? (I, i)

lowing this background information, the action begins. The fates of the Trojan women are decreed and Hector's young son, Astyanax, is sentenced to die.

The expository prologue in Euripides' *Medea* is a lamentation by Medea's nurse describing her mistress' murderous assistance in the past to help Jason steal the Golden Fleece followed by his present desertion of his family to marry the Princess of Corinth. Medea's sufferings and the Nurse's fears that violence may come prepare for the play's beginning. The Nurse says of Medea, "… I am afraid she may think of some dreadful thing,/For her heart is violent…. She's a strange woman…."

Modern Exposition

In contrast to the formal exposition of Greek plays, some modern plays begin with a telephone ringing; the person answering—for instance, a maid or butler in drawing-room comedy—gives the play's background information by talking to an unseen party about the family, its plans, and conflicts.

In most cases, plays begin with informational exchanges of dialogue to establish who, what, when, and where. Contemporary drama presents less information of this kind. Instead of asking who these people are and what is going to happen next, we usually ask: "What's going on now?" Absurdist plays raise more questions about the

(continued on page 163)

${\mathcal{E}}$uripides' Prologue in The Trojan Women

THE GREEKS, PRESENTED BY THE
ROYAL SHAKESPEARE COMPANY,
LONDON, 1979 In *The Trojan Women*,
Billie Whitelaw as Andromache
(foreground) with Eliza Ward as Hecuba
holding the child Astyanax in *Part One:
The War*. Production directed by John
Barton and designed by John Napier.

©Donald Cooper/Photostage Ltd.

The Trojan Women, written by Euripides and produced in 415 B.C. at the Theatre of
Dionysus, Athens, is, the third (and only surviving) play in his trilogy about Troy—its
destruction, the death of its defenders, and the enslavement of its women.

POSEIDON speaks:

....

I am Poseidon. Troy and its people were my city.

The ring of walls and towers I and Apollo built—
Squared every stone in it; and my affection has not faded
Now Troy lies dead under the conquering Argive spear,
Stripped, sacked and smouldering.
....

              Farewell, then, city!
Superb masonry, farewell! You have had your day of
Glory...

who, what, and why of a situation than they answer.

Point of Attack

The moment early in the play when the story is taken up is the point of attack. In *Macbeth*, the point of attack grows out of the victorious battle reports to King Duncan who, learning of the death of the traitorous Thane of Cawdor, rewards Macbeth with that title. In the very next scene Macbeth encounters the witches who greet him with many prophecies, including the title "Thane of Cawdor." Macbeth begins to believe the witches' prophecy that he will become the future king and writes to his wife, who plans the murder of King Duncan.

Complication, Crisis, Climax

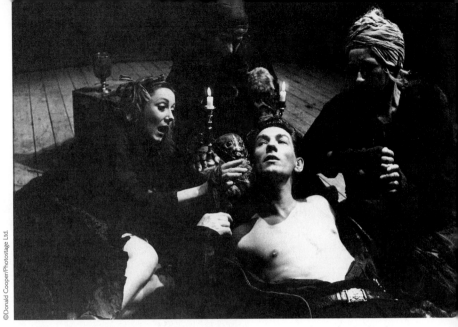

©Donald Cooper/Photostage Ltd.

The witches entice Macbeth (Sir Ian McKellen) with voodoo dolls, as they paint symbols on his body in the Royal Shakespeare Company (Stratford-upon-Avon, England) production of *Macbeth* (1976), directed by Trevor Nunn. The witches' prophesy the titles and royal throne that will be bestowed on Macbeth:

MACBETH: Speak, if you can. What are you?
1. WITCH: All hail, Macbeth! Hail to thee, Thane of Glamis!
2. WITCH: All hail, Macbeth! Hail to thee, Thane of Cawdor!
3. WITCH: All hail, Macbeth, that shalt be King hereafter! (I, iii)

The middle of a play is made up of complications—new information, unexpected events, or newly disclosed facts. Macbeth's unexpected encounter with the witches is the beginning of many violent complications. In *Ghosts*, Mrs. Alving overhears Oswald seducing Regina, the child of her husband and a servant, and, therefore, Oswald's half-sister. Mrs. Alving must deal with this complication.

A play's complications usually develop into a crisis, or turning point of the action. The crisis is an event that makes the resolution of the play's conflict inevitable. In *Macbeth*, the crisis is the murder of King Duncan by the Macbeths. They have killed an anointed king, and a universal bloodbath will follow until the murderers are punished and the rightful heir restored to the throne.

A play usually ends when the conflict is resolved in the climax, or highest point of intensity, and any loose strands of action are then tied off. In *The Trojan Women* the highest moment of intensity is when Hector's son, the heir to Troy, is sentenced to die and carried away to be executed. The consignment of the women to the Greek generals is almost anticlimactic because—without a male to procreate the tribe—Troy has no hope of future generations.

The climax of *Macbeth* is the appearance of the murdered Banquo's ghost at the banquet table—further evidence of Macbeth's ongoing bloody deeds and his unquiet conscience. After the ghost's appearance, forces turn against Macbeth, leading him finally to fight his rival Macduff; this secondary climax results in Macbeth's death and the restoration of the rightful heir to Duncan's throne.

(continued on page 165)

Shakespeare's Macbeth

Macbeth (Christopher Walken) confronts Banquo's ghost (Christopher Lloyd, at left) in the New York Shakespeare Festival's 1974 production.

The last of Shakespeare's four great tragedies (along with *Hamlet, Othello,* and *King Lear*), *Macbeth* (1606) was written when his creative powers were at their highest. Macbeth, King Duncan's noble warlord, hears witches prophesy that greatness will be his—that he will be king someday.

When his wife, Lady Macbeth, learns of the witches' prophecy, her imagination—overcharged with ambition—conceives the king's assassination. While he sleeps in their castle, the Macbeths murder Duncan, engendering a seemingly endless series of murders to conceal their original crime and to thwart other pretenders to the throne.

As the play progresses, the disintegrating effects of evil work on a once noble man and his wife. Macbeth's crimes distort his judgment; he is terrified by hallucinations of the ghosts of his victims, symbolizing a warning of retribution to come. He becomes increasingly isolated from his followers and his wife, whose guilty conscience eventually leads her to suicide. Pessimism and despair take hold of Macbeth as he contemplates his inevitable punishment. Only in the end does he revive a part of his former self, as he duels with his rival (Macduff) to a certain death.

This story of crime and punishment illustrates the destructive effects of power and ambition on the human psyche. Macbeth's self-awareness endows the action with its tragic dimension: He feels responsibility for the moral chaos he has created and he explores life's meaning in soliloquies that transcend his particular dilemma.

Resolutions or Endings

The resolution usually restores balance and satisfies the audience's expectations. The captive Trojan women are marched away to board the Greek ships; Medea flies away on her magical chariot with her dead children to find refuge in another land. Macbeth pays for his crimes with his life, and Duncan's son is crowned king of Scotland. In *A Streetcar Named Desire*, Blanche is taken to an asylum and the Kowalski household settles back into its routines of poker, beer, and Saturday-night bowling.

An absurdist play, like *The Bald Soprano*, usually completes a cycle in its resolution, suggesting that life's events repeat themselves over and over again. Some plays end with unanswered questions—for example, what is Nora Helmer's fate after she leaves her "doll's house"?—to stimulate audiences to think about the personal and social implications of the heroine's choice. Whatever the case, the resolution brings a sense of completed or suspended action, of conflicts resolved in probable ways, and of promises fulfilled.

Simultaneous Plots

Other dramatic conventions, such as simultaneous plots and plays-within-plays, relate past and present events and behavior. The Elizabethans used simultaneous or double plotting to represent life's variety and complexity. Two stories are told concurrently; the lives of one group of characters affect the lives of the other group. *Hamlet*, for instance, is the story of two families: Hamlet-Claudius-Gertrude, Laertes-Polonius-Ophelia. The secondary plot or subplot is always resolved before the main plot to maintain a sense of priority. For example, Laertes dies before Hamlet in the duel, thereby ending that family's story.

CONVENTIONS OF TIME

Dramatic Versus Actual Time

During a performance, audiences experience time on several levels. First, there is the amount of actual time that it takes us to see a play. Dramatic time, however, is a phenomenon of the playwright's text.

Within the fictional world of the play, time can be expanded or compressed. Dramatic time can be accelerated by using gaps of days, months, and even years; or it can be slowed down by interrupting the forward action with soliloquies and flashbacks. Episodes may be shown out of their chronological sequence, or they may be foreshortened so that they occur more quickly than they would in actuality. Shakespeare's battle scenes, requiring only a few minutes of swordplay on stage, would require days or even months in real time. In Samuel Beckett's plays, characters experience the relentless passage of time as they wait out their uneventful lives. Often in Beckett's plays, the experience of dramatic time is cyclical—day becomes night and night becomes day.

(continued on page 167)

Shakespeare's Hamlet

Hamlet (Albert Finney) stands above the wounded Laertes (Simon Ward) near the end of the duel. Laertes' death concludes the story of his family and the secondary plot in the 1976 production directed by Sir Peter Hall at London's Royal National Theatre.

Anthony Crickmay/V&A Picture Library

Shakespeare's greatest tragedy, *Hamlet* (c. 1601), tells the story of a man who confronts a task that seems beyond his powers. The play begins as the Danish court celebrates King Claudius' wedding to Queen Gertrude; her son Prince Hamlet still mourns the death of his father. His father's ghost appears and tells Hamlet that he was murdered by his brother Claudius. Hamlet swears to take vengeance, but he must first prove to himself that Claudius is guilty. He has a group of strolling players put on a play in which a similar murder is depicted. Claudius' reaction to the play betrays him, and Hamlet plots revenge.

By accident Hamlet kills Polonius, the Lord Chamberlain and father to Ophelia, a young woman who loves the prince. Hamlet is sent away for killing Polonius, and Ophelia is driven mad by her loss. Time passes and Hamlet returns.

Laertes, Polonius' son, vows revenge and challenges Hamlet to a duel. To ensure that Hamlet is killed, Claudius poisons Laertes' sword and prepares a cup of poison for Hamlet to drink during the duel. In the closing scene, Gertrude accidentally drinks from the poisoned cup and dies, Hamlet kills Claudius, and Laertes—after mortally wounding Hamlet—is killed by Hamlet with the poisoned sword. Hamlet's cousin Fortinbras is made king of Denmark.

Hamlet is a tragedy about the power of evil to corrupt the innocent, bring chaos to a kingdom, and paralyze the human will. It contains some of the greatest poetry written by Shakespeare.

Luigi Pirandello

©Bettman/CORBIS

Luigi Pirandello (1867–1936), the son of a rich owner of sulfur mines in Agrigento on the southern coast of Sicily, studied philosophy at the University of Rome and earned a doctorate at the University of Bonn in Germany. In his early years, he wrote poems and short stories for his own enjoyment. He married the daughter of his father's partner in an arranged marriage. Both families lost their fortunes when the mines flooded in 1904. To earn a living for his new family, Pirandello became an instructor at a teacher's college for women in Rome. Shortly thereafter, his wife became mentally ill. Refusing to place her in a public institution and too poor to afford a private one, Pirandello endured life with his wife's mental illness until her death in 1918. Writing to support the family, he attained international fame as a playwright by the 1920s. In 1925, he founded his own art theatre (*Teatro d'Arte*) in Rome and in 1934 was awarded the Nobel Prize for Literature.

Pirandello's plays demonstrate a brooding inquiry into the nature of reality. His belief that all experience is illusory and that life itself is a "sad piece of buffoonery" is best illustrated in *It Is So! (If You Think So)* (1917), *Henry IV* (1922), *As You Desire Me* (1930), and in his "theatre trilogy": *Six Characters in Search of an Author* (1921), *Each in His Own Way* (1924), and *Tonight We Improvise* (1930).

Time in the fictional universe of drama is highly malleable. Consideration of dramatic time has always played a large part in the different theories and rules of drama. In his *Poetics*, Aristotle briefly suggested that the amount of time it takes the actors to enact the story should ideally be concurrent with the actual time it takes to perform the play. This attention to a *unity of time*, as it was later called, is still found in modern realistic plays in which a situation develops and is resolved within twenty-four hours or less.

CONVENTIONS OF METAPHOR

The Play-Within-the-Play

Shakespeare used the play-within-the-play and it is still a common plot device, most notably in the work of as Bertolt Brecht, Luigi Pirandello, Peter Weiss, Tom Stoppard, and Michael Frayn. In *Hamlet*, the play-within-the-play (called *The Murder of Gonzago*, or "the mousetrap") is used in what is now thought of as a highly traditional way. The strolling players re-create a second play on stage for the entertainment of the

(continued on page 173)

Luigi Pirandello's Six Characters in Search of an Author *(with text)*

©Joan Marcus

PIRANDELLO'S "SIX CHARACTERS" MAKE THEIR MYSTERIOUS APPEARANCE IN THE PLAY-WITHIN-THE PLAY *Six Characters in Search of an Author* in the Arena Stage production, Washington, D.C., directed by Liviu Ciulei.

S*ix Characters in Search of an Author,* written in 1921 by Italian playwright Luigi Pirandello, begins with a rehearsal of a "Pirandello comedy" (called *Mixing It Up*) by a second-rate acting company. A family of six fictional characters intrudes upon a rehearsal and demands that their story be performed. They have been deserted by their author and left in limbo, so to speak. The actors agree to give one rehearsal to the characters' story, and chaos ensues in their tale of domestic tragedy that becomes the play-within-the-play. During the rehearsal, the characters insist that the actors cannot portray them in any meaningful way. Characters and actors bicker in a radical questioning of theatrical art. The paradoxes of play and reality, characters and actors, illusion and truth are played out in the rehearsal and in the characters' inner play.

Pirandello's influential *Six Characters in Search of an Author* anticipated the theatricalism of the modern theatre, along with the mood and questioning of absurdist drama.

Act I

At this point, the **Door-Keeper** has entered from the stage door and advances towards the manager's table, taking off his braided cap. During this manoeuvre, the **Six Characters** enter, and stop by the door at back of stage, so that when the **Door-Keeper** is about to announce their coming to the **Manager**, they are already on the stage. A tenuous light surrounds them, almost as if irradiated by them—the faint breath of their fantastic reality.

This light will disappear when they come forward towards the actors. They preserve, however, something of the dream lightness in which they seem almost suspended; but this does not detract from the essential reality of their forms and expressions.

He who is known as **The Father** is a man of about 50: hair, reddish in colour, thin at the temples; he is not bald, however; thick moustaches, falling over his still fresh mouth, which often opens in an empty and uncertain smile. He is fattish, pale; with an especially wide forehead. He has blue, oval-shaped eyes, very clear and piercing. Wears light trousers and a dark jacket. He is alternatively mellifluous and violent in his manner.

The Mother seems crushed and terrified as if by an intolerable weight of shame and abasement. She is dressed in modest black and wears a thick widow's veil of crêpe. When she lifts this, she reveals a wax-like face. She always keeps her eyes downcast.

The Step-Daughter, is dashing, almost impudent, beautiful. She wears mourning too, but with great elegance. She shows contempt for the timid half-frightened manner of the wretched **Boy** (14 years old, and also dressed in black); on the other hand, she displays a lively tenderness for her little sister, **The Child** (about four), who is dressed in white, with a black silk sash at the waist.

The Son (22) tall, severe in his attitude of contempt for The Father, supercilious and indifferent to The Mother. He looks as if he had come on the stage against his will.

DOOR-KEEPER [*cap in hand*]:   Excuse me, sir …

THE MANAGER [*rudely*]:   Eh? What is it?

DOOR-KEEPER [*timidly*]:   These people are asking for you, sir.

THE MANAGER [*furious*]:   I am rehearsing, and you know perfectly well no one's allowed to come in during rehearsals! [*Turning to the Characters.*] Who are you, please? What do you want?

THE FATHER [*coming forward a little, followed by the others who seem embarrassed*]:   As a matter of fact … we have come here in search of an author …

THE MANAGER [*half angry, half amazed*]:   An author? What author?

THE FATHER: Any author, sir.

THE MANAGER: But there's no author here. We are not rehearsing a new piece.

THE STEP-DAUGHTER [*vivaciously*]:   So much the better, so much the better! We can be your new piece….[3]

The Play-Within-the-Play: Traditional and Modern

Hamlet . **Six Characters in Search of an Author** .

The Caucasian Chalk Circle . **Marat/Sade** . **Noises Off**

Culver Pictures, Inc.

HAMLET BY WILLIAM SHAKESPEARE Laurence Olivier as Hamlet (seated at left) watches the king and queen during the theatrical "Mousetrap" that he has devised to prove Claudius' guilt. From the 1948 film of Shakespeare's play, also directed by Olivier.

170

SIX CHARACTERS IN SEARCH OF AN AUTHOR BY LUIGI PIRANDELLO Three of Pirandello's fictional "characters" rehearse their "inner" play for the Stage Manager in the 1988–89 Arena Stage production, directed by Liviu Ciulei, Washington, D.C.

THE CAUCASIAN CHALK CIRCLE BY BERTOLT BRECHT The players (center) perform Brecht's inner play about Grusha, Azdak, and the child for the benefit of the villagers and as a means of settling their dispute in the 1965 production at the Guthrie Theater, Minneapolis.

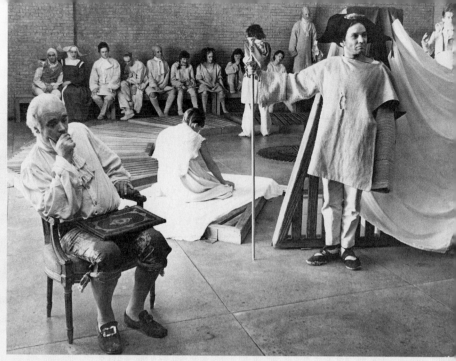

THE PERSECUTION AND ASSASSINA-
TION OF JEAN-PAUL MARAT AS
PERFORMED BY THE INMATES OF
THE ASYLUM OF CHARENTON UNDER
THE DIRECTION OF THE MARQUIS DE
SADE BY PETER WEISS The Marquis
de Sade (Patrick McGee) rehearses the
inner play with the inmates of Charen-
ton asylum in the 1965 production of
Marat/Sade, directed by Peter Brook for
the Royal Shakespeare Company (Strat-
ford-upon-Avon, England).

©Bruce Bennett

NOISES OFF BY MICHAEL FRAYN Actors (Linda
Larkin, seated, and Annalee Jeffries) in the inner
play rehearse their lines in the 1998 Alley Theatre
production, Houston.

court about the unusual murder of Hamlet's father. Claudius' violent reaction to it gives Hamlet proof of the King's guilt.

Brecht's *The Caucasian Chalk Circle*, like Pirandello's *Six Characters in Search of an Author* and Michael Frayn's *Noises Off*, is almost a play-within-the-play in its entirety. Brecht's singer-narrator links the outer play (the settling of the farmers' dispute over the ownership of the land) with the inner one (the stories of Grusha, Azdak, and the chalk-circle test). The long inner play manifests a kind of collective wisdom that has practical applications in the actual dispute over ownership of property (the outer play).

Recent playwrights use the play-within-the-play in more complex ways than either Shakespeare or Brecht to demonstrate that life is like theatre, and vice versa. The stage itself becomes a metaphor for the world's fictions and self-imposed illusions. The outer play retains the realistic convention that the stage is a real-life living room (or situation), but that real-life living room is also viewed as a "stage."

In the modern theatre, the play-within-the-play has become a means for demonstrating life's theatricality. The stage is the most accessible medium to show life's artifice, play-acting, and heightened moments of passion, anger, and even violence.

> Theatre is more than words: drama is a story that is lived and relived with each performance, and we can watch it live. The theatre appeals as much to the eye as to the ear.[4]
> EUGÈNE IONESCO
> *Notes and Counter-Notes: Writings on the Theatre*

DRAMA'S LANGUAGE

Words and Gestures

Playwrights, directors, designers, and actors use a "language" that is both visual and aural to organize our perceptions in the theatre.

Spoken language in the theatre is both like and unlike the way people talk in real life. First, it is the playwright's means for expressing what characters experience and for developing plot and action. Unlike conversation in real life, actors speak highly selective words. Shakespeare's soliloquies express thoughts and feelings in blank verse. This unusual and eloquent language is acceptable to us because it has its own reality, consonant with a world other than our own.

We are so used to equating language (and communication) with words that we must constantly remind ourselves that in the theatre, as in life, words are only a small part of the communications system. Peter Brook called the words spoken on stage only "a small visible portion of a gigantic unseen formation."[5] The playwright's words in the theatre are enhanced by a nonverbal language.

THE TEMPEST Caliban, wearing a mud mask from New Guinea, gestures to the frightened clowns in Shakespeare's *The Tempest*, directed and designed by Julie Taymor for the Theatre for a New Audience, New York City, 1986.

©Richard Feldman

Drama's Conventions and Language **173**

Drama's language has both verbal and nonverbal characteristics, and can be divided into the many ways that meaning is communicated to audiences. The diagram lists sixteen ways that stage language communicates the stage's living reality.

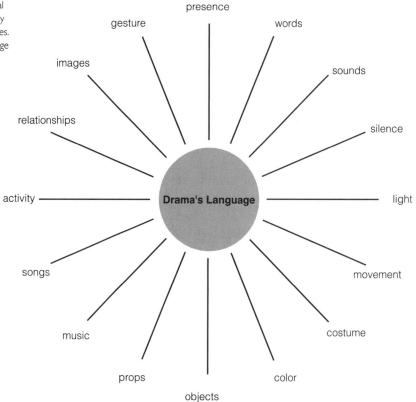

Physical gestures, costumes, colors, sounds, and lighting can speak eloquently to audiences of moods, attitudes, intentions, and meanings.

There is also in the theatre a direct connection between words and gestures. To repeat George Steiner's comment about this: "Drama is language under such high pressure of feeling the words carry a necessary and immediate connotation of gesture...."[6] Drama's language expresses not only the characters' thoughts, attitudes, and intentions, but also the active presence of human beings in a living world.

It has been argued that the language we use for communication in real life is also multifaceted and theatrical: Our clothes are costumes, we speak words and make gestures, we carry props (book bags or sunglasses), we wear makeup, and we are affected by the environment's sounds and silences. Although this is true, there is an important difference between language in the theatre and in life. In the theatre, language (both verbal and nonverbal) is selected and controlled. It shapes the action. Much more must happen in conversation, or dialogue, in the theatre than in ordinary life. Our conversations with friends are often random and purposeless. But language in the theatre is carefully arranged by the playwright into a meaningful pattern, and actors, directors, and designers provide elements of support for this pattern of words to be meaningful night after night.

Verbal and Nonverbal Language

On the page of a script, words are signs and symbols with the potential for making something happen in the theatre in an act of communication. Theatre's language is made up of words, sound, light, shape, movement, silence, activity, inactivity, gesture, color, music, song, objects, costumes, props, and visual images.

In communication theory, a sign has a direct physical relationship to the thing it represents—to its referent. Thunder is a sign of rain. It has a physical connection with changes in the atmosphere. Symbols differ from signs in that they have an arbitrary connection to their referents. The American flag, for example, is a symbol of our country, and most people associate everything good in America with the flag that represents the United States. During the Vietnam War, some people associated the flag with everything wrong with America. Today, flags have become issues of legal and social debate, further emphasizing their symbolism.

In the theatre, both verbal and nonverbal symbols and signs are used to enhance audience perception of the actors' living presence. In Anton Chekhov's *The Cherry Orchard*, the orchard is a verbal symbol variously interpreted as the passing of the old way of life and/or of the coming of a new social order. Characters refer to the orchard as a family treasure, a local tradition, a beautiful object, and valuable property to be sold in order to save the estate from auction. The orchard is symbolic of the ways Chekhov's characters deal with or fail to deal with life's demands. The sound of the ax cutting down the trees at the play's end is a nonverbal sign, communicating the destruction of the family's treasure and their way of life. But it also communicates the arrival of a new social order with new strengths and values. Verbal and aural symbols and signs in Chekhov's plays reinforce one another in communicating the play's meaning.

Martha Swope/TimePix

Actors with the American flag in the rock musical *Hair* (1967), directed by Tom O'Horgan Off Broadway, make a visual statement with their clothes, hats, and hair about the attitudes toward the establishment of counter-culture groups in the 1960s.

TYPES OF STAGE LANGUAGE

To understand communication in the theatre, we must ask basic questions: What do we hear? What do we see? What is taking shape before us? What growing image creates the life of the play? When the many elements of the stage's language work together, the audience experiences sensations, sounds, presence, and speech without particularly analyzing the experience in the moment.

Shakespeare's Verse

The *soliloquy* is a means of taking the audience into the character's mind to hear its contents and arguments with the self. Hamlet's "How all occasions do inform against

(continued on page 177)

Anton Chekhov's The Cherry Orchard

After some years abroad the widowed Madame Ranevskaya returns to her Russian estate to find that it has been heavily mortgaged to pay her debts, and that it is to be auctioned. Generous and irresponsible, she seems incapable of recognizing her financial situation. A half-hearted attempt is made to collect money owed her by a neighboring landowner, but he is also in financial straits. Gaev, Madame Ranevskaya's brother, makes some suggestions, but his chief hope lies in an uncertain legacy from a relative, or a rich marriage for Anya, Madame Ranevskaya's daughter. The only realistic proposal comes from Lopakhin, a merchant whose father was once a serf of the Ranevskaya family. He suggests cutting down the famous cherry orchard and dividing the land into plots for summer cottages. The family rejects the idea of destroying such beauty and tradition.

With no specific plan in mind for saving the estate, the family drifts aimlessly toward the day set for the auction. On the evening of the sale, Madame Ranevskaya gives a party she cannot afford. In the middle of the festivities, Lopakhin arrives; when questioned, he reveals that he has bought the estate and intends to carry out his plan for cutting down the orchard and subdividing the land.

With the estate and orchard now sold, the family prepares to leave. Forgotten in the confusion is the old and dying Firs, the devoted family servant. As the sound of the ax rings from the orchard, he lies down to rest and is soon motionless in the empty house.

The 1977 New York Shakespeare Festival production of *The Cherry Orchard*, directed by Andrei Serban at Lincoln Center Theater.

George E. Joseph

me" he begins with concern for his delayed revenge, then meditates on human nature, and on the "thing" to be done. The precision of Hamlet's argument with himself reveals the brilliance of a mind that perceives the cause, proof, and means of revenge. The speech's length betrays Hamlet's habit of mind that delays his revenge against Claudius and fills time and space with words rather than actions. Measuring himself against his kinsman, the soldier Fortinbras, the man of action, Hamlet finds the example by which to act.

It is meaningful that Hamlet's speech is written as a soliloquy. He is, indeed, alone in the charge from his father's ghost and in the eventual killing of Claudius.

The speech moves in thirty-five lines from inactivity to activity, concluding with: "O, from this time forth, / My thoughts be bloody, or be nothing worth!" Hamlet, the hitherto invisible man of action, takes shape before our eyes, ears, and minds in sixty lines of blank verse.

Anthony Crickmay/V&A Picture Library

THE ACTOR'S LANGUAGE Hamlet's costume in the final two acts is that of a man of action. He is no longer dressed in the "solemn black" of mourning, nor in the disheveled dress of his "antic disposition." In addition, the actor's speech, gestures, and movements convey the character's determination to rid Denmark of the corrupt king. Albert Finney plays Hamlet in the 1976 production at London's Royal National Theatre.

Chekhov's Sounds and Silences

Anton Chekhov ends *The Cherry Orchard* with verbal and nonverbal effects: sounds with silence, words with noise, physical activity with aural effects. Firs is the elderly valet left behind by the family in their hurried departure from the estate that has been sold at auction. His last speech is placed between stage directions suggesting offstage sounds of departure, of a breaking string, and the stroke of an ax. The pauses in Firs's speech indicate the ending of a life, and also of a way of life. The fact that he is alone, locked in the house, forgotten and dying, tells us more vividly that "life has passed him by" than his mutterings.

At the end of *The Cherry Orchard*, Firs, the elderly valet dressed in his livery, lies down alone—the final symbol of the passing of a way of life. The image of the dying man is reinforced by the sound effects that follow. From *The Cherry Orchard*, directed by Andrei Serban at Lincoln Center Theater in 1977.

George E. Joseph

Soliloquy from Hamlet

©Michal Daniel

HAMLET Directed by Andrei Serban, with Liev Schreiber as Hamlet, Diane Venora as Queen Gertrude, and Hamish Linklater as Laertes. New York Shakespeare Festival/Joseph Papp Public Theatre production, 1999.

©Michal Daniel

The Shakespeare soliloquy is a stage convention for expressing a character's inner thoughts and feelings: As the actor speaks, we overhear the way the character's mind works and understand those hidden thoughts that result in action.

In Chekhov's plays, what people do is frequently more important than what they say. More important than Firs's words is the sound of the breaking string in the distance juxtaposed against the immediate sound of the ax. Even the order of the sound effects is important. The breaking string's mournful sound, symbolic of the release of Firs's life and the passing of the larger way of life, subsides into silence *before* the axe stroke, the sound of the aggressive new order taking over, intrudes on the scene. At the end of *The Cherry Orchard*, the audience hears and sees a world in transition.

HAMLET: How all occasions do inform against
    me,
And spur my dull revenge! What is a man,
If his chief good and market of his time
Be but to sleep and feed? A beast, no more.
Sure, He that made us with such large
    discourse,
Looking before and after, gave us not
That capability and godlike reason
To fust in us unused. Now, whether it be

Bestial oblivion, or some craven scruple
Of thinking too precisely on the event,
A thought which, quartered, hath but one
    part wisdom
And ever three parts coward—I do not know
Why yet I live to say, "This thing's to do,"
Sith I have cause, and will, and strength, and
    means
To do't. Examples gross as earth exhort me.
Witness this army, of such mass and charge,
Led by a delicate and tender prince,
Whose spirit, with divine ambition puffed,
Makes mouths at the invisible event,
Exposing what is mortal and unsure
To all that fortune, death, and danger dare,
Even for an eggshell. Rightly to be great
Is not to stir without great argument,
But greatly to find a quarrel in a straw
When honor's at the stake. How stand I
    then,
That have a father killed, a mother stained,
Excitements of my reason and my blood,
And let all sleep, while to my shame I see
The imminent death of twenty thousand
    men
That for a fantasy and trick of fame
Go to their graves like beds, fight for a plot
Whereon the numbers cannot try the cause,
Which is not tomb enough and continent
To hide the slain? O, from this time forth,
My thoughts be bloody, or be nothing
    worth!

(4, iv)

Brecht's Gestic Language

Bertolt Brecht's stage language includes music, song, placards, film projections, and
gest. Brecht's concept of gest, or gestic language, is a matter of the actors' overall attitude toward what is going on around them and what they are asked to do within the
circumstances of the text. In a reversal of emphasis, Brecht insisted that words follow the gest of the person speaking. He wrote:

"Gest" is not supposed to mean gesticulation: it is not a matter of
explanatory or emphatic movements of the hands, but of overall atti-

*A*nton *Chekhov's Sound Effects in*
The Cherry Orchard

In the modern theatre, stage directions are a means by which playwrights communicate imaginative worlds to directors, actors, designers, and readers. In the final scene of *The Cherry Orchard*, Chekhov describes the stage's appearance as he saw it in his mind's eye: Firs's costume, manner, and words; and the final powerful sounds.

LYUBOV: We are coming. (*They go out.*)

> (*The stage is empty. There is the sound of the doors being locked up, then of the carriages driving away. There is silence. In the stillness there is the dull stroke of an axe in a tree, clanging with a mournful lonely sound. Footsteps are heard. Firs appears in the doorway on the right. He is dressed as always— in a pea-jacket and white waist-coat with slippers on his feet. He is ill.*)

FIRS (*goes up to the doors, and tries the handles*):   Locked! They have gone … (*sits down on sofa*). They have forgotten me…. Never mind … I'll sit here a bit…. I'll be bound Leonid Andreyevitch hasn't put his fur coat on and has gone off in his thin overcoat (*sighs anxiously*). I didn't see after him…. These young people … (*mutters something that can't be distinguished*). Life has slipped by as though I hadn't lived. (*Lies down*) I'll lie down a bit…. There's no strength in you, nothing left you—all gone! Ech! I'm good for nothing (*lies motionless*).

> (*A sound is heard that seems to come from the sky, like a breaking harp-string, dying away mournfully. All is still again, and there is heard nothing but the strokes of the axe far away in the orchard.*)

Curtain.[7]

---

tudes. A language is gestic when it is grounded in a gest and conveys particular attitudes adopted by the speaker towards other men. The sentence "pluck the eye that offends thee out" is less effective from the gestic point of view than "if thine eye offend thee, pluck it out." The latter starts by presenting the eye, and the first clause has the definite gest of making an assumption; the main clause then comes as a surprise, a piece of advice, and a relief.[8]

The Caucasian Chalk Circle
The characters' gestic language becomes visible in the test of the chalk circle. To decide who is worthy of rearing the child Michael, the judge orders that a circle be drawn on the floor and that the contestants pull the child from the circle. The mate-

©Ruth Waltz

rialistic attitudes of the lawyers and the governor's wife toward the child are contrasted with Grusha's humanity and love for the child. Grusha refuses to tug at the boy, while the governor's wife pulls the child from the circle two times. The wife's attitudes, words, and gestures betray the fact that her wealth and power depend upon her ownership of the child. We see that she is selfish and "grasping."

Brecht used music and song as well as dialogue to communicate his characters' thoughts and feelings. The narrator in *The Caucasian Chalk Circle* interrupts the play's action to sing songs that pinpoint social attitudes and injustices. He sings a song to reveal what Grusha thinks but does not say. As the Narrator sings, Brecht invites audiences to understand without becoming involved emotionally in the woman's selfless concern for the child.

THE SINGER: Hear now what the angry woman thought and did not say:
(*Sings*)
If he walked in golden shoes
Cold his heart would be and stony.
Humble folk he would abuse
He wouldn't know me.
Oh, it's hard to be hard-hearted

(continued on page 183)

SOUNDS AND SILENCE IN *THE THREE SISTERS* Director Peter Stein at the Schaubühne am Behniner Platz (Berlin), 1984, staged the ending of Chekhov's *The Three Sisters* so that the empty house, the trunks and valises, the dilapidated fence, the encompassing trees with open space beyond make a visual statement about leave-taking and endings. The total stage picture communicates parting, nostalgia, quiet change, and irreparable loss.

*P*laywright

Anton Chekhov

In *The Three Sisters* at the American Repertory Theatre, Cambridge, Mass., designer Beni Montresor created a playing space with mirrored floor, massive red velvet curtains in the rear, and banks of footlights on either side of the floor. The Prozorov house becomes a stage-within-a-stage where Chekhov's "poor players" strut and fret away their hours. All engage frantically in a dance, creating a striking visual image of people avoiding the inevitability of their lives. Directed by Andrei Serban.

Anton Pavlovich Chekhov (1860–1904) was born in southern Russia and studied medicine at Moscow University. During his student years he wrote short stories to earn money. He began his playwriting career in the 1880s with one-act farces, *The Marriage Proposal* and *The Bear. Ivanov* (1887) was his first full-length play to be produced.

Chekhov redefined stage realism during the years of his association with the Moscow Art Theatre (1898–1904). The meaning of his plays is not in direct, purposive action but in the representation of a certain kind of rural Russian life, which he knew firsthand. Director Konstantin Stanislavski's style of interpreting the inner truth of Chekhov's characters and the mood of his plays resulted in one of the great theatrical collaborations.

During his last years, Chekhov lived in Yalta, where he had gone for his health, and made occasional trips to Moscow to participate in the productions. He died of tuberculosis in a German spa in 1904, soon after the premiere of *The Cherry Orchard*, and was buried in Moscow.

During his short life Chekhov wrote four masterpieces of modern stage realism: *The Sea Gull, Uncle Vanya, The Three Sisters,* and *The Cherry Orchard.*

The Caucasian Chalk Circle, directed by Molly Smith, at the Perseverance Theatre, Alaska.

All day long from morn to night.
To be mean and high and mighty
Is a hard and cruel plight.
Let him be afraid of hunger
Not of the hungry man's spite
Let him be afraid of darkness
But not fear the light. (Scene xi)[9]

CONTEMPORARY TRENDS IN AMERICAN THEATRE

French playwright and theatre theorist Antonin Artaud (1896–1948) militated against traditional dialogue that furthers plot and reveals character. He favored inducing in audiences a shock reaction and a visceral response. He called for a *theatre of cruelty* to purge the audience's feelings of hatred, violence, and cruelty through use of non-verbal effects: sounds, lighting, unusual theatre spaces, and violent movements. Artaud wanted to assault the audience's senses, to cleanse the spectators morally and spiritually, for the improvement of humankind.

Influenced by Artaud's writings, American playwrights of the sixties assaulted the spectator's senses with sounds, violent images, and physicalization in works that grew out of protests against the political, military, industrial, and cultural establishments in the United States. By the end of the Vietnam War, American political consciousness was largely dissipated; the new performance techniques of experimental groups in the United States, like the Open Theatre, the Living Theatre, and the Performance Group, had become stale and predictable; and the games, transformations, and group

David Mamet's Wordsmiths
in Glengarry Glen Ross

Robert Prosky as Shelly Levene (left) argues for "leads" in the 1984 Goodman Theatre production, Chicago, of David Mamet's *Glengarry Glen Ross*, directed by Gregory Mosher.

Courtesy Brigitte Lacombe/Billy Rose Theatre Collection, The New York Public Library for the Performing Arts, Astor, Lenox and Tilden Foundations

David Mamet's wordsmiths, like real estate salesman Shelly Levene in *Glengarry Glen Ross*, articulate in monosyllabic words the panic and sheer poetry of their beleaguered lives. Mamet's emphases (the italicized words) in the text underscore the hard-sell core of the salesmen's lives as they fend off failure in the guise of loss of influence, respect, leads, sales, closings, bonuses, new deals, and even the job. In Mamet's writing, words bring to the surface the characters' fear, greed, and desperation.

improvisations of these companies had been appropriated by the commercial theatre as productions of *Hair* (1968) and *A Chorus Line* (1975) moved onto Broadway. Powerful new voices emerged in the 1970s and 1980s in the American theatre as a postwar wave of writers, including Edward Albee, John Guare, Beth Henley, David Mamet, Terrence McNally, Marsha Norman, Sam Shepard, August Wilson, Lanford Wilson, and many others. All tested the American character, family, and dreams, and found them wanting.

David Mamet's Wordsmiths

In language at once fragmented and profane, David Mamet explores the myths of American capitalism—the loss of individual and national enterprise—in the salesmen, confidence men, and tricksters that inhabit *American Buffalo* (1977), *Glengarry Glen Ross* (1983), and *Speed the Plow* (1988).

A booth at a Chinese restaurant, Williamson and Levene are seated at the booth.

LEVENE: John … John … John. Okay. John. John. Look: (*Pause.*) The Glengarry Highland's leads, you're sending Roma out. Fine. He's a good man. We know what he is. He's fine. All I'm saying, you look at the *board*, he's throwing … wait, wait, wait, he's throwing them *away*, he's throwing the leads away. All that I'm saying, that you're wasting leads. I don't want to tell you your *job*. All that I'm saying, things get *set*, I know they do, you get a certain *mindset*…. A guy gets a reputation. We know how this … all I'm saying, put a *closer* on the job. There's more than one man for the … Put a … wait a second, put a *proven man out* … and you watch, now *wait* a second—and you watch your *dollar* volumes…. You start closing them for *fifty* `stead of *twenty-five* … you put a *closer* on the …

WILLIAMSON: Shelly, you blew the last …

LEVENE: No. John. No. Let's wait, let's back up here, I did … will you please? Wait a second. Please. I didn't "blow" them. No. I didn't "blow" them. No. One kicked *out*, one I closed …

WILLIAMSON: … you didn't close …

LEVENE: … I, if you'd *listen* to me. Please. I closed the cocksucker. His *ex*, John, his *ex*, I didn't know he was married … he, the *judge* invalidated the …

WILLIAMSON: Shelly …

LEVENE: … and what is that, John? What? Bad *luck*. That's all it is. I pray in your *life* you will never find it runs in streaks. That's what it does, that's all it's doing. Streaks. I pray it misses you. That's all I want to say.

WILLIAMSON (*Pause*): What about the other two?

LEVENE: What two?

WILLIAMSON: Four. You had four leads. One kicked out, one the *judge*, you say …

LEVENE: … you want to see the court records? John? Eh? You want to go down …

WILLIAMSON: … no …

LEVENE: … do you want to go *downtown* … ? (Act 1)[10]

Mamet's characters are *wordsmiths* who invent lies, sell reassurance, tell stories, and command experience through words alone. His is a world composed of petty criminals (*American Buffalo*), dubious real estate salesmen (*Glengarry Glen Ross*), and second-rate Hollywood agents (*Speed the Plow*). His urban cowboys and gangsters speak a language that is self-serving, caustic, and exploitative as they hustle their "deals." These characters desperately wish to connect with one another, but they have forgotten how to do so except in their "business" relationships.

In *Glengarry Glen Ross*, Mamet contrives a neat paradigm (the real estate office) of a competitive capitalistic society. The play is set in and around a Chicago real estate office and takes its title from a subdivision ripe for the deal. The play concerns a group of none-too-successful real estate salesmen whose company has imposed a ruthless new regimen: The most successful salesman will receive a Cadillac, the runner-up a

SAM SHEPARD'S *BURIED CHILD*
In *Buried Child*, Bradley (Jay Sanders, right) is threatened with his own artificial leg by Vincent (Christopher McCann). Shelly (Mary McDonnell), Vincent's girlfriend, looks on. Off Broadway production, 1978.

set of steak knives, the loser will be fired. The key to success lies in securing the addresses of likely buyers ("the leads"), and the pressure to succeed encourages unscrupulous methods with respect to clients and even the company. Increasingly desperate, one of the salesmen, Shelly Levene, breaks into the office and steals the premium address list of potential clients. Police are called to investigate the "crime." By contrast, the salesmen's day-to-day activities as they go about deceiving their customers is regarded as good business tactics, sanctioned by the ethics of a world in which success is the ultimate achievement.

Mamet's salesmen talk in code, deploying the jargon of the trade: leads, deals, sales, closings, percentages, marks, streaks, and so on. They talk in incomplete sentences sprinkled with profanity. The characters are consummate storytellers—wordsmiths. When the need arises, they improvise a drama or create stories of total plausibility to turn a situation into advantage, a sale, and cash.

It should not be assumed that the ethical failures of Mamet's confidence men lose them either the playwright's sympathy or the audience's. Mamet's concern for the individual's alienation from his or her moral nature forces us to look at their neediness and vulnerability among fellow tricksters and unwary customers.

In David Mamet's work, there is a yearning for that very sense of trust denied by every betrayal in the petty wheeling and dealing that he documents. Somewhere at the heart of his characters' being is a sense of *need* that is the beginning of their redemption (and our sympathy for them). Their words may snap under the pressure of fear or greed; they may try to adjust themselves to the shape of myths and fantasies; they may deny or exploit the desire for companionship. Deep down, however, below the broken rhythms of speech and the four-letter words, beyond the failed gestures at contact, is a need for connection.

TRANSITION

Playwrights are among the most important of the theatre's "image makers." The writing of plays is their special way of imitating human behavior and events for the stage. Other theatre artists interpret the playwright's text in the theatre's three-dimensional space, giving it shape, sound, color, rhythm, image, activity, and human presence.

Since the time of ancient Greek festivals, the actor's role in the theatre has been celebrated. Although acting styles and training have changed over centuries, the actor joins the playwright as one of the theatre's earliest "image makers."

WEB SITES

Anton Chekhov on Writing
> http://mockingbird.Creighton.edu/NCW/
> chekwrit.htm

Complete Text of Shakespeare's Works, plus Other Information on Shakespeare
> http://www.tech-two.mit.edu/Shakespeare/

Full Texts of Works of Literature Publicly Available, Dating from A.D. 1500 to the Present
> http://www.etext.lib.Virginia.edu/uvaonline.html

The Theatre of Tennessee Williams: A Virtual Fact File
> http://www.sinc.sunysb.edu/class/thr525/index.htm

The Screenwriters/Playwright's Page (useful tips and resources on scriptwriting and playwriting)
> http://www.teleport.com/~cdeemer/scrwriter.html

These search terms are provided to assist you in exploring the topics introduced in this chapter at:

http//www.infotrac-college.com

dramatic conventions, exposition, play-within-the-play, double or simultaneous plots, soliloquy, dialogue, monologue, gestic language.

©Joan Marcus

The Image Makers: The Actor

Acting is the belief and technique by which the actor brings human presence and behavior into the theatre. Theatre is, after all, the art human beings make out of themselves.

Jerzy Grotowski's "poor theatre" reflects a trend in the modern theatre to reduce the theatrical experience to essentials. In the American theatre, the trend has its roots in the 1938 Broadway production of Thornton Wilder's *Our Town*. Director Jed Harris took Wilder's straightforward play about recognizable townspeople in Grover's Corner, U.S.A., and placed the actors on a bare stage framed by the theatre's back wall. Virtually no scenery was used, costumes were muted, and properties were minimal. The actors told the story using only those properties, such as chairs and umbrellas, that they could move on and off stage for themselves. The *actors* remained the one indispensable element of the theatrical experience.

For over sixty years, actors have re-created *Our Town*, bringing a new experience to audiences. When the only object of their focus is the actor, modern audiences *rediscover* the actor's presence and art.

ACTING—
THE ASTONISHING ART

Acting Is Doing

As defined by Sanford Meisner, acting is "living truthfully in imagined circumstances," and for Laurence Olivier acting "is an everlasting search for truth." That search for truthful behavior is the foundation stone of the actor's art.

This photo from the 1938 Broadway production of Thornton Wilder's *Our Town* reveals two essential theatrical elements: actors in the space.

At the outset, we can state what acting is not. Acting is not showing, narrating, illustrating, or exhibiting. Acting is not dressing up and displaying emotions. Acting is a creative process as old as the first actor who entered the ancient Greek festivals. As a creative artist, the actor (1) selects *sensory* responses (both physiological and emotional) in the search for (2) *selected* behavior pertinent to a character's needs within the (3) *given circumstances,* or human problems, contained within the play.[2]

Acting does not begin with performing on stage before an audience. It begins with an individual's talent, imagination, discipline, the need to express, and the process of observation through the sensory organs (eyes, ears, skin, tongue, nose). To prepare a role, the actor selects from memory and personal experience what he or she has seen, heard, felt, and experienced over a lifetime. "At its most rewarding," says British actor Ian McKellen, "acting involves an intense combination of intellect, imagination, and hard work, belying the popular distorted image of dressing-up, booming voices, and shrieking exhibitionism."[3]

THE ACTOR'S REALITY

Reduced to its simplest terms, the actor's goal is to tell the character's circumstances in the play's story as truthfully and effectively as possible. Those *circumstances* are the essential conditions in the play's world that include time (when), place (where), surroundings (what), and others (who) in the situation. The actor works in rehearsals to discover the truth of an individual's behavior in the circumstances existing among the play's characters. The actor must concentrate on the *truth* of the character's behavior—his or her sensory responses, psychological motives, and objectives—in the context of the play, not in the context of the performance or the audience's reactions.

Through meticulous "homework," the actor comes to believe in the reality of what he or she is doing on stage from moment to moment. To understand better the actor's truth or reality, let us compare the situation in a play with that in an event on the sports field. Like baseball, for example, a play has its own rules and regulations, the set dimensions of the playing area, a set number of persons on the field, and a coach. The interactions among the players are real, vital, and intense. For the playing time, the field is the players' whole universe. The game, like a stage play, has its own reality that is frequently "more real" and vibrant than everyday reality. Likewise, the actor is given a story, an identity, clothing, circumstances, relationships, motives, activities, and environs. The play sets the number of persons; the director and designer set the dimensions of the playing area; the playwright sets the circumstances under which the actor-as-character appears in the story. The play has its own reality that the actor finds in the exploration of the play's life and in the character's circumstances and needs.

The creative process that brings the actor to the "field of play" as the character Hamlet or Blanche DuBois, for example, is demanding and complex. Throughout stage history, actors have used both external technique and internal belief to create the character's reality on stage. *Technique* and *belief* are the fundamentals of the actor's craft. Sometimes, however, in the history of the profession one has been favored over the other.

External Technique

External technique is that activity by which an actor chooses, imitates, or outwardly illustrates a character's behavior. The mimetic actor approaches a role through a deep and passionate study of human behavior *in all its outward forms,* with an eye toward reproducing them in a disciplined and sensitive way.

The English actor David Garrick (1717–1779) approached acting as an imitation of life—he called acting *mimical behavior.* To prepare for the role of King Lear, for example, he studied the appearance and behavior of a friend who had been driven mad by his child's death. By his accurate reproduction of such behavior on stage, Garrick introduced what some called *naturalistic* acting into the English theatre. He believed that the actor could produce emotions by a convincing imitation and skilled projection of those emotions being imitated. He did not believe that the actor should actually experience anger or sadness or joy to project these emotions to an audience. The following words are ascribed to him: "… that a man was incapable of becoming an actor who was not absolutely independent of circumstances calculated to excite emotion, adding that for his own part he could speak to a post with the same feelings and expression as to the loveliest Juliet under the heaven."[4] His contemporaries wrote that on occasion he would delight them in relaxed moments with his face alone,

Irene Worth appears as Madame Ranevskaya in Chekhov's *The Cherry Orchard* in the 1977 New York Shakespeare Festival production, directed by Andrei Serban, Lincoln Center Theater.

George E. Joseph

GARRICK'S MACBETH Garrick played Macbeth in a contemporary military uniform. He was famous for the dagger scene; his contemporaries praised him for his ability to project the fact that be was "seeing" the dagger before him. It has been said that Garrick's "face was a language."

without any outward motivation or any inward feeling of personal emotion. In this external or purely technical approach, actors (like David Garrick), aim for a calculated *presentation* of a character's life on stage.

Many actors in England and Europe have followed Garrick's approach, thereby creating one school of thought on the matter of what distinguishes great acting. Throughout stage history, actors have been celebrated for their exceptional charisma, their theatrical skills, the bravado of their startling choices, and their ability to *illustrate* many different characters during a long a career. Included among these ranks are not only David Garrick but also Sarah Bernhardt and Laurence Olivier, to name only three among legions. These actors are notable for working from the "outside in." Laurence Olivier, celebrated in his lifetime as England's greatest actor, admitted being uncomfortable working in any other way. No one can deny the brilliance of Olivier's career, but he was often criticized for being "too technical." He defended his methods in interviews and autobiographical writings. One night, after playing in John Osborne's *The Entertainer,* his friends rushed backstage to congratulate him on a spontaneous and deeply moving performance. He admitted the spontaneity but said, "I don't like that kind of acting; I didn't know what I was doing."[5]

English actor John Gielgud—who was counted among the four greatest actors of his generation (Laurence Olivier, Peggy Ashcroft, and Ralph Richardson are the others)—says of his early days in the theatre that he slavishly imitated other actors:

> I imitated all the actors I admired when I was young, particularly Claude Rains, who was my teacher at dramatic school. I also understudied Noël Coward, whom I felt I had to imitate because he was so individual in his style…. naturally, the only way to say the lines was to say them as near to the way he said them as possible because they suited his style…. [Theodore Komisarjevsky, the Russian director] was an enormous influence in teaching me not to act from outside, not to seize on obvious, showy effects and histrionics, not so much to exhibit myself as to be within myself trying to impersonate a character who is not aware of the audience, to try to absorb the atmosphere of the play and the background of the character, to build it outward so that it came to life naturally….[6]

Today's actors, like Kenneth Branagh, Cherry Jones, and Ralph Fiennes, strive to find the physical reality of the character, to walk, talk, and look like the king, beggar,

David Garrick as MacBeth/Courtesy Theatre Museum/Victoria and Albert Museum or spinster they are playing. But they also reach into the truthful subtleties of the character's psychology and wholly embody the role, filling it with breath, blood, impulses, desires, and emotions so that we believe Ralph Fiennes when, as Hamlet, he says: "The time is out of joint. Oh, cursed spite/That ever I was born to set it right!" We forget that we are watching a working actor and become absorbed in the life and trials of Denmark's Prince.

Internal Belief

A second school of thought on acting emerged with those actors who astonish audiences with a creative process that is intuitive, subconscious, and subjective. Actors Uta Hagen, Paul Newman, Ellen Burstyn, and Al Pacino work "from the inside out" to select behavior pertinent to the character's needs within the play's imagined circumstances. These "realistic" actors allow personal behavior to develop out of the playwright's prescribed circumstances, knowing that their actions will involve a moment-to-moment subjective experience.

©T. Charles Erickson

Ellen Burstyn and Andrew McCarthy as Mary Tyrone and son James Tyrone Jr. in Eugene O'Neill's *Long Day's Journey into Night*, directed by Michael Wilson, Hartford Stage Company (Conn.).

A great deal of the actor's work is a searching within for emotional impulses from personal experience to give reality to the new existence or role. When, at the age of eighteen, Uta Hagen played the young, would-be actress Nina in Chekhov's *The Sea Gull*, she understood Nina as a naive middle-class girl from the country who is drawn into the life of her neighbor, a famous actress of whom she is in awe, and the actress' lover, a noted writer whom Nina hero-worships.

On stage with Lynn Fontanne as Madame Arkadina, Hagen found it easy to use her awe of the famous actress and her celebrated husband, Alfred Lunt. She said, "I was in awe of Miss Fontanne and hero-worshipped Mr. Lunt. These particular character relationships were mirrored in my own, and I used their reality directly for my role."[7]

Most modern theories of actor training address methods of working "from the inside out." Konstantin Stanislavski's "method" became the most famous and influential in modern times, especially among American actors.

The Actor's Tools

The actor's tools are the body, voice, impulses, emotions, concentration, imagination, and intellect. They must be flexible, disciplined, and expressive to communicate a wide range of attitudes, traits, emotions, feelings, and behaviors. The range of demands on the actor's abilities during a career is enormous. They must be adequate to re-creating classical and modern roles, such as Medea, Hamlet, Blanche DuBois, or Shelly Levene. In training and rehearsals, the actor works to understand the body and voice: how to control them; how to release psychological tensions and blocks that inhibit them; how to increase powers of imagination, observation, and concentration; and how to integrate them with the demands of the script and director. By using these tools, the actor combines an inner belief in the role with external techniques.

Successful acting combines belief and technique to create truthful behavior—of life taking place on stage, as if for the first time.

THE ACTOR'S TRAINING

For many years, European and American actors were trained in the theatre itself, beginning their careers as apprentices. A young man or woman who showed ability would be hired to play small parts in a provincial stock company. The older actors would coach the young person, prescribing voice and body exercises that had been handed down for generations. This kind of external training developed a voice capable of being heard in large theatres, exaggerated gestures, and skill in speaking verse. If actors showed talent, they would be given longer parts and eventually be invited to join the company.

When *realism* came into fashion late in the nineteenth century, this "large" style of acting seemed exaggerated and unconvincing. As the stage came to be thought of as a recognizable place with a reality that corresponded to what ordinary people observed around them, then scene design, stage decor, and acting styles changed. The play's world—the environment and characters—were represented as directly and in as lifelike a way as possible. A middle-class street, house, and living room represented on stage had to look like middle-class streets, houses, and living rooms outside the theatre. Actors were to be dressed like the businessmen or menial laborers that audiences encountered outside the theatre. So, too, the actor was called upon to set aside declamation and artificial gestures for the speech, walk, and behavior of a recognizable human being. To capture on stage and before an audience this sense of life being lived as it actually is, new methods for training actors had to be developed and new approaches arrived at for preparing a role.

Preparing the Role

Stanislavski's "Method"

At the turn of the nineteenth century, Konstantin Stanislavski, the Russian actor-director, set about developing a systematic approach to training actors *to work from the inside outward*. Today, his premises, developed over a lifetime, are accepted as the point of departure for most contemporary thinking about acting.

Stanislavski laid down the basis for a psychological understanding of acting and fused it with a deep sense of aesthetic truth. "The fundamental aim of our art," Stanislavski wrote in *An Actor Prepares*, "is the creation of [the] inner life of a human spirit and its expression in an artistic form."[8] To arrive at this truth, Stanislavski proposed that actors understand how men and women actually behave physically and psychologically in given cir-

STANISLAVSKI THE ACTOR
Stanislavski as Gaev in the 1904 Moscow Art Theatre production of Chekhov's *The Cherry Orchard.*

Billy Rose Theatre Collection, The New York Public Library for the Performing Arts, Astor, Lenox, and Tilden Foundations

cumstances. Stanislavski's approach asked the actor to study and experience subjective emotions and feelings and to manifest them to audiences by physical and vocal means. He also stressed that personal truth in acting had to be balanced by attention to the playwright's text, to imaginative realities outside the actor's immediate experience. The actor was called upon to enter "the imagined world of the play," not just to attend to his or her part.

Over the years, Stanislavski developed a means of training actors (his followers in America called it "the Method") whereby they would not only create a subjective reality of their own—an inner truth of feeling and experience—but would also represent the "outer" truth of the character's reality in the surrounding world of the play. Speaking of the "external" acting that he had seen and abhorred in his time, Stanislavski said that "the difference between my art and that is the difference between 'seeming and being.'"[9]

What distinguished Stanislavski's theory (and his lasting influence) was the actor's discovery of the purpose and objectives of his or her character's behavior and the successful "playing" of those goals.

Stanislavski developed rehearsal methods by which the actor would "live life" onstage. He developed a set of exercises and principles designed to help the actor call on personal feelings and experiences, along with the body and the voice, in the creation of the role. This aspect of his training was called the "psychotechnique." Through the development of self-discipline, observation, relaxation, and total concentration, his actors learned to recall emotions from their own lives that were analogous to those experienced by the characters they played. What mattered to Stanislavski was the *actor's truth:* What the actor feels and experiences internally expresses itself in what the character says and how the character reacts to given circumstances. Actors learned to experience what their characters experienced, *as if* it were actually happening to them.

The Magic If

Stanislavski called "the magic if" the method by which the actor thinks, "If I were in Othello's *situation,* what would I do?" Not, "If I were Othello, what would I do?" By "being" in the situation, the actor could give a performance that was a truthful, living experience, not merely the imitation of the experience.

Recalling Emotions

How does the actor create a reality of emotions in performance night after night? One of the early methods developed by Stanislavski was "emotional recall," or "affective memory," which became a subject of considerable dispute among his American followers. Strasberg interpreted emotional recall as the actor's conscious efforts to remember circumstances

JAMES EARL JONES AS OTHELLO Jones studied with Lee Strasberg at the Actors Studio and won Antoinette Perry "Tony" Awards as the boxer in *The Great White Hope* (1968) and Troy Maxson in *Fences* (1987). Here, he appears in the title role in the 1964 New York Shakespeare Festival Theatre production of *Othello*.

George E. Joseph

Lee Strasberg and the Actors Studio

Lee Strasberg (1901–1982), one of the best known acting teachers in America, transformed Stanislavski's system of acting into an American "Method."

In 1947, members of the Group Theatre (an ensemble of actors, directors, and playwrights that included Lee Strasberg, Elia Kazan, Robert Lewis, and Cheryl Crawford) started the Actors Studio (located today in a former church at 432 West Forty-Fourth Street, New York City) as a workshop for professional actors to concentrate on acting problems away from the pressures of the commercial theatre. Strasberg assumed leadership of the Studio in 1951. As a teacher and acting theorist, he revolutionized American acting, producing such remarkable performers as Marlon Brando, Marilyn Monroe, Julie Harris, Paul Newman, Geraldine Page, Robert DeNiro, Ellen Burstyn, and Al Pacino.

The methods of the Studio derived from Stanislavski were tailored by Strasberg for plays of American realism. He demanded great discipline of his actors, as well as great depths of character relationships and inner truthfulness. He once explained his approach in this way:

Courtesy Lee Strasberg Theatre Institute

> The human being who acts is the human being who lives. That is a terrifying circumstance. Essentially the actor acts a fiction, a dream; in life the stimuli to which we respond are always real. The actor must constantly respond to stimuli that are imaginary. And yet this must happen not only just as it happens in life, but actually more fully and more expressively. Although the actor can do things in life quite easily, when he has to do the same thing on the stage under fictitious conditions he has difficulty because he is not equipped as a human being merely to playact at imitating life. He must somehow believe. He must somehow be able to convince himself of the rightness of what he is doing in order to do things fully on the stage.[10]

In 1999, the Actors Studio led by its then artistic director Frank Corsaro (today, Estelle Parsons) established a joint master of fine arts degree program with the New School for Social Research in New York City to teach "beginning" actors the methods developed by Strasberg and others.

surrounding an emotion-filled occasion from the past in order to stimulate impulses and emotions that could be used on stage. The actor re-creates in the mind's eye all of the surrounding circumstances, the sensory and emotional detail, that were part of the remembered experience. For example, the actor uses a relative's death, or another sad event, to evoke memories that bring tears of sorrow. Julie Harris says that she conjures up something in her own life that produces tears when she is called upon to cry.

UTA HAGEN "PREPARING" THE ROLE OF BLANCHE DUBOIS
Uta Hagen, actress and teacher, described her preparations for performing the role of Tennessee Williams' heroine Blanche DuBois as a hunt for understanding the character's needs and desires. Williams' character struggles for perfection, gentleness, beauty, romantic love, and protection against the world's ugliness and brutality.

UTA HAGEN AS BLANCHE DUBOIS She succeeded Jessica Tandy as Blanche DuBois on Broadway in *A Streetcar Named Desire* in 1948.

In order to bridge the enormous distance between the actress' nature and the Williams' role, Hagen called upon sensory and psychological responses to animate her actions as Blanche. The actress recalled personal experiences that could be readily substituted for Blanche's desire for civility in her life. Hagen substituted personal responses to beautiful music, poetry, opera, and elegant dinner parties. In the absence of actually having lived in a plantation house in Mississippi, Hagen substituted her memories of visits to other mansions and found ways to build from her own experiences the impact of the cramped Kowalski apartment and the cacophonous street noises on Blanche's frayed sensibilities

Substitutions are central to the actor's creativity and craft in the building of a role. Through the substitution of remembered sensory and emotional details, many actors, like Uta Hagen, build emotions in sympathy with the character's circumstances. But the actor does not stop there. The character's emotional life must be reproduced in the theatre night after night with precise timing, on cue, and with a minimum of conscious thought.

Sanford Meisner's Foundation Technique

As another American approach to actor training, Sanford Meisner started the Neighborhood Playhouse School of Theatre in 1928 in New York City. As actor and teacher, Meisner evolved a "foundation" technique for training actors that sets out an approach to the creation of real and truthful behavior within the imaginary circumstances (the human problems) contained within the play.

As a founding member of the Group Theatre, Meisner was exposed to the ideas of Konstantin Stanislavski in the 1930s and emerged from the Group along with Lee Strasberg, Stella Adler, and Robert Lewis as a pre-eminent teacher of the "Method." Each developed his or her own approach to training actors. Meisner's foundation for the actor aims to ignite the actor's imagination and provide means for achieving the truth of human behavior. These techniques are built upon what Meisner calls "the reality of doing." His system of exercises provides actors with the means for calling upon inner impulses and instinctive behavior, freeing the imagination and strengthening

(continued on page 199)

Actor

Jack Mitchell/Courtesy of Barbara Hogen-son Agency

UTA HAGEN AND PAUL ROBESON IN *OTHELLO* Uta Hagen as Desdemona and Paul Robeson as Othello in the 1943 Broadway production of *Othello* directed by Margaret Webster for the Theatre Guild.

Uta Hagen

Richard Tucker/Billy Rose Theatre Collection, The New York Public Library for the Performing Arts, Astor, Lenox, and Tilden Foundations

Uta Hagen (b. 1919) was born in Göttingen, Germany, and, as a child, moved with her parents to the United States where her father was named head of the Art History Department at the University of Wisconsin, Madison. Inspired by a performance of Elizabeth Bergner as Saint Joan, she determined to be an actress and studied dance, piano, and eventually acting. Her first professional role was as Ophelia in Eva Le Gallienne's 1937 production of *Hamlet*. She played Nina on Broadway in the Alfred Lunt–Lynn Fontanne production of *The Sea Gull* in 1938 and played Desdemona opposite Paul Robeson in *Othello* on Broadway. She worked with such directors as Guthrie McClintic, Margaret Webster, Marc Connelly, Harold Clurman, and Alan Schneider. She subsequently appeared in *Key Largo, A Streetcar Named Desire, The Country Girl, Saint Joan, Who's Afraid of Virginia Woolf?, Mrs. Klein,* and *Collected Stories.* She can be seen in the film *Reversal of Fortune.*

Associated for over forty years as a teacher with the HB Studio, New York City, founded by her husband Herbert Berghof, she wrote two influential books on acting: *Respect for Acting* and *A Challenge for the Actor.* Hagen is known as an actor's actor for her masterly style, assertive presence, and resonant voice that promise enormous power held in reserve.

concentration, to achieve a "reality of doing." For Meisner, this "reality of doing" is the *foundation* of acting.

Meisner summarized his approach in this way: "My approach is based on bringing the actor back to his emotional impulses and to acting that is firmly rooted in the instinctive. It is based on the fact that all good acting comes from the heart...."[11]

Improvisation

Improvisation is useful in actor training and in rehearsals to free the actor's imagination and to strengthen concentration. Defined as "spontaneous invention," improvisation may be used with a group as warm-up exercises before classes or rehearsals. In rehearsal, improvisation may be used to establish rapport between actors, to solve acting problems, to spur spontaneity and release inhibitions, or to encourage new, instinctive responses to overly familiar circumstances.

Improvisation engages the actor's mind and body. Some exercises ask the actor to substitute his or her own words for the words in the script. As actors improvise arguments between two characters using their own words rather than the playwright's, the content of a difficult scene, its emotions and tensions, can be made clearer. The actor's newly found, inner emotional material can then be reapplied to the given circumstances of the playwright's scene.

Many improvisations involve physical interactions that release energy and focus strong feelings and gestures as verbal exchanges take place. The improvised physical activity may appear, at first, to have little relation to the written dialogue. However, the intensity of the physical work can support the equally intense verbal exchange required by the script.

There are many kinds of improvisational games. One such game is the repetition between two actors of the same word or phrase ("What time is it?," for example). Some are based on invented, or nonsensical, words. This made-up language spurs communication between actors. Some games are invented stories which one actor begins with a single word or sentence and other actors add to the developing storyline. In all, the actor learns to concentrate, react instinctually, and to work off the other actor moment to moment with real feelings.

Games and exercises condition actors to immerse themselves in given circumstances and to find new instinctual impulses and behavior that lead to real emotion. The end-product of improvisation is freeing the actor's creativity, honing concentration, and spurring commitment to finding the truth of behavior. Later, these instincts and impulses can be used in support of the demands of the text.

Practical Aesthetics

The Practical Aesthetics Workshop evolved out of a series of acting workshops given by David Mamet and W. H. Macy in the early eighties. These workshops mixed the

The Atlantic Theatre Company, a non-profit Off Broadway company, was formed in 1985 when David Mamet urged a group of students to form a company to "serve the play"—to do the job with respect and to create a theatre to serve society in a powerful and truthful way. Today, the ensemble has thirty-four members and a home in a Revival-style historic landmark building in Chelsea with a 182-seat theatre; its actor-training school is located on Sixteenth Street and is affiliated with New York University. Neil Pepe is the company's artistic director.

beliefs of ancient Stoics ("treat the endeavor with respect") with Stanislavski principles on acting ("to work truthfully within the given circumstances of the play"). The formation of the Atlantic Theatre Company in New York City in 1985 was the fruit of these acting workshops in Vermont, Chicago, and New York City.

The goal of "practical aesthetics" is to provide the actor with tools to prepare to go onstage with the freedom to be completely involved with the play as it unfolds. The focus of the training is on those things *within the actor's control:* voice, body, concentration, script analysis. The ultimate concern is "to find a way to live truthfully within the imaginary circumstances of the play."[12]

The training is based upon acting as a craft with a definite set of learned skills and tools combined with will, courage, and common sense to help the actor bring a living humanity to the playwright's circumstances. As set forth in *A Practical Handbook for the Actor,* practical aesthetics training is a process of making acting tools habitual in order to free the actor in rehearsals and performance to live truthfully and fully within the play's circumstances. In a letter to the company, David Mamet said that "a good actor sticks to his objective, no matter what. Emotion comes, sure, but it's a by-product of the larger action. It's all about serving the play."[13]

Physical and Vocal Training

The Actor's Body

Modern movement training provides actors with a wide range of physical choices in the creation of character. It is not simply a matter of physically demonstrating a pompous valet or a nervous debutante. In movement training ("stage movement" is the older term), the emphasis is on developing the actor's body as a more open, responsive, physical instrument by first eliminating unnecessary tensions and mannerisms. Movement training today is not the imposition of arbitrary positions or alignments, as it was when young actors copied the gestures of the leading actor. Rather, it is more a matter of sensitizing actors to the variety of possibilities of human movement *as an expressive signal* of character and intentions.

In recent years, movement training in the United States changed in two fundamental ways. First, the influence of psychology gave insight into the actor's inner world and consequently into how that world can be expressed through the body's motion. Second, numerous approaches to movement or physical training from many different cultures and traditions entered classrooms and rehearsal halls and have had an enormous impact on actor training over the last decade. They range from techniques in martial arts, fencing, yoga, tai chi, juggling and circus arts, stage combat, and mask training to Feldenkrais and the Alexander techniques. The best movement teachers are familiar with and work through one or more of these approaches.

Today's movement teacher is, above all, an acting teacher who chooses to work through the body. Our best teachers find ways to train actors to make fresh, often startling, choices—for movement grows from the urge to move as an expression of some-

thing that, until one critical moment, is hidden. The violent encounter between Stanley Kowalski and Blanche DuBois in *A Streetcar Named Desire* is an expression of Stanley's pent-up hostility and unconscious fear of his sister-in-law. He provokes a physical encounter—a fight and sexual assault—to express his fear and rage at the intruder who has disrupted his household and violated his sense of masculine authority. Blanche, on the other hand, fights for her dignity and sanity in what is clearly a rape encounter.

Truly expressive onstage movement, like the duel in *Hamlet*, begins with the character's inner needs. When those needs are well understood, it is always possible to create physical realities that are compelling—like Laurence Olivier's humpbacked Richard III (in Shakespeare's play) or James Earl Jones's Troy Maxson (in *Fences*), whose physical stance is that of an aging athlete.

To be convincing, the actor's movements must *embody* the character's attitudes or needs. In performance, all physical and vocal choices must serve those needs.

RON LIEBMAN IN *ANGELS IN AMERICA* Ron Liebman plays Roy Cohn, chief counsel to Senator Joseph R. McCarthy's investigative subcommittee on Communist activities in the United States during the 1950s and member of the Reagan administration's Justice Department, in Tony Kushner's *Angels in America: A Gay Fantasia on National Themes. Part 1: Millennium Approaches* (1993).

ANNE BOGART'S "VIEWPOINTS" Influenced by postmodern dance choreographer Mary Overlie, director Anne Bogart developed her own theory of movement technique, called "Viewpoints," which teaches actors to have greater awareness of their environment and enables them to express their impulses spontaneously through movement. Bogart's work is described as "dance done by actors in the service of dramaturgy."[14]

Bogart's "Viewpoints" are a philosophy of movement translated into techniques for training actors and creating movement on stage. The Viewpoints are a set of names given to certain basic principles of movement that make up a language for director and actor to talk about what happens or what works on stage. Primarily rehearsal techniques, they apply to tempo, space, duration of movement, repetitions, physical gestures, spatial relationships, and the physical stage.

The Actor's Voice

The voice is our means of communicating to others, presenting ourselves, expressing our personality, thoughts, and feelings. The function of the actor's speech, like our own, is to communicate needs. For example, if we are speaking trivialities, it is not the *triviality* that is important, it is the *need* to speak it that matters. Therefore, however ordinary, stylized, or heightened (as in poetry) stage language is, when the actor speaks lines from the dramatic text, he or she must root those lines in the *need* to speak in a particular fashion and with a particular choice of words.[15]

Voice training today happens only in relation to the acting process and involves the actor's entire being—the physical and the psychological. Vocal exercises practiced in the classroom are aimed at "freeing" the voice. These exercises involve relaxation, breathing, and increased muscularity of lips and tongue. These are followed by particular exercises on texts (Shakespeare's verse, for example) that stretch the voice, making it more responsive to the demands of the character.

(continued on page 203)

Director / Teacher

Anne Bogart

Brennan Cavanaugh

Anne Bogart was born in Newport, Rhode Island, in 1953. She graduated from Bard College in Annandale-on-Hudson, New York, and, while studying in a master's program at New York University's Tisch School of the Arts in the late seventies, she began writing and directing her own works for the theatre. As *New York Times* theatre critic Mel Gussow points out, "Depending on the point of view [Anne Bogart] is either an innovator or a provocateur assaulting a script."

Bogart won two Obie awards (for Off Broadway productions) for direction of her own *No Plays, No Poetry* (1988) and for Paula Vogel's *The Baltimore Waltz* (1992). She served briefly as artistic director of Trinity Repertory Company (R.I.), and in 1992 co-founded with Japanese director and acting theorist Tadashi Suzuki (creator of a rigorous physical and vocal discipline for actors called "the Suzuki Method") the Saratoga International Theatre Institute (SITI) based in Saratoga, New York. Their goal was to put into practice their artistic theories and "revitalize the theatre from the inside out." SITI began as a summer training program for actors in Saratoga and eventually established a year-round base in New York City. Since the company's beginning, SITI has performed throughout the world.

As a director Bogart's work divides roughly into four categories: new plays (*The Baltimore Waltz* by Paula Vogel and *In the Eye of the Hurricane* by Eduardo Machado); her own theatrical portraits of well-known cultural figures, such as Bertolt Brecht (*No Plays, No Poetry*), Andy Warhol (*Culture of Desire*), and Robert Wilson (*Bob*); iconoclastic interpretations of classic and popular plays (*A Streetcar Named Desire* set in a German Club with ten Stanleys and twelve Blanches, one of them a man); and original performance pieces that examine the history of popular entertainment in the United States—her trilogy *American Vaudeville* (1992), *Marathon Dancing* (1994), and *American Silents* (1997). In 1995, Bogart's work was featured at Actors Theatre of Louisville's Tenth Annual "Classics in Context" Festival: Modern Masters—Anne Bogart.

Bogart is an associate professor at the Graduate School of the Arts at Columbia University in New York City. Her recent works are *The Seven Deadly Sins* by Kurt Weill and Bertolt Brecht, *Songs and Stories from Moby Dick,* starring performance artist Laurie Anderson, and *War of the Worlds* based on the life of twentieth-century icon Orson Welles.

*V*oice Coach

Cicely Berry

Cicely Berry is Voice Director of the Royal Shakespeare Company, England. Trained at London's Central School of Speech and Drama, she taught voice and diction at the Central School for over twenty years. She then joined the Royal Shakespeare Company in Stratford-upon-Avon in 1969 at the invitation of then artistic director Trevor Nunn, where she was "Head of Voice" until 1991 with responsibility for all voice and text work with the company. An internationally renowned voice specialist, she has held workshops and given lectures in England, Australia, India, China, Canada, Korea, Zimbabwe, Italy, France, Russia, Poland, Croatia, Bulgaria, Yugoslavia, the Netherlands, Denmark, Columbia, Brazil, and the United States. In addition, she has a long history of training voice teachers, working in England's prisons, and directing workshop productions of Shakespeare. She was awarded the Order of the British Empire (O.B.E.) in 1991 for services to the theatre, and an Honorary Doctorate of Literature by the University of Birmingham, England, in 1999. In 1997, she became an Associate Artist of the Theatre for a New Audience in New York City.

Cicely Berry has worked with many actors, directors, and writers, including directors Peter Brook, Bernardo Bertolucci, Augusto Boal, Trevor Nunn, Adrian Noble, Terry Hands, Sam Mendes, and Julie Taymor; writers Edward Bond, Howard Brenton, and Arnold Wesker; actors Kenneth Branagh, Anthony Hopkins, Jeremy Irons, Derek Jacobi, and Emily Watson. Her award citation from the British Arts Council reads: "Cicely Berry's contribution to the place of voice in the live theatre is both innovative as well as invaluable, particularly in her enthusiastic response to the challenges posed by a technologically diverse and increasingly multi-cultural environment."

The primary objective in voice training is to open up the possibilities of the voice—its energy, its instinctive responses to what the actor has to say. Correcting one's speech (a regional accent, for example) is not as important in voice training today as it once was, although Standard American Speech is encouraged by the profession. The aim of vocal exercises is to keep the essential truth of the actor's own voice, yet make it large and malleable enough for projecting feelings to a large auditorium or modulating to the intimacy of a television studio. To get this balance between the size of the voice and its malleability, vocal work involves both technique and imagination. Unlike the singer whose "sound" is the message, the actor's voice is

Kathleen Widdoes as Maria Callas in Terrence McNally's *Master Class*, directed by Tazewell Thompson for PlayMakers Repertory Company, Chapel Hill, 1998. Producing Director Milly S. Barranger.

an extension of the person (and the character). Its possibilities are as complex as the actor's persona. Because actors deal with words that come off a printed page, they continually have to find ways to make those words their own. Voice training aims at establishing an ongoing process for the actor to become as sensitive as possible to the physical makeup of the voice in relation to the body (breath, diaphragm, ribs, head, neck). The goal is to merge techniques learned in voice exercises with the actor's imagination to communicate the character's needs through the words of the text. Hamlet's instructions to the Players on the use of the voice and the body—"Suit the action to the word, the word to the action"—are still appropriate to the actor's process.

Rehearsals and Performance

The work of rehearsals, which may last from two to ten weeks, is to condition the actor's responses so that during performance emotions flow from the actor's concentration on the character's objectives and the play's given circumstances. Rehearsals also bring the cast together with the director to "set" interpretation and physical movement under his or her guidance. Not until dress rehearsal, as a rule, is an actor able to work with a complete set of properties, furniture, scenery, costumes, makeup, sound, and lighting. However, rehearsal furniture is provided by stage management and special rehearsal clothes and properties, like eyeglasses, fans, walking sticks, long skirts, and capes, are also provided if they are significantly different from ordinary dress and handheld objects.

On each night of a play's run, the actor brings a living humanity with physical actions and the playwright's words and given circumstances to the stage. Everything the actor has analyzed, memorized, and made personal in rehearsals—objectives, mannerisms, vocal intonations, movements—stays (or should stay) much the same. But the actor's creativity continues within the boundaries set in rehearsal: This is the actor's freedom and art. Each performance requires the actor to give fresh life to the character's physical actions, responses, desires, goals—to concentrate anew on the character's speech, behavior, and theatrical effectiveness.

Actors' Equity Association (A.E.A.) is the independent union representing actors and stage managers who work in the professional theatre, and dancers in a Broadway show. Equity contracts are provided for Broadway, Off Broadway, Off Off Broadway, in Resident Theatre, Stock and Dinner Theatre, plus Special Contracts.

The Screen Actors Guild (SAG) is the independent union representing actors who work in the film and television industry.

The Actor in Film

Most actors today work in theatre, film, and television. Film acting requires the same discipline, preparation, and attention to relaxation, memory, concentration, and truthful behavior that actors bring with them on stage. Not the outdoor locations nor the vast hordes of technicians and onlookers during the shooting of a scene make the actor's work in film different from work in the theatre. The essential difference is always *the presence of the camera*. The camera listens to and records everything the actor does and says. The actor's credibility before this ever-present "eye" is what separates the successful film actor from the talented stage actor.

(continued on page 212)

Great Moments of Acting

Jessica Tandy . Bert Lahr . James Earl Jones

George Grizzard . Cherry Jones . Janet McTeer

Given 2,500 years of Western theatrical history, the names of great actors illuminating particular roles are legion. The list of celebrated actors of the modern theatre includes such names as Sarah Bernhardt, Eleanora Duse, John Barrymore, Ethel Barrymore, Sir John Gielgud, Eva Le Gallienne, Jean-Louis Barrault, Laurette Taylor, Sir Ralph Richardson, Dame Peggy Ashcroft, Jessica Tandy, Uta Hagen, Sir Laurence Olivier, and Rosemary Harris. Such legendary performances as Laurette Taylor's Amanda Wingfield, Laurence Olivier's Hamlet, or Jessica Tandy's Blanche DuBois grow out of rigorous training, keen sensitivity, vivid dramatic imagination, and an intelligence equal to the demands of text, director, and stage.

Director Peter Brook describes unforgettable moments in an actor's performance as "a flash of insight that comes from the confrontation of the performer's hidden world and the hidden world of character. For theatre to be seen at its most alive, there has to be a very, very exact balance between the living personality of the performer and the second personality, which is that of the character."[16] Great acting is a seamless integration of the actor's personality and the character in the context of the given circumstances of the play.

This photo essay captures a single moment in the work of six actors whose names are synonymous with certain roles: Jessica Tandy with Tennessee Williams' Blanche DuBois, Bert Lahr with Samuel Beckett's Estragon, James Earl Jones with August Wilson's Troy Maxson, George Grizzard with Edward Albee's Tobias, Cherry Jones with Ruth and Augustus Goetz's Catherine Sloper, and Janet McTeer with Henrik Ibsen's Nora Helmer.

205

JESSICA TANDY (1909–1994) as Blanche DuBois in the 1947 Broadway production of *A Streetcar Named Desire* with Marlon Brando as Stanley Kowalski and Kim Hunter as Stella in the background.

Tandy played Blanche, one of the longest and most exacting roles on record, for over two years on Broadway, establishing her as one of America's leading actresses. Critic Brooks Atkinson said of her performance: "She acts a magnificent part magnificently. She plays it with an insight as vibrant and pitiless as Mr. Williams' writing, for she catches on the wing the terror, bogus refinement, and intellectual alertness and the madness that can hardly be distinguished from logic and fastidiousness."

With her husband Hume Cronyn, Tandy formed a distinguished stage partnership. They appeared together on Broadway, at the Guthrie Theater, and at Stratford Ontario's Shakespeare Festival. Most notable was their work together in *The Fourposter* (1951), *The Gin Game* (1979), and *Foxfire* (1982). Tandy starred on Broadway as Amanda Wingfield in Williams' *The Glass Menagerie* (1984) and re-created the role of Miss Daisy in the film version of Alfred Uhry's play *Driving Miss Daisy* (1989), for which she won an Academy of Motion Picture Arts and Sciences ("Oscar") Award for Best Actress. During her distinguished stage career she won three Antoinette Perry ("Tony") Awards as Best Actress, for *A Streetcar Named Desire*, *The Gin Game*, and *Foxfire*.

Photo Essay

BERT LAHR (1895–1967) as Estragon (far right) in Beckett's *Waiting for Godot*. Beginning his stage career as a stand-up vaudeville comic, Lahr moved on to Broadway musical comedy, became identified with the role of the Cowardly Lion in the film *The Wizard of Oz* (1939), and closed his career as a distinguished actor best remembered for his performance as Gogo (Estragon) in Beckett's existential masterpiece.

Lahr created the role in the American premiere of Beckett's play in Miami, 1956, that continued on Broadway later that same year (directed by Herbert Berghof with E. G. Marshall as Vladimir, Kurt Kasznar as Pozzo, and Alvin Epstein as Lucky). These productions are described in *Notes on a Cowardly Lion* (1969), a perceptive biography by his son, John Lahr, a notable theatre critic.

As Estragon, Lahr was unfailing in his instincts to be clear, simple, and to the point. Audiences waited in vain for hints of the famous "cowardly lion," but Lahr refused to retread familiar ground. His warmth and common humanity extended across the footlights and caught up audiences in a shared experience. British critic Kenneth Tynan put it this way: "Mr. Lahr's beleaguered simpleton [Estragon], a draughts-player lost in a universe of chess, is one of the noblest performances I have ever seen."

The Image Makers: The Actors   **207**

JAMES EARL JONES (born in Arkabutla, Michigan) was educated at the University of Michigan, Ann Arbor, and studied acting in the late 1950s with Lee Strasberg and with the American Theatre Wing in New York City. He made his Broadway debut as an understudy in *The Egghead* (1957) and his London debut in *Paul Robeson* (1978), a one-man show.

Jones has performed a variety of stage and film roles. He has been seen as Othello, Claudius (in *Hamlet*), Macbeth, and King Lear with the New York Shakespeare Festival Theatre; as Jack Jefferson in *The Great White Hope* with Arena Stage, Washington, D.C., and Broadway in 1968; and as Troy Maxson (in *Fences*) with the Yale Repertory Theatre and Broadway in 1987. Jones won the Antoinette Perry ("Tony") Award for Best Actor in 1969 for *The Great White Hope* and the American Academy of Arts and Letters Medal for Spoken Language in 1981.

He has appeared in such major films as *Dr. Strangelove* (1964), *The Great White Hope* (1970), and *Hunt for Red October* (1990) and as the voice of Darth Vader in *Star Wars* (1977), *The Empire Strikes Back* (1980), and *Return of the Jedi* (1983).

The central character, Troy Maxson, in August Wilson's *Fences* has been described as the best role of James Earl Jones's career. His performance as Troy was called "mountainous," "magnificent," "towering." One critic called it one of Jones's "most powerful and riveting performances, rising to brilliant outbursts of anguish and irony."

William B. Carter

GEORGE GRIZZARD as Tobias in the Broadway revival of Edward Albee's *A Delicate Balance* with Rosemary Harris, Elaine Stritch, Elizabeth Wilson, John Carter, and Mary Beth Hurt. Winner of the 1996 Antoinette Perry "Tony" Award for Best Leading Actor in a Play, Grizzard's performance was called "triumphant."

Grizzard has had a distinguished stage career. Educated at the University of North Carolina, Chapel Hill, he made his Broadway debut in 1954 in *All Summer Long,* followed by award-winning performances in *Desperate Hours, Happiest Millionaire, Who's Afraid of Virginia Woolf?* (with Uta Hagen), *The Royal Family, California Suite, Man and Superman, Showboat,* and *Judgment at Nuremberg.*

Photo Essay

©Joan Marcus

©T.Charles Erickson

CHERRY JONES as Catherine Sloper in the 1995 Broadway revival of *The Heiress*, directed by Gerald Gutierrez, with Philip Bosco and Frances Sternhagen. Written in 1947 by Ruth and Augustus Goetz and based on Henry James's novel *Washington Square*, Cherry Jones played "the heiress" for 371 performances. One critic wrote that "Jones, radiant in hope, tragic in despair, chilling in conviction, resonates with passions that seem all the more vibrant for being suppressed…."

A graduate of the actor-training program at Carnegie-Mellon University, Cherry Jones made her Off Broadway debut in 1983 in *The Philanthropist*, followed by *A Light Shining in Buckinghamshire* and *The Baltimore Waltz*, and her Broadway debut in 1986 in *Stepping Out*. Most recently she has appeared in *The Night of the Iguana*, *Pride's Crossing*, and *Moon for the Misbegotten*.

©Joan Marcus

JANET McTEER as Nora Helmer in the Broadway production of *A Doll's House*, which transferred from London where she won the 1997 Olivier Award for Best Actress and also the 1997 Antoinette Perry "Tony" Award for Leading Actress in a Play. Janet McTeer's performance received critical praise for showing the depths of Nora's "pain and fear." Known in the London theatre for classical and contemporary roles, she played Elizabeth I in *Vivat! Vivat! Regina!*, Cecilia in Sam Shepard's *Simpatico*, Chekhov's heroines in *Uncle Vanya* and *The Three Sisters*, and Shakepeare's Beatrice (*Much Ado About Nothing*), Rosalind (*As You Like It*), and Imogen (*Cymbeline*). She can be seen in the film *Tumbleweeds*.

Michael Caine in *Sleuth* with Laurence Olivier (1972 film).

In his entertaining book on acting in film, Michael Caine says that "behaving realistically and truthfully in front of a camera is an exacting craft, one that requires steadfast discipline and application."[17] Hidden microphones pick up the smallest vocal nuance, close-ups record the slightest hesitation or uncertainty, scenes are shot out of sequence, and hordes of technicians (and often sightseers) provide distractions. Despite all, the actor must concentrate on "being" rather than "performing" because the camera transmits subtleties of emotion and thought and reveals in close-ups the character's thoughts. The film audience sees what the camera sees, and so the actor must be mentally prepared and thinking from moment to moment. The camera catches the smallest hesitation, failure of concentration, or verbal slip. The actor's readiness—preparation, relaxation, concentration, knowing lines, familiarity with set, properties, and placement of the "mark" (where the actor must stand to be filmed)—make the difference between staying in the film business or not.

The vocabulary of film acting has much in common with that of the theatre, but its purposes are often not the same. The film actor's audition is the "screen test" where the actor's potential before the camera is assessed. In the theatre, actors and directors use rehearsals to explore character, relationships, and interpretation. In film, rehearsals are most often for the director and cameraman to set blocking for the camera. Films are often made without an opportunity for actors to discuss the role with the director, with no time to meet others in the cast, and without rehearsals on the set. Given these conditions, the actor must be fully prepared to perform a scene when called upon and to repeat that scene over and over again until the director calls for "a wrap."

In film acting, the actor's relationship to other actors is different as well. The actor works only with those actors necessary to a scene. Back stage camaraderie often does not exist. Scenes are repeated many times, and the actor must listen and react as freshly as though each time were the very first. In this facet of the film actor's business, the best advice, according to Michael Caine, is to be completely in charge of "your craft, material, and yourself." At no time must the actor forget that the business of filmmaking is to make the film. Anything that slows down the film's schedule (the temperamental, unprepared, or late actor) will result in cost overruns and probably the quick end of a promising film actor's career.

TRANSITION

Actors bring living presence and human behavior to the stage. Their search for new depths of creative energy and truthful behavior keeps their performances fresh and lively night after night.

In turn, directors collaborate with actors and other artists to interpret the playwright's text. As captains of the production's theatrical ship, directors are the final arbiters of choice in the *creative* process.

In the final days of the nineteenth century, the director emerged as a transforming force in the theatre, and has remained so.

WEB SITES

Actingbiz (online resources for actors, with articles on every aspect of the business)
http://www.actingbiz.com/

Acting Workshop On-line (a site for beginners to learn about acting and actors)
http://www.execpc.com/~blankda/acting2.html

Actors' Equity Association (the union representing professional actors and stage managers who work in the theatre, and dancers in a Broadway show)
http://www.actorsequity.org

The Actors Studio (presented by TheatrGROUP, including a brief history of the Actors Studio, a lecture by Lee Strasberg, audition policies, and links to books about the Actors Studio)
http://www.actors-studio.com/

Arts International, Inc. (organization that promotes global connections in the visual and performing arts by providing support to artists and information services)
http://www.artsinternational.org

HOLA: Hispanic Organization for Latin Actors (HOLA serves as a link between Hispanic actors and the entertainment industry; it sponsors a referral service, touring programs, and showcases)
http://www.hellohola.org

The Lee Strasberg Theatre Institute (provides information on the institute, services, and training in New York City and Los Angeles)
http://www.strasberg.com

Non-Traditional Casting Project (works to increase participation of artists of color, women, and artists with disabilities in theatre, film, and television)
http://www.ntcp.org

Screen Actors Guild (the union representing professional actors who work in film and television)
http://www.sag.org

These search terms are provided to assist you in exploring the topics introduced in this chapter at:

http//www.infotrac-college.com

acting, American "Method" acting, Stanislavski's emotional memory, subtext, improvisation, Sanford Meisner's concentration exercises, scene study, actor training, voice training, stage combat, rehearsal, nontraditional casting, acting in film.

The Image Makers: The Director

The theatre of the future, if it is to hold us, will have to shake off a belief it has held only a relatively short time—the belief that it is showing us "a real room with real people." For the theatre's role is to present life not in it literal exact-ness but rather through some kind of poetic vision, metaphor, image—the mir-ror held up as 'twere to nature.[1]

ALAN SCHNEIDER

Director

Directors, in collaboration with playwrights and other artists and assistants, interpret and shape perfor-mances as theatrical metaphors of the world.

FORERUNNERS

In the 1860s in Europe, the practice of a single person guiding all aspects of the production process began to take hold. Before that time, leading actors, theatre managers, and sometimes playwrights "staged" the play, thereby set-ting actors' movements, dictating financial matters, and making decisions on casting, costumes, and scenery. During the first half of the nineteenth cen-tury, actor-managers (following the tradition of James Burbage in England and Molière in France) resembled the modern director in some respects. But the actor-manager was first of all an actor and considered the production from the perspective of the role he or she played. In the eighteenth century, David Garrick was one of England's most successful actor-managers. Although the theatre between 1750 and 1850 was immensely popular in Europe, most actor-managers—Garrick was an exception—maintained infe-rior artistic standards in their pursuit of large box office receipts.

This general condition in the theatre began to worry a growing num-ber of theatre people, who re-examined the production process. With the formation in 1866 of Duke Georg II of Saxe-Meiningen's company in Ger-many (known as the Meiningen Players), the director in the modern sense began to emerge. He exercised a central artistic discipline over the com-pany, serving as producer, director, and financial backer. By controlling design, he introduced a unified look in costumes and settings. The Duke's efforts to define the director's role were followed by those of André Antoine in France and Konstantin Stanislavski in Russia. Under their influence, the modern stage director's identity took shape in Europe: someone who understood all theatrical arts and devoted full energies to combining them into a unified, artistic whole.

Actor-Manager

Caroline Neuber

Caroline Neuber (1697–1760) was one of Europe's earliest women actor-managers. Together with her husband, actor Johann Neuber, she formed an acting company in 1727 in Leipzig, Germany. Shortly thereafter, they joined with Johann Gottsched, the leading German intellectual of his day, to work together to reform the theatre. Caroline Neuber's efforts were directed toward raising the artistic level of theatrical productions. She replaced the older plays with clowns as central figures with serious drama in imitation of French neoclassical writers. She also instituted reforms in the staging practices of her day: plays were staged with careful rehearsals and without improvisational material; actors were assigned added duties, such as painting scenery or sewing costumes; and the actors' personal lives were monitored in an effort to overcome moral prejudices against them.

Caroline Neuber's company had residencies in such cultural centers as Leipzig, Hamburg, Vienna, and St. Petersburg. At her death, her production techniques were being adopted by other companies and the new drama was being performed throughout Germany's theatrical centers.

THE DIRECTOR AS ARTIST

THE BEAUTY QUEEN OF LEENANE
Pauline Flanagan and Brendan O'Malley in *The Beauty Queen of Leenane* by Irish playwright Martin McDonagh, directed by Nagle Jackson. PlayMakers Repertory Company, Chapel Hill, 1998. Producing director Milly S. Barranger.

The director collaborates with playwright, actors, designers, and technicians to create on stage a carefully selected vision of life—a special mirror. Alan Schneider described the *theatre's* role from a director's viewpoint as presenting life not in its literal exactness but through some kind of poetic vision, metaphor, or image.

Depending upon the size of the theatrical organization the director can assume several roles, ranging from attending to budgets and box office details to creative interpretation of the playwright's text. In all cases, the director is the controlling artist responsible for unifying the production elements, including text, music, scenery, costumes, properties, sound, and visuals.

Although each director has his or her way of working creatively, in general three types of directors evolved over the years. On the first day of rehearsal, most directors give a speech

©Barry Slobin/PlayMakers Repertory Company

Duke of Saxe-Meiningen Georg II

Billy Rose Theatre Collection,
The New York Public Library for the
Performing Arts, Astor, Lenox and
Tilden Foundations

The Duke of Saxe-Meiningen, Georg II (1826–1914), transformed the Duchy of Meiningen's court theatre in Germany into an example of scenic historical accuracy and lifelike acting. As producer-director, the Duke designed costumes, scenery, and properties for historically authentic style, and worked for ensemble acting. The Duke was assisted by Ludwig Chronegk (1837–1891), an actor responsible for supervising and rehearsing the company. The Meiningen Players were noted throughout Europe for their crowd scenes, in which each member of the crowd had individual traits and specific lines. In rehearsals actors were divided into small groups, each under the charge of an experienced actor. This practice was in keeping with the company's rule against actors being stars and was the beginning of the new movement in 1874 toward unified production under the director's control. Saxe-Meiningen's example of the *single creative authority* in charge of the total production influenced Antoine and Stanislavski.

to the company describing the play and the approach to be taken to interpret and stage the text. One type of director treats actors and designers as "servants" to the director's concept; they are expected to deliver the "look" and "meaning" of the play's world as conceived by the director. Another type reverses this approach and acts as the creative coordinator of a group of actors and designers, thereby limiting his or her own vision to the suggestions, criticisms, and encouragements of the group.

The third functions as a guide, or helmsman, who senses at the outset the direction that the production will take but proceeds in rehearsals and design conferences to provoke and stimulate the actors and designers. This director creates an atmosphere in which actors dig, probe, and investigate the whole fabric of the play. Rehearsals are used to search out ("to harrow" in the original sense of the word *rehearse*), to listen, and to yield to suggestions. The "directorial conception" is what Alan Schneider refers to as the director's "poetic vision," and it precedes the first day's work. Nevertheless, the "sense of direction" only crystallizes into a consistent stage image as the process nears an end.

Unlike the theatre critics, a director's questions do not deal so much with "What's the event about?" as with the event's *potential*. This is the reason a director chooses one sort of theatrical material over another—because of its potential. This realization of a play's or production's potential motivates directors to find space, actors, and

Producer / Director

André Antoine

Billy Rose Theatre Collection, The New York Public Library for the Performing Arts, Astor, Lenox and Tilden Foundations

André Antoine (1858–1943) was founding producing-director of the Théâtre Libre, or "Free Theatre," in Paris. Beginning as a part-time actor, Antoine founded a theatre in 1887 and a naturalistic production style that became world-famous. The Théâtre Libre was a subscription theatre, one open only to members and therefore exempt from censorship. It became a showcase for new, controversial plays (Ibsen's *Ghosts* was one) and new realistic production techniques. Seeking authentic detail, Antoine set about reproducing exact environments. In one play he hung real beef carcasses on stage. In 1897, he opened his Théâtre Antoine, a fully professional theatre, and in 1906 he was appointed director of the Odéon Théâtre, a state-subsidized theatre in Paris.

In his efforts to stage "real" life, Antoine developed three important principles that influenced the direction of the European theatre: realistic environments, ensemble acting, and the director's authority.

---

forms of expression. Like the hunter or explorer, directors intuit that a potential exists within a work (or text) and yet explore the unknown with a sense of expectation and discovery, and with a deepening commitment to leading the creative team.

Imagine the potential of an untried script called *A Streetcar Named Desire* and the excitement of its first director, Elia Kazan, searching to find what he called the *spine* (or the through-line) of the play's action. In his notebook, he defined the play's *spine* as the "last gasp" of a dying civilization: "This little twisted, pathetic, confused bit of light and culture … snuffed out by the crude forces of violence, insensibility and vulgarity which exist in our South—and this cry is the play."[2]

Consider a director like Peter Brook who sets out, over a number of years, to explore an ancient Hindu epic (*The Mahabharata*). Brook's nine-hour theatrical realization presents humanity's greatest dilemma: human beings caught up in the conflict between divine and demonic forces. The storyline of this theatrical epic is essentially the quest for morality: how to find one's way in an age of global destruction. As director, Brook—with the assistance of collaborators, including writers, designers, musicians, and actors—guided the creation of a theatrical epic out of the ancient, sacred poem. In the case of *A Streetcar Named Desire*, Elia Kazan *interpreted* Tennessee Williams' text. Both Brook and Kazan as directors created theatrical "mirrors" that held up to human nature its many forms, varieties, and expressions.

216   *Chapter Nine*

Konstantin Stanislavski

Culver Pictures, Inc.

THE CHERRY ORCHARD A scene from the 1904 Moscow Art Theatre production of *The Cherry Orchard*, directed by Konstantin Stanislavski.

Konstantin Stanislavski (1863–1938) was producer-director-actor and co-founder of the Moscow Art Theatre. As a director, Stanislavski aimed for ensemble acting and the absence of stars. He established such directorial methods as intensive study of the play before rehearsals began, the actor's careful attention to detail and truthful behavior, and extensive research by visiting locales and museums to re-create the play's milieu. The Moscow Art Theatre's reputation was made with Anton Chekhov's plays depicting in realistic detail the lives of the rural landowning class in provincial Russia.

Stanislavski is remembered for his efforts to perfect a "truthful" method of acting. His published writings—*My Life in Art* (1924), *An Actor Prepares* (1936), *Building a Character* (1949), and *Creating a Role* (1961)—provide a record of the "Stanislavski System" as it evolved.

Early Responsibilities:
Play Selection, Casting, Conferences

In general, a director has six responsibilities: (1) selecting or creating a script, or agreeing to direct an offered script; (2) deciding on the text's interpretation and, with the designers, on the "look" and configuration of the stage space; (3) holding auditions and casting actors in the various roles; (4) working with other theatre artists, technicians, and managers to plan and stage the production; (5) rehearsing the acting company; and (6) coordinating all production elements into a unified performance.

(continued on page 219)

*D*irector

©Elisabetta Catalano

THE MAHABHARATA The archery contest in Peter Brook's 1986 production of the Hindu epic, *The Mahabharata,* which toured in the United States in 1987–88.

Peter Brook

Martha Swope/TimePix

Peter Brook (b. 1925) is founder of the International Centre for Theatre Research in Paris. Born in London and educated at Oxford University, he began his directing career in the 1940s. As co-director of England's Royal Shakespeare Company from 1962 to 1971, he directed acclaimed productions of *King Lear, The Tempest, Marat/Sade,* and *A Midsummer Night's Dream.* His activities with the Centre include *Orghast* for the Shiraz Festival in Persepolis (Iran), *The Ik* (based on Colin Turnbull's book *The Mountain People*), and *The Mahabharata.* He directed the film *The Lord of the Flies* (1963) and wrote influential books on theatre: *The Empty Space* (1968), *The Shifting Point: Theatre, Film, Opera 1946–1987* (1988), *The Open Door: Thoughts on Acting and Theatre* (1993), and his memoir *Threads of Time* (1999).

Known for his radical adaptations of familiar plays, Brook enjoys an enormous international reputation. Since founding the Centre in Paris, Brook has experimented with actor training and developed theatrical texts from myths, anthropology, and fables, producing *Conference of Birds, The Tragedy of Carmen, The Mahabharata,* and *The Man Who.*

None of the director's process is cut and dried. It is as variable as the names, faces, and talents of the director and the team players.

Casting and Auditions

Casting is matching an actor to a role. During auditions (and often with the help of a casting director), the director looks for actors whose physical appearance, personality, and acting ability flesh out the director's idea of the characters. In college and university theatres, auditions or tryouts are more or less standardized. Copies of the play (scenes or "sides") are made available and audition notices are posted. With the assistance of stage management, the director holds general auditions or private interviews, or a combination of the two. The director usually asks actors to come to the audition prepared to illustrate their talent and ability by performing selections either from plays of their own choosing, or from material assigned for the audition.

Beginning with the leading roles, the director narrows the choices for each part. If time and circumstances warrant, he or she calls back a final group of actors—the potential cast. This group reads together from the play so that the director can see how they relate to one another, how they work together, and how they complement one another in physical appearance and in vocal and emotional quality. Once the director decides on the members of the cast, the casting notice is posted, and rehearsals usually begin within a short period.

©T. Charles Erickson/Alley Theatre

THE DIRECTOR IN REHEARSAL
Gregory Boyd, artistic director of the Alley Theatre, Houston, works with Elizabeth Heflin (right) and Sherri Lee Parker in rehearsals for *The Greeks*.

The Director's Assistants

To prepare a play within a three- to ten-week rehearsal period, modern directors need assistants. The *assistant director* attends production meetings, coaches actors, and rehearses special or problem scenes. *Stage managers* compile the promptbook (a copy of the script with marginal space to record rehearsal notes); prepare rehearsal schedules; record stage business, blocking, lighting, sound, and other cues; take notes during rehearsals; coordinate rehearsals; and run the show after it opens. The *voice* and *dialects coach* works with actors in rehearsal to ensure audibility and clarity of meaning. The *movement coach* and/or *fight coordinator* works with actors for safety and expressive physical work. In musicals, the composer, musical director, and choreographer are also part of the director's team. In nonprofit theatres, the *production dramaturg* is also an integral part of the production team.

> **The Society of Stage Directors and Choreographers (SSDC)** *is an independent national labor union representing professional directors and choreographers who work in the theatre, and choreographers who work in the media. There are SSDC contracts for Broadway, Off and Off Off Broadway, resident theatres, and stock and dinner theatres, along with special contracts for members working in college/university theatre programs and in community theatres.*

Dramaturgy and the Production Dramaturg

The dramaturg's position was created in the eighteenth-century German theatre when playwright and critic Gotthold Ephraim Lessing joined the staff of the new Hamburg National Theatre in 1767. He declined the position of resident playwright but served instead as in-house critic where he advised on selection of plays and the company's productions, and published a journal of reviews and theories on drama. Thereafter, the position of dramaturg was firmly established in German and European theatres. In America, the dramaturg was introduced in the nonprofit theatres in the 1960s, and has since become a permanent member of the production staff in most.

How do dramaturgs serve the production? Early in the process, they may select the version of the text to be performed (a Shakespeare or a Brecht text, for example), prepare a translation or adaptation, and cut and rearrange the script that is to be the production script. They usually research background on a playwright's life and his or her other plays and writings, explore the surrounding period or culture, and offer script analysis. In a word, they increase understanding of the play, the writer, and the world that shaped both.

In rehearsals, dramaturgs serve as a critical "eye" for directors and provide feedback on how well the author's and director's intentions are being realized onstage. The theatre also asks dramaturgs to manage outreach programs to educate audiences: hold "talk back" sessions with audiences, prepare materials for school programs, and prepare other materials (playbill inserts and newsletters) that elaborate on script interpretation and production values.

In all, dramaturgs serve productions and their creative teams in advisory and critical ways to ensure that both playwright's and director's intentions are complementary and meaningful to audiences.

DIRECTING APPROACHES AND STYLES

At the most basic level, the director helps the actor find the character's inner life and project this life vocally and visually to the audience. Many directors preplan the actor's movements in each scene (called blocking) and, like a photographer composing a group photograph, arrange the actors in the stage space to show their physical and psychological relationships. Not unlike the photographer, some directors compose pictures with actors on stage to show relationships and attitudes. In all instances, directors concern themselves with conveying truthful human behavior and telling the playwright's story.

Stage Vocabulary

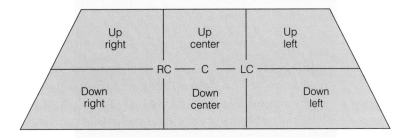

Stage vocabulary is a language that developed over the years between director and actor to communicate quickly to each other in rehearsals. It is a kind of stage shorthand in which *all directions are to the actor's left or right.*

Upstage means toward the rear of the acting area. *Downstage* means toward the front. *Stage right* and *stage left* refer to the performer's right or left when he or she faces the audience. The stage floor is frequently spoken of as though it were divided into sections: *up right, up center, up left, down right, down center, down left.*

Body positions are also designated for work largely on the proscenium stage. The director may ask the actor to *turn out,* meaning to turn more toward the audience. Two actors are sometimes told to *share a scene,* or to play in a profile position so that they are equally visible to the audience. An actor may be told to *dress the stage,* meaning to move to balance the stage picture. Experienced actors take directions with ease and frequently make such moves almost automatically.

Audiences are almost never aware that the actor is taking a rehearsed position. But the actor's speech and movements, along with lighting and sound, often control what we see and hear onstage.

Preplanned Approach

Some directors use early rehearsals to *block* the play. In blocking rehearsals, the director goes through each scene, working with actors on when to enter or exit, where to stand or sit, and which lines to move on. As they go through the scenes, the actors write down this information in their scripts along with stage business (specific actions, such as answering a telephone or turning on a radio).

Directors vary a great deal in their approach to beginning rehearsals. Some give full directions immediately; others leave much of the detail to be worked out later as the actors try out their lines and reactions to one another. Almost any director makes adjustments in later rehearsals as director and actors discover better ways of moving and reacting and generally shaping their work into a meaningful performance.

Collaborative Approach

A second approach, which many directors favor, is the *collaborative* approach. This method involves director and actors working together in rehearsals to develop movement, gestures, character relationships, stage images, and line interpretations. Rather than entering the rehearsal period with entirely preset ideas, the director watches, listens, suggests, and selects as the actors rehearse.

The importance of the rehearsal process is to discover a unity, rhythm, and meaning for the production. At some point in the rehearsal period, the director sets the performance by selecting from what has evolved in rehearsals. In this second approach, improvisation or game playing is often an important director's tool.

Improvisation

Improvisation is primarily a *rehearsal* tool, not a performance technique. How much improvisation is used in rehearsal depends upon the director's skill with it and the actors' needs.

Improvisational exercises are oftentimes an actor's road to freedom. They are exercises designed to free an actor's imagination and body for spontaneous storytelling. Often directors use improvisations early in rehearsals to release inhibitions and spark the actors' imaginations, behaviors, reactions, and moods as they begin working together. In later rehearsals, improvisations can be used to increase concentration, discover new actions, clarify character relationships, and develop good working relations among actors.

While rehearsing *A Midsummer Night's Dream,* Peter Brook's actors practiced circus tricks each day along with comic improvisations to encourage inventiveness and

A MIDSUMMER NIGHT'S DREAM
Peter Brook used circus tricks and techniques borrowed from puppet theatre and English music halls in his acclaimed production of Shakespeare's comedy. Trapezes and a feathered bower create the magical forest as Titania makes love to Bottom, who wears a clown's red nose. The Royal Shakespeare Company's 1970 production.

©Max Waldman Archives

Bertolt Brecht's Approach to Directing

The methods of German playwright and director Bertolt Brecht have been described in this way:

> During rehearsals Bertolt Brecht sits in the auditorium. His work as a director is unobtrusive. When he intervenes it is almost unnoticeable and always in the "direction of the flow." He never interrupts, not even with suggestions for improvement. You do not get the impression that he wants to get the actors to "present some of his ideas"; they are not his instruments.
>
> Instead he searches, together with the actors, for the story which the play tells, and helps each actor to his strength. His work with the actors may be compared to the efforts of a child to direct straws with a twig from a puddle into the river itself, so that they may float.
>
> Brecht is not one of those directors who knows everything better than the actors. He adopts towards the play an attitude of "know-nothingism"; he waits. You get the impression that Brecht does not know his own play, not a single sentence. And he does not want to know what is written, but rather how the written text is to be shown by the actor on the stage. If an actor asks: "Should I stand up at this point?", the reply is often typically Brecht: "I don't know." Brecht really does not know; he only discovers during the rehearsal.[3]

---

playing for the sake of playing. With the "rude mechanicals," Brook organized realistic improvisations to give the actors as working-class men in the story a down-to-earth reality.[4]

Director's Ground Plan

The modern director uses many tools in rehearsal to stimulate the actors' imaginations. The director's and scene designer's agreed-upon *ground plan* defines the size

(continued on page 228)

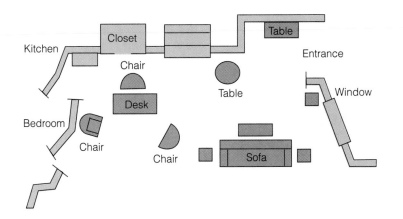

THE GROUND PLAN Director and scene designer work out the play's environment, noting on a floor (or ground) plan doorways, windows, stairs, levels, walls, and furniture. This landscape is then outlined in tape on the rehearsal-room floor by stage management so that actors can visualize and work within the dimensions of the environment during rehearsals.

The Director as Creator

Peter Brook . Ariane Mnouchkine . Andrei Serban . Julie Taymor . Robert Wilson

©Richard Feldman

JULIE TAYMOR, as director and designer, created the puppets for the 1988 Off Broadway production of *Juan Darién: A Carnival Mass*, based on a Latin American story by Horacío Quiroga.

©Richard Feldman

©Joan Marcus

ANDREI SERBAN directed the 1984 production of *The King Stag* with costumes and masks by Julie Taymor for the American Repertory Theatre, Cambridge, Massachusetts. The long arms of the bird-magician (front) were inspired by the flowing sleeves of Korean garments.

JULIE TAYMOR directed and designed masks and puppets for *The Green Bird*, a play by Carlo Gozzi, at the New Victory Theatre, New York City, in 1996. The production was restaged on Broadway in 2000.

Martha Swope/TimePix

PETER BROOK'S production of *The Mahabharata*, based on the Hindu epic *The Bhagavad Gita*, was staged in 1988 at *Les* Bouffes du Nord Théâtre in Paris. Brook's actors create their story with simple props and stylized gestures. Brook's colorful staging emphasized the elements: fire, water, earth, air.

Martha Swope/TimePix

The Image Makers: The Director

ROBERT WILSON'S *The Black Rider: The Casting of the Magic Bullets* brought together Wilson, Tom Waits, and William Burroughs in a collaboration based on a German folk tale of a man who, to succeed as a marksman and win his bride, casts magic bullets with the help of the devil. With direction and scene design by Robert Wilson, *The Black Rider* was part of the 1993 Next Wave Festival, Brooklyn Academy of Music, New York.

Klaus Schreiber (opposite) in *The Black Rider.*

226   *Photo Essay*

©Richard Feldman

ROBERT WILSON conceived and directed *the CIVIL warS: a tree is best measured when it is down.* Actors and puppets are juxtaposed in pinpoints of light. American Repertory Theatre production, Cambridge, Massachusetts, 1985.

ARIANE MNOUCHKINE removed Shakespeare's play from a traditional Western performance style. As conceived, her version of *Richard II* relies on Kabuki traditions of setting, costumes, props, makeup, and movement. Théâtre du Soleil production, Paris, 1981.

©Martine Franck/Magnum, Inc.

©Michele Laurant/The Liaison Agency

ARIANE MNOUCHKINE'S costumes and makeup for the chorus members of *Iphigenia in Aulis* resonate with Kathakali and other Eastern theatrical traditions in the Théâtre du Soleil production of *Les Atrides,* Paris, 1992.

and shape of the playing space, including walls, windows, furniture, doors, stairs, and so on. Some areas will have greater access for movement than others. Other areas will restrict and isolate. As actors physically inhabit the ground plan, they discover physical relationships that further the emotional life and meaning of the text. As the director and actors add storytelling details of gesture and speech, the characters' emotional truths come alive visually and vocally and the living quality of the play takes shape.

THE DIRECTOR'S VISION

As creative artists, some directors serve the playwright by translating the script as faithfully as possible into theatrical form. Elia Kazan, for example, interpreted Arthur Miller's and Tennessee Williams' plays with a faithful concern for the playwright's "intentions." Other playwrights, like Edward Albee, Brian Friel, Athol Fugard, David Mamet, and María Irene Fornés, direct their own plays. Many directors seek out a controlling idea, image, or sound to define the production's emotional and political meaning. Mike Nichols, in directing Neil Simon's comedies, searches for what he calls the "Event"—the truthful moment or series of moments that will illuminate the author's meaning, that will reveal "real people living their lives." In contrast, JoAnne Akalaitis allows events from the real world, such as songs, pictures, or magazine articles, to trigger the creative process for her. Often seen as an iconoclastic director, Anne Bogart seeks mystery and danger in dramatic texts in her search for imaginative ways to renew theatrical experience at the start of a new millennium.

Many directors today, taking their cues from such great experimental directors as Vsevolod Meyerhold, Bertolt Brecht, and Peter Brook, fashion the script into a wholly new and directorially original work of art. In this role, the director alters the play—changes the historical period, cuts the text, rearranges the scenes—and practically takes over the role of author.

THE NEW COLLABORATORS

Pina Bausch, Martha Clarke, Robert Wilson

Directors Martha Clarke, Pina Bausch, and Robert Wilson are grounded in non-narrative theatrical traditions. Their work has its inception in images, sounds, and movement, not in verbal texts. For this reason (among others) their work differs from

A MIDSUMMER NIGHT'S DREAM Peter Brook took Shakespeare's play out of period costumes, painted scenic backdrops, and green forests. The actors performed the text in a white box while balancing on trapezes, juggling plates, hurling streamers, and walking on stilts.

Max Waldman Archives

*D*irector

Elia Kazan

*A STREETCAR NAMED
DESIRE* Marlon Brando as
Stanley (left) prepares to throw
his cup and plate to the floor
during Blanche's birthday party
in *A Streetcar Named Desire*,
directed in 1947 by Elia Kazan.
Jessica Tandy as Blanche (center)
and Kim Hunter as Stella (right)
are seated at the table.

Elia Kazan (b. 1909 in Istanbul, Turkey) was educated at Williams College and Yale University. As a member of the Group Theatre, he acted in their productions of Clifford Odets' *Waiting for Lefty, Paradise Lost,* and *Golden Boy.*

He is best known today for his direction of plays by Tennessee Williams and Arthur Miller: *A Streetcar Named Desire* (1947), *Death of a Salesman* (1949), *Camino Real* (1953), *Cat on a Hot Tin Roof* (1955), and *Sweet Bird of Youth* (1959). Kazan also directed films of *A Streetcar Named Desire, On the Waterfront,* and *East of Eden.*

Along with designer Jo Mielziner, Kazan established *selected realism* as the dominant American theatrical style during the 1950s. This style combined acting of intense psychological truth with simplified but realistic scenery. Marlon Brando as Stanley Kowalski embodied the acting style for which Kazan's productions were famous. Kazan described his working methods in his autobiography, called *A Life* (1988).

---

other contemporary directors, such as Elia Kazan, Daniel Sullivan, Lynne Meadow, and Emily Mann. Their theatre pieces grow out of intense collaborations with different types of theatrical artists, including designers, composers, choreographers, actors, musicians, dancers, and singers.

Martha Clarke's Theatre-Dance Pieces

Martha Clarke connects hundreds of imagistic fragments in her theatrical works. First, she asks singers and dancers to move to music and develop fragmentary scenes. Later

*E*lia *Kazan's Director's Notebook*
for A Streetcar Named Desire

The following is taken from Elia Kazan's *Director's Notebook* (dated August 1947) kept before and during rehearsals of *A Streetcar Named Desire:*

A thought—directing finally consists of turning Psychology into Behavior.

Theme—this is a message from the dark interior. This little twisted, pathetic, confused bit of light and culture puts out a cry. It is snuffed out by the crude forces of violence, insensibility and vulgarity which exist in our South—and this cry is the play.

Style—one reason a "style," a stylized production is necessary is that a subjective factor—Blanche's memories, inner life, emotions, are a real factor. We cannot really understand her behavior unless we see the effect of her past on her present behavior.

This play is a poetic tragedy. We are shown the final dissolution of a person of worth, who once had a great potential, and who, even as she goes down, has worth exceeding that of the "healthy," coarse-grained figures who kill her.

Blanche is a social type, an emblem of a dying civilization, making its last curlicued and romantic exit. All her behavior patterns are those of the dying civilization she represents. In other words her behavior is *social*. Therefore find social modes! This is the source of the play's stylization and the production's style and color. Likewise, Stanley's behavior is *social* too. It is the basic animal cynicism of today. "Get what's coming to you! Don't waste a day! Eat, drink, get yours!" This is the basis of his stylization, of the choice of his props. All props should be stylized: they should have a color, shape and weight that spell: style.

An effort to put poetic names on scenes to edge me into stylizations and physicalizations. Try to keep each scene in terms of Blanche.

1. Blanche comes to the last stop at the end of the line.

---

in the collaborative process among the various artists, she superimposes other parts onto the scenes. If the pieces connect, she then weaves them into the fabric of the total work that is shaped and reshaped in six months or more of rehearsal. *The Garden of Earthly Delights* is Clarke's theatrical interpretation of painter Hieronymus

ENDANGERED SPECIES The production, conceived and directed by Martha Clarke with designs by Robert Israel, had a large cast of individuals and circus animals—all "endangered species." The 1990 Next Wave Festival at the Brooklyn Academy of Music, New York.

Martha Swope/TimePix

2. Blanche tries to make a place for herself.

3. Blanche breaks them apart, but when they come together, Blanche is more alone than ever!

4. Blanche, more desperate because more excluded, tries the direct attack and makes the enemy who will finish her.

5. Blanche finds that she is being tracked down for the kill. She must work fast.

6. Blanche suddenly finds, suddenly makes for herself, the only possible, perfect man for her.

7. Blanche comes out of the happy bathroom to find that her own doom has caught up with her.

8. Blanche fights her last fight. Breaks down. Even Stella deserts her.

9. Blanche's last desperate effort to save herself by telling the whole truth. The truth dooms her.

10. Blanche escapes out of this world. She is brought back by Stanley and destroyed.

11. Blanche is disposed of.

The style—the real deep style—consists of one thing only: to find behavior that's truly social, significantly typical, at each moment. It's not so much what Blanche has done—it's how she does it—with such style, grace, manners, old-world trappings and effects, props, tricks, swirls, etc., that they seem anything but vulgar.

And for the other characters, too, you face the same problem. To find the Don Quixote character for them. *This is a poetic tragedy, not a realistic or naturalistic one. So you must find a Don Quixote scheme of things for each.*

Stylized acting and direction is to realistic acting and direction as poetry is to prose. The acting must be styled, not in the obvious sense. (Say nothing about it to the producer and actors.) But you will fail unless you find this kind of poetic realization for the behavior of these people.[5]

Bosch's fifteenth-century triptych. A one-hour evocation of the Garden of Eden and the netherworld, *The Garden* is inhabited by ten dancers and musicians who at times are earthbound and at others celestially somersaulting through the air on cables.

Clarke is the chief creator of her theatre pieces, which are not narrations of a storyline but expressions of her subconscious. They link the points between inspiration and a volatile inner emotional life. Commenting on her collaborative process, she says:

> … If you watched a rehearsal of mine, you would see that nine-tenths of it is in such disarray. I flounder…. I'm foggy a lot of the time. And the actors and dancers have to search as much as I do. We're all children dropped on another planet at the beginning of this process and, tentatively, hand-in-hand, we find our way through this mire to whatever. The day-by-day process couldn't be more collaborative.[7]

Robert Wilson's "Visual Book"

Robert Wilson is author, designer, and director of nearly one hundred theatre, opera, dance, film, and video works. He is best known for such innovative productions as *Einstein on the Beach* (a 1976 collaboration with composer Philip Glass),

"I'm a very instinctive person and I feel my way around like someone blindfolded in the attic. I stumble the piece into shape and often don't get a vision until late in the process. Then I take out my scissors and my paste and in the very last moments before a first preview it falls together."[6]
MARTHA CLARKE
Director/Choreographer

*D*irector

©1984 Newsday, Inc. Reprinted with
permission.

WAITING FOR GODOT The first
American production of Samuel Beckett's
Waiting for Godot was directed by Alan
Schneider in 1956 at the Coconut Grove
Playhouse, Miami. Tom Ewell played
Vladimir (center) and Bert Lahr was
Estragon.

Alan Schneider

Alan Schneider (1917–1984) was born Abram Leopoldovich Schneider in Kharkov,
Russia, the son of medical students. The Schneiders emigrated to the United States
during the Russian Revolution and settled in Maryland. Educated at Johns Hopkins
University and Cornell University, Alan Schneider made his acting debut on Broadway in a Maxwell Anderson play. He first worked as a director at Arena Stage, Washington, D.C., where he began a directing career that alternated between professional
regional theatres and Broadway.

The invitation to direct the American premiere of *Waiting for Godot* was the turning point of his career. Bringing Samuel Beckett's plays to the public's attention
became Schneider's lifelong crusade. He directed the American premieres of Beckett's *Krapp's Last Tape, Happy Days, Endgame, Not I,* and *Rockaby.* He directed the
original Broadway productions of Edward Albee's *Who's Afraid of Virginia Woolf?,
Tiny Alice,* and *A Delicate Balance.* Amid this flurry of activity, he became head of the
Juilliard Theatre Center in New York City. At the time of his death, he was artistic
director of Juilliard's Acting Company.

Few directors have been so consistently involved with plays of quality and significance. Few have worked with so many seminal playwrights.

the CIVIL warS: a tree is best measured when it is down (with author Heiner Müller and
composer David Byrne, 1988), *The Days Before: Death, Destruction and Detroit III* (with
composer Ryuichi Sakamoto, 1999); and new stagings of Ibsen's *When We Dead Awaken*
(1991), Buchner's *Danton's Death* (1992), and Strindberg's *A Dream Play* (2000).

(continued on page 234)

Director / Choreographers

Martha Clarke and Pina Bausch

Courtesy of Martha Clarke

Born in Baltimore, Maryland, in 1944, **Martha Clarke** entered the theatre through dance training at the Juilliard School, New York City, and as a member of Anna Sokolow's dance company and later the Pilobolus Dance Theatre. The New York–based Music Theatre Group funded Clarke to develop her own theatrical form. The result was a series of increasingly complex works: *The Garden of Earthly Delights* (1984), *Vienna: Lusthaus* (1986), *Endangered Species* (1990), and *Dammerung* (1993). Awarded a MacArthur "genius" grant in 1990, she has since worked on *Alice in Wonderland* for the Royal National Theatre, London, and created a new work based on Anton Chekhov's short stories, called *Vers la Flamme.*

©Gert Weigelt

Pina Bausch creates surreal dance-theatre spectacles. She lives in Germany and works largely in Europe with her Tanztheater Wuppertal company. In 1999, two of her acclaimed dance-theatre works toured the United States: *Nelken,* a carnation-strewn extravaganza; and *Danzon,* staged on a carpet of dirt piled high with red bauhinia blossoms. Bausch is a deft social critic. In her work, she often remarks upon societal inequities that deal with the disparity between classes, anxiety over aging, and the violent side of love. Against a backdrop of a film featuring exotic yellow and blue fish swimming about, *Danzon* is an image-saturated work about the inevitability of nature: the joys and fears surrounding birth and death, greetings and farewells, innocence and its loss. Bausch's work combines dance, film, music, tableaux, narrative, and some dialogue to create visually stimulating pieces about the human condition.

©Gert Weigelt

PINA BAUSCH'S *DANZON*

ROBERT WILSON Director/designer
Robert Wilson working with his
collaborators.

Wilson's work is grounded in what he calls the "visual book." He say, "I'm not a writer of words…. I usually find a form before I have content. Before I've gathered material, I have a form. Once I have a form, it's a question of how to fill the form."[8] He then proceeds in workshops and rehearsals to structure time and episodes, to visualize landscapes, and to add themes and reference.

Describing his workshop/rehearsal period, Wilson uses the analogy of cooking a meal to describe the process:

I've said many times it's like making a dinner. The four of us here at this table are now going to make a dinner. Well, I know I can make a salad, and that's about it. You can make coffee. But maybe he knows how to make pasta, and she knows how to make something else, and then we have this dinner based on what we can do. So Heiner Müller [writer] can do one thing and Darryl Pinckney [writer] can do another, and David Byrne [composer] can do another, and maybe they're all very different, with different aesthetics, different viewpoints. But we make a work together. We have to try to figure out how we can take these different people and make this meal. And then we offer it.[9]

Unlike directors who faithfully interpret the playwright's world, the "new" collaborators, like Martha Clarke, Pina Bausch, Robert Wilson, Philip Glass, and Anne Bogart, develop their own texts or reconceive older texts with collaborators. These works are sometimes called a "theatre of visions." They are the stagings of the creators' visions of new theatrical realities. There is no concern for verbal analysis, no attention to plausibility, no question of conveying information or of generating meaning. Of ultimate importance to these new collaborators is the act of imparting an *artistically created vision* together with a sense of its visual significance and excitement.

DANTON'S DEATH Actor Richard Thomas as the revolutionary Danton surrounded by supporters in Georg Buchner's *Danton's Death*, reconceived and directed by Robert Wilson. Alley Theatre, Houston, 1992.

TRANSITION

Before the emergence of the director in the nineteenth century, leading actors, managers, and playwrights ran the theatres, dictated production elements, and took care of financial matters. A coordinating specialist—the director—became necessary with advancing technology and changing subject matter brought about by new currents in social, aesthetic, and political thought.

Today's audiences experience theatrical works through the director's imagination and intellect often to such a degree that the modern director has become almost as distinct a creative force as the playwright.

Other indispensable artists—set, costume, lighting, and sound designers—also entered the theatre in the last century to transform the theatrical experience with their creative energies and skills.

WEB SITES

The Director's Guild of America (DGA)

The Guild represents directors of theatrical, industrial, educational, and documentary films, as well as television (live, filmed, taped), radio, videos, and commercial films.

http://www.dga.org/

The Drama League

The League's national Directors Project provides training, assistant directorships, and Equity production opportunities for early-career directors.

http://www.echonyc.com/~diny

Literary Managers and Dramaturgs of the Americas

A national membership organization, LMDA serves literary managers, dramaturgs, and other professionals through conferences, a job phone line, and an early-career dramaturg program.

http://www.lmda.org

New York Public Library for the Performing Arts

The *Theatre on Film and Tape Archive* contains a collection of theatrical productions on video; also documents on popular entertainment, including scripts, promptbooks, photographs, reviews, books, and personal papers.

http://www.nypl.org

Society of Stage Directors and Choreographers (SSDC)

This independent national labor union represents professional directors and choreographers.

http://ssdc.org

What Is a Dramaturg?

A description of position and responsibilities.

http://www.dramaturgy.net/dramaturgy/

These search terms are provided to assist you in exploring the topics introduced in this chapter at:

http//www.infotrac-college.com

actor-manager, Meiningen Court Theatre, Moscow Art Theatre, Théâtre Libre, Konstantin Stanislavski, André Antoine, Peter Brook, Ariane Mnouchkine, auditions, rehearsal methods, dramaturgy/dramaturg, promptbook, *modelbuch,* dance-theatre.

©Richard Feldman

CHAPTER 10

The Image Makers: The Designers
Scenery, Costumes, Makeup, Masks, Wigs & Hair

Designers of theatrical scenery, costumes, masks, puppets, hair, and wigs realize the playwright's and director's intentions in visual terms. They are visual artists working in a variety of materials, ranging from wood and steel to fabrics, metals, and found objects.

D esigners collaborate with the director to focus the audience's attention on the actor in the theatrical space: the stage. Designers shape and fill the stage space. They create a three-dimensional environment for the actor and make the play's world *visible* and *interesting* for audiences. Sometimes one person (the scenographer) designs scenery, lighting, and costumes. But in most instances in today's theatre, scenery, costumes, lights, and sound are designed by individual artists, whose efforts are considered separately in this discussion.

THE SCENE DESIGNER

Background

The scenery or set designer entered the American theatre over 100 years ago. The designer's nineteenth-century counterpart was the resident *scenic artist,* who painted large pieces of scenery for theatre managers. Scenery's main function in those days was to give the actor a painted background and to indicate place. Scenic studios staffed with specialized artists were set up to turn out scenery on demand. Many of these studios conducted a large mail-order business for standard backdrops and scenic pieces. By the middle of the nineteenth century, realism had come into the theatre, and the job of making the stage environment look real became more complex.

Edward Gordon Craig /Courtesy The Victoria & Albert Museum

EDWARD GORDON CRAIG'S
HAMLET This is one of Edward
Gordon Craig's design models for the
famous setting of *Hamlet* for the
1912 Moscow Art Theatre production.
Craig designed huge white screens to
be sufficiently mobile so that the
appearance of the scene could be
changed without closing the front
curtain. Unfortunately, the screens did
not function with the efficiency he
envisioned.

By the late nineteenth century, theatre was dominated by a naturalistic philosophy that insisted life could be explained by the forces of environment, heredity, economics, society, and the psyche. This being the case, theatre had to present these forces as carefully and effectively as possible. If environment (including economic factors) really did govern people's lives, then it needed to be shown as they actually experienced it. The demands of realism called for the stage to look almost photographically like actual places and rooms. The responsibility for creating this stage environment shifted from the scene painter to the set designer.

Realism has been the dominant convention of the theatre in our time. However, many new and exciting movements in the modern theatre came about as reactions to this direct representation of reality, which pretends that the stage is not a stage but someone's living room and that the audience (seated in a dark auditorium) observing the play is really not there beyond the invisible "fourth wall." Leaders of many avant-garde or new movements in stage design argued that the stage living room and box set were themselves unnatural. They set about pioneering other kinds of theatrical reality for the stage—expressionism, symbolism, and selected realism.

Before the First World War in Europe, Adolphe Appia and Edward Gordon Craig became self-proclaimed prophets of a new movement in theatre design and lighting. They were concerned with creating mood and atmosphere, opening up the stage for movement, and unifying visual ideas; they assaulted the illusion of stage realism and led the way to a rethinking of theatrical design. In his *Music and Stage Setting*, Appia called for theatrical art to be expressive. And today, in the same spirit, many modern set designers have extended the traditional media of wood, canvas, and paint to include steel, plastics, projected images, pipes, ramps, light, platforms, and steps to *express* the play's atmosphere and imaginative life instead of attempting to *reproduce* realistic details of time and place.

Appia and Craig influenced the young American designers of the 1920s, Robert Edmond Jones, Lee Simonson, and Norman Bel Geddes, who dedicated themselves to

*D*esigners

Appia and Craig

Billy Rose Theatre Collection, The New York Public Library for the Performing Arts, Astor, Lenox and Tilden Foundations

Adolphe Appia (1862–1928) and **Edward Gordon Craig** (1872–1966) built the theoretical foundations of modern expressionistic theatrical practice. For the Swiss-born Appia, *artistic unity* was the basic goal of theatrical production. He disliked the contradiction in the three-dimensional actor performing before painted two-dimensional scenery, and he advocated the replacement of flat settings with steps, ramps, and platforms. He thought the role of lighting was to fuse all visual elements into a unified whole. His *Music and Stage Setting* (1899) and *The Work of Living Art* (1921) are early source books for modern stage-lighting practices.

Edward Gordon Craig was born into an English theatrical family (he was the son of actress Ellen Terry and architect and scene designer Edward Godwin) and began his career as an actor in Henry Irving's company. The 1902 exhibit of his work as a stage designer and the publication of his *The Art of the Theatre* in 1905 created controversy throughout Europe; indeed, his entire theatrical life was a storm of controversy. He thought of theatre as an independent art that welded action, words, line, color, and rhythm into an artistic whole created by the single, autonomous artist. Many of his ideas on simplified decor, three-dimensional settings, moving scenery, and directional lighting prevailed in the new stagecraft that emerged after the First World War.

bringing the "new stagecraft" to Broadway. Two generations of American scene designers followed their lead. Prominent among them are Jo Mielziner, the designer of *Death of a Salesman, A Streetcar Named Desire,* and *The King and I;* Boris Aronson, the designer of *Cabaret, Company,* and *Pacific Overtures;* Oliver Smith, designer of *Brigadoon, The Sound of Music,* and *Plaza Suite;* Ming Cho Lee, designer of *Hair, for colored girls who have considered suicide/when the rainbow is enuf,* and *K2;* and John Lee Beatty, designer of *The American Daughter* and revivals of *The Heiress* and *Chicago.*

The Designer's Training

Over sixty years ago the designer, like the actor, was trained in stock and repertory theatres. The scenic artist, with only a rough knowledge of theatrical settings, was concerned almost solely with painting. Design training consisted of an apprenticeship in a scenic studio. With the emergence of the director as artistic coordinator, the concept of the scene designer

"When I sit alone in a theatre and gaze into the dark space of its empty stage, I'm frequently seized by fear that this time I won't manage to penetrate it. And I always hope that this fear will never desert me. Without an unending search for the key to the secret of creativity, there is no creation. It's necessary always to begin again. And that is beautiful."[2]

JOSEF SVOBODA
The Secret of Theatrical Space

EXPRESSIONISTIC DESIGN The skeleton scene in the 1922 New York production of German playwright Georg Kaiser's *From Morn to Midnight*, designed by Lee Simonson, is a good example of expressionistic design and production style, which stressed imaginative lighting (a tree has been transformed into a human skeleton), symbolic decor on an almost empty stage, and the distortion of natural appearances. Notice how the actor is dwarfed by the huge projection.

as a collaborative, interpretive artist with responsibility for all visual and technical elements developed as well. In the 1920s, American universities became the training ground for theatrical designers—the set, costume, lighting, and later, sound designers.

Designing for the Theatre

Scene designers use one of five basic methods to design stage settings:

- Start with a real room or unlocalized place, select from it, change the dimensions, and reshape it for a particular stage.
- Start with the play's most important events and then add platforms, shapes, and voids.
- Start with the play's mood and find the lines, shapes, and colors that will reflect it.
- Design the scene as an idea or metaphor—in the 1920s, the expressionists in Germany sought to reflect the nightmarish outlook of the disturbed mind in their stage settings.
- Organize the entire space, including actor and audience, as environment.

The environmentalist begins with the notion that the production will both develop from and totally take place in a given space. There is no effort to create an illusion or imitation; rather, the performer and audience, space and materials, exist as what they are: people, ramps, platforms, ladders, stairs, mazes.

The design process can take months. The designer usually begins by studying the script in much the same way as the director, visualizing details of place, movement,

Designers

Ming Cho Lee and John Lee Beatty

Hsu Ping, Taipei/Courtesy of Ming Cho Lee

Ming Cho Lee (born 1930 in Shanghai and educated at Occidental College and UCLA) designed his first Broadway show, Eugene O'Neill's *Moon for the Misbegotten,* in 1962. Since then, he has designed settings for Broadway, Off Broadway, regional theatres, opera and dance companies. For over ten years he was the principal designer for the New York Shakespeare Festival. He also designed for the Metropolitan Opera Company and the Martha Graham Company.

Speaking of his methods, Ming Cho Lee says: "I generally read the script once just to get an impact from which I will try to form some kind of visual concept.... I always design for the total play and let the specifics fit in. The total play demands some kind of expression through materials, and this is something I always first ask a director.... And then, I would make the choice as to whether it is a realistic play that requires very literal settings or if it's a play that requires a nonliteral approach and essentially you present it on a platform—you create a framework on which to hang your visual statement."[3]

Courtesy of John Lee Beatty

John Lee Beatty (b. 1948) grew up in Palo Alto, California, and attended Brown University (R.I.) and the Yale University School of Drama, where he studied with designer Ming Cho Lee. Beatty has designed more than 100 professional productions, including Broadway's *Ain't Misbehavin', Chicago, Footloose, Once Upon a Mattress, An American Daughter, The Heiress, The Last Night of Ballyhoo,* and *A Delicate Balance.* He also works with Lincoln Center Theater, the Manhattan Theatre Club, and the City Center Encores! Series. He is winner of Antoinette Perry "Tony," Drama Desk, and Outer Critics Circle Awards.

Known for designs of poetic realism and playful theatrical settings, Beatty says of his process: "My job as a designer is to design the scenery and to give a designer's point of view... Coming up with the design is what is hard. I normally do a group plan and a rough sketch first... I usually show a fairly simple sketch to a director... It's important to let the director know it's a work in process."[4]

and objects in space. The designer asks certain questions about the script's and director's requirements: How will the director approach the play? Is there a concept? Where does the play take place? What is the play's historical period? How does the play proceed in time and seasons? What kinds of movements do the characters make? What elements from life are essential parts of the play's world? What is the play's spatial

A REAR ELEVATION A rear elevation is a two-dimensional drawing used for construction purposes. The elevation shows the overall dimensions of a unit of scenery from the back.

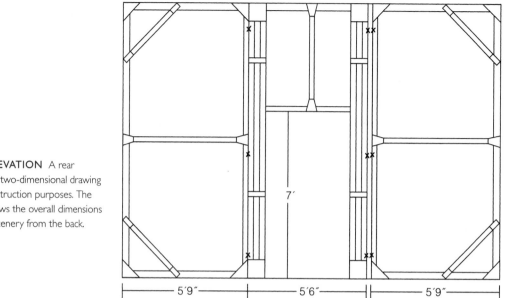

PAINTER'S ELEVATION The scenic artist, or scene painter—in nonprofessional theatres usually the designer—is a specialized artist who paints the scenery following painter's elevations and a model provided by the designer. The scene painter's art provides color, perspective, depth, shape, and texture.

relationship to the audience? Is it close up or far away? Are the play and the audience in the same space? How are character relationships expressed in the space? How much playing space is needed? Is the action to be violent or sedate? What is the play's mood? How many exits, properties, and essential pieces of furniture are needed?

As the designer visualizes the space, details are established in *sketches,* a *ground plan,* and a *model. Sketches* (or rough pencil drawings) are made in the early period when both the director and the designer are visualizing the stage floor and theatrical space. When their ideas reach some degree of concreteness, they confer and agree on the *ground plan:* the shape and dimensions of the playing area as seen from above with entrances, exits, and windows. The *model* is a small three-dimensional reproduction of the design, in scale, with movable cutouts for scenic pieces, furniture, and actors.

The designer also researches the play's historical period, background, and style, including architecture, furniture, and decor. Over the next weeks or even months, sketches, color chips or suggestions, and a three-dimensional model follow until the director and designer (and the producer) have arrived at the look, details, and costs of the scenery.

The designer, or an assistant, then prepares a $\frac{1}{2}$-inch scale model, front elevations (two-dimensional drawings outlining the scenic pieces as they appear to the eye), and paint elevations to give to the theatre's production manager, technical director, and shop foreman. The designer's drawings are then converted into technical drawings, showing how the scenic pieces are to be constructed, their dimensions, and materials.

Scenery is basically two- or three-dimensional, framed or unframed. It is built from technical drawings and moved onto the stage as scheduled. (This effort is commonly called "put-in.") The drawings detail the profile and outer dimensions of all scenic elements, showing where and how they function and the order in which they will appear onstage.

Scenery must be strong, portable, and dependable. As audiences look at the scenery from the house, they are usually not aware of types of scenery, how it fits together, how it is moved about during scene changes—unless the moving is done for theatrical effect.

Joan Marcus /Courtesy Arena Stage

ELEVATIONS FOR *K2* The elevations for this rock and ice face resembled a government geological survey map. Fifty thousand board feet of plastic foam were used to build the wall over a wooden frame armature. Finishing touches included an oil fog mist and nightly avalanche of snow from a theatrical supply house. (*K2* opened in 1982 at Arena Stage, Washington, D.C., and moved to Broadway.)

(continued on page 247)

Modern Stage Designs

Jo Mielziner's *A Streetcar Named Desire* and *Death of a Salesman* . Teo Otto's *Mother Courage and Her Children* . Josef Svoboda's *Oedipus the King* . John Lee Beatty's *The Heiress*

JO MIELZINER (1901–1976) pioneered, along with director Elia Kazan, "selective realism" in scenic design. Of his type of design Mielziner said: "If you eliminate nonessentials, you've got to be sure that the things you do put in are awfully good. They've got to be twice as good, because they stand alone to make a comment…. I got to feel that even realistic plays didn't need realistic settings necessarily."[5]

In the final scene of *A Streetcar Named Desire* (1947), Stanley Kowalski's friends play poker while Blanche DuBois (right) is taken away to an institution for the mentally ill. In the foreground are the selected realistic details of Mielziner's setting: living spaces on different levels, beds, tables, and chairs.

©Eileen Darby/Billy Rose Theatre Collection, The New York Public Library for the Performing Arts, Astor, Lenox and Tilden Foundations

Billy Rose Theatre Collection, The New York Public Library for the Performing Arts, Astor, Lenox and Tilden Foundations

For Arthur Miller's *Death of a Salesman* (1949), Mielziner designed the salesman's house on several levels (kitchen, sons' bedroom, porch, and forestage). The actors' movements with area lighting were the only scene-change devices. The large backdrop upstage was painted to show tenement buildings looming over Willy Loman's house in the play's present time. When lighted from the rear, the buildings washed out to be replaced with projections of trees with leaves, suggesting Willy's remembered past with its bright sunshine and cheerful ambience.

The Berliner Ensemble's 1949 production of Brecht's *Mother Courage and Her Children* in (former) East Berlin was originally designed by TEO OTTO. In this final scene, Mother Courage's wagon is the main set piece, which actress Helene Weigel as Courage, alone in the harness, pulls toward yet another war.

KaiDib Films International.

BERTOLT BRECHT'S favorite designers—Teo Otto, Caspar Neher, and Karl von Appen—did not create illusions of real places but provided background materials (projections on a rear cyclorama, placards, signs, and set pieces, like Mother Courage's wagon) that commented on the play's historical period and the characters' socioeconomic circumstances. The setting itself (the open theatrical space) was used to make the dramatic action and individuals appear strange or unfamiliar. Outwardly, they resembled little that was familiar in our daily lives. Brecht did not disguise the fact that all was taking place in a theatre under exposed lighting instruments, creating "white light," and before an audience.

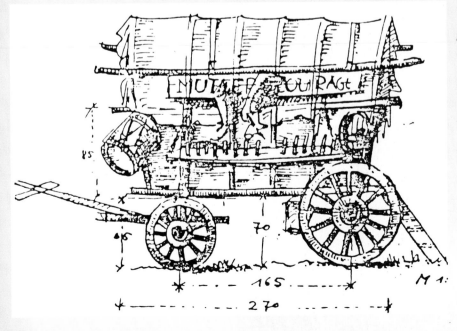

For the Berlin production of *Mother Courage and Her Children* at the Deutsches Theater in 1949, Brecht used the set model devised by TEO OTTO for the 1941 Zurich production. The wagon and movable screens were the main set pieces of the design.

JOSEF SVOBODA, chief designer at Prague's National Theatre in the Czech Republic and artistic head of Laterna
Magika, is Europe's most celebrated scenographer. He
makes highly imaginative use of an array of contemporary
technologies, including computerized slide and film projections, laser beams, moving platforms, plastics, and netting.
His trademark is the use of surfaces to project images
around the actor, creating what he calls "dramatic space" as
"psychoplastic." "The goal of the designer," Svoboda has
said, "can no longer be a description of a copy of actuality,
but the creation of its multidimensional model."[6]

Oedipus the King, designed by Josef
Svoboda and directed by Miroslav
Machacek at the National Theatre,
Prague, in 1963. The setting was a
vast flight of stairs, starting in the orchestra pit and reaching almost out of sight. The stairs were
punctuated by platforms that thrust out from the stairs themselves. The actor playing Oedipus
appears on a platform. "At the end Oedipus was left alone. Virtually all the flat levels disappeared.
He climbed an endless staircase made of acoustically `transparent' material (the orchestra was
located beneath the risers), into sharp counterlighting."

The Heiress, the 1995 Broadway revival of
the play by Ruth and Augustus Goetz,
directed by Gerald Gutierrez with sets by
JOHN LEE BEATTY and costumes by Jane
Greenwood. Beatty created an upper-class,
richly appointed 1850s parlor with large windows, chandeliers, lamps, fireplace, and staircase rising to the upper level of the large
house on Washington Square, New York.

THE COSTUME DESIGNER

Costume design has been compared by American designer Patricia Zipprodt to a car trip in which unpredictables of life pop up—unavailable fabric, the inadequate budget, the temperamental actor. The designer, like the car's driver, remains in a constant state of problem solving.

The Costume

Costumes include all the character's garments and accessories (purse, cane, jewelry, handkerchief), all items related to hairdressing, and everything associated with face and body makeup, including masks.

Costumes tell us many things about the characters and about the nature, mood, and style of the play. As visual signals, they add color, style, and meaning to the play's environment. Costumes establish period, social class, economic status, occupation, age, geography, weather, and time of day. They help to clarify the relationships and relative importance of various characters. Ornament, line, and color can tie together members of a family, group, faction, or party. Changes in costume can indicate alteration in relationships among characters or in a character's psychological outlook. Similarities or contrasts in costumes can show sympathetic or antagonistic relationships. Hamlet's black costume, for instance, is contrasted with the bright colors worn by the court and speaks eloquently of his altered attitude toward the court. Designer Lucinda Ballard's costumes for *A Streetcar Named Desire* express Blanche DuBois' self-image of Southern gentility. Jessica Tandy's costume for Blanche's evening with Mitch includes tasteful summer dress, pearls, hat, gloves, handbag, bracelet, and bouquet.

Years ago, the actor, manager, or person in charge of stage wardrobe was responsible for costumes. But in the last eighty years, the new stagecraft has required designers trained to select and control these visual elements with great attention to detail. Designers are involved in costume research and in sketching, preparing costume plates, assessing color choices, choosing fabric, and sometimes overseeing construction. Depending upon the size of the theatre's budget, there can be many assistants involved in cutting, sewing, fitting, and making shoes, boots, and accessories.

Today, costume design and construction have become a major industry. Professional designers work in film, fashion, theatre, opera, television, dance, commercials, and extravaganzas (ice shows, nightclubs, circuses, and dance revues). The large costume houses, such as Dodger Costumes, Ltd., and Broadway Costume Rental, Inc. (located in Queens, N.Y.), Western Costume Company (North Hollywood), Warner

COSTUME BY DESIGNER LUCINDA BALLARD
Blanche DuBois' famous party costume was created by Lucinda Ballard for the 1947 Broadway production of *A Streetcar Named Desire*. Tennessee Williams described the dress as a "somewhat soiled and crumpled white satin evening gown and a pair of scuffed silver slippers with brilliants set in the heels." Stanley Kowalski calls Blanche's dress "a worn-out Mardi Gras outfit." A rhinestone tiara, bracelet, and faded corsage completed the costume.

©Eileen Darby/Billy Rose Theatre Collection, The New York Public Library for the Performing Arts, Astor, Lenox and Tilden Foundations

The Image Makers: Designers　　**247**

Costume Designer

Patricia Zipprodt

Courtesy of Constance Zipprodt-Zonka.

Patricia Zipprodt (1925–1999) studied at Wellesley College (Mass.) and the Fashion Institute of Technology (New York City). She designed costumes for regional theatres as well as Broadway musicals and plays, including *Sunday in the Park with George* (with Ann Hould-Ward), *Brighton Beach Memoirs, Fiddler on the Roof, Cabaret, Zorba, Sweet Charity, 1776, The Little Foxes, Plaza Suite, Pippin, Chicago, Cat on a Hot Tin Roof,* and *Shogun.* She won nine Drama Desk Awards and was nominated for the Antoinette Perry ("Tony") Award ten times, winning three. She also designed costumes for opera, dance, and film: the Metropolitan Opera's acclaimed *Tannhäuser* and *The Barber of Seville,* Jerome Robbins' ballets *Les Noces* and *Dybbuk Variations,* and such films as *The Graduate* and *1776.* She was inducted into the Theatre Hall of Fame in 1992.

She was once overheard saying that "velcro" is the costume designer's favorite word.

Patricia Zipprodt's elaborate period costumes for Molière's *Don Juan* in the 1981 Guthrie Theater production, directed by Richard Foreman.

Bruce Goldstein/Courtesy Guthrie Theatre

Studios (Burbank, Calif.), and Malabar Ltd. (Toronto), rent and build costumes on demand. (They do not buy from closing Broadway and touring shows but accept donations instead.) The Costume Collection and Odds Costume Rental & Fur (both in New York City) do not build costumes but rent to nonprofit organizations like regional, community, and university theatres. A visit to these collections is not only

(continued on page 253)

Broadway Set and Costume Designers at Work

John Lee Beatty . **Bob Crowley** . **Jane Greenwood** . **William Ivey Long** . **John Napier** .
Ian MacNeil . **Martin Pakledinaz** . **Anthony Powell** . **Robin Wagner** . **Tony Walton**

© Joan Marcus

CAROUSEL The 1994 revival of Richard Rodgers and Oscar Hammerstein's musical *Carousel* at Lincoln Center Theater, New York City, directed by Nicholas Hytner. Sets and costumes for this production were designed by **Bob Crowley,** who used the theatre's large, open stage with colorful scenic pieces and background cyclorama to re-create Billy Bigelow's world of violence, love, and redemption.

SUNSET BOULEVARD The lavish scenery for the 1994 Andrew Lloyd Webber musical *Sunset Boulevard,* starring Glenn Close, was designed by **John Napier** with costumes by **Anthony Powell** and lights by Andrew Bridge.

© Joan Marcus

© Joan Marcus

AN INSPECTOR CALLS The 1994 revival of J. B. Priestley's play opened on London's West End and moved to Broadway with Rosemary Harris and Philip Bosco in the leading roles. The spectacular moving set, designed by **Ian MacNeil,** unfolds onstage to disclose a realistic interior and collapses at the play's end (below). Directed by Stephen Daldry with costumes by **Ian MacNeil.**

© Joan Marcus

Martha Swope/TimePix

THE SISTERS ROSENSWEIG The English living room set for Wendy Wasserstein's *The Sisters Rosensweig* was designed by **John Lee Beatty** with costumes by **Jane Greenwood** and lighting by Pat Collins. The 1993 production was directed by Daniel Sullivan.

KISS ME KATE The 1999 Broadway revival of the Cole Porter musical with book by Sam and Bella Spewack, featuring Marin Mazzie and Brian Stokes Mitchell. Set design by **Robin Wagner** and costume design by **Martin Pakledinaz.** Directed by Michael Blakemore.

© Joan Marcus

© Joan Marcus

AIDA **Bob Crowley** designed sets and costumes for this spectacular production of *Aida* with music and lyrics by Elton John and Tim Rice. The 2000 Broadway production was directed by Robert Falls.

*C*ostume *Designer*

Theoni V. Aldredge

Courtesy Theoni V. Aldredge

The final musical number of *A Chorus Line* (1975), conceived by Michael Bennett and costumed by Theoni V. Aldredge.

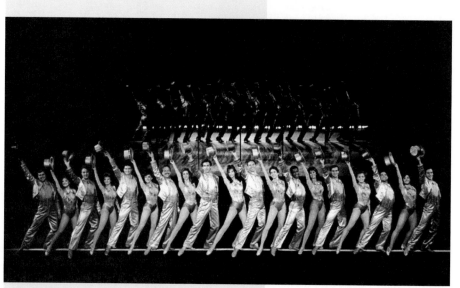

Martha Swope/TimePix

Theoni **V. Aldredge** (b. 1932), one of theatre's most gifted and respected designers, has produced more than 1,000 costumes and designed costumes for five hit musicals that ran simultaneously on Broadway: *A Chorus Line, 42nd Street, Dreamgirls, La Cage aux Folles,* and *The Rink.* She designed costumes for other Broadway shows, including *Nick and Nora, The Secret Garden, Annie Warbucks, The Flowering Peach, Putting It Together,* and *Annie.* She begins her creative process by studying the characters and the cast of any given production: "To me, good design is design you're not aware of. It must exist as part of the whole—as an aspect of characterization. Also, a designer must be flexible and extremely patient…. A performance will suffer if an actor doesn't love his costume, and it's your job to make him love it."

For *A Chorus Line,* the story of a Broadway audition, Aldredge closely observed the personalities of the dancers and singers and the outfits they wore to rehearsals. Of this long-running musical, conceived and directed by Michael Bennett, she said: "I took millions of snapshots of what the kids came in wearing, and adapted what they had on for my costumes. I didn't depart too much, because it's what made each of them so unique. The only real transformation came with the golden chorus line at the end of the show, which, incidentally, Michael had wanted it to be a red chorus line. But I felt red was too definite a color. I thought it should be a fantasy number. I told him it ought to be the color of champagne—of celebration—and that's what we did."[7]

Costume Designer

Jane Greenwood and William Ivey Long

Courtesy Jane Greenwood

Jane Greenwood (b. 1934 in Liverpool, England) is one of the American theatre's premier costume designers. She designed her first professional costumes at the Oxford Playhouse (England) and worked in Canada at the Stratford (Ontario) Festival for three seasons. In New York City she made her Broadway debut in 1963 with *The Ballad of the Sad Café*. Her many Broadway credits include *The Prime of Miss Jean Brodie, California Suite, The Last Night of Ballyhoo, Master Class, Passion, Same Time Next Year, The Scarlet Pimpernel,* and *James Joyce's The Dead.* She has designed off Broadway and in regional theatres, and her costumes are seen in such films as *Arthur, The Four Seasons, 84 Charing Cross,* and *Glengarry Glen Ross.* She has designed for the Alvin Ailey and Martha Clarke dance companies and the world premiere of the opera *The Great Gatsby.* Her many awards include twelve Antoinette Perry "Tony" Award nominations, the Irene Sharaff Award for Lifetime Achievement, the ACE Award, and the American Theatre Wing Design Award. She teaches costume design at the Yale University School of Drama.

William Ivey Long (b. 1947) studied history at The College of William and Mary College (Va.) and set and costume design at the Yale University School of Drama. His costume designs for *Nine* and *Crazy for You* received Antoinette Perry "Tony" Awards. His design credits include musical revivals of *Chicago, 1776, Smokey Joe's Cafe, Guys and Dolls, Cabaret, Annie Get Your Gun, The Music Man, Contact, Seussical, Swing!,* and *The Producers.* He designed costumes for Siegfied and Roy, Rolling Stones, and for the Peter Martins, Paul Taylor, and Twyla Tharp dance companies.

Jane Wexler/Courtesy of William Ivey Long

an exciting adventure in itself, but also serves as a tour through the history of theatrical design.

The Designer's Process

Set and costume designers work with directors to make visible the world in which the play's characters live. They explore verbally and with rough sketches many different approaches and ideas that might bring that world into theatrical focus onstage. Designers reinforce with concrete visual elements the director's concepts and, in

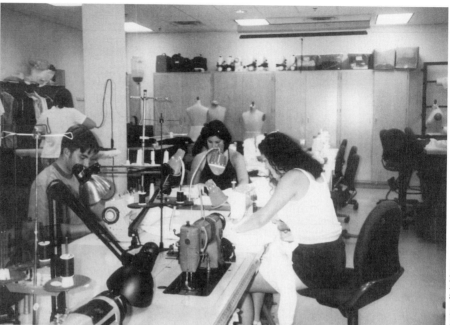

A COSTUME SHOP CONSTRUCTS A SHOW The costume technician's tools—industrial sewing machines and irons, work tables, dress forms, movable racks, and storage cabinets—are available in the modern costume shop. (Photo courtesy of Judy Adamson, Costume Director, PlayMakers Repertory Company, Chapel Hill).

so doing, often inspire the director to think in a different way about the play. Award-winning designer Theoni V. Aldredge says about costumes: "The costumes are there to serve a producer's vision, a director's viewpoint, and an actor's comfort."

Like the director and the scene designer, the costume designer begins by studying the script and taking note of the story, mood, characterization, visual effects, colors, atmosphere, geography, period, and season. Then the designer asks the practical questions: How many costumes (including changes) and accessories are required? What is the costume budget? What actors have been cast? What stage actions, such as fighting, will affect the construction or wear of the costumes?

The Design Conference

The overall plan of the production is worked out in design conferences. The costume designer brings sketches, color plates, costume charts, accessory lists, and fabric swatches to these meetings to make his or her visual concept clear to the director and scene designer. The costume designer must be specific to avoid later misunderstandings and costly last-minute changes.

Sometimes a brilliant costume design develops through trial and error. While designing the costumes for the Broadway production of the musical *Pippin*, Patricia Zipprodt and director Bob Fosse had difficulty deciding on the right look for the strolling players. The musical is performed by a group of actors costumed as some kind of theatrical caravan, who relate the story of Charlemagne's eldest son, Pippin,

Costume Construction

Barbara Matera

© John-Francis Bourke

Barbara Matera's list of shows constructed in her shop reads like a history of the contemporary American theatre. Born in England, Matera learned her craft by first studying art and then working as a junior designer, draper, and cutter. She joined the costume shop at the Stratford Festival in Canada and then moved to New York City, where in 1967 Barbara and Arthur Matera founded the most venerable of New York City's costume construction shops—Barbara Matera Ltd.

Over the years, Matera's has created costumes for theatre, opera, dance, and film; for designers Theoni V. Aldredge, Tony Walton, Irene Sharaff, Raoul Pene du Bois, Patricia Zipprodt, and Santo Loquasto; and for such shows as *A Funny Thing Happened on the Way to the Forum, Grand Hotel, Beauty and the Beast,* and *Aida.*

---

an idealist journeying through courts, battles, and love's intrigues. The script said, "Enter strolling players of an indeterminate period." Zipprodt remembers:

> Now, to me, this meant exactly nothing. I did a lot of sketches, which everybody seemed to like. On the day I was supposed to present finished sketches, time ran short. Instead of fully coloring the costumes of the strolling players as was planned and expected, I just painted beige and off-white washes so that Fosse could read the sketches more easily. I put the whole group of 14 or 15 in front of him and was just about to apologize for not getting the color done when he said, "That's just brilliant, exactly the colors they should be. How clever of you." The minute he said it, I knew he was right.[8]

But more often, the final designs are selected after numerous alternatives have been explored.

Costume Construction

After approving the sketches and plans, the director turns full attention to rehearsals, and the costume designer arranges for construction, purchase, or rental of costumes, and schedules measurements and fittings with the actors. If the costumes are being constructed in the theatre's shop (as is most often the case in college, university, and resident theatres), actors are measured, patterns cut, dyeing and painting of fabric done, garments constructed, and accessories built or purchased. After several individual fittings with the actors, the costumes are ready for the *dress parade,* during

CATS The "cats" in the musical wore costumes and makeup designed by John Napier and wigs designed by Paul Huntley.

Martha Swope/TimePix

which designer and director examine the costumes on the actors before the dress rehearsal begins.

To accomplish this work, the professional designer will have assistant designers, shop supervisors, cutters, drapers, seamstresses, wigmakers, milliners, and other assistants to cut, sew, dye, and make hats, footwear, and wigs. Often in small costume shops this personnel doubles up on the responsibilities. In the New York theatre, the construction of costumes is jobbed out to such businesses as Barbara Matera Ltd., where designs are turned into costumes and delivered to the Broadway companies.

Dress Rehearsal and Wardrobe Personnel

The dress parade and dress rehearsal (where costumes, makeup, and masks are worn onstage with full scenery and lights) usually take place a week before opening night. It is not unusual to discover that the color of a fabric doesn't work under the lights or against the scenery. In this event, the designer may redesign the garment, select another fabric or color (or both), and have the costume reconstructed or dyed almost overnight and ready for the next rehearsal or opening performance.

Once costumes and accessories are finished, the costumes leave the shop and the wardrobe crew takes charge of them during dress rehearsals and performances. Their responsibility is to mend, press, clean, and maintain the costumes for the length of the play's run. Although in the professional theatre there is a clear-cut division between these two groups, in college and university theatres the construction and wardrobe crews may be many of the same people.

Before dress rehearsals begin, the wardrobe supervisor (long ago called the wardrobe master or mistress), or crew head, makes a list of the costumes and accessories worn by each actor. These lists are used by crew members and actors to check that each costume is complete before each performance. The wardrobe "running" crew helps each actor dress and make quick changes and is responsible for costumes before, during, and after each performance. Wardrobe routines are established during the dress rehearsal period and are strictly followed during production. The crew is also responsible for "striking" the costumes when the production closes. Costumes are cleaned, laundered, and returned to the rental houses or placed in storage along with accessories, such as hats, wigs, handbags, shoes, and jewelry.

MAKEUP, MASKS, WIGS & HAIR

Makeup

Makeup enhances the actor and completes the costume. It is essential to the actor's visibility. In a large theatre, distance and lighting makes an actor's features without makeup colorless and indistinct. Like the costume, makeup helps the actor reveal character by giving physical clues to age, background, ethnicity, health, personality, and environment.

In the ancient Asian and Greek theatres, actors used a white-lead makeup with heavy accents, or linen or cork masks. Today, basic makeup consists of a foundation and color shadings to prevent the actor from looking "washed out" beneath the glare of the stage lights. Pancake makeup has replaced greasepaint, or oil-base makeup, as the foundation for the actor's basic skin color. Cake makeup—less messy and more flexible than greasepaint—comes in small plastic cases like everyday makeup and is applied with a damp sponge. Color shadings with rouge, lipstick, liners, mascara, and powder are applied with pencils and brushes. A well-equipped makeup kit (which can be purchased inexpensively from theatrical-supply houses) includes standard foundations and shading colors plus synthetic hair, glue, solvents, wax, and hair whiteners.

Straight, Character, and Fantasy Makeup

Makeup is classified as *straight* and *character*. Straight makeup highlights an actor's normal features and coloring for distinctness and visibility. Character makeup transforms the actor's features to reveal age or attitude. Noses, wrinkles, eyelashes, jawlines, eyepouches, eyebrows, teeth, hair, and beards can be added to change the actor's appearance. Character (sometimes called *illustrative*) makeup can make a young actor look older, can give the actor playing Cyrano his huge, bulbous nose, and can transform Laurence Olivier into Othello the Moor. When misused, makeup can destroy the actor's characterization by giving an external look that conflicts with the character's inner life. The actor must know, then, the basics of makeup as an art and how to work with hair and wigs.

Makeup is applied by the actor. In fantasy productions, such as the musicals *Cats* and *Beauty and the Beast,* makeup, hair, wigs, and masks are the final responsibility of the designer.

How does the actor make up? There is no substitute for practice with a basic makeup kit; every actor comes to know his or her face in a new way as soon as practice begins. Each face is different, catching and reflecting light in a different way. Each character presents a new set of challenges in which pancake makeup, rouge, liners, mascara, false eyelashes, wigs, facial hair (usually made from crepe wool), nose putty, and various prosthetic materials for aging, scarring, and disfiguring the skin's appearance are used to accent the character's expressions and attitudes. For this reason, actors should apply their own makeup, since actors know best the expressions, lines, and shadows their characters use.

MODERN MASKS IN _LES ATRIDES_
The chorus of baboon-faced dogs with pointed snouts are costumed in masks designed by Erhard Stiefel for _The Eumenides_, the final part of Ariane Mnouchkine's production of _Les Atrides_ (Paris, 1992).

Masks

Ancient and Modern Masks

In the early theatre, masks had many uses. They enlarged the actor's facial features so that the character's image would be apparent at great distances. The Greek masks expressed basic emotions: grief, anger, horror, sadness, pity. But most important for us today, the masked actor creates an altogether different _presence_ onstage than the actor without a mask. Although a masked actor may lose something in subtlety of expression, the presence of the actor-with-mask can be stately, heroic, awesome, or

THE _COMMEDIA DELL'ARTE_ MASK All characters in Italian _commedia_, with the exception of the young lovers, wore masks. Unlike classical masks and those of China and Japan, commedia masks did not express any particular emotion like joy or sorrow. Instead, they gave a permanent expression to the character, such as cunning or avarice. The mask's expressiveness varied with the angle from which it was seen.

Pantalone, one of the chief _commedia_ characters, was a miserly merchant. His mask, brown with a hooked nose, gray, sparse moustache, and pointed white beard, has a fixed expression of crafty greed.

Illustration of Pantalone from Jacques Callot's etchings, c. 1622, of commedia actor

©Joan Marcus

THE GREEN BIRD Director/designer Julie Taymor designed the bird puppet and masks for *The Green Bird* (Broadway 2000) based on an eighteenth-century Italian play by Carlo Gozzi, who championed *commedia dell'arte* traditions.

mysterious; the actor may move the audience simply by standing onstage and reflecting light. Nor is the masked actor totally deprived of the facial subtlety available to the actor whose facial muscles move and change expression. By changing the mask's position (if the mask is made with this effect in mind), by angling the head and catching the light, different emotional responses can be evoked.

Mask-making is an ancient art dating from early cultures where masks were objects of fear; they were thought to have supernatural powers. Masks have been used in the Greek and Roman theatres, by the *commedia dell'arte* in Renaissance Italy, in Japanese Noh, and in the modern theatre. In addition to an artful exterior, a mask must be comfortable, strong, light, and molded to the contours of the actor's face. Today, in colleges and some regional theatres, the costume designer creates the masks as part of the costume, designing for color, durability, and expressiveness.

Wig & Hair Design

The creation of theatrical wigs starts with a meeting between the wig designer (or maker) and the costume designer to determine the needs and style of hair and wigs. This meeting is followed by another with the costume designer and actor during which measurements of the actor's head are taken using a plastic cap. A discussion of color

A MODERN *COMMEDIA* MASK This modern mask was designed for Théâtre du Soleil's production of *L'Age d'Or* (Paris, 1975).

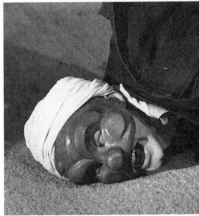

© Martine Franck/Magnum Photos, Inc.

Wig and Hair Designer

Paul Huntley

Courtesy Paul Huntley Enterprise

Paul Huntley, whose career as a wigmaker spans thirty years, started out as an actor in England. He developed an interest in theatrical hair, wigs, and makeup and went to work for Wig Creations, where he learned the history and traditions of hairstyles throughout the ages. "It's really very good for the wigmaker to know about dressing hair," he said, "… you start as a wig-maker and then you become a hair-dresser. In other words, you learn to *address* the hair."[9]

Huntley came to New York City in 1971 to make wigs for director Mike Nichols' film *Carnal Knowledge.* He then launched a Broadway, film, and television career that includes wigs and hair for *Cats, Nine, Amadeus, My Fair Lady, 42nd Street, Evita, Dreamgirls, Once Upon a Mattress, Kiss Me, Kate, Jekyll and Hyde, The Scarlet Pimpernel, Chicago, Cabaret,* and *Contact.*

While the wigs for *Amadeus* and *Jekyll and Hyde* are stylized, Huntley prefers designing "natural wigs," like the wig he created for Mia Farrow in the Woody Allen film *Broadway Danny Rose.*

PAUL HUNTLEY'S WIGS AND HAIR FOR *CATS* The yak-hair wigs for *Cats* were first ventilated and then dyed. Additional, bolder coloring was required for some wigs to stand out under the theatrical lighting.

Martha Swope/TimePix

follows along with an understanding of what happens with the character during the play. Will a hat be worn, for example? Will the hair be let down for a bedroom scene?

The base of the wig is then made of lace, the hair is prepared, and the next step is to "ventilate" the wig (or knot the strands of hair in place). Designer Paul Huntley says that a good wig has very little hair, which gives it better balance and is lighter on the head.

In the second and final fitting with the actor, the wig is styled. A third is called only if major alterations are needed.

TRANSITION

All good theatrical design enhances the actor's presence and supports the director's interpretation of that world—developing, visualizing, illuminating, and enriching it. Lighting and sound designers complete the roster of theatrical designers and find support for their endeavors among the theatre's production personnel and technology.

WEB SITES

The Costume Gallery's Research Library

A central location to study costume and fashion.

http://costumegallery.com/research.htm

Costume Institute of the Metropolitan Museum of Art, New York City

The Costume Institute houses more than 75,000 costumes and accessories covering seven centuries and five continents. The holdings include dress accessories (hats, shoes, gloves, buttons), eighteenth-century men's wear, twentieth-century haute couture, and contemporary fashions.

http://www.metmuseum.org/collections/index.asp?dep=8

The Costumer's Manifesto

Advice on "how to."

http://www.costumes.org/

The Costume Site—Online Costuming Sources for Historical, Science Fiction, and Fantasy Costumers

http://milieux.com/costume/costume1.html

Entertainment Design: The Art and Technology of Show Business

Formerly *Theatre Crafts;* contains Designer Profiles.

http://www.etecnyc.net

Masks.org

Digital library devoted to masks.

http://masks.org/index.htm

Museum of the City of New York

The Theatre Collection covers theatrical activity in New York City from the late eighteenth century to the present day. The Collection includes original scenery and costume renderings, elevations, and set models by such notable designers as Jo Mielziner, Robert Edmond Jones, and Patricia Zipprodt; original scripts by Eugene O'Neill and others; more than 5,000 costumes and props; significant drawings and photographs; and a major Yiddish Theatre collection.

The Costume and Textiles Collection includes Broadway Theatre Costumes and all aspects of New York City costume history, including clothing and inaugural gowns.

http://www.mcny.org/theater.htm

United Scenic Artists, L.U. 829

The union for designers and artists for the entertainment industry with links to web pages displaying their works.

http://www.usa829.org

United States Institute for Theatre Technology

The association of design, production, and technology professionals in the performing arts and entertainment industry.

http://www.usitt.org

These search terms are provided to assist you in exploring the topics introduced in this chapter at:

http//www.infotrac-college.com

scenic design, expressionistic scenic design, realism in scenic design, perspective painting, scenography, costume design, costume construction, costume rental companies, fantasy makeup, masks, mask-making, wig-making, *commedia dell'arte,* historic costume collections.

©T. Charles Erickson/Hartford Stage

The Image Makers: The Designers
Lighting, Sound, and Computer Technologies

In today's theatre, lighting, sound, and computer technologies affect what we see, how we see, how we hear, how we feel, and often what we understand. As areas of theatrical design, lighting and sound along with the new "machines" are essential to the modern stage's theatrical effectiveness.

THE LIGHTING DESIGNER

Stage lighting is a powerful theatrical tool to focus an audience's attention, to enhance their understanding, and to give aesthetic pleasure. It is sometimes surprising to learn that the "lighting" designer emerged in the theatre well before the invention of electricity.

Background

The Greeks called their theatres "seeing places." These were outdoor theatres and performances took place chiefly during daylight hours, but they were not without some attention to lighting effects. Playwrights, who were also the earliest directors, called for dramatic effects with torches, fires, and even sunlight. Aeschylus in *Agamemnon,* which tells the story of the King's return at the close of the Trojan War, begins with a Watchman standing atop the palace to watch for beacons shining from distant mountaintops that will signal Agamemnon's return to Argos. Most interpreters think that the Watchman's speech begins virtually in the early morning mist and that his recognition of the signal flames coincides with the actual sunrise over the stage house in the Theatre of Dionysus. Certainly, the effect would be spectacular. Since the plays lasted throughout the day, it is also logical that the red rays of sunset in the Attic sky could

Lighting Designer

Jennifer Tipton

Courtesy of Jennifer Tipton

Stage lighting controls what we see and often what we hear. Jennifer Tipton's lighting design for the 1977 production of *Agamemnon* at Lincoln Center Theater, New York City, creates a somber atmosphere while directing attention to the bodies of Agamemnon and Cassandra lying before the palace doors.

George E. Joseph

have simulated the destructive flames of the burning Troy, or even the cessation of military or personal struggles in the last rays of sunlight.

Again, in the medieval outdoor theatres, torches, cauldrons of flame and smoke, and reflecting metals focused the surrounding audience's attention on important events in the Biblical stories. As productions of morality plays during the late Middle Ages moved indoors within manor houses and public halls, oil lamps, candles, and reflecting colored glass provided illumination and effects.

By the Renaissance, Italian painters and architects in Italy and France created general illumination with tallow or wax candles in chandeliers and wall sconces, and spectacular effects with oil lamps, panes of colored glass illuminated from behind, colored lanterns, transparent veils of cloth, along with the astonishing outdoor display of fireworks to climax festival events in Florence or Versailles with incendiary brilliance.

Between 1660 and 1800 in England, the general practice was to light the onstage candles before the curtain opened and to snuff them out when the play ended. Chandeliers above the auditorium remained lighted from start to finish. Diarist Samuel Pepys in the mid-seventeenth century complained of candle wax dripping onto spectators and of the candlelight hurting his eyes. There were other inventions, such as footlights, around 1672. The Argand, or "patent" oil lamp, in 1785 produced a brighter and steadier light and superseded the use of candles. But the invention of gaslight in the early nineteenth century, followed shortly thereafter by the development of electricity, completely transformed the theatrical experience.

Jennifer Tipton, born 1937 in Columbus, Ohio, grew up in Knoxville, Tennessee, where she briefly studied dance with Martha Graham and José Limón. A graduate of Cornell University, she eventually found her way with the help of designer Thomas Skelton into a career as a lighting designer for choreographers Paul Taylor, Robert Joffrey, Jerome Robbins, and Twyla Tharp.

Beginning in the late sixties, she worked consistently as a lighting designer for regional theatres, for dance and opera companies, and on Broadway. In 1976 she won the Drama Desk Award for lighting design in Ntozake Shange's *for colored girls who have considered suicide/when the rainbow is enuf* and Antoinette Perry "Tony" Awards for *The Cherry Orchard* at Lincoln Center in 1977 and for *Jerome Robbins' Broadway* in 1989. She designed lighting for Robert Wilson's *the CIVIL warS* at the American Repertory Theatre, Cambridge, Massachusetts, and for the 1997 revival of Eugene O'Neill's *The Hairy Ape,* starring Willem Dafoe, for the Wooster Group, New York City. In 1989, she again received the Drama Desk Award for lighting design in *Jerome Robbins' Broadway, Long Day's Journey into Night,* and *Waiting for Godot.* In 1991 she made her directing debut at the Guthrie Theater, Minneapolis, with *The Tempest.* She teaches lighting design at the Yale School of Drama in New Haven, Connecticut.

Tipton's use of light is characterized by "textured and sculptured space" and by use of a palette based on white. She summarizes the essence of the lighting designer's art by saying, "While 99.9 percent of an audience is not aware of light, 100 percent is affected by it."

First, the ease and flexibility of control with gas lighting provided for the first time general illumination on American and European stages rather than simply showy or spectacular effects. An operator at a "gas table," very much like a modern control board, could adjust a valve and increase or decrease the intensity of light, or even control all of the lights. Gas lighting had its drawbacks, not the least of which were unpleasant fumes, intense heat, and the danger of live flame on stage, which not infrequently resulted in the burning down of such theatres as Drury Lane in London. In addition, the heat, smoke, and carbon pollution from gaslights caused the deterioration of scenery and costumes, and affected the eyes of actors and spectators alike. Thomas Edison's invention of the incandescent lamp in 1879 was almost immediately adopted as the means of lighting the entire stage. It was an answered prayer to end the disastrous theatre fires caused by open gas flames.

Electricity transformed overall possibilities for lighting design in the theatre. It made possible complete control of a range of intensities and colors; it provided the ability to lighten or darken different areas of the stage; it provided a source of mood for the actor and atmosphere for the play; and it also made possible spectacular effects. London's Savoy Theatre in 1881 was the first to be fully lighted with electricity.

Enter the modern lighting designer. At the turn of the twentieth century, Swiss designer Adolphe Appia understood the artistic possibilities of lighting for the theatre. In *Music and Stage Setting* he argued that light should be the guiding principle of all design and set down modern stage lighting practices. He believed that light

A view of a control booth with computerized control consoles and monitors.

©Richard Feldman

could unify or bring into harmony all production elements, including two- and three-dimensional objects, actors, and inanimate objects, shapes, and things. Appia established light as an artistic medium for the theatre and defined the role of the modern lighting designer.

The Art of Light

Designer Jean Rosenthal (1912–1969) defined lighting design as "imposing quality on the scarcely visible air through which objects and people are seen." One rule of lighting maintains that *visibility* and *ambience* (the surrounding atmosphere) must be inherent to the total theatrical design, including scenery and costumes. The light designer's tools, other than the instruments themselves, are form (the shape of the lighting's pattern), color (the mood achieved by filters—thin, transparent sheets of colored plastic, gelatin, or glass—or by varying degrees of intensity, or by both), and movement (the changes of

DESIGNER'S LIGHT PLOT A light plot created by designer Robert Wierzel for *The Cherry Orchard* illustrates the positioning of 250 instruments around three sides of the thrust stage, as well as the overhead chandelier and backlighting behind the rear doorways. Wierzel's design for PlayMakers Repertory Company, Chapel Hill. Producing director Milly S. Barranger.

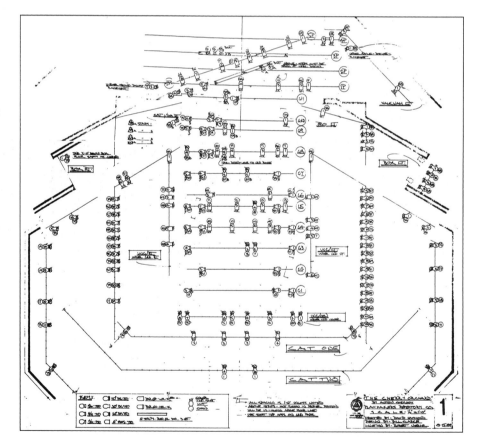

forms and color by means of dimmers, motorized instruments, and computerized control consoles).

The Designer's Process

The lighting designer's first step in the design process is to read the script and meet with the director followed by meetings with set and costume designers. In these conferences there are basic questions to be answered. What degree of reality does the director want to suggest? Where are the important scenes, or areas, within the set? What restrictions are there? What forms, moods, color patterns, and movements are required by the play and director? Are special effects needed?

Armed with information about the production, the designer drafts a *light plot,* which is basically a map showing the shape of the stage and auditorium, as seen from above, with the location of the lighting instruments to be used, including type, size, wattage, wiring, and connection to appropriate dimmers or circuits. There are no set rules. Any particular instrument may or may not be used in any location. The only limitations in lighting design are those imposed by the director, by the physical nature of the theatre, by the theatre's available technology, and by safety concerns.

The Designer's Working Methods

Plotting, Focusing, and Cueing

It often takes weeks to transfer successfully the designer's light plot from paper to the stage. A finished light plot shows: (1) the location of each lighting instrument to be used; (2) the type of instrument, wattage, and color filter; (3) the general area to be lighted by each instrument; (4) circuitry necessary to operate the instruments; and (5) any other details necessary for the operation of the lighting system. For example, if a wall fixture is needed onstage so that an actor can "turn on" a light, or an overhead chandelier is required, the position and circuitry of the fixtures are shown on the light plot.

Once the lights specified by the designer are hung in the theatre, they are then focused, that is, pointed in a precise direction to illuminate areas, actors, or objects. Hundreds of instruments of different types and wattages as well as colored gels and dimmers may be necessary to achieve the desired effects in production. During technical rehearsals, the lighting will be fine-tuned to account for the changing presence of the actors, the costumes, and the scenery.

After the instruments are hung, circuited, angled, and focused, the lighting designer is ready to "cue" the show. A handwritten or computer-generated cue sheet (or chart of the control console indicating

LIGHTING FOR *THE CHERRY ORCHARD* Robert Wierzel designed the lighting for this production of Chekhov's *The Cherry Orchard* for a thrust stage with set design by Bill Clarke. In this scene, the house is open, window shades raised, and the lighted chandelier indicates that it is evening.

Courtesy Bill Clarke Designs

Jennifer Tipton says that the directors who have meant the most to her are the ones who have stimulated her to use darkness. Andrei Serban who directed the revival of Chekhov's The Cherry Orchard for which Tipton won her first Antoinette Perry "Tony" Award insisted on "darkness." He said, "No, darker, darker, darker, darker." "And it got very dark, so people were almost invisible," Tipton said, "which made voices ring out even more clearly than when the lights were on. The fact that he [Serban] had made me go that dark at that moment meant that the whole composition over time changed…. Because the darkness was there, the brightness had to be brighter, and there had to be other darker moments. Serban didn't tell me to do that. I just did it. It had to be. Any one thing you do, any change you make, affects everything in the whole production."[2]

instrument settings and color with each cue numbered and keyed to the script) is provided in advance to the operators at the control console. During technical rehearsals, the designer asks for various intensities of light and makes changes until satisfied. With each change of lighting, a notation (the light cue) is made that tells how to set the control board and at what point in the stage action to change intensity and color. In the past, these changes were performed manually during each performance. Computers now permit changes to happen smoothly, and light cues for the entire show to be programmed. All is done in consultation with the director.

Special Lighting Effects

Special lighting effects range from the simple to the complex, from mirror balls, searchlights, and lightning to projections, holograms, fireworks, and Tinkerbell's moving light in *Peter Pan*. The plan, budget, and rehearsal with equipment and staff are essential to preparing special effects. The most frequently seen special effects relate to the use of *gobos* (a slide inserted into the gate of a spotlight) to project images of trees, clouds, water, windows, abstract shapes, and so forth; rear projections to throw images on backdrops and screens; color wheels to produce changing color effects; twinkling star effects on backcloths; and moon effects perfected in the Victorian theatre with a box with lights inside. More complicated and costly effects are related to projections, holograms, and lasers.

Commercial devices can be purchased to achieve most effects but require designers and technicians to ensure that they are credible, effective, and safe.

Both lighting and sound designers are usually involved to perfect explosions, fireworks, and sudden apparitions of Shakespeare's ghosts and witches. Today's effects in the theatre and film are notable for their emotional impact on audiences rather than, with some exceptions, the quantity of the "magic."

The Designer's Assistants

The professional lighting designer usually has an assistant designer to help prepare sketches and light plots, compile instrument schedules, act as liaison with the theatre's stage electrician and other technicians, and locate special equipment. The assistant designer also aids in supervising the installation of the instruments, compiling cue sheets, and programming the light design.

Courtesy Will Owens/Playmakers Repertory Company

DEATH OF A SALESMAN A revival of Arthur Miller's *Death of a Salesman* with Judd Hirsch and Eva Marie Saint, directed by Jeffrey Hayden with lighting by Mary Louise Geiger, PlayMakers Repertory Company, Chapel Hill. Producing director Milly S. Barranger, 1994.

Lighting Designers

Jules Fisher, Peggy Eisenhauer, and Tharon Musser

©Peter Simon

Jules Fisher and **Peggy Eisenhauer** are among the American theatre's leading lighting designers. Educated at Pennsylvania State University and Carnegie Institute of Technology, Fisher (b. 1937) has designed lighting for Broadway's *Hair, Pippin, Jesus Christ Superstar, Chicago, La Cage aux Folles,* and *Grand Hotel,* among others. Since 1986, he and Ms. Eisenhauer (educated at Carnegie-Mellon University) have designed numerous productions jointly including *Victor Victoria, Ragtime, Jane Eyre,* and *Bring in 'da Noise, Bring in 'da Funk,* for which they received the Antoinette Perry "Tony" Award. Ms. Eisenhauer also designed the lighting for the recent revival of *Cabaret.* In the music industry, her concert production designs have been seen internationally in twenty-six countries.

Jules Fisher provided the lighting design and production supervision for the 1975 *Rolling Stones* Tour. Today he is a principal of a theatrical consulting firm, Fisher Dachs Associates, and also partner in an architectural lighting firm, Fisher Marantz Stone.

Tharon Musser (b. 1925) is another influential lighting designer. A graduate of Berea College, Kentucky, and the Yale University School of Drama, she, like Jean Rosenthal and Jennifer Tipton, did most of her early lighting work for dance companies. Her Broadway career began in 1956 with José Quintero's production of *Long Day's Journey into Night,* and since 1971, she has designed the lighting for all of Neil Simon's Broadway productions. She is credited with lighting more than 125 Broadway productions, receiving three Antoinette Perry "Tony" Awards. She is most renowned for her collaborative work on *A Chorus Line* with Michael Bennett (director and choreographer), Robin Wagner (scene designer), and Theoni V. Aldredge (costume designer), which became one of the longest running productions to appear on Broadway. Other Broadway works include *Mame, Follies, A Little Night Music, 42nd Street, Dream Girls,* and *Laughter on the 23rd Floor.*

Courtesy of Tharon Musser, Lighting Designer

Most theatres have a master electrician on staff (or a lighting crew head) who works closely with the designer when equipment is installed and instruments adjusted. This individual oversees safety issues, checks and maintains equipment before each performance, and deals with all lighting issues during the run. In the professional theatre, the master electrician and lighting crew are members of the International Alliance of Theatrical Stage Employees union (IATSE). In the nonprofessional theatre, crews are usually made up of students and volunteers.

(continued on page 272)

Lighting Instruments, Control Consoles, and Accessories

Ellipsoidals . Fresnels . Follow Spotlights . Striplights . Control Consoles . LCD Displays and Monitors . Dimmer Racks

FRESNEL The fresnel produces a short throw, soft-edged beam of light that varies in diameter from 4.2 feet to 21 feet at a throw distance of 15 feet. The fresnel is used in theatres for acting areas where beam shaping is not required, in television studios for back lighting, or in museums where soft edge controlled lighting is required.

ELLIPSOIDAL Fixed focus ellipsoidal instruments provide a sharp projection of light. The low wattage, high output elipsoidals (called "lekos") are found in theatres, night clubs, and television studios.

Photos courtesy of Altman Lighting, Inc.

FOLLOWSPOT The rugged, long throw followspot produces a narrow hard or soft edge beam at distances of 150 feet. The instrument is used in any situation where manual control of a lighting beam is required to follow a performer and to vary beam size, quality, and color.

STRIPLIGHTS Striplights and borderlights are used when a general wash of light is needed, but the available space is small. Each compartment holds lamps and is fitted with filter frames for color.

Courtesy of High End Systems

Courtesy of High End Systems

LIGHTING CONTROL CONSOLES The light plot, fixtures, groups, palettes, and multiple cues can be programmed into the computerized control console. The two touch screens, key pad and function buttons provide ease in control of conventional and moving lighting, enter levels and times, and edit cues or palettes. Designers and technicians control moving lights with keystrokes, modify groups of lights, or access special effects for stage, television, concert events, and theme parks.

Courtesy of Leviton, NSI-Colortran Division

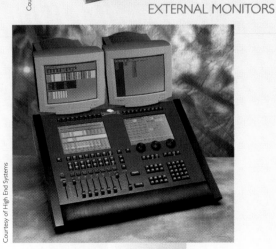

Courtesy of Leviton, NSI-Colortran Division

CONSOLES WITH EXTERNAL MONITORS

DIMMER BAYS WITH POWER PATCH BAY The rolling rack dimmer system makes for mobility and ease of placement in small spaces. This unit provides two dimmer bays and one power patch bay to support 96 dimmers.

Courtesy of High End Systems

The Image Makers: The Designers

CAROUSEL The revival of Richard Rodgers' and Oscar Hammerstein's *Carousel* was directed by Nicholas Hytner with sets and costumes by Bob Crowley, lighting by Paul Pyant, and sound by Steve Canyon Kennedy. Presented by Lincoln Center Theater, New York City, 1994.

In all types of theatres, the lighting crew installs, operates, and generally maintains all lighting equipment and shifts any electrical equipment that must be moved during performance. The control board operator executes the lighting cues during performances and maintains the designer's work. All backstage technicians are responsible to the production stage manager during performance.

Successful stage lighting complements and unifies the whole without calling attention to itself unless for special effects, for example, or to give greater emphasis to a stage area, or to illuminate the ghost of Hamlet's father. It contributes to the play's interpretation with visibility and ambience—controlling what we see (and even hear) and how we see what is taking place onstage.

THE SOUND DESIGNER

The Art of Theatrical Sound

Sound has always been a part of the theatrical event. In earliest times, music (pipes, drums, lyres), choral chanting, and actors' voices provided the chief sound effects. Until the use of disc recordings in the 1950s and more recently CDs, all sound effects in the theatre were produced live offstage; many—such as gunfire, door bells, and door slams—still are. In Elizabethan times, "thunder machines" (a series of wooden troughs for cannonballs to rumble down), "thundersheets" (suspended sheets of tin that when rattled made a rumbling sound), and "thunder runs" (sloping wooden troughs for rolling cannonballs down with a large crashing sound at the end) were

*S*ound *Designer*

Abe Jacob

©Carol Rosegg

Abe Jacob pioneered today's theatrical sound designer in the American theatre along with the sound credit on the title page of playbills. He got his start mixing sound for rock-and-roll stars in San Francisco in the 1960s, working with Jimi Hendrix, The Mamas and the Papas, and Peter, Paul, and Mary. His Broadway career began with a canceled preview performance of *Jesus Christ Superstar* due to technical problems. Director Tom O'Horgan, who had worked with Jacob on a West Coast production of *Hair,* asked him to help. His Broadway work continued with Bob Fosse on *Pippin, Chicago,* and *Big Deal;* Michael Bennett on *Seesaw* and *A Chorus Line;* Gower Champion on *Mack and Mabel* and *Rockabye Hamlet.* He credits these directors with being among the first supporters of sound design as a legitimate art form. More recently, he championed the cause to acquire union representation for sound designers and technicians in the Broadway theatre within Local 922 of the International Alliance of Stage Employees (IATSE).

Jacob also pioneered sound design in opera, serving as sound consultant for the New York City Opera Company. Acknowledging that the opera world is unfriendly to sound designers, he said, "When I started in theatre, it was almost immediate that the critics started making comments about the sound in the theatre, and how it was going to bring about the death of the American musical as we knew it, and they've been saying it ever since. And now they're saying it about opera, so I guess," he laughs, "I have the distinction of being able to destroy both art forms."[3]

---

invented to simulate tremendous storms, such as the storms in *Twelfth Night, The Tempest,* and *King Lear.* A cannon was fired from the roof of Shakespeare's theatre to convince audiences of fierce battles taking place, and musicians with trumpets sounded "flourishes," and so forth.

With the invention of electricity, most theatres since 1900 have used electric telephone or doorbell ringers (a battery-powered bell mounted on a piece of wood) and a door slammer (a small doorframe and door, complete with knob and latch) to simulate real-life sounds. Assistant stage managers usually created or supervised these manual "sound effects." But in the 1970s and 1980s with the development of audio recording and playback technologies, a virtual revolution in sound creation emerged along with a new theatre artist: *the sound designer.*

Theatres today have the capability for both live and recorded sound. Augmented sound, including the actor's voice, is routinely used even in nonmusical performances. Microphones are placed across the front of the stage, or actors wear miniature wireless microphones (usually concealed in their hair or beneath wigs). In the musical *Rent,* there is no attempt to conceal the wireless microphones that the actor's wear and, in effect, they become part of the "rock" costumes. There is much debate today over the electronic amplification of speaking and singing voices in Broadway musicals and nonmusical plays by those who prefer a "more natural" sound. The sound mixing board has become a permanent fixture in the rear of the orchestra rows of most Broadway theatres and a visual reminder that sound technology is an important part of enhancing the "aliveness" of the living theatre.

The use of live or recorded sounds serves many purposes. Those include

information	location
to establish locale	foghorns
time of day	chimes on the hour
time of year	birds in springtime
weather conditions	rain or thunder
street sounds	car horns, screeching brakes
realism	ambulance siren, toilet flushing, television sounds
mood	ominous sounds for scary moments
onstage cues	telephones, door knocks
special effects	the "breaking string" at the end of *The Cherry Orchard,* or the helicopter sequence in *Miss Saigon*

Sound Requirements in A Streetcar Named Desire. Tennessee Williams' text of A Streetcar Named Desire *details a number of specific sounds: barroom music with a "tinny piano," called a "blue piano," and muted trumpet, street sounds, cathedral bells, cats screeching, rumba music from an onstage radio, trains passing by, polka music, running water in an offstage bathtub, a distant revolver shot, policeman's whistle, Varsouviana music, hot trumpet and drums, cries and noises of the jungle.*

Music also serves many purposes, such as evoking mood, establishing period, heightening tension, intensifying action, and providing transitions between scenes and at endings. Today, music is often composed for a production and played "live" during the performance, or music is derived from copyrighted recordings (the use rights must be acquired by the theatre and licensing fees paid) and then played through the theatre's sound system. The sound designer oversees the implementation of all of these elements. Sometimes the sound designer is also the musical composer and holds copyright to the music he or she writes for the production. For example, John Gromada was both sound designer and composer for the production of *Camino Real* at Hartford Stage in 1999 and wrote music and lyrics for Betty Buckley to sing.

Whatever the source or quality of the sound, sound designers and technicians are responsible for it: music, abstract sounds, gunshots, rain and thunder, airplanes passing overhead, trains in the distance, telephones and doorbells ringing, sounds of nature (bird calls, crickets chirping), even military bands marching offstage, as Chekhov requires at the end of *The Three Sisters.*

Cue #	Page	Tape 1	Tape 2	Tape 3	Tape 4
1	61	Magic noise			Storm background
2	61		Thunder #1		
3	61			Thunder #2	
4	61	Wind blast			
5	61		Wave crash		
6	62			Thunder #3	
7	62	Thunder #4			
8	62		Ropes crash		
9	62			Bosun cry!	
10	62	Wave crash 2			
11	62		Thunder #5		
12	62	Wave crash 3		Big crash	
13	63		Thunder #6	Voices	
14	63	Split #1	Split #2		
15	63	Rocks crash	Wave #4	↓	
16	63			Magic noise	
17	63	Distant storm	Rumble		
18	63			Waves	

SOUND CUE SHEET FOR *THE TEMPEST* A sound cue sheet listing sound effects cues, locations on tape, and the page number of the script for a production of Shakespeare's *The Tempest*.

In consultation with the director, the sound designer plots the effects required by the script (and often added by the director). The new sound technology available to the sound designer in the 1940s included audio-tape recorders and playback units, audio cartridges that provided exact cueing of individual sounds, and speaker

*S*ound *D*esigners

Jonathan Deans

Courtesy Jonathan Deans

Jonathan Deans is involved in the development of the use of digital sound processing technology for mixing live (real-time) performances and automation (timed) performances. He has designed more than 120 musicals, plays, operas, Las Vegas spectaculars, and theme park attractions. Recent credits include *Ragtime, Fosse, Parade, King David, Candide, EFX,* and *Cirque du Soleil* at the Bellagio Hotel and *Mystère* at Treasure Island Hotel in Las Vegas.

FOSSE ON BROADWAY *Fosse,* a musical based on the choreography of Bob Fosse, with set and costume design by Santo Loquasto, lighting by Andrew Bridge, and sound by Jonathan Deans. The musical opened at the Broadhurst Theatre on West Forty-Fourth Street, Broadway, in 1999.

Courtesy of Milly S. Barranger

systems. More recently, digital audio (compact disc, digital audio tape), multichannel replay devices, and multiple-output samplers (digital and analog) permit operators to program dozens of individually recorded sounds onto the control keyboard, where each can be instantly recalled and played individually or in combination. Today, theatrical sound systems include speakers of high quality and versatility placed throughout the auditorium, a patch bay (a means of connecting tapes and microphones to any outlet), and a control board. Almost any sound can be programmed

Sound Design

Laurie Anderson and *Moby Dick*

©Frank Micoletta/Image Direct

LAURIE ANDERSON in a virtual voyage aboard Captain Ahab's ship "The Pequod" in *Songs and Stories from Moby Dick*, directed by Anne Bogart. (1999 Next Wave Festival at the Brooklyn Academy of Music.)

Performance artist Laurie Anderson created a virtual voyage called *Songs and Stories from Moby Dick* with a custom-built MIDI-controlled "talking stick," prerecorded musical tracks (vocals and keyboards), in-ear monitoring system plugged into a wireless microphone system, loudspeakers, mixing console, and digital playback devices. There are no literal whale sounds in the show. Anderson's sound track is basically an abstract landscape of sounds. The visuals, designed by Anderson herself, project images like the opening of pages of a book, large gold coins, underwater bubbles, and various abstractions. At one point, Anderson with short spiky hair, black clothes, and red shoes sits in a huge armchair, a lone voice in a vast sea. Sound, images, and lighting provide the audience with a road map into her interpretation of Herman Melville's famous novel.

into a sampler with the exception of gunshots—which are still performed "live" with blanks because they are too loud for most sound systems. The use of guns on or off stage must meet precise conditions specified by fire and safety authorities.

The Designer's Working Methods

Like the lighting designer, the sound designer studies the script, noting effects implied or detailed in the text; holds discussions with the director, other designers, the composer, and technicians; researches sound effects libraries; records sounds and music; prepares a sound track; develops a cue sheet indicating the placement of each sound in the script, the equipment involved, sound levels, control levers, and timing of sounds; and determines placement of speakers and microphones. The sound designer also has assistants to help with preparations and crews to run the show.

Special Effects with Sound

Special sound effects capture the audience's attention for a theatrical moment and/or increase the emotional impact of a scene. A sound effect may be an offstage noise like the sound of a car door shutting as preparation for an actor's entrance. Or it may be recorded music underscoring an emotional scene onstage. Whatever the sound effect, it grows out of a preconceived need on the part of playwrights, directors, and designers to enhance the overall quality of the production.

Sound effects in the theatre date from the use of music and human voices to enhance the storytelling in the classical Greek theatre. Shakespeare wrote sound effects into his plays. They are mostly battle and storm sounds that could be re-created with percussion instruments and simple backstage devices like thunder and wind machines. The English theatre during the Victorian era built other machines to reproduce the sounds of weather, horse-drawn carriages, trains, and disasters. These mechanical effects were handled by the property master rather than a sound engineer. In the modern theatre such sounds as telephones ringing, gunshots, door slams, doorbells, and breaking dishes are still created manually backstage by a member of the crew. Less than twenty-five years ago, the introduction of electronic amplification followed by recording and playback systems, microphones and loudspeakers, and digital audio technology created the need for a "sound designer." Abe Jacob introduced the sound designer into the American musical theatre, and now all Broadway, Off Broadway, and regional theatres hire sound designers and/or sound technicians to create and oversee this element of theatrical design.

COMPUTER-AIDED DESIGN: SCENERY, COSTUMES, LIGHTING, AND SOUND

For centuries, theatrical designers worked with the same tools as other visual artists: drafting table, paper, charcoal, pencils, colored paints, rulers, squares, and slide rules. Not until personal computers became readily available did theatre artists and technicians gain a remarkable new tool of far-reaching potential. In the mid-1980s, computer-aided design (CAD) and computer-aided manufacture (CAM) were widely adopted by the industry and became the fastest-growing technology for the stage.

This "machine" with its developing software has the capacity for configuring (and reconfiguring) spaces, angles, shapes, colors, perspectives, and measurements in response to the designer's imagination, research, and artistic choices. Computer-aided design is a remarkable asset in the design studio. First, computers reduce the drudgery of the scene designer's drawing mechanics. With the click of a mouse, they reconfigure spaces, change colors, lengthen lines, add walls, raise platforms, insert windows, reconfigure instruments on the lighting grid, and redesign or resize costumes. A click of the mouse also edits a text, adds director's notes, and inserts sound cues. Indeed, the computer saves many hours of painstaking drafting, copying, researching art collections, and creating final designs (and in color).

Vast visual and aural databases are literally at the designers' fingertips. Virtual libraries of art, sound effects, and music are found on CD-ROMs; and virtual catalogues of sculpture, decorative arts, chandeliers, and clothing and wardrobe collections from historical and modern periods have been digitized for computer retrieval. Re-use of another artist's theatrical designs can be subject to legal copyright considerations, and always require investigation.

Three-dimensional models of scenery can be created with computerized scenographic modeling. While this computer-enhanced technique has not replaced traditional ground plans and elevations, the computer models provide perspectives from above and from the left, right, and center of the house. Although computing equipment for such modeling is expensive, it is often cheaper than rebuilding scenery when a director or designer decides at the last minute to move a door.

The future use of computers holds out the promise of an "integrated computer design" whereby a design team can present at early conferences the scenic model, computerized costume renderings, colored lighting from calibrated lighting positions, and music and sound effects.

Computerized inventories of clothing, hats, wigs, shoes, and accessories have also revolutionized costume management and shops. For the costume designer the advantage of the new tool is the freedom to cut, paste, and combine elements of clothing before actually purchasing and cutting the cloth. With the computer, a designer can change sleeves on a garment or shorten the skirt without sewing a single stitch. Through the use of the actor's photo and measurements, a "virtual actor" can be dressed in the entire costume design before fabric is cut and sewn. By the same token, the wig designer can "virtually" change color and styles before the first fitting with the actor.

In all cases, the reality of the computer age is instantaneous communications. Designs can be sent instantly across the United States by digital electronic transmission, reducing travel costs and conference time. However, as designer Jennifer Tipton warns, "Technology … is only as good as the person using it." The designer's creativity and imagination are not imperiled by the new technology, as some have argued. Greater experimentation and innovation are made possible by the ease and speed of computer-enhanced design.

(continued on page 282)

New Stage Technologies

Automated Lighting Instruments . Intercom Systems .
Portable Sound Systems

In the Broadway theatre, the new automated lighting instruments have reduced inventory (and rental costs). The motorized beam redirection and color changers solve many of the problems of limited space for hanging instruments in the older New York theatres.

Courtesy of High End Systems

Courtesy of High End Systems

THE INTELLABEAM® WITH ROTATING MIRROR
Lighting designers were reluctant to use the new instruments at first. They were noisy, costly to buy or rent, and had high maintenance costs as well. With improvements in automated lighting that resulted in 1989 in the Intellabeam®, designers were convinced. The quieter instrument with a rotating mirror in front redirected its beam of light to focus on cue. The new engineering allowed multiple internal color changes that provided many color choices and the ability to change colors in less than three-tenths of a second.

AUTOMATED OR REMOTE-CONTROLLED MOTORIZED LIGHTING INSTRUMENTS
The needs of rock concerts to have moving, color-changing spotlights brought about one of the major changes in modern stage lighting. The first of these instruments, the VARI*LITE® VL1™ spot luminaire, was a single instrument that could light different areas of the stage from different angles on timed cues under the control of a computerized console. Their advantages were many: they reduced the lighting instrument inventory, which, in turn, affected costs and set-up time; they reduced the number of crew members needed; they increased the designer's control over changing color with an internal mechanically rotating wheel of colors; and they created spectacular effects with a number of instruments moving at the same time.

© 2001, Vari-Lite Inc. Photo by Lewis Lee

280

Courtesy of Clear Com

INTERCOM SYSTEMS WITH BELT-PACKS AND HEADSETS Intercom systems and accessories worn by managers, supervisors, technicians, and crews provide instant backstage communication among key personnel.

Courtesy of Sennheiser Electronic Corporation

INFRARED WIRELESS SYSTEMS WITH LAVALIER MICROPHONES The bodypack transmitter with omnidirectional clip-on microphone fulfills professional demands for sound quality and rugged handling. This system is suitable for areas of live work where a small and unobtrusive microphone is required for vocal and speech amplification.

Courtesy of Sennheiser Electronic Corporation

"SPEAKER ON A STICK" A complete, self-contained sound system designed for fixed or portable use. The "speaker on a stick" is a newly designed public address system for use in theatres, meetings, churches, schools—to be used with or without an external mixer.

TECHNICAL PRODUCTION

Without the *production team*—managers, technicians, craftspeople, and crews—no theatre has the capacity to organize the production, build and install scenery, create sound, light and costume a production, and run the show from start to finish. Depending upon the size of the theatre's organization, these individuals often outnumber the director, designers, and actors, and they shoulder responsibility for the production night after night.

The Production Team

Just as with any complex organization, the theatre has an established hierarchy of production managers and technicians charged with responsibility for supervising a large number of specialists: electricians, carpenters, stagehands, properties artisans, cutters, drapers, stitchers, milliners, wigmakers, shoemakers, wardrobe, dressers, makeup artists, light and sound operators, and running crews. A backstage hierarchy of management and technical practices—of what works and what does not—evolved over centuries.

Until the twentieth century, technical crafts were learned through apprenticeships in the theatre. Today, the "technical arts," called technical production and costume production, are taught in college and university theatre departments and students serve their "apprenticeships" within university theatre shops—the scene shop, the costume shop, the props shop, the sound and light studios. Each of these specialty shops serves as a working unit of the theatre as well as a laboratory for instruction. Key professional personnel command these shops and contribute through their expertise to the artistic enterprise as a whole—the production.

Production Manager

The technical production team is led by the *production manager* (*PM*) and seconded by the *technical director* (*TD*). The position of production manager has grown in importance over the last two decades, especially in professional regional theatres.

The production manager coordinates the staffing, scheduling, and budgeting of every element in the production, including building, installation ("load-in"), and operation ("running") of all design and technical elements. The PM is sensitive to the artistic needs of director, designers, and technicians throughout the production process and struggles with the complex problems of integrating the many disparate elements of the production, including the needs of the theatre's shops. Safety procedures, accounting policies, legal codes and union practices, and time management are part of the PM's knowledge and expertise.

Technical Director

The technical director (TD) has charge of the management of the scene shop and the construction and operation of scenery and stage machinery, such as hydraulics for moving scenery or trapdoors for special effects or entrances. Following the build

The Production Team

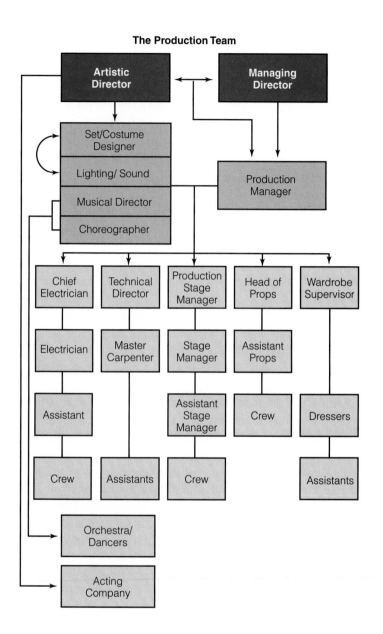

period, which requires conferences with the set designer, the TD oversees the moving of scenery into the theatre, plans adequate "stage time" for the various scenery and paint crews to complete their jobs, and establishes policies and directives for scene shifting, special effects, and "strike" (the final removal of scenery from the theatre or into storage at the close of the production). The TD coordinates the build, the "put-in," and "strike" schedules in tandem with

International Alliance of Stage Employees (IATSE). *The union that serves production managers, technical directors, and technicians in theatre, opera, film, and television, and employees in some sound studios. Sound designers are represented by IATSE as well.*

the other units of the theatre. In small theatres, lighting and sound installation and operation, for example, are often the responsibility of the TD as well.

Costume Shop Manager

The *costume shop manager* has a function parallel to that of the TD, with responsibility for the management of the costume shop, its inventory, budgets, the buying of fabrics, and building, buying, and/or renting of costumes and accessories, including hats, wigs, and shoes. Following a comparable build period during which conferences are held with the costume designer and craftspeople, the shop manager is responsible for the scheduling of the tasks of the various personnel and crews in order to complete the costumes, maintain them during the run, and "strike" them according to the theatre's policies at the close of the show.

Production Stage Manager

As we come to the role of the *production stage manager* (*PSM*)—formerly called the *stage manager* (*SM*)—and the *assistant stage manager* (*ASM*), we find a highly responsible and artistically sensitive position. The PSM coordinates the director's work in rehearsals with the actors and the technical departments. For example, the use in rehearsals of furniture, props, and clothing will be coordinated by stage management. At the beginning of rehearsals, the PSM organizes and schedules calls and appointments, records the blocking of actors, anticipates technical concerns for quick costume changes and scenery shifts, and organizes and annotates the "calling" of the show—that is, the system by which actors' entrance cues, and lighting, sound, and scene-shift cues are initiated. During performance, the PSM has full responsibility for the running of the show and has final authority over the entire onstage and backstage operation. The ASM is usually positioned backstage during the performance with responsibility for the smooth operation of technical systems and the actors' exits, entrances, and costume changes.

The PSM also conducts understudy rehearsals and maintains the precision of the production in the director's absence during the run of a professional production. For example, if line rehearsals are needed, the cast is brought together and while seated and without scripts they say or "run" their lines of dialogue with attention to accuracy. The PSM calls those rehearsals as well. Professional stage managers are members of Actors' Equity Association (A.E.A.).

Technical Assistants and Running Crews

Just as designers have their assistants, key technical management people have assistants with such titles as assistant stage manager, assistant production manager, assistant technical director, assistant costume shop manager, and so on. These individuals are invaluable in the supervision of the many, varying elements within a production. In turn, they will be the next generation of stage managers, production managers, technical directors, and so on. The running crews, as their name implies, are the technicians and personnel who "run" the show from night to night.

TRANSITION

All design elements in the theatre serve the play and enhance the storytelling quality of the theatre. In collaboration with the director, designers (in tandem with actors) transform the "empty space" into the living world of the production. The theatre's production and stage managers, along with the many technicians, provide the technical support system without which no theatre can open its doors.

WEB SITES

Arts, Crafts, and Theater Safety

A not-for-profit organization concerned with artists' health and safety, including safety laws in the U.S. and Canada.

http://www.caseweb.com/acts/

BBC Sound Effects Library

2,250 sound effects on CDs, fully indexed.

http://www.films.com

Design Image Online

A collection of web sites of theatrical and entertainment designers.

http://www.performance-design.com/dol/desimage.html.

Glossary of Technical Theatre Terms

http://www.ex.ac.uk/drama/tech/glossary.html

Lighting Links Page

Links to lighting resources and much more.

http://waapa.cowan.edu.au/lx/

Professional Lighting and Sound Association

http://www.plasa.org/publishing/

The Theatre Design and Technical Jobs Page

Free list of job openings.

http://home.earthlink.net/~pshudson/jobs/jobs.htm

Theatre Sound Design Directory and Resource

http://www.theatre-sound.com/tsindex.html

United States Institute of Theatre Technology (USITT)

See Chapter 10.

http://www.usitt.org

These search terms are provided to assist you in exploring the topics introduced in this chapter at:

http//www.infotrac-college.com

theatre design history, lighting design, lighting technology, lighting effects, sound design, sound technology, sound effects, holographs, computer-aided design, scenic technology, technical production, theatre health and safety.

There's no business like

show business ...

IRVING BERLIN

Composer and Lyricist

The Image Makers: The Producer

The producer is responsible for financing the production, for hiring and firing the artistic and managerial personnel. The producer is frequently all things to all people: money machine, mediator, friend, tyrant, boss, enemy, gambler, investor, consultant. In a word, the producer's job is to make the play happen.

Many contribute to the making of theatre, a highly complex, collaborative art form. The producer is that anomalous person who, in the highly competitive and risky business of theatre, deals with plays, investors, artists, theatre owners, trade unions, agents, contracts, taxes, rentals, deficits, grosses, and the bottom line. The producer is rarely an artist but rather an astute businessperson with creative judgment who knows the demands of the commercial theatre. In answer to the question "What exactly do you do?" producer Cheryl Crawford said: "I find a good play or musical, I find the money required to give it the best physical form on a stage, I find the people to give it life, I find a theatre and try to fill it."[1]

PRODUCING ON BROADWAY

The Broadway Producer

There are thirty-six Broadway theatres at the present time. At least sixteen are owned by the Shubert Organization of major New York producers. Because of the high cost of producing on Broadway—over $8 million for a musical; $800,000+ for a dramatic play—many Broadway producers are seasoned veterans and are collaborating more frequently with one another in their producing efforts. Eight producers joined forces to bring *Angels in America: A Gay Fantasia on National Themes* to Broadway in 1993. As the costs of producing on Broadway continue to skyrocket (*Ragtime* cost $10 million in 1998, and *Aida* $15 million in 2000), producers

Courtesy of Milly S. Barranger

DUFFY SQUARE TICKET BOOTH (TKTS) The TKTS booth, located on Broadway's Duffy Square at Forty-Seventh Street, sells discounted tickets on the day of the performance for Broadway and Off Broadway shows.

commingle their know-how and assets. They employ general managers, accountants, and lawyers to assist with the business of financing a Broadway play from option to opening.

Why is theatre, and especially the commercial Broadway theatre, so costly? Analysts agree that theatre is a service business in which most of the cost of the product is labor—actors, musicians, stagehands, ushers, and so on. As wages rise with general living standards across the country, most businesses turn to technology rather than to people to blunt the cost of inflation. However, in the theatre, the opportunities for saving labor costs are still limited. It takes just as long for actors to stage *Hamlet* in the year 2000 as it did in Shakespeare's day and just as long to design and build *The Cherry Orchard* as it did in Chekhov's. Unlike the film industry, the multimillion-dollar production cannot be put in a "can" and distributed to tens of thousands of moviehouses to offset the original costs. One solution is the creation of national touring companies of *Ragtime* and *Titanic,* for example, as a means of broadening distribution.

Courtesy of Milly S. Barranger

BROADWAY'S SHUBERT THEATRE The Shubert Theatre on West Forty-Fourth Street with the revival of *Chicago* on the marquee.

The Broadway Option

Once a play is written, the playwright's agent contacts producers, who may eventually option the play. The *option*—a payment advanced against royalties to the playwright—is the starting point on that long road to opening night. It is an agreement that grants producers the right to produce a play or musical within a specified period of time in exchange for a fee paid to the writer or to the composer/lyricist. The amount paid, the length of the option, and what the money buys are all negotiable.

Another approach is to send the script directly to the artistic director of a regional theatre in the hope that there will be some interest in the play. Regional and Off Broadway theatres produce new plays and musicals, and today many Broadway hits are first seen elsewhere. For example, August Wilson's *Fences* was first produced at the Yale Repertory Theatre in New Haven (Conn.) before transferring to Broadway. The same has been true of *Angels in America* (Mark Taper Forum, Los Angeles), *Rent* (La Jolla Playhouse, San Diego), *Death of a Salesman* and *Moon for the Misbegotten* (Goodman Theater, Chicago), *Aida* (Alliance Theatre Company, Atlanta), and *The Full Monty* (Old Globe Theatre, San Diego).

All plays produced on Broadway by an American author are optioned by producers under the Dramatists Guild contract. There are separate contracts for musicals, dramatic productions, stock tryouts, and collaborations.

When a commercial producer options the exclusive rights to a play for Broadway, the playwright works on the script during workshops, rehearsals, out-of-town tryouts, and previews. Workshops, tryouts, and previews are the testing ground for commercial productions. On the basis of critical notices and audience response during this period, the play is reworked and sometimes completely rewritten before the official New York opening. There is enormous pressure on the playwright to satisfy various interest groups, including director and producer.

(continued on page 292)

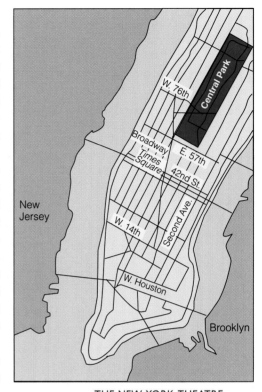

THE NEW YORK THEATRE DISTRICTS: BROADWAY, OFF BROADWAY, OFF OFF BROADWAY As a general rule, Actors' Equity Association makes a distinction between Broadway theatres (theatres with 500 seats or more), Off Broadway (100 to 499 seats), and Off Off Broadway (99 seats or less).

Martha Swope/TimePix

JELLY'S LAST JAM With book and direction by George C. Wolfe and music by Jelly Roll Morton, *Jelly's Last Jam* featured Gregory Hines as the legendary jazz musician. With sets by Robin Wagner, lighting by Jules Fisher, and masks/puppets by Barbara Pollitt. Broadway 1992.

Broadway's "Hottest" Property: The Musical

Aida . The Lion King . Fosse . Chicago . Rent . The Phantom of the Opera

©Joan Marcus

AIDA Elton John and Tim Rice's *Aida* with Sherie René Scott as Amneris, directed by Robert Falls. Scenery and costumes designed by Bob Crowley. Broadway 2000.

©Joan Marcus

THE LION KING With music and lyrics by Elton John and Tim Rice and others, *The Lion King* opened with Tsidii Le Loka, Samuel E. Wright, John Vickery, and Heather Headley. With costumes by Julie Taymor, masks and puppets by Julie Taymor and Michael Curry, directed by Julie Taymor. Broadway 1997.

©Joan Marcus

FOSSE With original choreography by Bob Fosse, conceived by Richard Maltby Jr., Chet Walker, and Ann Reinking, *Fosse: The Musical* was co-directed by Richard Maltby Jr. and Ann Reinking with artistic advisor Gwen Verdon. Broadway 1999.

©Carol Rosegg

CHICAGO The revival of John Kander's and Fred Ebb's *Chicago* with original choreography by Bob Fosse. The revival is directed by Walter Bobbie with choreography by Ann Reinking in the style of Bob Fosse. Bebe Neuwirth stars as Velma Kelly. Broadway 1996.

THE PHANTOM OF THE OPERA Directed by Harold Prince, *The Phantom of the Opera* opened in 1988 and remains one of the longest-running musicals on Broadway.

©Peter Cunningham

©Joan Marcus

RENT With music, book, and lyrics by Jonathan Larson, *Rent* starred Adam Pascal and Daphne Rubin-Vega in the original cast. Directed by Michael Greif. Broadway 1996.

*P*roducer

Cameron Mackintosh

Michael Le Poer Trench/Courtesy
Cameron Mackintosh, Ltd.

CATS Cameron Mackintosh
produced the long-running
Andrew Lloyd Webber
musical on Broadway.

Martha Swope/Time Pix

Born 1946 in Enfield in North London, **Cameron Mackintosh** is a leading producer in the commercial theatre on both sides of the Atlantic Ocean—on London's West End and Broadway. His name is synonymous with such award-winning musicals as *Cats, Les Misérables, The Phantom of the Opera, Miss Saigon, Whistle Down the Wind, The Witches of Eastwick,* and the London revival of *Oklahoma.* Knighted in 1996 for "services to the British theatre," Sir Cameron Mackintosh owns seven theatres in London's West End.

Alexander H. Cohen on Producing. *"I function in the commercial world, I have to live in the commercial world, I have to finance the productions I do—not by writing a check on what Mr. Ziegfeld left me because he knew I was coming, but by going out and hustling to get the money to produce plays on Broadway...."*[2]
ALEXANDER H. COHEN
Producer

An initial option usually lasts for one year from the date of delivery of the completed script. There are permissions for extending the option (if a star is unavailable for six months, for example, or if there is a wait of four to six months to move into a choice Broadway theatre), but that can be expensive.

In 1938, producer-director Jed Harris used an unusual strategy to open *Our Town* on Broadway. Convinced that Thornton Wilder's play could not open in just any theatre, but not wanting to extend the option, Harris gambled on a suitable theatre becoming available once the show had opened. He opened the play in a theatre that was available for only one week, reasoning that if the play was a success, another theatre would materialize. And so it did. When the play proved to be a hit, the favored theatre magically became available.

The producer enters into comparable arrangements with the director, actors, and designers. In addition, the producer will be concerned with potential touring companies, foreign productions, recordings, television, and video and film rights.

Since producing a Broadway show is an expensive, high-risk investment, the producer usually seeks assistance from co-producers, associate producers, and general managers in raising the money and in handling other business details. Backers, or "angels," are sought to invest in the show, with the full knowledge that they can lose their total investment.

Associations and Craft Unions

The Broadway producer deals with a variety of organizations. The League of American Theatres and Producers, an association of producers and theatre owners, was founded in 1930 to oversee the common interests and welfare of theatre owners, lessees, operators, and producers. The League's primary function is to act as bargaining representatives for theatre owners and producers with the many unions and associations, ranging from ticket sellers to press agents.

Casting and the Casting Director

Casting in the professional theatre (commercial and nonprofit) is conducted by *casting directors* in association with producers, directors, playwrights, and composers (for new musicals).

At the outset, the casting director receives a "breakdown" of roles to be cast and those qualities needed for each part. This information is posted with agents through the Breakdown Services and audition space rented. Agents then submit actors' names and resumés to the casting director, who selects those actors to audition based on their training, past work, and performances that the casting director may have seen. The casting director also searches office files for actors he or she may have seen for past projects and who might be appropriate for the current one. (Special auditions may also be held to "screen" unknown actors before the main audition.) Then, the casting director schedules the actors for their auditions, gives them the materials (or "sides"), and tells them time and place.

During auditions, the casting director sits with the show's director and producer, and may also be part of the discussion to select the final cast. The director and producer make the *final* casting decisions. If it is a new work, the creators (playwright and composer of a musical) also have casting approval. Most casting directors are located in New York City or Los Angeles, although large nonprofit theatres, like the Manhattan Theatre Club and Lincoln Center Theater, have casting directors as part of the theatre's permanent staff. Names and addresses of casting directors are listed in the *Ross Reports* and are members of the Casting Society of America (C.S.A.).

Courtesy of Milly S. Barranger

THE MARQUEE FOR *AIDA* At Broadway's Palace Theatre on Forty-Seventh Street, the marquee for *Aida* overlooks Duffy Square.

Actors' Equity Association contracts. *Actor's Equity Association, the union for actors and stage managers, has three basic contracts: a standard minimum contract for actors and stage managers, a standard minimum contract for chorus members, and a standard run-of-play contract. (All of these are spelled out in the Actors' Equity Rules Handbook.) Once assembled for rehearsals, the cast elects a deputy to represent Equity members in dealing with the producer over any breach of agreements and other employment issues. Chorus singers and dancers have separate deputies.*

SUNSET BOULEVARD The Andrew
Lloyd Webber musical, *Sunset Boulevard*,
based on the Billy Wilder film, opened
on Broadway with Glenn Close in 1993.

Nontraditional Casting

Nontraditional casting involves casting actors in roles for which they might not have been considered in the past for reasons of ethnicity, gender, or physical impairment. *Colorblind casting* ignores race or ethnicity and casts actors solely on the basis of talent and suitability to a role. Those who oppose colorblind casting base their arguments on the fact that it ignores cultural differences and absorbs other cultures into the majority white, Eurocentric culture.

Conceptual casting alters the race or ethnicity of characters to bring about a new perspective on the play. The *Othello* produced by the National Asian-American Theater Company changed the historical obsession with racial and class differences in Shakespeare's text, and substituted a nonracial contest between a great warrior and a confederate of boundless evil.

Casting inversions involve issues of injustices to minority actors by denying them ethnic roles. While it is no longer the practice to cast white actors in nonwhite roles, the issue of nontraditional casting erupted into an international controversy when Actors' Equity Association objected to the casting of a white British actor, Jonathan Pryce, as the Eurasian narrator in *Miss Saigon*. Pryce had played the role in the successful London musical, but as it was transferred to Broadway the union took issue with producer Cameron Mackintosh and called for an Asian actor in the role. Eventually, Actors' Equity gained other concessions and permitted Pryce to play the lead on Broadway.

Nontraditional casting is now common practice in professional companies and university theatres and is not likely to be ignored in the future.

The Agent

When asked "What does an agent do?", Audrey Wood, possibly the most famous playwrights' agent of the last fifty years, answered as a character in Arthur Kopit's play *End of the World:* "This is a question I am asked all the time. In *theory,* an agent is sup-

OTHELLO The National Asian-
American Theater Company produced
Shakespeare's *Othello* with American
actors of Asian descent, including
Korea, China, Japan, and the Philippines.
Joshua Spafford as Othello and Joel de
la Fuente as Iago, directed by Jonathan
Bank, at the Connell Theater, New York
City, 2000.

Broadway Contracts

Contracts negotiated by the League of American Theatres and Producers for Broadway include the following:

- Theatre Protective Union, Local No. 1, IATSE: basic theatre house crews, including electricians, carpenters, curtain and property people.

- Treasurers and Ticket Sellers Union, Local No. 751: all box office personnel involved in ticket selling.

- Legitimate Theatre Employees Union, Local No. B-183: all ushers, doormen, ticket takers.

- Theatre, Amusement and Cultural Building Service Employees, Local No. 54: custodians, cleaners, matrons, and the like.

- International Union of Operating Engineers (affiliated with the AFL-CIO), Local No. 30: employees involved in operation and maintenance of heating and air-conditioning systems.

- Mail and Telephone Order Clerks Union Local B-751: all mail clerks and telephone operators employed by theatres.

- Actors' Equity Association: actors, stage managers, singers, dancers.

- Theatrical Wardrobe Attendants Union, Local No. 764: wardrobe supervisors, assistants, and dressers.

- The Society of Stage Directors and Choreographers: directors and choreographers.

- The Dramatists Guild Minimum Basic Production Contract: authors.

- The United Scenic Artists, Local No. 829: set, lighting, costume designers and assistants.

- Associated Musicians of Greater New York, Local No. 802, American Federation of Musicians: musicians.

- Association of Theatrical Press Agents and Managers, Local No. 18032: press agents, house and company managers.

---

posed to find her client *work!* Now, while this has certainly been *known* to happen, fortunately, for all concerned, we do much, much more."

An agent, whether for playwright, director, actor, or designer, acts on behalf of that artist to find theatre, film, television, commercials, and publishing contracts. For a fee, the agent looks after the livelihood of the artist, negotiates contracts and

Playwrights' Agent

Audrey Wood

Playwrights' agent **Audrey Wood** (1905–1985) helped to define the American theatre by representing and guiding the careers of Tennessee Williams, William Inge, Robert Anderson, Clifford Odets, Carson McCullers, Preston Jones, Arthur Kopit, and many others.

Wood discovered Tennessee Williams through his entry in a playwriting contest sponsored by the Group Theatre. It took her eight years to sell the script of *The Glass Menagerie,* but when she did, it launched Williams' international career. When "her" playwrights were young and struggling, she found them work and grants and often lent them money herself. She was known for her extraordinary devotion to her clients and was tireless in her calls on their behalf to producers and influential people. Moreover, she was the first agent in the American theatre to be given billing in the program: "Mr. Williams' Representative—Audrey Wood." In her autobiography, *Represented by Audrey Wood* (1981), she said: "The theater is a venture (one hesitates to call it a business) built on equal parts faith, energy and hard work—all tied together with massive injections of nerve."[3]

royalties, and writes checks. The agent is as much a part of the artist's professional life and success in the commercial theatre as the director or producer, because it is through the agent that the actor or playwright is usually seen and heard by directors and producers. As the artist's lifeline into the commercial theatre, the agent is frequently friend, mentor, counselor, parent, psychiatrist, and investment broker.

Preview or Out-of-Town Tryout

Until recently, almost every Broadway show had a trial run in New Haven, Boston, or Philadelphia before its New York opening. The purpose was to get audience response and to "fix" the script and casting problems before subjecting the production to the scrutiny of Broadway critics. Today, out-of-town tryouts, as they were conceived in the past, are so expensive that many producers use other options, such as the *preview* (usually of one to three weeks); another is transferring with commercial producers a play or musical that has had a successful debut in a regional theatre directly to Broadway (*A Chorus Line, Big River, Rent, The Full Monty*); or recreating the successful commercial London production (*Cats, Les Misérables, The Phantom of the Opera*).

Courtesy of Milly S. Barranger

The Broadway preview, like the pre-Broadway production, brings the show into its permanent theatre, thereby avoiding the expenses of touring, and provides a period of time for Broadway audiences to respond to the show and generate favorable word-of-mouth publicity before its official opening.

Broadway Openings and After

Those late opening-night parties at Sardi's restaurant in New York City where everyone connected with the show waits to learn the critics' verdict are legendary. Will the show have a run, or won't it? Tension mounts as those involved with the show wait to learn their fate. Usually the show's press agent or publicity manager downloads the reviews from the Internet on a Palm Pilot or has the reviews faxed from early newspaper editions. They are read aloud to the assembled group.

The morning after an opening, there is a customary meeting among producers, press agent, and general or company manager (and sometimes an attorney). If the show receives rave reviews, as did *The Phantom of the Opera, The Producers,* or *The Lion King,* the job of planning advertising expenses is an easy one. If the reviews are "pans," the decision to close is equally easy. However, if the reviews are mixed, decisions are difficult. There's always a chance that the show can make it, but figuring out how much money to spend to keep it running until expenses can be made is tricky.

Neither is it an easy decision to close a show if the possibility exists of developing business at a later date. So many jobs, from stage electricians to actors, depend on this decision. Advance sales to theatre parties have to be weighed against current box office sales. Generally, when a show is panned, it has little chance of making its costs, much less returns on investments.

KISS OF THE SPIDER WOMAN
Directed by Harold Prince with book
by Terrence McNally, *Kiss of the Spider
Woman* opened on Broadway in 1993.
The musical became a star vehicle for
Chita Rivera as the bygone film star,
Aurora, who lives in the imagination of
a homosexual prisoner, played by
Brent Carver.

National Touring Companies

When shows are hits on Broadway, touring companies are financed through guarantees
from various theatres across the country where they will appear. A smash hit in New York
City can gross over $800,000 a week in Chicago, Houston, Detroit, Los Angeles, Philadel-
phia, Washington, D.C., and Toronto. During 1999, the highest-grossing national companies were all musicals: *Jekyll & Hyde, Fosse, Beauty and the Beast,* and *Titanic.*

PRODUCING OFF BROADWAY

Once a haven from the high costs of Broadway commercial contracts and unions, Off
Broadway is now a smaller, less expensive version of its namesake. There is a League
of Off Broadway Theatres and Producers; the Dramatists Guild and Actors' Equity
have developed Off Broadway contracts, which apply to the smaller theatres (100 to
499 seats) and the smaller box office potential.

At one time it was said that producing Off Broadway was unlike anything else in
the world, since contractual arrangements were loosely defined. However, Off Broadway today mirrors the larger enterprise. It all begins when the producer options the
play for an Off Broadway production.

Co-producers and associate producers also appear on the Off Broadway scene,
since money is always required. A co-producer enters into a joint venture (or limited
partnership, as it is called) to assist the producer in raising money for the production:
now a minimum of $500,000 for a small, nonmusical play.

(continued on page 300)

Chapter Twelve

Daryl Roth

Daryl Roth

Daryl Roth produces plays that deal with serious issues and taboo subjects. She has three Pulitzer Prize–winning plays in five years to her credit. *Wit* by Margaret Edson (about ovarian cancer), *How I Learned to Drive* by Paula Vogel (about incest), and *Three Tall Women* by Edward Albee (about dying). "My criteria is to do things that instinctively say something to me," she says. "That's all I have to go by. If I hear something, and it touches me, then I think it will touch other people of like mind."[4]

Daryl Roth is revered today as a producer who helps nonprofit theatres move their plays to commercial theatres. In 1996, she bought a former bank building in New York City's Union Square and created her own theatre (the Daryl Roth Theatre), thus helping to revitalize the neighborhood. Playwrights Paula Vogel, Margaret Edson, and Jane Anderson, whose play *Defying Gravity* about the Challenger space shuttle disaster was produced by Roth, credit the producer with nurturing their work. Commenting on her choice of plays with very serious subjects, she says that "theatre is basically a very safe place yet we are able to experience something that isn't very safe within its confines."

Christopher Gross/SCR

WIT Written by Margaret Edson, *Wit* was originally produced at the South Coast Repertory Theatre, Costa Mesa (Calif.), in 1995. The Off Broadway production opened at the Union Square Theatre (1999), produced by Daryl Roth.

THE WHO'S *TOMMY* The award-winning musical from the 1993 Broadway season with music, lyrics, and book by Pete Townshend, a member of the British musical group *The Who*, and directed by Des McAnuff.

©Joan Marcus

Why use a co-producer? A certain amount of "front money," or risk capital, is needed immediately to pay for the option and printing scripts, for making payments to lawyers and general managers, and to pay for backers' auditions, where potential investors are invited to sample the play. The backers' audition is key to money-raising. The playwright or director tells the storyline, actors present scenes from the script, musical numbers are sung, and major investors from all areas of the business world are often forthcoming. Associate producers also join up for a percentage to get others to invest in the show, and they get billing credits for their efforts.

Once the money is reasonably assured, the producer proceeds to hire a general manager (who oversees the budget and takes care of all financial transactions), rent a theatre, and hire a press agent, an advertising agency, accountants, lawyers, a director, a casting director, designers, stage managers, and actors. For a musical, additional personnel—a musical director, musicians, arrangers, choreographers, dancers, and singers—are needed.

Today there is little difference, other than the scale of the production and the amount of the investment, between producing on and off Broadway. The language is the same, contracts similar, key personnel identical, and risks ever-present.

PRODUCING IN REGIONAL THEATRES

In regional theatres—sometimes called resident theatres or companies—the producer is called an artistic director or producing director (the titles vary from theatre to theatre). As the theatre's leader, this person deals with a board of directors or trustees, corporations, foundations, federal and state agencies, patrons, and subscribers. Together with the company's managers, he or she plans the theatre's season and hires the artists.

Although Broadway remains the mecca for American commercial theatre, nonprofit professional theatres have proliferated beyond Broadway and throughout the United States. Beginning in the late fifties, the regional theatre movement established a network of more than sixty nonprofit professional theatres across the country. They formed a national alliance known as the League of Resident Theatres (LORT), which negotiates contracts with theatre unions, including Actors' Equity, under which all nonprofit professional theatres operate. It is unusual to find a major city that does not have one or more professional resident theatres, although the majority are clustered in the Northeast.

The terms *resident* and *regional* are used interchangeably to describe nonprofit professional theatres located from coast to coast. Today, there are more than 136 theatres with operating budgets ranging from $250,000 to more than $25 million. In the 1998 season, they gave more than 38,369 performances and attracted over 12 million people to the theatre. Most schedule seasons of from five to ten months, generally to subscription audiences. Many have school touring programs. Others have outreach programs for audiences of all ages, which are models for community-wide social and cultural organizations. They all offer employment opportunities for writers, directors, designers, actors, and technical staff that are, for the most part, unavailable in New York City and Los Angeles.

The regional theatres have an inherent mandate to develop new works. Because New York productions boast prohibitive staging costs, astronomical ticket prices ($35 to $100 for a single ticket), and mercurial critics, writers increasingly prefer to have their works initially produced by regional companies. There, during a guaranteed rehearsal period and a four- to six-week run, writers have time to make changes without the threat of closing notices being posted on opening night.

BOY MEETS GIRL: Magazine writer Theresa Bedell (Mary Beth Fisher) meets her blind date Tony (Ian Lithgow) in this scene from the Goodman Theatre's production of Rebecca Gilman's *Boy Meets Girl*. Directed by Michael Maggio, Chicago, 2000.

©Liz Lauren/Goodman Theatre (pictured are: Mary Beth Fisher and Ian Lithgow)

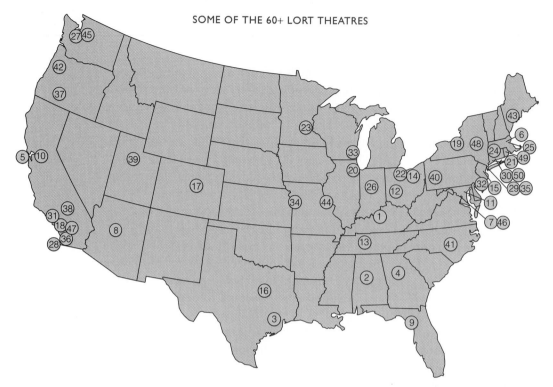

SOME OF THE 60+ LORT THEATRES

Theatre	City	Producing/Artistic Directors
① Actors Theatre of Louisville	Louisville, KY	Marc Masterson
② Alabama Shakespeare Festival	Montgomery, AL	Kent Thompson
③ Alley Theatre	Houston, TX	Gregory Boyd
④ Alliance Theatre Company	Atlanta, GA	Susan Booth
⑤ American Conservatory Theatre	San Francisco, CA	Carey Perloff
⑥ American Repertory Theatre	Cambridge, MA	Robert Woodruff
⑦ Arena Stage	Washington, D.C.	Molly D. Smith
⑧ Arizona Theatre Company	Tucson, AZ	David Ira Goldstein
⑨ Asolo Theatre Company	Sarasota, FL	Howard J. Millman
⑩ Berkeley Repertory Theatre	Berkeley, CA	Tony Taccone
⑪ Center Stage	Baltimore, MD	Irene Lewis
⑫ Cincinnati Playhouse in the Park	Cincinnati, OH	Edward Stern
⑬ Clarence Brown Theatre Company	Knoxville, TN	Blake Robison

Our regional theatres have developed such writers as Pearl Cleage, Christopher Durang, Rebecca Gilman, Beth Henley, Terrence McNally, David Mamet, Marsha Norman, David Rabe, Sam Shepard, Paula Vogel, Wendy Wasserstein, Cheryl L. West, and August Wilson, among others. In 1999, even established playwrights like Arthur Miller, Edward Albee, and Lanford Wilson unveiled their new plays in regional theatres.

Theatre	City	Producing/Artistic Directors
(14) The Cleveland Playhouse	Cleveland, OH	Peter Hackett
(15) Crossroads Theatre Company	New Brunswick, NJ	Hal Scott
(16) Dallas Theatre Center	Dallas, TX	Richard Hamburger
(17) Denver Center Theatre	Denver, CO	Donovan Marley
(18) Geffen Playhouse	Los Angeles, CA	Gilbert Cates
(19) GeVa Theatre	Rochester, NY	Mark Cuddy
(20) Goodman Theatre	Chicago, IL	Robert Falls
(21) Goodspeed Opera House	East Haddam, CT	Michael P. Price
(22) Great Lakes Theater Festival	Cleveland, OH	James Bundy
(23) Guthrie Theater	Minneapolis, MN	Joe Dowling
(24) Hartford Stage Company	Hartford, CT	Michael Wilson
(25) Huntington Theatre Company	Boston, MA	Nicholas Martin
(26) Indiana Repertory Theatre	Indianapolis, IN	Janet Allen
(27) Intiman Theatre Company	Seattle, WA	Bartlett Sher
(28) La Jolla Playhouse	La Jolla, CA	Des McAnuff
(29) Lincoln Center Theater	New York City	André Bishop
(30) Long Wharf Theatre	New Haven, CT	Douglas Hughes
(31) Mark Taper Forum	Los Angeles, CA	Gordon Davidson
(32) McCarter Theatre for the Performing Arts	Princeton, NJ	Emily Mann
(33) Milwaukee Repertory Theatre	Milwaukee, WI	Joseph Hanreddy
(34) Missouri Repertory Theatre	Kansas City, MO	Peter Altman
(35) The Joseph Papp Public Theatre/ New York Shakespeare Festival Theatre	New York City	George C. Wolfe
(36) The Globe Theatre	San Diego, CA	Jack O'Brien
(37) Oregon Shakespeare Festival	Ashland, OR	Libby Appel
(38) The Pasadena Playhouse	Pasadena, CA	Sheldon Epps
(39) Pioneer Theatre Company	Salt Lake City, UT	Charles Morey
(40) Pittsburgh Public Theatre	Pittsburgh, PA	Ted Pappas
(41) Playmakers Repertory Company	Chapel Hill, NC	David Hammond
(42) Portland Center Stage	Portland, OR	Elizabeth Huddle
(43) Portland Stage Company	Portland, ME	Anita Stewart
(44) Repertory Theatre of St. Louis	St. Louis, MO	Steven Woolf
(45) Seattle Repertory Theatre	Seattle, WA	Sharon Ott
(46) The Shakespeare Theatre	Washington, D.C.	Michael Kahn
(47) South Coast Repertory	Costa Mesa, CA	Martin Benson
(48) Syracuse Stage	Syracuse, NY	Bob Moss
(49) Trinity Repertory Company	Providence, RI	Oskar Eustis
(50) Yale Repertory Theatre	New Haven, CT	Stan Wojewodski, Jr.

New York City has its own resident, nonprofit theatres: Manhattan Theatre Club, Playwrights Horizons, Lincoln Center Theater, The Joseph Papp Public Theater/New York Shakespeare Festival, Classic Stage Company, Roundabout Theatre Company, Signature Theatre Company, Vineyard Theatre, Pan Asian Repertory Theatre, Repertorio Español, Jewish Repertory Theatre, Theatre for a New Audience, and many more.

THE PLAY ABOUT THE BABY
Written and directed by Edward Albee,
this play had its American premiere
with Earle Hyman and Marian Seldes at
the Alley Theatre, Houston, in 1999.

These theatres provide stages for the talents of such writers as Jon Robin Baitz, Christopher Durang, Charles Fuller, A. R. Gurney Jr., David Henry Hwang, Tina Howe, Terrence McNally, Suzan Lori-Parks, Wendy Wasserstein, and George C. Wolfe.

The producer's job in the regional theatre is both similar to and different from the Broadway producer's job. He or she deals with Actors' Equity through the special LORT contract; in the New York, Boston, Chicago, and Los Angeles areas, some even deal with craft unions. However, the artistic director (or producing director) produces not a single play but a season of plays spanning eight to eleven months. This individual is in charge of planning a season of six to ten plays, sometimes in two or more theatres, including classical and modern works, musicals, lesser-known European works, and new plays. The artistic director may direct one or more plays within a season and hires other directors to complete the season. The regional theatre producer develops a projected budget to cover all contingencies:

- artistic salaries and fees
- administrative salaries and costs
- travel and housing (for casting and artists)
- marketing and development costs
- production and personnel expenses
- equipment, facilities maintenance, and services

In this milieu, producing is also precarious. Although there is usually continuity of administrative and artistic leadership within regional theatres, no continuous financial support system exists from season to season, although some theatres have developed endowments to offset annual operating costs. The regional theatres and

(continued on page 306)

Literary Management and Literary Managers

In the United States, *literary managers* are most often found in professional non-profit theatres. This individual finds and develops new plays. While the literary manager's responsibilities may vary from one company to the next, the essential job is to read new scripts and develop the most promising. Almost every professional theatre receives a large number of unsolicited scripts each season. Many companies read only those scripts submitted by agents, or brought to them by known writers and other professionals.

Literary management most often includes new play development. This is a highly sensitive and lengthy undertaking since it involves working with playwrights to realize the full potential of their scripts. In this capacity, the function of the literary manager merges with that of the dramaturg. Oftentimes, the process is taken over by a director, but usually late in the developmental process. Director Daniel Sullivan suggested "substantial changes" to Rebecca Gilman's script for *Spinning into Butter* (already "developed" at the Goodman Theatre) before its New York premiere at Lincoln Center Theater.

In the process of developing new plays, the literary manager talks with and advises playwrights to clarify intentions and shape the action. Then, readings of the new play are held for key theatre personnel (especially for directors and producers), followed by workshops to test the stage-worthiness of the new piece. Many established writers voice concerns about well-intentioned literary managers (and dramaturgs) "rewriting" their plays. Many have highly productive relationships with literary managers and directors to whom they return again and again with new scripts. In recent years, there have been legal disputes over "authorship." Perhaps the most publicized dispute involved the late playwright Jonathan Larson and dramaturg Lynn Thomson, who, together, developed the popular musical hit *Rent*. There was no contractual arrangement between Larson and Thomson at the moment of his untimely death. She sued the playwright's estate for a percent of the royalties on the grounds of her contributions to the project as co-collaborator. The court ruled in favor of the estate based on the absence of a contract. Despite the notoriety of this case, legal disputes between collaborators are rare in the professional regional theatres because of the contractual arrangements exercised by theatres with playwrights.

Because literary managers make critical decisions on the readiness of new scripts for production and their appeal (and even appropriateness) for the theatre's audience, they are often involved in the planning of a theatre's new season.

Some theatres are renowned for their new play development programs. In this category are the South Coast Repertory Theatre (Costa Mesa, Calif.), Actors Theatre of Louisville (Ky.), and Playwrights Horizons (New York City).

A MOON FOR THE MISBEGOTTEN

Cherry Jones as Josie Hogan and Gabriel Byrne as James Tyrone, Jr. in Eugene O'Neill's *A Moon For The Misbegotten* at the Goodman Theatre, Chicago, 2000. Directed by Daniel Sullivan.

their producers depend on a delicate balance of federal and state dollars, foundation and corporation money, and subscribers' dollars. The producer must at all times juggle the season's budgeted expenses against real and projected income. Although most theatres hire permanent administrative staff and artistic leadership, few have been able to fund a resident company for the entire season, as is the practice in Britain, France, and Germany. At best, a small core of actors returns year after year, playing a variety of roles. They are matched with other performers who are hired on a show-by-show basis. The artists themselves often support the theatre by accepting minimal salaries until they grow tired and move into film and television, or leave the theatre entirely. New actors replace them, and the cycle begins again. This talent drain is wearing at best and discouraging at most.

Despite the lack of permanent funding and resident companies, the regional theatre movement is strong. One way a number of producers have chosen to counterbalance the fiscal difficulties has been to re-establish connections with the New York commercial theatre. In the last decade, Broadway has been enlivened by shows that established themselves first with regional audiences (a variation on the out-of-town tryout) and then move with added capital (and co-producers) onto Broadway. A short list includes: *A Chorus Line* from the New York Shakespeare Festival Theatre, *Death of a Salesman* and *A Moon for the Misbegotten* from the Goodman Theatre in Chicago, *Proof, The Tale of the Allergist's Wife,* and *A Class Act* from the Manhattan Theater Club in New York City, *Having Our Say* and *Electra* from the McCarter Theatre in Princeton, and *Not About Nightingales* from the Alley Theatre in Houston.

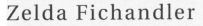

*P*roducing *D*irector

Zelda Fichandler

Annalisa Kraft/Courtesy Arena Stage

Zelda Fichandler, former producing director of Arena Stage and former artistic director of The Acting Company, discusses the distinction between a producer and a manager: How do you define the difference between a producer and a manager? "Well in my way of thinking (and I'm like the Red Queen, when I use words they mean exactly what I mean them to mean—no more, no less) in my way of thinking, as the Red Queen, they don't belong in the same category, they're two different functions. The producer does what the title says. He or she leads out, leads forth, leads through. The producer is the total organizing human being who generates the impulse from the organization: what direction is it going to take? When is it necessary to move in another direction? The style of the work; are you going to do only new works? Are you going to do only female playwrights between the ages of forty and forty-five? Are you going to do only dead playwrights? Who can come to rehearsals? Are you going to increase your deficit and say 'To hell with it, let's see what happens'? Are you going to cut costs? Are you going to have two theatres? Which twin has the Toni?—all of the big questions. The manager, it seems to me, has a very important function. But the manager works within the compass design, works within the full circle to manage whatever area. We're lousy with managers—we've got a box office manager, a house manager, a theatre manager, a production manager. A manager is an executor of the design set by somebody else, in my view...."[5]

Broadway producer Alexander H. Cohen said that the commercial and nonprofit theatre share something in common:

> *What's good succeeds.* If the material is good—if it addresses the nature of our society—then it will succeed in either the commercial or nonprofit theatre, or, in both, as the case may be. There's a great deal of trial and error in choosing material and producing it. But finally the dross sinks beneath its own undistinguished weight and the meaningful, imaginative, and exciting continue on our stages.

Out of the commercial and nonprofit theatres, and out of producers' visionary risk-taking, have come such American classics as *A Streetcar Named Desire, Death of a Salesman, A Raisin in the Sun, Who's Afraid of Virginia Woolf?, A Chorus Line, Cabaret, Chicago,* and *Angels in America: A Gay Fantasia on National Themes.*

*A*rtistic *D*irector

Gregory Boyd

Courtesy of Alley Theatre

Gregory Boyd became artistic director of the Alley Theatre in Houston in 1989. He has focused on developing a core company of actors, and an internationally known group of Associate Artists, including Edward Albee, Robert Wilson, and Frank Wildhorn. Under his artistic leadership, the Alley Theatre co-produced *Not About Nightingales,* an early Tennessee Williams' play, with the Royal National Theatre in London, which came to Broadway in 1998 for a limited run; and the Frank Wildhorn musicals *Jekyll & Hyde* and *The Civil War,* which were developed and opened in Houston before Broadway debuts.

THE REAL THING Tom Stoppard's *The Real Thing* with John Feltch and Elizabeth Heflin, directed by artistic director Gregory Boyd, Alley Theatre, Houston, 2000.

©T. Charles Erickson/Alley Theatre

Boyd has also engaged in an ongoing collaboration with such influential artists as Anne Bogart, Tony Kushner, Corin Redgrave, and Vanessa Redgrave. A typical season at the Alley includes Arthur Miller's *A View from the Bridge,* Eve Ensler's *Lemonade,* Charles Dickens' *A Christmas Carol,* Margaret Edson's *Wit,* Shakespeare's *The Comedy of Errors,* Noël Coward's *Hay Fever,* Douglas Carter Beane's *As Bees in Honey Drown,* and Tom Stoppard's *The Real Thing.* In 1996, the Alley Theatre was given the "Special 'Tony' Award for Outstanding Regional Theatre" in recognition of one of the nation's most innovative professional resident theatres.

TRANSITION

The producer's job, as the title implies, is to *produce*. Many business people are attracted to "show biz" and to investing for a variety of reasons, most of them the wrong ones: the glamour of associating with Broadway and "stars," and the get-rich-quick dream of an overnight "hit."

But producing means making a lot of difficult, educated decisions about art, people, and money, and carrying them out. It is not for the dilettante or the faint of heart. Producing is frequently painful. It can mean firing your favorite actor, director, or designer who turns out not to be right for the show. A producer has to have the personality and experience to influence people, raise money, hire, dismiss, mediate disputes, encourage and assist, option wisely, sell expediently, soothe bruised egos, and be all things to all people. Most important is the ability to extract money from investors—in a word, *to produce the show*.

WEB SITES

The League of American Theatres and Producers

The national trade association for the Broadway theatre industry is made up of theatre owners, producers, presenters, and general managers.

http://www.broadway.org

League of Chicago Theatres

Comprising members from the commercial, not-for-profit, and educational theatres, the league promotes the Chicago theatre industry.

http://www.theaterchicago.org

Theatre Bay Area

A group dedicated to strengthening and promoting theatre and dance in the San Francisco Bay Area.

http://www.theatrebayarea.org/

Web sites for up-to-date information on the New York theatre industry, including shows, cast lists, reviews, and ticket prices.

Broadway Theatre

http://www.broadway.com

Broadway and Off Broadway Theatre

http://www.theatermania.com

Curtain Up

http://www.Curtainup.com

The New York Theatre Experience

http://www.nytheatre.com

New York Today

http://www.nytoday.com/theater

The Off Off Broadway Review

http://www.oobr.com

Playbill

http://www.playbill.com

Theatre.com

http://www.theatre.com

TheatreLink

http://www.theatrelink.org

Theatre Reviews Limited

http://www.theatrereviews.com

These search terms are provided to assist you in exploring the topics introduced in this chapter at:

http//www.infotrac-college.com

Broadway, Off Broadway, Off Off Broadway, Broadway grosses, producers, commercial theatre, musical theatre, nonprofit theatre, casting director, agent, nontraditional casting, regional theatre, resident theatre, literary manager, theatre manager, previews, national touring companies, arts management.

Re-imaging Cultures: Theatrical Diversity

I think when you spend time outside of your own culture, you are so stimulated that you are given tremendous perspective on yourself and your own world.[1]

JULIE TAYMOR

Director and Designer

The re-imaging of world cultures by international companies and solo performers in the late twentieth century brought cultural diversity onto our stages in a defining way. The fusion of performance styles from many cultures and the reflection upon global moral, social, and economic issues engaged the theatre anew in the fundamental issues of our times—racism, barbarism, hunger, disease, terrorism, discrimination, injustice, and environmental hazards.

CULTURAL LINKS

Since its beginnings, theatre moved beyond the borders of specific cultures by way of itinerant players, traveling audiences, touring companies, and universal subjects. In the final decades of the twentieth century, the theatre assumed a large role in the desire of artists and societies to demonstrate their openness to world cultures. In effect, the theatre's unique ability to blend cultures in the creation of distinctive aesthetic forms positions theatre at the forefront of the current debate on cultural diversity and intercultural artistic expression.

This discussion of the theatre's re-imaging of cultures begins with the cultural buzzwords of the nineties—*multiculturalism, transculturalism,* and *interculturalism*—and examines leading international companies and solo performers who are in the vanguard of artistic efforts to confront the moral, social, and political issues of our time. This new trend in world theatre brings new styles and neglected issues onto our stages, and new audiences into our theatres.

In the late 1980s, new influences in the ease of world travel, along with the cross-fertilization of aesthetic forms among European and Asian artists and the awakening of America to the riches of a multiracial society, opened doors to new performers, bold texts, and intercultural artistic expression. Intercultural productions by Peter Brook, Julie Taymor, and Ariane Mnouchkine transcended borders, languages, and ethnicity. Solo performers, especially in the United States, took up issues of race, class, and self-identity in America and created a new avant-garde for the nineties.

Multiculturalism

Webster's *Dictionary* says that *multiculturalism* means "of or pertaining to a society of varied cultural groups." In our newspapers, magazines, and university curriculums, the term has been utilized in two ways: first, to acknowledge the rich diversity of American society—its cultural fusions of traditions, learning, and art; and second, to redress the heavy emphasis on the importance, achievements, and values of Western culture. What is at issue here is the desire to emphasize cultural differences—that is, to allow all cultures self-expression, autonomy, and power.

It is fashionable to say that the American effort to emphasize the multicultural is the inversion of the "melting pot" idea. Multiculturalism celebrates the *separateness* and *distinctions* of diverse groups existing side by side. Culturally diverse groups set about in today's world to retain their own distinct ethnic qualities: African American, Asian American, Latino/a, Native American, Korean, Irish, Hasidic, Jamaican, and so on. Nor is the multicultural idea limited to ethnicity. It also includes orientations and ideologies—gay, lesbian, feminist, environmentalist, creationist, and so on.

Interculturalism

Interculturalism is another way of understanding a diverse society, its similarities and differences. Theorists argue that intercultural performance aims to *bridge* two cultures—for example, East and West.[2]

Interculturalists directly confront power arrangements and struggles between ethnic groups. They explore the confrontations, fears, disturbances, and difficulties at the points where fissions occur—where cultures collide, overlap, and pull away. Interculturalism happens in art, literature, and scholarship when writers and performers examine the causes of conflicts among culturally diverse groups.[3] Performance artist Guillermo Gómez-Peña lives between two cultures—Mexico and the United States—and makes art out of the contradictions. David Henry Hwang's play, *M. Butterfly,* a drama based on the libretto of a nineteenth-century Italian opera, examines Chinese and American culture through the eyes of a Chinese actress who is, in fact, a man.

The terms *multicultural* and *intercultural* are favored today to describe cross-cultural theatrical expression. A third term is used to refer to the "blenders," the *transculturalists,* who borrow forms and styles from various cultures to create new cultural contexts to speak to large issues that embrace all humankind. The works of Peter Brook, Ariane Mnouchkine, and Julie Taymor are very much transcultural in this sense: they blend Eastern, European, African, American, and Hispanic cultures—texts, styles, traditions, nationalities, and languages—in the making of new theatre pieces that speak with *universal voices* on issues common to all humankind in the twenty-first century.

Transculturalism

Since its beginnings in ancient Greece, theatre transcended specific cultures with its concern for the universality of the human condition. Greek writers confronted issues of tribal wars and international imperialism. Aeschylus in *The Persians,* produced in

472 B.C., treated the nation's enemies from the East with deep sympathy and turned their story into a parable on the dangers of pride that goes with power. Euripides in *The Trojan Women,* written one year following the Athenian army's destruction of the population of the island of Melos (all male inhabitants were put to death and women and children sold into slavery), condemned Greek barbarity through portraits of war's universal victims—women and children. Twenty-five hundred years later, these ancient theatrical worlds are not far removed from the tribal and religious conflicts in Eastern Europe, the Near East, and Africa.

Such large universal issues that transcend specific cultures inform the work of Peter Brook, Julie Taymor, and Ariane Mnouchkine, who base their efforts on Eastern, Latin American, African, and Greek texts to speak to all cultures about good and evil, war and peace, and the common ground of human desires and needs. In a word, transculturalism refers not so much to a theatrical aesthetic of expression as to "seeing" those universal themes spanning all cultures.

PETER BROOK AND *THE MAHABHARATA*

In a rock quarry in southern France in 1985, Peter Brook first staged the twelve-hour performance of *The Mahabharata,* a cycle of three plays (*The Game of Dice, The Exile in the Forest,* and *The War*) adapted by Jean-Claude Carrière in French from the Sanskrit poem dating from 400 B.C. The epic poem compiles the myths, legends, wars, folklore, ethics, history, and theology of ancestral India, including the Hindu sacred book *The Bhagavad Gita.* From high in the quarry's rock wall, the piercing fanfare of the nagaswaram, an instrument that is half trumpet and half pipe, announces the approach of the first play. Brook's multinational company of twenty-one players lends diverse qualities of physical virtuosity, intelligence, humor, and cultural differences.

> "A [theatre] is like a small restaurant whose responsibility is to nourish its customers.... There is only one test: Do the spectators leave the playhouse with slightly more courage, more strength than when they came in? If the answer is yes, the food is healthy."[4]
> PETER BROOK
> *The Threads of Time*

In staging this epic struggle between two opposing sets of cousins in an ancient Indian dynasty, Brook begins with the narrative voice of the symbolic poet Vyasa, who is writing a poem about the history of his ancestors (and by inference, the story of humankind). His story is recorded by the elephant-man Ganesha, who is also the god Krishna, the supporter of the good and the brave. Throughout, there is the innocence of the young boy who, just as the spectators, listens to the storyteller, watching, questioning, searching. What begins as an austere bargain and a lesson in the right way of life proceeds through adventures that carry an inconsolable sense of loss but ends with a vision of paradise as a gentle place of music, food, cool waters, pleasant conversation, and harmony. At the close, the blind can see, the wounded and slaughtered are restored, and all animosity is forgotten.

Brook achieves the stylization of this global war by minimal, yet spectacular, choices. He makes dramatic use of the elements (earth, fire, and water) along with brightly patterned carpets, swirling fabrics of red and gold, and masks to transform

(continued on page 315)

The Mahabharata

Martha Swope/TimePix

THE GAME OF DICE The dice players toss to determine the fate of the Pandavas in *The Mahabharata,* directed by Peter Brook, at Les Bouffes du Nord Théâtre, Paris, 1986.

The Mahabharata, based on the ancient Hindu poem and first produced at the Avignon Festival in France in 1985, is a cycle of three plays: *The Game of Dice, The Exile in the Forest,* and *The War.*

Part I introduces the main characters, their mythic origins, their characteristics and aims, the role of the gods (especially Krishna), and the growing discord between the Pandavas and the Kauravas, two branches of the Bharata clan. In a game of dice, which the Pandava leader loses to his cousins, the Pandavas forfeit all their property and worldly possessions and are exiled to a forest.

In Part II, the Pandavas live a primordial existence in the forest, while procuring arms for the inevitable battle to come.

In Part III, the devastating war that threatens the entire universe is unleashed—a war foreordained and controlled by the god Krishna. After a gruesome massacre, Pandava regains his rights and is later reconciled with his enemies in heaven. Vyasa, the storyteller, warns that this is "the last illusion," referring to earth and/or the play. According to Hinduism, life is God's dream and, as rendered by God, is an illusion.

At the cycle's end, the actors, dressed in pure white, drop their personae, eat delicacies, and exit, signaling that the game and the performance are over.

actors playing half-animal or half-divine creatures. Staging techniques are adopted from Eastern theatre—a billowing cloth represents newborn children, and a single large wooden wheel stands for Krishna's chariot. Battles are conveyed by acrobatic displays of Eastern martial arts; dozens of white arrows fly through the air; and, with the flutter of a hand, a god creates a solar eclipse.

The common ground shared by *The Mahabharata* and Western literature are those associations with Oedipus found in the wanderings of the blind prince Dhritarashtra, with the Old Testament in the forest exile of Pandavas, with Shakespeare in the wars of ruling dynasties, and with the *Iliad* and *Odyssey* in the moral struggle of ideal heroes representing divine forces of good arrayed against demonic ones.

Brook's production represents a culmination of his lifelong search for theatrical expression of humankind's greatest dramas and deepest dilemmas. His efforts to transform Hindu myth into universalized art, accessible to any and all cultures, are triumphant. Embedded in the ancient text are eternal philosophical questions on the paradox of the human condition: Why do people lust for power? What are the causes of humankind's destructiveness? Will humanity survive armageddon? Does the individual have a choice? What is God's game and are we pawns?

"Of course, the basic themes are contemporary," Brook says. "One of them is how to find one's way in an age of destruction. What is brought out in *The Mahabharata* is that there is a certain world harmony, a cosmic harmony, that can either be helped or destroyed by individuals…. We, too, are living in a time when every value one can think of is in danger."[5]

JULIE TAYMOR AND *JUAN DARIÉN*

Julie Taymor and her collaborator, composer Elliot Goldenthal, tell the story of a jaguar cub transformed into a boy in a performance piece about faith and superstition, compassion and revenge, civilization and savagery.

Juan Darién, first produced Off Broadway in 1988, is a compelling narrative, based on the Latin American story by Uruguayan writer Horacio Quiroga, that deals with the bestiality of humans and the humanity of beasts. Taymor's production utilizes puppets, masks, movement, and a musical score sung in Latin and Spanish. Her subjects include maternal love and bereavement, the primitiveness of the natural world, and the malevolence of the human one. Subtitled "A Carnival Mass," the work is described as a "passion play, a ritualized chronicle of the martyrdom of innocence by bigotry."[6]

Opening images display the play's themes: The deteriorating walls of a mission church are overtaken by giant jungle leaves, while the distant voices of a Latin chorus singing the *Agnus Dei* are drowned out by the buzzing of dragonflies. Taymor describes *Juan Darién* as "a visual dance of images that have a clear story line, with music—not language—motivating the action."[7]

Creator

Julie Taymor

©Elisabetta Catalano

©Joan Marcus

JUAN DARIÉN A carnival scene from *Juan Darién* (1988).

Juan Darién tells the story of a young jaguar who is transformed by motherly love into a boy, then cruelly executed by superstitious and vengeful villagers, and finally retransformed into the feared jaguar of jungle lore. Understanding the fear of jaguars by people living at the edge of civilization, Julie Taymor says, is paramount to understanding this instance of human savagery.[8]

Interludes between scenes, called "Tiger Tales," reinforce the culture's obsession with the jaguar as enemy. The "Tales" are a series of shadow puppet plays depicting struggles between humans and beasts presided over by Mr. Bones, the master of ceremonies, a life-size skeleton puppet topped with a black bowler hat. These tales serve to break the linear flow of the story, interrupt the tension, and introduce crude jokes. In one instance, a jaguar eats a baby who then drives the animal mad with its loud and ceaseless crying. The jaguar tries to stop the sound within his stomach by covering his various orifices and finally blows his head off, whereupon the baby emerges giggling and gurgling. These interludes range from the sublime to the ridiculous.

The story begins with images of a tiny church whose windows crumble into lush foliage that descends until the stage becomes a jungle with strange serpentine creatures, night sounds, and flying lizards. A mother jaguar is slain by hunters, and her cub stands forlornly in the wilderness. The jungle disappears and an entire hill town in miniature, dotted with houses and with a road that winds to a graveyard at the hill's

Julie Taymor (b. 1952) grew up in a suburb of Boston. She traces her initial interest in puppetry and masks to the École du Mime de Jacques Le Coq in Paris, where she studied before attending Oberlin College in Ohio. She traveled to Eastern Europe, Japan, and Indonesia, where she lived for four years. In Indonesia, she formed her own international company, Teatr Loh (*loh* means "the source" in Javanese), with performers skilled in traditional dance, t'ai chi, improvisation, shadow puppetry, mask-making, acting, and singing. Her first major work, *Way of Snow,* used masks and puppets to take spectators on a cross-cultural journey from the tale of an Eskimo shaman into the modern world of speeding buses and telephone operators.

Returning to the United States in 1979, she designed sets, costumes, puppets, and masks for productions in regional theatres. In 1988, she won her first *Village Voice* ("Obie") award for the stage version of *The Transposed Heads,* based on a Thomas Mann novella. She received a MacArthur Foundation "genius" award in 1991. Her various projects include *The Tempest, Liberty's Taken, Tirai* (1981 Maharan Theatre Design Citation), *The Taming of the Shrew, Titus Andronicus, Visual Magic* (1985 Obie award), *Juan Darién* (1988 Obie Award for writing, directing, and designing), *The King Stag, Savages, Black Elk Speaks, The Haggadah,* a revised *Juan Darién* (1997 nomination for five Antoinette Perry "Tony" Awards), *The Lion King* (1998 "Tony" Awards for best directing and costumes, including the 2000 Olivier Award for costume design), and *The Green Bird* (1996, revised Broadway 2000); *Fool's Fire* (television); *Oedipus Rex, The Magic Flute, Salomé,* and *The Flying Dutchman* (operas); and *Titus* (feature film). A major retrospective of Julie Taymor's work opened in 2000 at the National Museum of Women in the Arts in Washington, D.C.

peak, moves downstage. This magical landscape captures Taymor's large themes: birth and death, faith and superstition, civilization and savagery.

Juan Darién is a mélange of cultural influences that Taymor absorbed in the early seventies in Europe, Japan, and Indonesia. First, there is the Latin American fable, then music from the Roman Catholic Mass, life-size Bunraku-type puppets manipulated by three handlers, monumental puppets that recall the Bread and Puppet Theatre, Indonesian shadow puppets, European Punch-and-Judy-style puppets, and Mayan masks. A variety of musical instruments are used: Japanese taiko drums, African shakers, Indian temple gongs, Mayan clay flutes, an Australian didgeridoo, Western trumpets, marimbas, tuba, and an upright piano.

Only the actors playing the mother and the boy are identifiable in an ensemble of eleven. With this ensemble, Taymor captures the story's sense of living at the border between the jungle, with its natural beauty and savagery, and civilization, with its refinement and cruelty.

Juan Darién is also a story of transformation. The boy is transformed five times. First, he

TIGER TALES The life-size skeleton puppet, Mr. Bones, presides over the interludes (called "Tiger Tales") in Julie Taymor's *Juan Darién.*

©Joan Marcus

©Richard Feldman

appears as a jaguar cub (a rod and string puppet); second, he becomes an infant (a hand-manipulated doll) cradled by a mother who has lost her own child to disease; at age ten, he transforms into a four-foot-tall Bunraku puppet with realistic features; upon the death of his mother, he becomes a flesh-and-blood child. This is the pivotal moment. From this point on, Juan is the only human (unmasked) actor in the play. When he is accused by the villagers of being a dangerous jaguar, we realize that everyone around him wears a mask. Unlike Juan, the masked villagers appear not quite human. The final transformation occurs when the child is burned alive on the Bengal lights (fireworks) and metamorphoses into a jaguar once again. This time, the child's face can be seen through the open mouth of the animal mask, his hands are covered by large paws, and his naked torso has blood-red stripes received during a brutal whipping.[9] The final lesson is that human beings, through abominable acts of torture and murder, unwittingly make beasts of others.

> "A puppet is a sort of poetic abbreviation, a distillation to a character's essence. It is more archetype than individual, an ideogram for Vulgarity, Brutality, Helplessness, Despair. That these creatures are inanimate only enhances that concentration of meaning."[10]
>
> JULIE TAYMOR
> *Director and Designer*

Taymor's work is a blend of Eastern and Western theatre: puppetry, masks, performance styles, and minimal scenery. The stage is transformed into a poetic realm of myth, dreams, nightmares, and childlike storytelling, where puppets and actors concentrate meaning on universal issues that extend beyond specific cultures.

ARIANE MNOUCHKINE AND *LES ATRIDES*

French director Ariane Mnouchkine's ten-hour cycle of Greek tragedy combined Aeschylus' *Oresteia* (*Agamemnon, The Libation Bearers, The Eumenides*) with Euripides' *Iphigenia in Aulis* in the 1992 Théâtre du Soleil production in Paris. This presentation excavates the savage, disaster-cursed story of the House of Atreus, whose central players are Agamemnon, Clytemnestra, Menelaus, Orestes, and Electra.

In borrowing from the classical texts and from the arts and crafts of Eastern cultures, Mnouchkine and her collaborators reshaped the form and substance of Aeschylus' story by beginning the cycle with *Iphigenia in Aulis* as a prologue to the causes of genocide-like wars, the death of families, and the role of women in the dissolution and resurgence of civilizations. She combined music, rhythms, costumes, makeup, movements, and acting styles from Europe, Africa, China, and India with actors recruited from various ethnic groups and nations. Like Peter Brook, Mnouchkine creates a world theatre informed by behaviors common to all humankind.

Mnouchkine's company, not unlike Brook's, adheres in performance style and visual silhouette to the cultural influences of both East and West. In seeking a "look" for the Greek cycle that was both ancient and modern, Mnouchkine emphasized Eastern antiquity with the ancient Indian tradition of *Kutiyattam*, the only surviving tradition for presenting Sanskrit drama. At least as old as the tenth century, Kutiyattam gave rise to the modern Kathakali dance drama. The result is an amalgam of many cultures and forms of theatre and dance in the colorful costumes and stylized makeup dominated by the Kathakali. Actors surrounded by kinetic choruses, colorful non-Western costumes and painted faces, bloody tableaux, and Eastern sounds of string and percussive instruments underscore the mixing of cultural influences from East and West.

Mnouchkine also brings a modern feminine sensibility to the reading of the classical Greek texts. Her story of the Atridae centers on Clytemnestra, who married into the accursed clan and whose doomed passion is central to three of the plays. Prefaced by *Iphigenia in Aulis,* in which Clytemnestra is tricked into bringing her daughter to Aulis—where the Greek fleet is becalmed. There, her daughter is sacrificed to enable the fleet to sail to Troy. This modern version becomes the story of women betrayed by male ambition, power politics, and their own emotions.

The Eumenides, the final part of *Les Atrides,* is key to Mnouchkine's intentions. Shockingly modern with its nonhuman chorus of leaping, barking dogs, this final episode is presided over by Athene, the goddess of peace and wisdom, who makes peace with the forces of vengeance. She is a fragile, becalmed figure dressed in an East Indian costume of white trousers and tunic. Like a slender reed of peace, she positions herself between the audience as democratic populace and the howling forces of barbarism, the perennial "dogs of war." Athene literally stands between the audience and the forces of darkness before which civilizations for 2,400 years have collapsed into savagery and death. However tentative Athene's presence, her pacifying influence is witnessed as the dogs (actors costumed with elaborate baboon-faced masks adorned with swept-back coifs of black hair and pointed snouts) begin to stand on two legs as symbolic of the influence of the enlightened way that has led civilizations out of barbarism and savagery.

The entire production takes place in a forty-foot-wide bullfighting arena of a neutral sand color, textured with painted smears of "aged blood." It is a ritualized "killing

Martine Franck/Magnum

IPHIGENIA IN AULIS Clytemnestra (Juliana Carneiro da Cunha), Agamemnon's wife, and Achilles (Simon Abkarian), the warrior, in *Iphigenia in Aulis,* the first of the four plays in *Les Atrides.*

THE LIBATION BEARERS The chorus consoles Clytemnestra in the third part of *Les Atrides.*

field." A place for confrontation and violence, the arena is surrounded by three walls with six partitions for the "picadores" and "matadors" to escape to safety from the ensuing violence. There is safety only behind or on top of the arena walls, not within the barren and merciless killing field occupied by the doomed protagonists.

Mnouchkine confessed that she began rehearsals without an "image" of the playing space. Gradually, the arena formed in her imagination with its "wooden enclosure and the spaces where the matador can step away in order to seek protection from the wounded beast sensing its death and seeking the death of its opponent."[11] Boxlike platforms—rectangular second stages— glide into the arena through the rear gates, suggesting alternately a ship, chariot, dais, bed, or monument and carrying its cargo of child, returning warriors, the dead, and the goddess. To complete the landscape (and to provide quick exits and entrances), a raked trolley is pushed by stagehands through the audience to the front of the stage area. As the central characters step onto the trolley, they stand in telling friezelike postures and exit into an invisible area of unmitigated violence and death. Clytemnestra stands, for example, enfolded in Agamemnon's arms as they are transported to his arranged death.

Mnouchkine and her company are like archaeologists excavating the Greek texts to uncover an ancient civilization of history, myth, and legend. Of the company's choice of the Greek cycle, she said: "It shows that war is fratricidal, that we kill those who are closest to us, members of our own family…. Humanity is a cursed family. Why do we make war? Why so many civil wars? That is the theme of the Théâtre du Soleil."[12]

CULTURAL DIVERSITY AND PERFORMANCE ART

Theatre artists in the United States also respond to diverse cultural values and political issues that extend beyond the borders of current debates over political correctness, affirmative action, equal opportunity, and racial quotas. Today's cultural pluralism resulted, first, in a re-examination of America's predominantly European tradition in culture and the arts. The new pluralism resulted in our awakening to African American, Hispanic, Native American, and Asian American artists, issues, and traditions. Today, we have the plays of Lynne Alvarez, Maya Angelou, Philip Kan Gotanda, David Henry Hwang, Eduardo Machado, Suzan-Lori Parks, José Rivera,

(continued on page 323)

Re-imaging Cultures

Peter Brook . Ariane Mnouchkine . Andrei Serban . Julie Taymor

The *Mahabharata, Les Atrides, The King Stag,* and *Juan Darién* are productions that transcend national borders, language, ethnicity, and serve as examples of the "re-imaging of cultures."

Martine Franck/Magnum

AGAMEMNON The chorus of old men dance around Clytemnestra (Juliana Carneiro da Cunha) as she waits for Agamemnon's entrance and his death in the second part of *Les Atrides.*

Influenced by Eastern dress and makeup, MNOUCHKINE staged the story of the House of Atreus in a wooden enclosure resembling a bullfighting arena where violence and death reign in a killing field occupied by the doomed protagonists—Iphigenia, Agamemnon, Clytemnestra, and Orestes. A colorful blue and white canopy arches above the playing space, like a changeable sky bearing witness to human destiny.

Martine Franck/Magnum

THE LIBATION BEARERS The chorus of women in colorful costumes and makeup adapted from Kathakali dance drama.

Martha Swope/TimePix

The nine-hour Sanskrit epic, *The Mahabharata,* directed by PETER BROOK, captures the art, culture, and spiritual life of the ancient culture.

THE MAHABHARATA One of the many startling images from Peter Brook's production based on the Sanskrit poem.

321

Rumanian-born director ANDREI SERBAN came to the United States in 1969 at the invitation of Ellen Stewart to work at La Mama Experimental Theatre Club. He participated in Peter Brook's International Centre of Theatre Research productions both in Paris and Shiraz (Iran), and directed to great acclaim *Fragments of a Trilogy* (*Electra* and *The Trojan Women*) for La Mama ETC, a production that overcame barriers and borders of languages and countries. His collaboration with Julie Taymor on *The King Stag* also spans theatrical traditions of East and West.

THE KING STAG In an effort to bring monsters and magical creatures to the American theatre, Julie Taymor designed gigantic flying creatures along with costumes and masks for Andrei Serban's 1984 production of *The King Stag* at the American Repertory Theatre (Cambridge, Mass.).

©Richard Feldman

JULIE TAYMOR'S artistic signature is apparent in *Juan Darien, The Lion King,* and *The Green Bird.* She openly reveals the theatricality of puppetry, singer-narrators guiding the story, and the visible presence of musicians. She draws on the arts and crafts of many cultures to tell age-old mythic stories about young people growing up in the face of adult evil and hostile environments.

JUAN DARIÉN Juan (Lawrence Neals Jr.) talks with one of Julie Taymor's creature puppets designed for the 1988 Off Broadway production.

©Joan Marcus

THE LION KING Taymor mixed Javanese rod puppetry, Balinese headdress, African masks, American and British music (much of it written by Elton John) with African music (from Soweto with songs written by Lebo M.), and the click language of Xhosa performed by Tsidii Le Loka (center) from South Africa.

Actress and solo performer Anna Deavere Smith in *Fires in the Mirror*, first performed in 1992 at the Joseph Papp Public Theatre, New York.

San Francisco Chronicle

Milcha Sanchez-Scott, and August Wilson. Likewise, today's audiences mirror a diverse and complex society as well.

Performance art and solo performers explore America's cultural diversity and social pluralism. At a time when theatre has been forced by film and television into the margins of cultural life, individual artists have stepped forward to call attention to the marginalized of society: the poor, nonwhite, gay, old, young, ill, homeless, and abused.

Performance artists have lead the American theatre's avant-garde in the nineties. There subjects are the excluded, the ostracized, the isolated, and the abandoned.

The solo performer exists on the fringes of the establishment, call it the commercial theatre or the larger political system. In form and substance, the solo performer's antecedents stretch back to shamanistic practices in early cultures and forward to modern art forms, including vaudeville, cabaret, stand-up comedy, music, poetry readings, dance, and European cubism, dadaism, and futurism. What these performers share in common is their singular presence and their active participation with audiences. These solo artists are positioned not so much on the aesthetic outskirts of the community as on its moral and social fringes. The solo explorations of Laurie Anderson, Eric Bogosian, Lenny Bruce, Karen Finley, Guillermo Gómez-Peña, Spalding Gray, Holly Hughes, and Anna Deavere Smith—as challenging as they might seem artistically—are functions of their overriding concerns with class, ethnicity, gender, sexuality, environment, and, indeed, with the entire political, social, and natural environment of American life.

(continued on page 326)

©Joan Marcus

Eric Bogosian, performance artist.

> "The model of cross-cultural interdisciplinary collaboration is still a very effective one. Sharing resources and skills, artists from different cultural backgrounds and métiers can effectively negotiate a common ground that supersedes temporarily our/their differences."[13]
>
> GUILLERMO GÓMEZ-PEÑA
> *Performance Artist*

> "The question often comes up: Why is the solo show so endemic in the '90s? It would miss the heart of the artist's impulse to create solo work to simply echo the oft-cited bottom-line reasons—diminishing government funding for the arts, paucity of ensemble-size venues, the obvious showcase potential for an actor as a stepping stone to larger or more commercial work. Perhaps the primary reason for the proliferation of solo work in this decade lies in the great appeal for artists of having total aesthetic control of their material...."[14]
>
> JO BONNEY
> *Director*

Eric Bogosian, Eve Ensler, Karen Finley, Guillermo Gómez-Peña, Holly Hughes, John Leguizamo

Photo by Ivan Kyncl/Courtesy of Eric Bogosian

Eric Bogosian developed savagely comic performances—what he has called "explosions of expression"—of America's low-life characters. In his solo performances of *Men Inside, Funhouse, Drinking in America, Sex, Drugs, and Rock & Roll, Pounding Nails in the Floor with My Forehead, SubUrbia,* and *Wake Up and Smell the Coffee,* his characters are pimps and whores, addicts and sellers, talk-jocks and rock stars. His first play, *Talk Radio* (1985), was made into a film directed by Oliver Stone, and his book *Notes from Underground* has been a best-seller.

Eve Ensler—an award-winning playwright, activist, and screenwriter—compiled and performed *The Vagina Monologues* as an anthology on women and won a 1997 Obie Award. The world tour of *The Vagina Monologues* initiated V-Day, a movement to stop violence against women. This piece can be performed solo or with several actresses. Ensler's stage works include *The Depot, Floating Rhoda and the Glue Man, Extraordinary Measures, Ladies, Scooncat, Cinderella Cendrillion* (directed by Anne Bogart), *Lemonade,* and *Conviction.* There have been performances of *Necessary Targets* to benefit Bosnian women refugees on Broadway, at The John F. Kennedy Center in Washington, D.C., in Sarajevo and London. Ensler's satirical comedy is angry, poignant, and deeply committed to women's issues.

©1997 Susan Johann

©Timothy Greensfield-Sanders

Karen Finley became the center of controversy when the National Endowment for the Arts rescinded her grant to create performance art. Her work was considered offensive by local and national legislators for its obscene language, sexuality, nudity, and attacks on political and religious figures. In *We Keep Our Victims Ready,* about the degradation of women, Finley stripped nude and smeared her body with chocolate while comparing women to penned-up calves. In 1998 she toured the country with her *Return of the Chocolate-Smeared Woman* to continue her protest against government censorship of the arts.

Photo by Eugenio Castro/LA POCHA
NOSTRA

Guillermo Gómez-Peña. Born and raised in Mexico City, Gómez-Peña came to the United States in 1978. He is a performance artist who also engages in video, audio, and installations along with writing poetry and critical essays on cultural theory. His performance pieces are politically charged critiques of xenophobia and U.S. imperialism. He is as likely to be found performing in marginally funded community centers as in museums and galleries. By way of irony, humor, poetry, and wit, he uses performance to enter into dialogue on such complex issues as censorship, immigration, and Anglo-American attitudes toward Latinos and others. Through it all, he projects a range of tensions, hopes, and fears that characterize U.S./Mexican relations and envisions a utopian future where people live without borders. His performance work includes *The End of the Line, The Dangerous Border Game, The Mexterminator Project,* and *Borderscape 2000.*

Holly Hughes is another performance artist whose grant from the National Endowment for the Arts was rescinded for the allegedly indecent content of her work. She has since become a crusader against censorship of the arts. Credited with reinventing lesbian theatre, her solo performances explore her identity as a woman and lesbian. From her satires of detective fiction, *The Lady Dick* and *The Well of Horniness,* to her confrontational "queer theatre" pieces *World Without End* and *Clit Notes,* Holly Hughes has been called "the poster child for indecent art."

Kelly Campell/Courtesy of Holly Hughes

The Everett Collection

John Leguizamo was born in Columbia, South America, and grew up in Jackson Heights (Queens, N.Y.). *Spic-o-Rama* and his best-known *Freaks* are comic, satirical, and poignant journeys through his Latino neighborhood in Queens in which he plays a dozen different characters—male and female, young and old. Leguizamo and *Freaks* reached Broadway, and he was nominated for a 1998 Antoinette Perry "Tony" Award; *Freaks* was directed by Spike Lee as an HBO comedy special.

THE SOLO PERFORMANCE

Fires in the Mirror: Crown Heights, Brooklyn, and Other Identities; Twilight: Los Angeles 1992; and *House Arrest* by Anna Deavere Smith

Created by writer and actress Anna Deavere Smith, *Fires in the Mirror* brought her national attention for its deft biography of people involved in the 1991 Crown Heights riots in Brooklyn, New York. Her solo works (*Fires in the Mirror* and *Twilight: Los Angeles 1992*) are part of a series begun in 1983 as *On the Road: A Search for American Character* in which she brings onto the stage the "voices of the unheard"—the invisible in America. In each of these performance pieces, Smith takes on the roles of the many people she interviewed. "I try to represent multiple points of view and to capture the personality of a place by showing its individuals," she said. In effect, her solo performances are a demonstration of the American character, what she calls "a parade of color," and her theatrical solos create a new framework from which to assess race and class in America.[15]

Both *Fires in the Mirror* and *Twilight: Los Angeles 1992* are based on historical incidents. The racial conflict between the Lubavitcher and black communities in Crown Heights, Brooklyn, that resulted in the riots of 1991 became the subject for *Fires in the Mirror.* Racial divisions in Los Angeles between the Rodney King incident of March 3, 1991, and the federal trial that ended in April 1993 with the conviction of two Los Angeles policemen for violating King's civil rights provided the topic for *Twilight.* Of these communities, Anna Deavere Smith says, "They all have a very clear sense of their own difference. I'm interested in capturing the American character through documenting these differences."[16]

Anna Deavere Smith as the Rabbi Joseph Spielman in her award-winning *Fires in the Mirror: Crown Heights, Brooklyn, and Other Identities* produced by the Berkeley Repertory Theatre, California, 1994.

San Francisco Chronicle

Fires in the Mirror: Crown Heights, Brooklyn, and Other Identities

This solo piece grew out of 100 interviews with a variety of participants and witnesses from the black and Lubavitcher communities in Crown Heights. Out of these many voices, Anna Deavere Smith crafted a coherent performance by using the words of those she interviewed, thereby developing unique and often contradictory insights into a complex series of events. As the conflict unfolds, the voices of the Crown Heights community are heard: the Reverend Al Sharpton, civil rights activist; Robert Sherman, New York City's Commissioner on Human Rights; Norman Rosenbaum, Yankel Rosenbaum's brother; and Roz Malamud, a Crown Heights resident. It becomes apparent that there are no simple answers to the questions surrounding the controversy.

Anna Deavere Smith

San Francisco Chronicle

Anna Deavere Smith (b. 1951), actress, playwright, and performance artist, grew up in Baltimore, Maryland, as the daughter of Deavere (pronounced "da-veer") Young, a coffee merchant, and Anna Young, an elementary school principal. She trained as an actress at the American Conservatory Theatre in San Francisco, graduating with a Master of Fine Arts degree in 1976. She taught at Carnegie-Mellon University, New York University, and the University of Southern California–Los Angeles before joining the faculty at Stanford University in California.

In 1983 she began a series of solo performances, entitled *On The Road: A Search for American Character.* She gained national attention with the award-winning *Fires in the Mirror* in 1992 at the Joseph Papp Public Theater and on tour, and with *Twilight: Los Angeles 1992* at the Mark Taper Forum in Los Angeles in 1993 and on Broadway in 1994. She appeared in the films *Dave* and Jonathan Demme's *Philadelphia.* She collaborated in 1994 on a ballet called *Hymn* for the thirty-fifth anniversary season of the Alvin Ailey American Dance Theater. *House Arrest,* begun during the 1996 presidential campaign with Smith as a member of the Clinton campaign's press corps, opened as a solo performance in March 2000 at the Joseph Papp Public Theater, New York City, with a book version, called *Talk To Me.*

Anna Deavere Smith's solo pieces are sophisticated explorations of race, class, and politics in contemporary America.

What Anna Deavere Smith clearly demonstrates, however, is that each person's perspective on the incidents is a reflection of his or her background and experience of race, religion, and gender, and is worthy of being heard and understood.

The historical moment occurred on August 9, 1991, in the Crown Heights section of Brooklyn when one of the cars in a three-car procession carrying the Lubavitcher Hasidic *rebbe* (spiritual leader) ran a red light, hit another car, and swerved onto the sidewalk, killing Gavin Cato, a seven-year-old child from Guyana, and seriously injuring his cousin.

Rumors spread throughout the community that a Hasidic-run ambulance service helped the driver and his passengers while the children lay bleeding and dying on the sidewalk. Members of the district's black community reacted violently against the police and the Lubavitchers. That evening a group of young black men fatally stabbed Yankel Rosenbaum, a twenty-nine-year-old Hasidic scholar from Australia. For three days, blacks and Hasidic patrols fought one another and the police.

San Francisco Chronicle

Anna Deavere Smith as Sonny Carson, activist, in *Fires in the Mirror*. In this series of monologues (using minimal props and costume pieces) she presents a compelling portrait of a society unraveling at the seams of race and class.

This conflict reflected long-standing tensions in the Crown Heights community as well as the pain, oppression, and discrimination these groups have historically experienced. Many of the Crown Heights black community were Caribbean immigrants from Jamaica, Guyana, Trinidad, and Haiti. They had experienced discrimination on the basis of their color and their national origin. The Lubavitchers—members of an Orthodox Jewish sect that fled the Nazi genocide of Jews in Europe during the Second World War—were particularly vulnerable to anti-Jewish stereotyping because of their religion, style of dress, and insular community. Both communities felt victimized by the police, the press, and the legal system. Many viewed the jury acquittal of Yankel Rosenbaum's accused murderer as a stark example of this mistreatment and injustice.

Anna Deavere Smith interviewed people engaged at all levels of this conflict. She distilled the interviews into a ninety-minute solo performance in which she speaks the words, thoughts, and emotions of eighteen people—male and female, black and Jewish, activist and resident, parent and teacher.

As a creator and performer, Smith sets out to use the words of the voiceless and the powerful in society, creating a sophisticated and poetic dialogue about race relations in contemporary America. Onstage among the clutter of chairs and tables, Smith, barefoot with hair pulled back to make the changes of costume and gender easier, gives shape to the voices and words of others. She shows culturally diverse people struggling to make coherent their sense of rage, pain, and disbelief. She listens not for the facts but for the inner conflicts of the soul expressed in everyday speech. "I'm interested," she said, "in how language and character intersect."[17]

Fires in the Mirror, like *Twilight,* captures a multicultural America at the edge of consciousness about the death, pain, and guilt generated by racism and class. *House*

©Michal Daniel

HOUSE ARREST Anna Deavere Smith portrays a range of political figures from Thomas Jefferson and Franklin Delano Roosevelt to Anita Hill and William Jefferson Clinton in *House Arrest.* Directed by Jo Bonney, The Joseph Papp Public Theater, New York City, 2000.

Arrest, performed in 2000, is a departure for Smith. Using historical documents and original interviews, she explores the presidencies of Thomas Jefferson, Abraham Lincoln, Franklin Delano Roosevelt, and William Jefferson Clinton to strip away the myths created by history, political systems, and newspaper headlines. "House arrest" refers to the captivity of the U.S. President who inhabits the White House.

Staging Ethnic Diversity

Beginning in the early seventies, small and ethnically diverse theatre companies emerged throughout the United States. Many took their names from the ethnicity that was the sounding board of their founders, writers, artists, and political coalitions. Today, these producing organizations mirror America's growing awareness of ethnic diversity; frame the overriding political, economic, and social issues of the minority culture they represent; and, in turn, are radically changing both American culture and society.

African American Theatre Companies: New Federal Theatre, Penumbra Theatre Company, St. Louis Black Repertory Company, Crossroads Theatre Company

As producing organizations, the New Federal Theatre, Penumbra Theatre Company, St. Louis Black Repertory Theatre, and Crossroads Theatre Company are measures of the successful emergence of the African American experience onto the national stage. The creation of African American theatre companies paralleled the civil rights movement of the sixties. Amiri Baraka (LeRoi Jones) formed Spirit House in Newark, New Jersey, in 1966 to create a black "separatist" theatre "by us, about us, for us." The New Lafayette Theatre, founded in 1967 by Robert Macbeth, became a Harlem cultural center with Ed Bullins as resident playwright, associate director, and editor of *Black Theatre* magazine. The magazine functioned as an information service for black artists. Disagreements within the company brought about its dissolution in 1973. The Free Southern Theatre (New Orleans), founded in 1963 by Gilbert Moses and John O'Neal as an extension of the civil rights movement in the South, has also dissolved. The Negro Ensemble Company (NEC), created by Douglas Turner Ward in 1968 in New York City, produced works about the black experience but the plays were not always written by African Americans. The company's most influential works were *A Soldier's Play, Ceremonies in Dark Old Men, Home, The Sty of the Blind Pig,* and *River Niger.*

The works of Lorraine Hansberry, Amiri Baraka, and Ed Bullins shaped the writing of serious plays about the black experience in mid-century America. August Wilson has since become perhaps the most distiguished African American playwright writing in the final decades of twentieth century.

NEW FEDERAL THEATRE, NEW YORK CITY Among the most successful companies to achieve artistic and financial stability as a producing organization is, first, the New Federal Theatre, founded by producing director Woodie King, Jr. in 1970, in New York City. Now in its thirtieth season, the New Federal Theatre officially began at the Henry Street Settlement and today serves minority audiences in New York's Lower East Side and sponsors a variety of ethnic theatre groups and events.

PENUMBRA THEATRE COMPANY, ST. PAUL Founded in St. Paul, Minnesota, in 1976 by Lou Bellamy, the Penumbra Theatre Company encourages the staging of plays that address the African American experience and increase public awareness of the

AIN'T MISBEHAVIN' The musical by Murray Horwitz and Richard Maltby Jr., with J. Samuel Davis and Eddie Webb, produced by the St. Louis Black Repertory Company, 2000.

significant contributions of black artists to a diverse and all-inclusive America. Plays by Rita Dove, Pearl Cleage, Langston Hughes, Amiri Baraka, August Wilson, and John Davidson are featured.

ST. LOUIS BLACK REPERTORY THEATRE, MISSOURI Committed to producing works by African American and Third World writers, the St. Louis Black Repertory Theatre was founded in 1976 by Ronald J. Himes. It has since created ongoing arts programs, expanded the season to include six productions and touring shows, and workshops and residences, to heighten the community's social, cultural, and educational awareness. Ruby Dee, Charles Fuller, Wole Soyinka, Laurence Holder, August Wilson, Ossie Davis, and Cheryl L. West are among the writers featured in the company's seasons.

CROSSROADS THEATRE COMPANY, NEW BRUNSWICK, NEW JERSEY The Crossroads Theatre Company received the 1998 Regional Theatre Award presented during the annual Antoinette Perry "Tony" Awards on Broadway. The theatre was founded in 1978 by Ricardo Khan and L. Kenneth Richardson to provide a safe haven for African American artists—writers, directors, actors, and designers—to stage their dreams. Crossroads spawned a new generation of artists: Avery Brooks, Harold Scott, Ntozake Shange, Cheryl L. West, and George C. Wolfe, whose *The Colored Museum* was originally staged by Crossroads in 1986.

Almost 200 African American theatre companies exist today throughout the United States. The outcome of the growing availability of companies and stages dedicated to the American black experience has been the increase in opportunities for African American playwrights, actors, directors, and designers over four decades. Such names as Tazana Beverly, Clinton Turner Davis, Ossie Davis, Ruby Dee, Gloria Foster, Allen Lee Hughes, Derek Anson Jones, Marion I. McClinton, Novella Nelson, Lloyd Richards, Seret Scott, Paul Tazewell, Regina Taylor, Tazewell Thompson, and Jane White lead a pantheon of African American artists, many of whom found their way into mainstream commercial theatres.

Asian American Theatre Companies: East West Players, Ping Chong and Company, Pan Asian Repertory Theatre

Asian workers were imported into the United States in the mid-nineteenth century to help build the railroads. Many workers and their families remained clustered in neighborhoods within major port cities, such as San Francisco, New York City, Chicago, Los Angeles, and Seattle. Many communities developed their own entertainments that featured Asian players and many Asians were featured in films, although chiefly as racial stereotypes. The inscrutable detective "Charlie Chan" and the "Dragon Lady" were two among many stereotypical characters in films and television, but this was to change. The Korean and Vietnam wars increased the number of Asian immigrants to the United States, American soldiers married Asian women, and the plight of Vietnamese boat people developed further awareness of Asian culture and traditions. International theatre artists like Antonin Artaud and Bertolt Brecht drew heavily on Asian theatrical traditions. They were followed by Jerzy Grotowski, Peter Brook, Ariane Mnouchkine, Harold Prince, Andrei Serban, and Julie Taymor, whose work owes a great debt to Asian stage and puppet traditions.

In the late sixties and early seventies in the wake of the civil rights movement, Asian American artists formed small theatre companies in major cities to tell their own stories with authentic voices. The earliest, East West Players (1965) in Los Angeles; the Asian Exclusive Act (1973), later renamed Northwest Asian American Theatre Company; the Asian American Theatre Workshop (1973) in San Francisco; Ping Chong and Company (1975), founded by current artistic director Ping Chong in New York City; Pan Asian Repertory Theatre (1977), founded by current artistic director Tisa Chang; and the Ma-Yi Theatre Ensemble (1989) in New York City. These companies nurtured such writers and artists as Tisa Chang, Daryl Chin, Frank Chin, Ping Chong, Tim Dang, David Henry Hwang, Philip Kan Gotanda, Maxime Hong Kingston, Fabian Obispo, Hans Ong, Jon Shiroto, Diana Son, Ching Valdes-Aran, B. D. Wong, and Laurence Yep.

©Lia Chang

KWAIDAN Directed and adapted by Ping Chong from novelist Lafcadio Hearn, *Kwaidan* was presented by Ping Chong and Company, New York City, 1999.

EAST WEST PLAYERS, LOS ANGELES East West Players, founded in 1965, is the oldest of the present group of Asian American companies producing in the United States today. Created as a home to promote Asian Pacific American works, the company first operated out of a storefront facility on Santa Monica Boulevard in Silver Lake. In 1996, it moved into the Union Center for Arts in downtown Los Angeles and performs to 40,000 annually. Under the leadership of actor-director Mako, the group concentrated on plays by Asian Americans and showcased Asian American actors in classical plays. Today, under the artistic leadership of Tim Dang, the company features about four plays a season by such influential writers as David Henry Hwang, Philip Kan Gotanda, Jon Shirota, and Euijoon Kim; and it also produces American classics (*The Zoo Story*,

Photo by Michael Lamont/East West Players production of GOLDEN CHILD by David Henry Hwang 1/26–2/20, 2000. Left to right: Kerri Higuchi*, Connie Kim, Annette Lee, Amy Hill*, Daniel Dae Kim*, Melody Butiu*, Ming Lo, Emily Kuroda* (*=Members of Actors Equity Association)

GOLDEN CHILD David Henry Hwang's play was produced by the East West Players and directed by Chay Yew. Los Angeles, 2000.

A Chorus Line, Follies, The Fantasticks) with Asian casts. EWP distinguished alumni include Mako, John Lone, B. D. Wong, David Henry Hwang, Philip Kan Gotanda, Freda Foh Shen, Wakako Yamauchi, and many others.

PING CHONG AND COMPANY, NEW YORK CITY   Founded by performance artist, choreographer, writer, director, and designer Ping Chong in 1975, this company exists at the intersections where race, culture, history, art, and technology meet. The clash of these forces is the source of Ping Chong's artistic investigations that have earned an international reputation for the company. Resisting being "ghettoized as an Asian-American artist," he has said, "I am an American artist. I believe that it is important to be inclusive; a free society should allow for a multiplicity of views." Ping Chong views his company's work as "an ongoing dialogue with the 20th century." He creates about four pieces a season with the company, including *American Gothic, Secret History, Elephant Memories,* and *Kind Ness.*

PAN ASIAN REPERTORY THEATRE, NEW YORK CITY   Since founding the company in 1977, artistic director Tisa Chang produced works by Asian American playwrights, Asian masterworks translated into English, and innovative adaptations of Western classics. In 1987, she established a resident ensemble—one of the few companies in the United States to do so. Engaged today in intercultural projects and music theatre, Chang envisions programs that transcend geographic and ethnic boundaries; *Cambodia Agonistes* is one such endeavor.

Latino/Hispanic/Chicano Theatre Companies: El Teatro Campesino, Repertorio Español, Bilingual Foundation of the Arts, GALA Hispanic Theatre

Theatre historians record that the first play to be staged in the United States was performed by Spanish soldiers in 1598 near what is now El Paso, Texas. In the late nineteenth century, Spanish-language theatre was commonly found, first in California, then in Texas, and by the early twentieth century in the territories bordering Mexico. By 1918, Los Angeles had five professional Spanish-language theatres, but the economic depression of the 1930s, along with the popularity of the new medium, film, ended these professional troupes.

The political unrest of the 1960s again brought attention to U.S. Latino/a theatre. Luis Valdez's El Teatro Campesino ("The Farmworkers' Theatre"), a bilingual Chicano company, formed in 1965 in Delano to call attention to the plight of migrant farm workers in California. Other groups followed, including Repertorio Español (New York City), Thalia Spanish Theatre (Sunnyside, N.Y.), and cultural centers such as the INTAR Hispanic American Arts Center (New York City), Bilingual Foundation of the Arts (Los Angeles), and GALA Hispanic Theatre (Washington, D.C.). Their agendas serve to bring attention to their Hispanic heritage and new works by emerging Latino/a playwrights.

EL TEATRO CAMPESINO, SAN JUAN BAUTISTA, CALIFORNIA

El Teatro Campesino, founded in 1965 by Luis Valdez under the wing of the United Farm Workers' organization to dramatize the plight of agricultural workers in California, subsequently devoted itself to plays focused on broader issues of Mexican American culture, consciousness, and pride. It is the earliest and best-known Chicano theatre.

At first, Valdez staged improvised, didactic *actos* to dramatize the exploitation of the farm workers by their bosses; these short plays were in themselves political acts and performed in Spanish and in English, on flatbed trucks, on farms, in marketplaces, and at political rallies. About these *actos*, Valdez said, "Our theatre work is simple, direct, complex and profound, but it works."

During the 1970s, the work performed by a mostly student group broadened to include Mexican American issues on education, culture, and religion. A vivacious performance style informed the *carpa* (itinerant tent shows), *corridos* (narrative ballads), and *mitos* (myths). The long history of the group's collective work ended in 1980. Luis Valdez, a prolific writer, has since written a number of full-length plays about the heritage and lives of contemporary Mexican Americans. *Los Vendidos, Corridos, Zoot Suit, I Don't Have to Show You No Stinking Badges,* and *Bandito* have been performed throughout California, and on national and European tours. Valdez' film work, especially *La Bamba,* has also brought him and his theatre international acclaim.

Courtesy El Teatro Campesino

LA CONCIENCIA DEL ESQUIROL
Founding artistic director and playwright Luis Valdez (right) plays the *Esquirol,* or Scab, in one of El Teatro Campesino's early *actos* presented at nightly rallies of the Farmworkers Union.

REPERTORIO ESPAÑOL, NEW YORK CITY

Founded by artistic director René Buch and Gilberto Zaldívar in 1968, Repertorio Español produces year-round in the Gramercy Arts Theatre (New York City). The repertory company presents more than twelve productions a year, from classics to modern and new plays. Since 1981, a musical company introduced *zarzuelas* (light operettas) and other music from Mexico, Puerto Rico, Cuba, and Spain. The Spanish dancer Pilar Rioja has been a guest artist since 1973. The repertory has included classics by Pedro Calderón de la Barca, Federico García Lorca, and Gabriel García Marquez, and new plays by Dolores Prida, Emilio Carballido, Abelardo Estorino, and Gloria Gonzalez.

BILINGUAL FOUNDATION OF THE ARTS, LOS ANGELES

Founded in 1973 in Los Angeles by Margarita Galban (artistic director), Estela Scarlata, and Carmen Zapata (producing director), the Bilingual Foundation of the Arts aims to present the rich diversity of Hispanic history, traditions, and culture in classic and contemporary plays written in Spanish and in English. BFA provides an "artistic doorway," writes Margarita Galban, "through which the rich diversity of Hispanic literature may be experienced by people of all cultures." BFA operates three theatres and produces year-round such

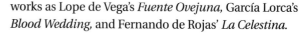

BLOOD WEDDING Suzanna Guzman and María Bermudez in Frederico García Lorca's *Blood Wedding*, directed by Margarita Galban, was produced by the Bilingual Foundation of the Arts, Los Angeles, 1999.

works as Lope de Vega's *Fuente Ovejuna,* García Lorca's *Blood Wedding,* and Fernando de Rojas' *La Celestina.*

GALA HISPANIC THEATRE, WASHINGTON, D.C. Founded in 1976 by producing director Hugo J. Medrano and Rebecca Read Medrano, GALA Hispanic Theatre promotes Hispanic culture by presenting bilingual theatre. Since its beginnings GALA has produced more than 100 plays and other arts programs in Spanish and English. With associate producing director Abel Lopez, a professional company of actors performs an average of four classic and contemporary plays a season. An award-winning producing organization, GALA has appeared at international festivals in Costa Rica, El Salvador, Venezuela, and Cuba. A recent season included classics by Pablo Neruda and Tirso de Molina and new works by Rudolfo Walsh and Alberto Pedro Torriente.

Other producing organizations that encourage *multicultural* performances are La Mama Experimental Theatre Company under the artistic leadership of Ellen Stewart and the Joseph Papp Public Theater under the direction of George C. Wolfe. The Signature Theatre Company in New York City dedicated its 1999–2000 season to a retrospective of the works of Cuban-born María Irene Fornés. Puerto Rican-born José Rivera (*Marisol*); Chicano authors Josefina Lopez (*Real Women Have Curves*), Carlos Morton (*The Miser of Mexico*), and Nilo Cruz (*Two Sisters and a Piano*); and Cuban-born Eduardo Machado (*The Floating Island Plays*) have found producers among the professional regional theatres for their works.

Native American Theatre Companies: Native American Theatre Ensemble, Spiderwoman Theatre

POWER PIPES A production by Spiderwoman Theatre, *Power Pipes* with Lisa Mayo, Muriel Miguel, and Gloria Miguel premiered at the Brooklyn Academy of Music in 1992.

There are only a handful of Native American theatre companies in existence. The theatrical heritage is rooted in the outdoor dance performances of Native Americans in the telling of their inherited myths and traditions to unite communities and reinforce traditional beliefs. What plays there are aim to sustain that heritage and build pride among Native American peoples. Many of these Western-style dramas have found productions in established producing organizations, such as the Denver Theatre Center, the Great American History Theatre (St. Paul), the Mixed Blood Theatre Company (Minneapolis), the Montana Repertory Theatre (Missoula), and the Perseverance Theatre (Douglas, Alaska). Nonetheless, there is only a small body of literary plays written by Native Americans, and performances by Native Americans about their native culture and traditions are infrequent. Only a few Native American authors have written plays. They are Rollie Lynn Riggs, Hanay Geiogamah, William S. Yellow Robe, N. Scott Momaday, and sisters Muriel and Gloria Miguel and Lisa Mayo.

NATIVE AMERICAN THEATRE ENSEMBLE   The Native American Theatre Ensemble (originally called the American Indian Theatre Ensemble), founded by writer-director-choreographer Hanay Geiogamah in 1972, was the first all–Native American repertory company to present plays based on traditional myths and contemporary life for Native American audiences. Their aim was to promote ethnic pride. The Ensemble found support in Ellen Stewart's La Mama Experimental Theatre Club in New York City, where Geiogamah's plays *Body Indian* (1972) and the musical *49* (1982) were produced. In recent years, Geiogamah transformed the company into the American Indian Dance Theatre, which performs an intertribal repertory with members drawn from a dozen tribes. *Kotuwokan,* by Geiogamah, is a dance-drama about a Native American boy's efforts to find his way in the contemporary world.

SPIDERWOMAN THEATRE   Spiderwoman Theatre (named after the Hopi Goddess of Creation) was founded in 1975 by three Kuna-Rappahannock sisters—Muriel Miguel, Gloria Miguel, and Lisa Mayo—to promote both Native American and feminist concerns. The three women worked with the Minnesota Native American AIDS Task Force as teachers and artists. As artistic director of Spiderwoman, Muriel Miguel developed more than twenty shows in the late seventies. The success of the first piece, *Women in Violence,* led to an invitation to perform at the World Festival Theatre in Nancy, France, and elsewhere in Europe. Their work reveals a storyweaving technique—spinning together words and movement. These loosely structured pieces range from satires on sexuality and violence against women adapted from Aristophanes and Chekhov (*Lysistrata Numbah, The Three Sisters from Here to There*) to explorations of the Native American heritage, spirituality, racism, and politics (*Sun Moon and Feather* and *Power Pipes*). Spiderwoman Theatre is unique in the blending of Native American ritual traditions and myths and modern feminist concerns. It is one of the most important Native American theatre groups performing today in the United States and Canada.

Cultural Separatism or Cultural Fusion?
Debating the Issues: August Wilson and Robert Brustein

A televised debate was sponsored by *American Theatre* magazine of the Theatre Communications Group at New York City's Town Hall on the evening of January 27, 1997. For many months playwright August Wilson (arguably today's most celebrated African American playwright) and critic Robert Brustein had previously debated issues of race, funding, and multiculturalism in the pages of the *New York Times* and *American Theatre.* The formal town-hall debate, called "On Cultural Power," was moderated by Anna Deavere Smith.

August Wilson set forth the case for increased financial support of African American professional theatres to permit them to explore their history and culture outside of the dominant culture. He also pointed out that mainstream "white" theatres received external funding to produce minority plays as a token part of their seasons,

Playwright August Wilson (right) and critic Robert Brustein (left), moderated by playwright-actress Anna Deavere Smith, "Debate the Issues" at New York City's Town Hall.

thereby diverting funds from minority theatres. He also denounced "colorblind" casting that placed African American actors in roles written for whites (thereby "denying us our own humanity"), and, as he has done in the past, called for African American plays to be directed *only* by African Americans.

Critic and former artistic director of the American Repertory Theatre, Robert Brustein, charged that August Wilson advocated "cultural separatism" and called for a theatre of inclusion that would achieve "a single value system." The debate, as moderated by Anna Deavere Smith, was heated. Ideas were exchanged, but the positions advocated by these two theatrical giants remained largely unchanged.

As an observer, artistic director and head of New York University's Graduate Acting Program Zelda Fichandler regarded the debate as a "non-event" in which two distinguished men revealed themselves as "chained together in their separate rigidities" and unable to "venture outside their fixed positions." Speaking with some regret, she said:

> We were looking for guidance, some opening into wisdom, into hope, so that we could better move forward as a theatre community to solve some of these knotty problems of race, economics, the development of our talented artists, and the role each of us might play in the design of the future.[18]

The case was not made either for "cultural separatism" or for "cultural fusion," but for "self-determinism" in the arts for 34 million African Americans in the United States. What emerged from the debate was the call for more and better financed theatres led by African Americans to be self-determining, to express their own culture, and to reflect the needs of their communities. In these arenas, African American artists would decide for themselves what they wanted to produce and with what artists. In effect, what was gained in the debate for and against cultural separatism versus cultural fusion was "one small step" for a national, theatrical community.

TRANSITION

In the final decades of the twentieth century, *cultural diversity* is one of the defining issues in society and the arts—especially in the United States. What we have called the "re-imaging of cultures" by world theatre artists refers for the most part to the *fusion* of performance styles and traditions from Eastern and Western cultures in the creation of new artistic expressions. The purpose is often to engage us anew in a sisterhood of issues on hunger, disease, racism, and injustice, and to blend cultures in the creation of distinctive, new aesthetic forms. In contrast to the "fusion of cultures," performance artists and ethnically centered theatre companies more directly confront the voices, words, identities, and experiences of people caught up in historical moments of *colliding* cultures. Most important is the theatre's ability to deal with issues of prejudice and injustice and to establish *common ground* with all peoples and audiences.

WEB SITES

Asian American Theatre Revue

http://www.abcflash.com/a&e/r_tang/AATR.html

Black Theatre

Links to black theatre artist profiles and theatres, related resources, and online education in black theatre.

http://www.bridgesweb.com/blacktheatre.html

"By Definition, Being an Artist Means Taking Risks": A Conversation with Theater, Dance, and Video Artist Ping Chong

http://www.fas.Harvard.edu/~ofa/spectrum/sep99/ping.html

El Teatro Campesino

http://www.elteatrocampesino.com/campesin/campesin.html

Guillermo Gómez-Peña

http://www.telefonica.es/fat/egomez.html

Native American Women Playwrights Archive

http://stafrf.lib.muohio.edu/nawpa/

The pErfOrmAncE aRt Front

http://www.sirius.com/~jenny/PAF/Performance artfront.html

Spiderwoman Theatre

http://staff.lib.muohio.edu/nawpa/Spiderwoman.html

Theatre Communications Group

TCG publishes annually a *Theatre Directory* containing web sites for member not-for-profit theatres.

http://www.tcg.org

Wakiknabe: Inter-tribal Native Theatre

http://members.xoom.com/Wakiknabe/mission.htm

Women of Color/Women of Words

http://www.scils.rutgers.edu/~cybers/home.html

These search terms are provided to assist you in exploring the topics introduced in this chapter at:

http//www.infotrac-college.com

cultural diversity, multiculturalism, interculturalism, transculturalism, ethnicity, cross-cultural exchange, solo performance artists, fringe theatre.

VLADIMIR: *Moron!*
ESTRAGON: *Vermin!*
VLADIMIR: *Abortion!*
ESTRAGON: *Morpion!*
VLADIMIR: *Sewer-rat!*
ESTRAGON: *Curate!*
VLADIMIR: *Cretin!*
ESTRAGON: *(with finality)*
Crritic![1]

SAMUEL BECKETT

Waiting for Godot

CHAPTER 14

Viewpoints

Critics add new dimensions to our awareness and appreciation of theatre. They acquaint readers and audiences with both good and bad productions. At best, they hope to connect the truly good work with audiences and to preserve it for future generations.

CRITICISM

There are two kinds of criticism for the theatre. *Drama criticism* comments on the written text from a literary and cultural-historical-theoretical perspective. *Theatre criticism* gives us a professional assessment of what we see on stage. Theatre criticism, or theatre reviewing, most often deals with plays-in-performance.

Present-day theatre criticism found in newspapers and magazines reflects the fact that we live in a consumer-oriented society. The business of professional reviewers writing for the *New York Times,* the *Los Angeles Times,* the *Chicago Tribune,* the *Washington Post,* or *Variety* is to appraise productions found on Broadway, Off Broadway, and in civic and regional theatres. Other reviewers who work on the staffs of local newspapers in our cities and communities throughout the country also cover college, community, and touring productions.

Theatre criticism is more than appraisal. It is also an economic force (although many critics deny this fact). In the commercial theatre, theatre critics often determine whether a play will continue for months or close after opening night. It is a fact that critics for the *New York Times* and other metropolitan newspapers and television stations have the power to close a Broadway play or keep it running for months. It is, therefore, important to consider how the critic's viewpoint affects the quality of our national theatre and the plays that we see. It is also interesting to reflect on our own roles as critics in which we are cast by simply attending a show.

SEEING THEATRE

Audiences as Critics

After the curtain comes down and the applause is over, we often go with friends to our favorite restaurant or hangout to talk about the production we have just seen. It's hard to shut our minds to a powerful performance of a play, whether we've just experienced Blanche DuBois' dependence on "the kindness of strangers" or the Orgon family's triumphant return to a peaceful house after their ordeal with Tartuffe. It's also difficult to rid our memories of those abiding questions raised by great plays. Is the world a stage? What's in a name? Must "attention be paid" to the Willy Lomans of the world? Can we depend on the kindness of strangers? And so on.

We also talk about the production—about the acting, the directing, the costumes, scenery, lighting, and sound effects. These conversations generally bring us to questions about the truthfulness of the acting. Were we aware of the actors "playing" their parts, or did they convince us that they were the Loman family? Were the costumes appropriate, or did Blanche's Mardi Gras gown seem new rather than old and worn? Were the sound effects too loud, calling unnecessary attention to themselves as effects?

A well-performed and meaningful play remains in our thoughts and emotions long after the curtain falls. As we pick up our playbills and leave the theatre, we discuss our likes and dislikes with friends. In other words, we become critics.

All audiences are critics by virtue of seeing a play performed. We may like the play and not the performance; or like the performance and not the play; or like neither or both. We may even praise certain strong scenes or single out powerful performances by certain actors. It is generally agreed that audiences bring at least four viewpoints to their theatre going experience: We relate to a play's human significance, its social significance, its artistic qualities, and its entertainment value, but not necessarily in any particular order.

AUDIENCES AT AN OUTDOOR THEATRE Audiences seated before the thrust stage at the outdoor Delacorte Theatre, located in Central Park, New York City. They are seeing a production of *The War of the Roses* (*Henry IV*, 2 parts, and *Richard III*), directed by Stuart Vaughn, for the New York Shakespeare Festival, 1970.

THE GRAPES OF WRATH The thirty-five-member cast at the curtain call for the 1998 Steppenwolf Theatre Company Production, Chicago.

Audience Viewpoints

Human Significance

Playwrights and other theatre artists connect audiences with a common humanity. Great plays confront us with life's verities, conveying the hope, courage, despair, compassion, violence, love, hate, exploitation, and generosity experienced by all humankind. They show us ways of fulfilling ourselves in relationships; they also show us the possibility of losing our families and property through accidents or catastrophes of war. The best plays explore what it means to be human beings in special circumstances. These circumstances can be bizarre, like the witches' fortuitous appearances before Macbeth, or recognizable, like an unwanted relative appearing at a New Orleans tenement building. Theatre is an extraordinary medium that links us as audiences with actors as characters. They become reflections of ourselves, or what potentially could be ourselves. Theatre's best achievements lead us to discoveries and reflections about our own personalities, circumstances, desires, choices, and anxieties.

> "I have looked at some of my earlier stuff and said, 'I can't believe how harsh this was, and how unforgiving it was, and how I was so concerned with artistic principles that I forgot that there was any kind of humanity involved.'"[2]
>
> FRANK RICH
> Former theatre critic for the New York Times

Social Significance

Of all the arts, theatre has an inherent relationship to society; by definition, an audience is an assembled group of spectators, a social unit. We become part of a community as we see theatre. Communities vote, express themselves at town council meetings, and respond to local, national, and international events.

Since the days of the classical Greek theatre, the playing space has served as an arena wherein to discuss social and political issues, popular and unpopular. Euripides and Aristophanes were often scorned because of their unpopular pacifist beliefs in a time of great nationalistic fervor among Athenians. The modern theatre likewise deals with controversial issues. The theatre section of any Sunday edition of the *New York Times* lists plays that deal with almost every imaginable social issue: drug addiction, abortion, racism, gay rights, sports scandals, investment fraud, family strife,

Arthur Miller's Death of a Salesman

Judd Hirsch as Willie Loman in Arthur Miller's *Death of a Salesman*, directed by Jeffrey Hayden, for PlayMakers Repertory Company, Chapel Hill, 1993. Producing director Milly S. Barranger.

Courtesy PlayMakers Repertory Company

Linda Loman reprimands her sons (and the world) for not paying attention to the worthiness of an average man like Willie Loman. Arthur Miller's celebrated play, *Death of a Salesman,* calls attention to the *human significance* of average people in this world.

LINDA LOMAN: … I don't say he's a great man. Willy Loman never made a lot of money; his name was never in the paper; he's not the finest character that ever lived. But he's a human being, and a terrible thing is happening to him. So attention must be paid. He's not to be allowed to fall into his grave like an old dog. *Attention,* attention, must be finally paid to such a person....[3]

discrimination, financial hardship, incest, terminal disease, mental illness, capital punishment, political chicanery, and so on. The best plays present social issues as fuel for thought, not as propaganda.

Playwrights and their artistic collaborators focus our attention, compassion, and outrage on social injustices and political corruption. *Tartuffe* celebrates triumph over

(continued on page 344)

Tony Kushner's Angels in America, Part Two: Perestroika

ANGELS IN AMERICA: A GAY FANTASIA ON NATIONAL THEMES by Tony Kushner with Ellen McLaughlin as the Angel and Stephen Spinella as Prior Walter in *Part Two: Perestroika*, directed by George C. Wolfe, Broadway, 1993.

Angels in America: A Gay Fantasia on National Themes. At the end of Part One, titled *Millennium Approaches,* the central figure Prior Walter is visited by an angel with spreading silver wings in a shower of unearthly light and sounds of triumphal music who announces that "The Great Work Begins." At the close of Part Two, Prior, seated before New York City's Bethesda Fountain in Central Park with its stone angel commemorating the Union navy's war dead rising above him, delivers Kushner's "coda" on the world's ills and its salvation.

PRIOR: … This disease will be the end of many of us, but not nearly all, and the dead will be commemorated and will struggle on with the living, and we are not going away. We don't die secret deaths anymore. The world only spins forward. We will be citizens. The time has come.
Bye now.
You are fabulous creatures, each and every one.
And I bless you: *More Life.*
The Great Work Begins.[4]

chicanery and injustice, and *Macbeth* deplores subversion and murder by evil forces and personal ambition. Playwrights stimulate social awareness and put us, as audiences, in touch with our own thoughts and feelings about issues—both as individuals and as communities. The aim of great playwriting is to give us new perspectives, to expand our consciousness, on old and new social issues and human behaviors.

Aesthetic Significance

Each of us has aesthetic standards. We know what we like and what we don't like. We have seen a lot of television shows and many films. As we attend more and more plays, we quickly come to recognize honesty in acting and writing. We see the gimmicks for what they are—tools for manipulating our emotions. We sense the miscasting and the awkward moments.

There is no reliable checklist for what makes one performance more effective, provocative, or moving than another, but there are a number of questions we can ask ourselves about any play or performance. Does the play, as performed, excite or surprise us? Does it barely meet our expectations, or worse? Does it stimulate us to think? Are the actors convincing? Or are they more than just convincing, are they mesmerizing? Does the performance seem wooden or lively? Does what we are seeing seem in any way original, or does it seem a carbon copy of something else? Is it complete and logically sound? Are we caught up in the characters' lives, or are we simply looking at our watches and waiting for the play to end?

As we see more and more theatre, we develop a more sophisticated awareness of sights, words, characters, actions, actors, sounds, and colors. We appreciate balance and harmony—beginnings, middles, and ends. We admire situations that defy our expectations, amuse, and speak to our sense of the bizarre and ridiculous in human behavior. We also appreciate stage performances that exceed our expectations—that reveal issues and viewpoints that we did not know existed, and in theatrical ways we did not anticipate.

Entertainment

Great theatre is always amusing or diverting in one or more ways. Although we think of entertaining theatre as comedy and farce because of the foolish behavior, the clever lines, the laughable gags, and the pratfalls, even tragedy delights us in unusual ways. Aristotle called the tragic way catharsis, or the cleansing of the emotions by pity and fear. In addition, tragedy has its share of just plain thrills. *Hamlet* and *Macbeth* offer ghosts, witches, murders, and duels, but they also please us at a deeper level. By witnessing the trials and hearing the poetic insights of the heroes, we are liberated from despair over the senselessness of human deeds.

Comedy and farce openly entertain us with romance, pratfalls, gags, misunderstandings, wit, and nonsense while assuring us that wishes can be fulfilled (and even if our wishes cannot, farce assures us that it's safe at least to wish for the unheard of, or for the socially unacceptable). Comedy and farce persuade us that society is really

(continued on page 346)

Tennessee Williams' The Glass Menagerie

In 1945, Laurette Taylor stunned audiences with her performance as Amanda Wingfield in Tennessee Williams' first major success. The Wingfield family, isolated in their St. Louis apartment, captures William's understanding of the "beauty and meaning in the confusion of living." Clinging to her illusions of a more genteel life in the Mississippi Delta, the mother, Amanda Wingfield, incarnates pretensions, pride, disappointment, and desperation. Williams' human "menagerie" displays the oppressed, the fragile, the needful, and the desperate.

Amanda, trying to make a little money selling magazine subscriptions, telephones one of her former subscribers:

AMANDA [*on the telephone trying to sell magazine subscriptions*]: Ida Scott? This is Amanda Wingfield! We *missed* you at the D.A.R. last Monday! I said to myself: She's probably suffering with that sinus condition! How is that sinus condition? Horrors! Heaven have mercy!—You're a Christian martyr, yes, that's what you are, a Christian martyr!

Well, I just now happened to notice that your subscription to the *Companion's* about to expire! Yes, it expires with the next issue, honey!—just when that wonderful new serial by Bessie Mae Hopper is getting off to such an exciting start. Oh, honey, it's something that you can't miss! You remember how *Gone with the Wind* took everybody by storm? You simply couldn't go out if you hadn't read it. All everybody *talked* was Scarlett O'Hara. Well, this is a book that critics already compare to *Gone with the Wind*. It's the *Gone with the Wind* of the post-World-War generation!—What?—Burning?—Oh, honey, don't let them burn, go take a look in the oven and I'll hold the wire! Heavens—I think she's hung up![5]

THE GLASS MENAGERIE
A revival of Tennessee Williams' *The Glass Menagerie* with Andrew McCarthy as Tom Wingfield, directed by Michael Wilson for the Hartford Stage Company (Conn.), 2001.

© T. Charles Erickson

THE INVENTION OF LOVE The American premiere of Tom Stoppard's comedy about the poet A. E. Housman with Jason Butler Harner (left) as young Housman and James Cromwell as the older poet. Directed by artistic director Carey Perloff, American Conservatory Theatre, San Francisco, 2000.

not so bad after all. In effect, they affirm that society will survive humanity's bungling.

In short, theatre is a dependable source of pleasure, laughter, tears, and companionship in an uncertain world. It is a place where we meet friends and join with them (and also strangers) in a collective experience: We laugh together, we cry together, and we applaud together. Theatre entertains by involving us in a social situation with others on stage and seated around us in the auditorium.

THE PROFESSIONAL CRITIC

The Critic's Job

The writing of criticism about theatrical performance takes place after the fact. After the curtain comes down on the opening-night performance, critics begin their formal work—writing the review for publication in the next morning's newspaper, or preparing their sound bites for late-night television. These are the reviews read by producers, managers, or directors during those opening-night parties at Sardi's restaurant in the Broadway district. Recently, some New York newspaper critics began attending preview performances two or three days before opening night to write their reviews at a more leisurely pace. However, these reviews are still published in the morning newspaper following the official opening-night performance.

The critic's education, background, experience in the theatre, and analytical skills make it possible for him or her to produce reviews in a short time span for radio and television or to write many paragraphs for the newspaper deadline. Those critics writing for Sunday editions or for weekly or monthly magazines have more leisure and usually write longer reviews. Outside of New York City, some newspaper critics take several days to write a review, but most producers are aware of the schedule for the review's publication. However, in all instances the professional critic has deadlines and a specific number of words allotted for the review.

Critic Stanley Kauffmann, formerly of the *New Republic,* gives an interesting viewpoint on the critic's work. He calls the theatre critic "a kind of para-reality to the theater's reality...."

His [the critic's] criticism is a body of work obviously related to but still distinct from what the theatre does; possibly influential, possibly not, but no more closely connected than is political science to the current elections. The critic learns that, on the one hand, there is the theatre, with good and bad productions, and, on the other hand, there is criticism, which ought to be good about both good and bad productions. Life is the

Today's Leading Critics

Ben Brantley, *New York Times*

Dan Sullivan and Jan Breslauer, *Los Angeles Times*

Richard Christiansen, *Chicago Tribune*

Bernard Weiner, *San Francisco Examiner*

Bruce McCabe, *Boston Globe*

Amy Gamerman, *Wall Street Journal*

Benedict Nightingale, *London Times*

Charles Isherwood, *Variety*

John Lahr, *The New Yorker*

John Simon, *New York Magazine*

Linda Winer, *Newsday*

Richard Zoglin, *Time*

---

playwright's subject, and he ought to be good about its good and bad people; the theatre is the critic's subject, and he ought to be good about its good and bad plays.[6]

Theatre, according to Kauffmann, is a subject that critics often approach with an attitude of open hostility. That hostility is frequently requited by artists, producers, and managers. They often resent the critic's power to sit in public judgment on productions. The resentment is not so much against the individual critic, or the review, but against the very practice of theatre criticism. In *Love's Labour's Lost,* Shakespeare has Berowne speak of "A critic; nay, a night-watch constable." Chekhov, according to one report, referred to critics as "horse-flies … buzzing about anything." And Max Beerbohm acknowledged in "The Critic as Pariah": "We are not liked, we critics." When he was leading critic for the *New York Times,* Frank Rich was called "The Butcher of Broadway." In contrast, Broadway theatres were named for revered critics Brooks Atkinson and Walter Kerr, suggesting the industry's admiration for their distinguished service.

Critics actually perform many services for the theatre-going public, its artists, and producers. They recognize and preserve the work of good artists for future generations.

"THE CRITIC SEES" Artist Jasper Johns demonstrates his sense of irony in "The Critic Sees" (1961, sculpmetal on plaster with glass).

© Jasper Johns/Licensed by VAGA, New York, NY

Plays that receive favorable critical attention are usually published, which in turn creates a wider audience. Critics are also publicists of the good and the bad, separating the wheat from the chaff. They help the public decide which productions to see. Critics serve as mediators between artists and audiences. They also serve as historians of sorts. Analyses of professional productions by Brooks Atkinson, Kenneth Tynan, Claudia Cassidy, Margaret Croyden, Ben Brantley, Benedict Nightingale, Mel Gussow, and many others provide historical accounts of theatre seasons, theatrical events, and performances. Many, like Frank Rich and Mel Gussow, publish collections of their criticism, which serve as social and theatrical records of the times. Finally, critics discover new playwrights and artists and call attention to electrifying performances.

The Critic's Creativity

The most brutal (and dishonest) argument levied against theatre critics is that they are no more than failed artists. As the saying goes, "If you can't do it, you write about it." This is also said of literary, art, music, opera, and architecture critics. Sometimes first-rate criticism is written by second-rate artists; often the reverse is true. George Bernard Shaw excelled in both. Criticism is a true talent, combining artistic sensibilities, writing ability, performance insights, and knowledge of theatre past and present. It requires a special creative flair. Stanley Kauffmann defines the critic's creativity in this way: "… [as] the imaginative rendering of experience in such a way that it can be essentially re-experienced by others." This is why the critic writes and why the reader (although he or she may not go to the theatre very often) reads reviews. Finally, the critic holds a mirror up to theatre's nature, serving in the long run even those who most resent the role of the critic in the theatre.

The Critic's Questions

Theatre criticism evaluates, describes, or analyzes a performance's merits and a production's effectiveness. Since the time of the early-nineteenth-century German playwright and critic Johann Wolfgang von Goethe (1749–1832), the theatre critic traditionally asks three basic questions of the work:

- What is the playwright trying to do?
- How well has he or she done it?
- Is it worth doing?

The first question concedes the playwright's creative freedom to express ideas and events. The second question assumes that the critic is familiar with the playwright, as well as with the forms and techniques of the playwright's time. The third question demands a sense of production values and a general knowledge of theatre. These questions show up in varying degrees of emphasis in reviews.

If critics work with these essential questions (and each usually generates more questions about the performance), they first consider the imaginative material, the

SEVEN GUITARS A scene from *Seven Guitars* by August Wilson with Alex Morris as Bluesman Floyd "Schoolboy" Barton and band members Ken La Ron and Jernard Burks. Directed by Lloyd Richards, Seattle Repertory Theatre, 1997.

concept, and the themes. Second, they judge how well the performance accomplishes the playwright's intentions. Storyline, character, acting, directing, sets, costumes, lighting, and sound may be considered, depending on their relative contributions to the effectiveness of the production. Third, the response to the question "Was it worth doing?" is the most sensitive and influential aspect of the review, for critical standards are on the line as well as the fate of the production. Claudia Cassidy and Brooks Atkinson had the innate good judgment to know that Tennessee Williams had said something significant about human vulnerability and anger in *The Glass Menagerie* and *A Streetcar Named Desire.* Their reviews demonstrate the critical standards and evaluations that get at the heart and substance of great plays and performances.

Whatever the order of the critic's essential questions about the performance, theatre criticism describes, evaluates, and assesses to one degree or another, depending on the critic's tastes, talents, and preferences. Where the critic places his or her emphasis also depends on the production itself. Is it an old play dressed out in fresh designs and interpretations, as was Peter Brook's production of *A Midsummer Night's Dream*? Unless the critic describes that new "look," the reader will not understand the critic's estimation of the production.

Performance Notes

American Theatre, The Drama Review, Theatre Journal, and the *Performing Arts Journal* publish critical descriptions of distinguished productions in the not-for-profit theatre both in the United States and Europe. These performance notes provide, first, a record of productions. The critical viewpoints stress experimental qualities in acting, directing, and design, along with new interpretations that emerged from texts and staging. The notes are usually accompanied by photographs to give a visual sense of performance style.

Performance notes offer impressions of trends in the avant-garde theatre, as well as familiarity with directors whose tastes and styles are gradually finding their way

Theatre Critics

George Jean Nathan, Claudia Cassidy, Brooks Atkinson, Ben Brantley, Mel Gussow

© CORBIS

For many years, leading theatre critic **George Jean Nathan** (1882–1958) wrote largely for New York City newspapers and magazines. He fought for a drama of ideas in America, and championed plays by Henrik Ibsen, George Bernard Shaw, and August Strindberg. He discovered the great American playwright Eugene O'Neill, and published his early work in *The Smart Set*, a magazine he edited with H. L. Mencken. Nathan's more than thirty books on theatre include the volumes on the New York season that he produced annually for many years. One of the most prestigious awards for criticism carries his name: the George Jean Nathan Award for Dramatic Criticism.

One of the first women to serve as a long-term theatre critic on large metropolitan newspapers—the *Chicago Journal of Commerce,* the *Chicago Daily Sun,* and then the *Tribune*—**Claudia Cassidy's** (1905–1996) name is part of the legendary success story of Tennessee Williams' *The Glass Menagerie.* Cassidy praised the new play, which had its premiere in Chicago in 1944, and its leading actress, Laurette Taylor. When audiences failed to turn out for the play, she mounted a crusade to convince them to attend a theatrical event of first importance. As a result, *The Glass Menagerie* became a Chicago hit, proceeded to Broadway, and became one of the most celebrated of modern American plays. Until her retirement, she wrote a daily column called "On the Aisle."

Courtesy of The Chicago Tribune

into the commercial theatre. A glance at a collection of performance notes from recent theatrical seasons turns up such directors' names as Anne Bogart, Robert LePage, Lee Breuer, Martha Clarke, Robert Wilson, Andrei Belgrader, and JoAnne Akalaitis; such international companies as the Berliner Ensemble, Cirque du Soleil, and Théâtre de Complicité; and such American companies as the Oregon Shakespeare Festival, Ashland, and the Steppenwolf Theatre Company, Chicago.

Educated at Harvard University, **Brooks Atkinson** (1894–1984) attended George Pierce Baker's Workshop 47 at Harvard. Beginning a career as a reporter on the Springfield (Mass.) *Daily News,* he moved to the *Boston Daily Evening Transcript* as assistant drama critic. In 1922, he became book review editor for the *New York Times* and succeeded Stark Young as the newspaper's theatre critic in 1926.

When the Second World War broke out, Atkinson took an overseas assignment, later receiving a Pulitzer Prize in 1947 for his reports on the Soviet Union. After the war, he returned to reviewing the Broadway theatre and became the most respected theatre critic of his generation. At his retirement in 1960, the Mansfield Theatre was renamed in his honor. His books include *Broadway Scrapbook* (1948), *Brief Chronicles* (1966), *Broadway* (1970), and *The Lively Years: 1920–1973* (1973).

Ben Brantley succeeded Frank Rich and David Richards in 1996 as the leading theatre critic for the *New York Times.* His influence determines the fate of multimillion dollar investments in one of the world's major theatre capitals—New York City.

Mel Gussow (b. 1933) writes about theatre and film for the *New York Times* with emphasis on Off Broadway and Off Off Broadway theatre. His collected writings are published in *Theater on the Edge: New Visions, New Voices* (1998); he also wrote the award-winning biography of Edward Albee called *A Singular Journey* (1999). He is a recipient of the George Jean Nathan Award for dramatic criticism.

Theatre Scholarship

The majority of scholarly critics in the United States are university teachers and/or professional dramaturgs. They bring a range of intellectual backgrounds on historical, social, and cultural issues to their subjects. They analyze plays and productions within rigorously researched critical contexts. They theorize about large issues of dramaturgy, uncover hidden aspects of a text's meaning, and analyze social, philosophical, linguistic, and cultural resonances. Criticism is no longer simply the study of the text of the play. The new generation of scholarly critics considers staging, performance, financing, audiences, and their social and political surroundings.

Scholarly critics ordinarily write with a comprehensive knowledge of a specific subject. That subject may be a playwright's body of work, performance theories and practices, historical periods, and intercultural and gender studies. Traditional scholarly methodologies included studies of dramatic character, analyses of play forms, examinations of staging and theatrical styles, and detailed interpretations of texts. The great writers of dramatic criticism in the West have also created literary works of lasting value, beginning with Aristotle's *Poetics* and continuing through Harold Bloom's *Shakespeare: The Invention of the Human.*

In recent years, changing intellectual fashions of academic life introduced new methodologies that draw heavily upon the fields of linguistics, anthropology, and cultural and critical theory. These new areas include applications of theory and vocabulary from linguistics, semiotics, structuralism, post-structuralism, and deconstructionism. The celebrated French critic Roland Barthes has revisited traditional texts and arrived at startling insights.

Critical Standards

It takes years of seeing theatre to develop critical standards. The best professional critics remain open and flexible even in their immense knowledge of theatre. George Jean Nathan, writing in the twenties and thirties, got at the heart of the matter when he said, "… Criticism, at its best, is the adventure of an intelligence among emotions."[7]

After all is said and done, theatre criticism is the encounter of one person's sensibility with the theatrical event. Thus, it is important that the critic tells us about the performance, humankind, society, and perhaps even the universe in the course of evaluating the production. Critic and director Harold Clurman once said that whether the critic is good or bad doesn't depend on his opinions but on the reasons he can offer for those opinions.

THE LION KING Marquee and box office for Walt Disney's *The Lion King* at the New Amsterdam Theatre on Broadway.

Courtesy of Milly S. Barranger

WRITING THE THEATRE REVIEW

Although there is no general agreement on criteria for judging a performance, the first step in writing theatre criticism is *the ability to see.* If we can describe what we see in the theatre, then we can begin to arrive at critical judgments. The play or production, or both, determines the approach: the organization of the review and the critical priorities. If the staging justifies a detailed account of what we observe, then the review incorporates a great deal of

(continued on page 355)

Critics at Work

Critics Brooks Atkinson, Margaret Croyden, Robert Brustein, and Ben Brantley challenge readers and audiences to appreciate new and difficult works by arguing the presence of profound truths on stage along with the awesome power of amazing theatrical works.

"... to establish some perspective by which 'Streetcar' may be appreciated as a work of art. As a matter of fact, people do appreciate it thoroughly. They come away from it profoundly moved and also in some curious way elated. For they have been sitting all evening in the presence of truth, and that is a rare and wonderful experience. Out of nothing more esoteric than interest in human beings, Mr. Williams has looked steadily and wholly into the private agony of one lost person. He supplies dramatic conflict by introducing Blanche to an alien environment that brutally wears on her nerves. But he takes no sides in the conflict. He knows how right all the characters are—how right she is in trying to protect herself against the disaster that is overtaking her, and how right the other characters are in protecting their independence, for her terrible needs cannot be fulfilled."

©Eileen Darby/Billy Rose Theatre Collection, The New York Public Library for the Performing Arts, Astor, Lenox and Tilden Foundations

BROOKS ATKINSON
The *New York Times*, 14 December 1947

"[Peter Brook] treated *The Mahabharata* with unabashed grandeur and daring theatrics. He evoked every theatrical mode at his command and used all the aspects of his years of travel and research in Asia and Africa—ritual theater, Oriental storytelling, Indian classical theater, magic and clowning, the broad scope of epic staging, the tone and timbre of Shakespearean tragedy and the savagery of the theatre of cruelty....

"At the end of the performance, many in the audience—like the boy—were full of wonderment and awe at what they had seen. For them, Mr. Brook's theatrical magic had worked, evoking the possibilities of live theatre with grand themes in the hands of a master magician."

MARGARET CROYDEN
The *New York Times*, 25 August 1985

Martha Swope/TimePix

353

© Joan Marcus

"*Angels in America* [*Part One, Millennium Approaches*] is, first and foremost, a work about the gay community in the Age of AIDS—an urgent and timely subject fashionable enough off Broadway, now ripe for the mainstream. It is also a 'national' (that is, political) play in the way it links the macho sexual attitudes of redneck homophobes in the '80s with those of red-baiting bullies in the '50s. It is a 'fantasia' not only in its hallucinated, dreamlike style but in the size and scope of its ambitions…. And it is a very personal play that distributes blame and responsibility as generously among its sympathetic gay characters as among its villains."

ROBERT BRUSTEIN
The *New Republic*, 24 May 1993

"Suddenly, you're 4 years old again, and you've been taken to the circus for the first time. You can only marvel at the exotic procession of animals before you: the giraffes and the elephants and the hippopotamuses and all those birds in balletic flight. Moreover, these are not the weary-looking beasts in plumes and spangles that usually plod their way through urban circuses but what might be described as their Platonic equivalents, creatures of air and light and even a touch of divinity….

"Such is the transporting magic wrought by the opening 10 minutes of 'The Lion King,' the director Julie Taymor's staged version of the Midas-touch cartoon movie that has generated millions for the Walt Disney Company. And the ways in which Ms. Taymor translates the film's opening musical number, "Circle of Life," where an animal kingdom of the African plains gathers to pay homage to its leonine ruler and his newly born heir, is filled with astonishment and promise…."

BEN BRANTLEY
The *New York Times*, 14 November 1997.
(Copyright © 1997 by the New York Times Co. Reprinted by permission.)

© Joan Marcus

Photo Essay

description. However, what we see in the theatre must connect with the play's meaning. For these reasons, *all theatre criticism involves both description and evaluation.*

Since theatre is an event *perceived* by audiences, writing about performance should be based on sensory impressions. As audiences, we are exposed to many significant details, sounds, and images, and only from them do we derive concepts or abstract meanings. Because we build critical concepts on the foundation of our perceptions, we can begin the process of seeing theatre critically by learning to describe our perceptions. A model for writing a theatre review might follow the points listed below:

1. Heading or logo
2. Substance or meaning of play
3. Setting or environment
4. Acting (actor or character)
5. Language   *Select and*
6. Stage business   *prioritize*
7. Directing   *these elements*
8. Costumes
9. Lighting and sound effects
10. Other significant human details

A MOON FOR THE MISBEGOTTEN by Eugene O'Neill with Gabriel Byrne, Roy Dotrice (center), and Cherrie Jones, directed by Daniel Sullivan, Goodman Theatre, Chicago, 2000.

In writing any commentary it is necessary, first, to identify the production early in the review. Brooks Atkinson identifies both play and playwright in the first paragraph of his review of *A Streetcar Named Desire.* Frank Rich identifies actress, play, and playwright in the two short opening paragraphs of his review of *Rockaby.* Margaret Croyden identifies the Hindu poem and the clashing dynasties in her review of Peter Brook's *The Mahabharata.*

AMERICAN BUFFALO
By David Mamet; directed by Neil Pepe; set by Kevin Rigdon; costumes by Laura Bauer; lighting by Howard Werner; fight director, Rick Sordelet; production stage manager, Darcy Stephens; production manager, Richard Burgess; general manager, Bardo S. Ramírez. Presented by the Atlantic Theater Company, Mr. Pepe, artistic director; Hilary Hinckle, managing director. At 336 West 20th Street, Manhattan.

WITH: Philip Baker Hall (Don), Mark Webber (Bobby) and William H. Macy (Teach).

THEATRE REVIEW HEADINGS Newspapers, like the *New York Times*, use a standardized format for summarizing the details of the production, including play title, author, artists, stage managers, producers, location of the theatre, and cast list. This *New York Times* logo for *American Buffalo* was published on March 17, 2000.[9]

Next, commentary on the play's substance or meaning informs the reader about the playwright's particular perspective on human affairs. Third, the performance involves what J. L. Styan calls "an environment of significant stimuli": sights, sounds, color, light, movement, space.[8] These stimuli can be described by answering questions related to setting, costumes, sound, lighting, acting, and stage business. Is the stage environment open or closed, symbolic or realistic? What are the effects of the stage's shape on the actor's speech, gesture, and movement? Is the lighting symbolic or suggestive of realistic light sources? What details of color, period, taste, and socioeconomic status are established by the costumes? What use is made of sound, music, or lighting effects? What details separate the actor-at-work from his or her character-in-situation? What do the characters do in the play's circumstances? What stage properties do the actors use? Are they significant? Finally, what visual and aural images of human experience and society develop during the performance? How effective are they?

Frank Rich on Beckett's *Rockaby*

ROCKABY Billie Whitelaw in Samuel Beckett's *Rockaby*, directed by Alan Schneider at the Samuel Beckett Theatre, New York City, 1984.

In his review of *Rockaby*, Frank Rich describes the actress seated in the single piece of furniture (the rocking chair), and the recorded sounds of her voice in contrast to the single word that she speaks ("more"). The stark stage environment, the lighting (or the absence thereof), the rocking movements of the woman in the chair, and the death-mask-like makeup Billie Whitelaw wears precede any concern for the "meaning" of it all. The critical properties are clear. The look of the seated actress and the minimal speech project an image of the playwright's meaning: "… the tortured final thrashings of a consciousness" before her death, or, as Beckett writes, before "the close of a long day."

THREE WORKING CRITICS

Brooks Atkinson, Kenneth Tynan, and **Edith Oliver** wrote significant first-night reviews of three plays that made stage history: *A Streetcar Named Desire, Look Back in Anger,* and *American Buffalo.* Atkinson reviewed a play enthusiastically embraced by critics and audiences; Tynan, in contrast, found himself a lone voice supporting a play most critics had vilified; and Edith Oliver argued for an appreciation of David Mamet as an "original and true" voice in the American theatre.

These highly influential critics said to their readers, "I have just seen a masterpiece, and so should you." Let us examine the choices that each made as they set about to persuade and organize the elements of their reviews.

Brooks Atkinson on *A Streetcar Named Desire*

The opening-night reviewers for three of the New York newspapers—the *Post,* the *Daily News,* and the *Herald Tribune*—were unanimously ecstatic, calling Williams' new play "brilliant," "powerful," and "a smash hit." They compared him to Eugene

STAGE: BILLIE WHITELAW IN THREE BECKETT WORKS
By Frank Rich

It's possible that you haven't really lived until you've watched Billie Whitelaw die.

The death occurs in "Rockaby," the last of three brief Beckett pieces that have brought the English actress to the newly named Samuel Beckett Theater. In "Rockaby," she plays a woman in a rocking chair, rocking herself to the grave. The assignment looks simple. The only word Miss Whitelaw speaks on-stage is "more," repeated four times. The "mores" are separated by a litany of other words—the tortured final thrashings of a consciousness, as recorded by the actress on tape. Then there is no more.

At that point, Miss Whitelaw stops rocking. The long light that picks her face out of the blackness starts to dim, and, in the longest of Beckett pauses, we watch the light within the face's hollow eyes and chalky cheeks dim, too. During the long silence, the actress doesn't so much as twitch an eyelash—and yet, by the time the darkness is total, we're left with an image different from the one we'd seen a half minute earlier. Somehow Miss Whitelaw has banished life

from her expression; what remains is a death mask, so devoid of blood it could be a faded, crumbling photograph. And somehow, even as the face disintegrates, we realize that it has curled into a faint baby's smile. We're left not only with the horror of death, but with the peace.

And there you have it. With no words, no movement and no scenery, the world's greatest playwright and one of his greatest living interpreters have created a drama as moving as any on a New York stage. Indeed, one might almost say that the entire Beckett canon is compressed into this short coda to a 15-minute play. In the long pause, we feel the weight of the solitary, agonizing, seemingly endless night of living. In Miss Whitelaw's descent to extinction, we see the only escape there can be—and we feel the relief. Death becomes what it must be in a Beckett play: a happy ending.

Like the other works of this evening, "Rockaby" is late Beckett. . . . The author's dramatization of stasis has been distilled to its most austere, pitch-black quintessence; the writing is so minimalist that even the scant, incanta-

tory language has been drained of color, vocabulary and at times even of feeling. Yet if "Rockaby" (1980) and its predecessor on the bill, "Footfalls" (1976), make unusual demands on the audience, they are riveting theater. Or so they are as performed by Miss Whitelaw, for whom Mr. Beckett wrote them, and as impeccably directed by Alan Schneider. . . .

In "Rockaby," the actress continues to create variations within a tiny palette. Each of the four "mores" becomes more fearful: the speaker's "famished eyes" more and more dominate her face. Though the recorded speeches that follow the request for "more" tend to sound alike, subtle differences in both the writing and the performance gradually unfold the desolate tale of a woman's terrifying search for "another creature like herself"—for "one other living soul." An echoed phrase— "time she stopped"—serves as a refrain in each speech until we at last reach the "close of a long day." Then Mr. Beckett and Miss Whitelaw make time stop, and it's a sensation that no theatergoer will soon forget.

The *New York Times* review of Samuel Beckett's *Rockaby*, published February 17, 1984.[10]

O'Neill, Clifford Odets, and William Saroyan. In the *New York Times,* Brooks Atkinson, then dean of New York reviewers, best put the play in perspective.

In an unusual approach, Atkinson wrote two reviews of *Streetcar.* The first appeared after opening night. The second, and more famous, appeared ten days later, on Sunday, December 14, 1947. In both reviews Atkinson recognized that Williams' play did not address the great social issues of the times, that it solved no problems and arrived

STREETCAR TRAGEDY: MR. WILLIAMS' REPORT ON LIFE IN NEW ORLEANS
By Brooks Atkinson

By common consent, the finest new play on the boards just now is Tennessee Williams' "A Streetcar Named Desire." As a tribute to the good taste of the community, it is also a smash hit. This combination of fine quality and commercial success is an interesting phenomenon. For if the literal facts of the story could be considered apart from Mr. Williams' imaginative style of writing, "Streetcar" might be clattering through an empty theatre. It is not a popular play, designed to attract and entertain the public. It cannot be dropped into any of the theatre's familiar categories. It has no plot, at least in the familiar usage of that word. It is almost unbearably tragic.

After attending a play of painful character, theatregoers frequently ask in self-defense: "What's the good of harrowing people like that?" No one can answer that sort of question. The usual motives for self-expression do not obtain in this instance. There is no purpose in "Streetcar." It solves no problems; it arrives at no general moral conclusions. It is the rueful character portrait of one person. Blanche DuBois of Mississippi and New Orleans. Since she is created on the stage as a distinct individual, experiences identical with hers can never be repeated. She and the play that is woven about

her are unique. For Mr. Williams is not writing of representative men and women; he is not a social author absorbed in the great issues of his time, and, unlike timely plays, "Streetcar" does not acquire stature or excitement from the world outside the theatre.

Character Portrait

These negative comments are introduced to establish some perspective by which "Streetcar" may be appreciated as a work of art. As a matter of fact, people do appreciate it thoroughly. They come away from it profoundly moved and also in some curious way elated. For they have been sitting all evening in the presence of truth, and that is a rare and wonderful experience. Out of nothing more esoteric than interest in human beings, Mr. Williams has looked steadily and wholly into the private agony of one lost person. He supplies dramatic conflict by introducing Blanche to an alien environment that brutally wears on her nerves. But he takes no sides in the conflict. He knows how right all the characters are—how right she is in trying to protect herself against the disaster that is overtaking her, and how right the other characters are in protecting their independence, for her terrible needs cannot be

fulfilled. There is no solution except the painful one Mr. Williams provides in his last scene.

For Blanche is not just a withered remnant of Southern gentility. She is in flight from a world she could not control and which has done frightful things to her. She has stood by during the long siege of deaths in the family, each death having robbed her of strength and plunged her further into loneliness. Her marriage to an attractive boy who looked to her for spiritual security was doomed from the start; and even if she had been a super woman she could not have saved it.

By the time we see her in the play she is hysterical from a long and shattering ordeal. In the wildness of her dilemma she clings desperately to illusions of refinement—pretty clothes that soothe her ego, perfumes and ostentatious jewelry, artifices of manners, forms and symbols of respectability. Since she does not believe in herself, she tries to create a false world in which she can hide. But she is living with normal people who find her out and condemn her by normal standards. There is no hope for Blanche. Even if her wildest dreams came true, even if the rich man who has become her obsession did rescue her, she would still be lost. She will always have to flee reality.

at no general moral conclusions. Nor did it deal with "representative" men and women. But, as Atkinson wrote, it was a work of art. Its audiences sat in the "presence of truth."

Atkinson's review is organized to deal, first, with *the play's truthfulness* about the human beings portrayed. Then, he takes up Williams' "poetic language," directing and scenic details, the performances of the actors, and finally, Williams' career as the author of two Broadway successes in two years: *The Glass Menagerie* and *A Streetcar Named Desire.*

Poetic Awareness

Although Mr. Williams does not write verse nor escape into mysticism or grandeur, he is a poet. There is no fancy writing in "Streetcar." He is a poet because he is aware of people and of life. His perceptions are quick. Out of a few characters he can evoke the sense of life as a wide, endlessly flowing pattern of human needs and aspirations. Although "Streetcar" is specific about its characters and episodes, it is not self-contained. The scenes of present time, set in a new Orleans tenement, have roots in the past, and you know that Mr. Williams' characters are going on for years into some mysterious future that will always be haunted by the wounding things we see on stage. For he is merely recording a few lacerating weeks torn out of time. He is an incomparably beautiful writer, not because the words are lustrous, but because the dialogue is revealing and sets up overtones. Although he has confined truth to one small and fortuitous example, it seems to have the full dimension of life on the stage. It almost seems not to have been written but to be happening.

"Streetcar" deserves the devotion of the theatre's most skillful craftsmen and, not entirely by accident, it has acquired them. Elia Kazan, who brilliantly directed "All My Sons" last season, is versatile enough to direct "Streetcar" brilliantly also. He has woven the tenderness and the brutality into a single strand of spontaneous motion. Confronted with the task of relating the vivid reality of "Streetcar" to its background in the city and to its awareness of life in general, Jo Mielziner has designed a memorable, poetic setting with a deep range of tones.

Excellent Performances

The acting cannot be praised too highly. Marlon Brando's braggart, sullen, caustic brother-in-law, Karl Malden's dull-witted, commonplace suitor, Kim Hunter's affectionate, level-headed sister are vivid character portraits done with freshness and definition. As Blanche DuBois, Jessica Tandy has one of the longest and most exacting parts on record. She plays it with an insight as vibrant and pitiless as Mr. Williams' writing, for she catches on the wing the terror, the bogus refinement, the intellectual alertness and the madness that can hardly be distinguished from logic and fastidiousness. Miss Tandy acts a magnificent part magnificently.

It is no reflection on the director and the actors to observe that Mr. Williams has put into his script everything vital we see on the stage. A workman as well as an artist, he has not only imagined the whole drama but set it down on paper where it can be read. The script is a remarkably finished job: it describes the characters at full length, it foresees the performance, the impact of the various people on each other, the contrasts in tone and their temperaments and motives.

In comparison with "The Glass Menagerie," "Streetcar" is a more coherent and lucid drama without loose ends, and the mood is more firmly established. "Summer and Smoke," which has not yet been produced in New York, has wider range and divides the main interest between two principal characters. If it is staged and acted as brilliantly as the performance of "Streetcar," it ought to supply the third item in a notable trilogy. For there is considerable uniformity in the choice of characters and in the attitude toward life. That uniformity may limit the range of Mr. Williams' career as a playwright: so far, he has succeeded best with people who are much alike in spirit. In the meantime he has brought into the theatre the gifts of a poetic writer and a play that is conspicuously less mortal than most.

Kenneth Tynan on *Look Back in Anger*

Following the opening of John Osborne's *Look Back in Anger* by the English Stage Company in London on May 8, 1956, critic Kenneth Tynan found himself in the minority, defending a play that many considered offensive and dismissed as self-indulgent drivel.

Not unlike Brooks Atkinson writing on *A Streetcar Named Desire*, Kenneth Tynan focused on the play's central character and Jimmy Porter's "desperate conviction that

LOOK BACK IN ANGER AT THE ROYAL COURT
By Kenneth Tynan

Kenneth Tynan reviewed *Look Back in Anger* for the *Observer*, London. Osborne's play, produced by the English Stage Company, opened at the Royal Court Theatre, London, on May 8, 1956.[12]

"They are scum" was Mr. Maugham's famous verdict on the class of State-aided university students to which Kingsley Amis' Lucky Jim belongs; and since Mr. Maugham seldom says anything controversial or uncertain of wide acceptance, his opinion must clearly be that of many. Those who share it had better stay away from John Osborne's *Look Back in Anger*, which is all scum and a mile wide.

Its hero, a provincial graduate who runs a sweet-stall, has already been summed up in print as "a young pup," and it is not hard to see why. What with his flair for introspection, his gift for ribald parody, his excoriating candour, his contempt for "phoneyness," his weakness for soliloquy, and his desperate conviction that the time is out of joint, Jimmy Porter is the completest young pup in our literature since Hamlet, Prince of Denmark. His wife, whose Anglo-Indian parents resent him, is persuaded by an actress friend to leave him; Jimmy's prompt response is to go to bed with the actress. Mr. Osborne's picture of a certain kind of modern marriage is hilariously accurate; he shows us two attractive young animals engaged in competitive martyrdom, each with its teeth sunk deep in the other's neck, and each reluctant to break the clinch for fear of bleeding to death.

The fact that he writes with charity has led many critics into the trap of supposing that Mr. Osborne's sympathies are wholly with Jimmy. Nothing could be more false. Jimmy is simply and abundantly alive, that rarest of dramatic phenomena, the act of original creation, has taken place: and those who carp were better silent. Is Jimmy's anger justified? Why doesn't he *do* something? These questions might be relevant if the character had failed to come to life; in the presence of such evident and blazing vitality, I marvel at the pedantry that could ask him. Why don't Chekhov's people *do* something? Is the sun justified in scorching us? There will be time enough to debate Mr. Osborne's moral position when he has written a few more plays. In the present one he certainly goes off the deep end, but I cannot regard this as a vice in a theatre that seldom ventures more than a toe into the water.

Look Back in Anger presents post-war youth as it really is, with special emphasis on the non-U intelligentsia who live in bed-sitters and divide the Sunday papers into two groups, "posh" and "wet." To have done this at all would be a signal achievement; to have done it in a first play is a minor miracle. All the qualities are there, qualities one had despaired of even seeing on the stage—the drift towards anarchy, the instinctive leftishness, the automatic rejection of "official" attitudes, the surrealist sense of humor (Jimmy describes a pansy friend as "a female Emily Brontë"), the casual promiscuity, the sense of lacking a crusade worth fighting for, and, underlying all these, the determination that no one who dies shall go unmourned.

One cannot imagine Jimmy Porter listening with a straight face to speeches about our inalienable right to flog Cypriot schoolboys. You could never mobilise him and his kind into a lynching mob, since the art he lives for, jazz, was invented by Negroes; and if you gave him a razor, he would do nothing with it but shave. The Porters of our time deplore the tyranny of "good taste" and refuse to accept "emotional" as a term of abuse; they are classless, and they are also leaderless. Mr. Osborne is their first spokesman in the London theatre. He has been lucky in his sponsors (the English Stage Company), his director (Tony Richardson), and his interpreters: Mary Ure, Helena Hughes, and Alan Bates give fresh and unforced performances, and in the taxing central role Kenneth Haigh never puts a foot wrong.

That the play needs changes I do not deny: it is twenty minutes too long, and not even Mr. Haigh's bravura could blind me to the painful whimsey of the final reconciliation scene. I agree that *Look Back in Anger* is likely to remain a minority taste. What matters, however, is the size of the minority. I estimate it at roughly 6,733,000, which is the number of people in this country between the ages of twenty and thirty. And this figure will doubtless be swelled by refugees from other age-groups who are curious to know precisely what the contemporary young pup is thinking and feeling. I doubt if I could love anyone who did not wish to see *Look Back in Anger*. It is the best young play of its decade.

LOOK BACK IN ANGER John Osborne's play opened at the Royal Court Theatre (London) in 1956, with Alan Bates, Mary Ure, Helena Hughes, and Kenneth Haigh.

AP/Wide World Photos

the time is out of joint...." Praising the character as an act of original creation on Osborne's part—a truthful portrait of postwar youth—he wrote, "Mr. Osborne is their first spokesman in the London theatre...." Tynan emphasized the human, social, and political significance (in that order) of Osborne's young people as characters never before seen on the British stage.

Edith Oliver on *American Buffalo*

American Buffalo was first produced Off Broadway at St. Clement's Theatre in February 1976, for a limited engagement; then it transferred on February 16, 1977, to Broadway's Ethel Barrymore Theatre with Kenneth McMillan, John Savage, and Robert Duvall. It received the New York Drama Critics Circle 1977 citation as Best American Play. Edith Oliver found herself introducing a new playwright with a limited track record to readers of *The New Yorker*. Her conviction that she was in the presence of a remarkable new writer with an aptitude for lowlife dialects and pawnshop characters sustained her throughout the review.

In her "Off Broadway" column, Edith Oliver reviewed *American Buffalo* for *The New Yorker* on February 9, 1976.[13]

DAVID MAMET, whose "Sexual Perversity in Chicago" and "Duck Variations" made such a remarkable evening several months ago, is back at St. Clements with "American Buffalo," which will run from February 4th through February 7th. The setting is the cluttered pawnshop, presumably in Chicago, of one Donny Dubrow. Before the action starts, a coin collector has been in and paid more than fifty dollars for a buffalo-head nickel that Dubrow had considered worthless, and then departed, leaving his card. The plot is entirely concerned with the plans of Dubrow—aided by a young man who works for him and a crony called Teach—to break into the customer's safe and steal his collection. Dubrow and Teach, we learn, are given to a bit of petty thievery, but they are really innocents of a sort, to put it as kindly as possible, and inexperienced in serious crime.

"Sexual Perversity" and "Duck Variations" were very funny plays with an underlying sadness, which never quite surfaced; "American Buffalo" is just as funny, and this time the undercurrent of greed and treachery is so far under (or else we are so diverted from it by laughter at the conversation—the marvelous idiom—of Dubrow and Teach) that the play's violent ending comes as a shock. It is all but inconceivable that these two clucks, however edgy, could turn so ruthless and cruel. Much of the conversation is a matter of obscenities used as casually and wholeheartedly as if they were the only words available. Dubrow is a portly soul of philosophical manner; Teach is nervous, distrustful, and touchy to the point of tears at imagined offenses. They are very well acted by Michael Egan and Mike Kellin. J. T. Walsh plays the young man with a quiet, subtle sincerity that is also very impressive. But the evening belongs to the dramatist. Mr. Mamet has now shown an aptitude for vernacular and character in three contrasting milieus, and although one can perhaps notice traces of the influence of the Second City in his work, he is original and a true humorist. —EDITH OLIVER

Theatre criticism—carefully weighed by the reader—adds a new dimension to our discovery of theatre. To become skilled critics is to hone our perceptions of the *when, where,* and *how* of the event taking place before us. As we gain experience seeing theatre, we become skilled in arranging our critical priorities, describing those details that enhance the performance and omitting those that contribute little to it. We develop criteria for judging the play's and the performance's effectiveness. We share our insights with others. In a word, we become *critics.*

AMERICAN BUFFALO A revival of David Mamet's *American Buffalo* with William H. Macy and Philip Baker Hall, directed by Neil Pepe, at the Atlantic Theatre Company, Off Broadway 2000.

TRANSITION

For the professional critic, the play in performance is the end-product of the theatre's creative process. At best, the critic enhances our understanding of the production or theatre event by enabling us to read about the theatrical experience from a perspective other than our own, or that of our friends. *Theatre criticism*—carefully weighed by the reader—adds a new dimension to our discovery and understanding of theatre.

WEB SITES

All newspapers have web sites. Listed below are web sites for national newspapers noted for their influential critics and theatre reviews:

Boston Globe

  http://www.boston.com/globe

Chicago Tribune

  http://www.chicagotribune.com

Los Angeles Times

  http://www.latimes.com

New York Times

  http://www.nyt.com

Variety

  http://www.variety.com

Washington Post

  http://www.washingtonpost.com

Daily Digest of Arts and Culture Journalism

  This collection of current topics on arts-and-culture-related news from around the world covers music, theatre, dance, publishing, and the visual arts. There are also topics on the issues and people that shape the cultural world.

  http://www.artsjournal.com/

These search terms are provided to assist you in exploring the topics introduced in this chapter at:

http//www.infotrac-college.com

theatre criticism, audience theory, aesthetics, entertainment, creativity, theatre scholarship, cultural theory, critical theory, performance, post-performance, theatre reviews.

GLOSSARY

Absurdism A post–Second World War movement in Europe, absurdism grew out of existentialism as a philosophical viewpoint. The absurdist begins with the assumption that the world is irrational. Such writers as Samuel Beckett and Eugène Ionesco show the irrationality of the human experience without suggesting remedies. The sense of absurdity in their plays is heightened by nonsensical events, ridiculous effects, and language that fails to communicate rational meaning.

Aesthetic distance The term implies a detachment (or "distance") between the work of art and the spectator. In order to experience a play as a work of art and not as life, there must be some sort of "psychical distance" between the viewer and the theatre event or art object itself. If we become too involved in a play for personal reasons (perhaps the subject matter is too painful based on a recent experience), then we may be able to view the play only as a real-life experience and not as art.

Aesthetic distance does not mean that we are unmoved by a play, a performance, or a painting. It means we are aware of ourselves as receptors and can experience with a new interest the work of art as something that is like life, but is not life. Simply put, aesthetic distance is the emotional and intellectual distance between the spectator and the work of art.

Agon A Greek word meaning contest or debate between opposing characters and viewpoints in Greek tragedy and comedy. The fierce debate between Oedipus and Teiresias in *Oedipus the King* is called an *agon*.

Alienation effect (Verfremdungseffekt) Bertolt Brecht called his theory and technique of distancing or alienating audiences from emotional involvement with characters and situations an "alienation effect." Brecht wanted a thinking audience rather than an emotionally involved audience. To break down emotional involvement Brecht used theatrical effects such as white light, placards, loudspeakers, projections, loosely connected scenes, songs, and music to make things on stage appear unfamiliar, even strange, so audiences would observe and think about what they were seeing.

Allegory A narrative in which abstractions, such as virtue, charity, and hope, are made concrete for the purpose of communicating a moral. In a drama, like *Everyman* (written around 1500), characters are personified abstractions, a device typical of a morality play for teaching lessons to audiences. In *Everyman*, the most famous dramatic allegory of its time, we find Good Deeds, Beauty, Five Wits, Death, and more, represented on stage by actors.

Amphitheatre Today, the term refers to a building with tiers of seats around a central area, such as a stadium, arena, or auditorium. The term originated to describe a Roman building of elliptical shape, with tiers of seats enclosing a central arena, where gladiatorial contests, wild beast shows, and staged sea battles took place. The first amphitheatre was probably built by Julius Caesar in 46 B.C. The most famous is the Colosseum in Rome, completed in A.D. 80, and which is a tourist attraction today.

Anagnorisis (Recognition) Aristotle introduced *recognition* in the *Poetics* as a simple recognition of persons by such tokens as footprints, clothes, birthmarks, and so on. The term also has a larger meaning to include the tragic hero's self-understanding. All of Shakespeare's tragic heroes have great moments of recognition wherein they realize who they are, what they have done, and what their deeds mean for others as well.

Antagonist The character in a play who commonly opposes the chief figure, or *protagonist*. The *agon* in Greek tragedy is usually centered on the debate between protagonist and antagonist; for example, in *Oedipus the King* the great antagonists to Oedipus in various debates are Teiresias, Creon, Jocasta, and the Shepherd.

Apron A large forestage used in proscenium theatres in England and Europe built in the late seventeenth century. In England, theatres like Covent Garden and Drury Lane had two doors, called proscenium doors, that opened onto the apron, allowing actors to exit and enter with greater ease.

Arena stage See **Stages**.

Aside A short statement made by a character directly to the audience to express a personal attitude or to comment upon another character or event. The convention is that the aside cannot be overheard by another character.

Audition The opportunity for actors to "try out" for a role. The date, place, and time are announced, and "sides" (parts to be read) are provided by the theatre. During the audition a reader assists the actor by reading dialogue with him or her. In the professional theatre, auditions are scheduled for actors with their agents by the casting director.

Black box See **Stages**.

Box set An interior setting, such as a living room or a dining room, using flats to form the back and side walls and often the ceiling of the room. The Moscow Art Theatre settings for Chekhov's *The Three Sisters* and *The Cherry Orchard* used box settings.

Broadway Broadway is one of the longest streets in Manhattan, extending diagonally the length of the island. However, for theatregoers, "Broadway" is the thirty to forty theatres clustered between Forty-First and Fifty-Fourth Streets two or more blocks to the west and east of the thoroughfare. Most Broadway playhouses were built at the turn of the century, tending to have small foyers, proscenium stages, outmoded equipment, and drafty dressing rooms. Called the "Great White Way" for its glittering lights and lighted marquees, Broadway remains the area where the most important commercial theatre in the world is produced. When it has a dud of a season, it is then referred to as "the fabulous invalid."

Bunraku The doll or puppet theatre (*ningyo shibai*) first came into prominence in Japan during the seventeenth century. As the dolls became more complex with the addition of hands, feet, and movable fingers and eyes, the number of handlers increased from one to three men—all visible to the audience. Chikamatsu Monzaemon, Takedo Izumo, and Chikamatsu Hanji were its most popular playwrights. As interest in doll theatre declined in the late seventeenth century, Uemura Bunrakuken restored its vitality in Osaka, and the name *Bunraku* is used by present-day doll or puppet theatres.

Today, the future of Bunraku has been secured by the Bunraku Association (formed in 1963) to manage all aspects of the art. In addition to performing in Osaka, the troupe plays four months each year in a small theatre created in 1966 in the National Theatre in Tokyo.

Catharsis Aristotle considered *catharsis* the release of twin emotions of pity and fear in the audience as it experienced tragedy. Catharsis is thought of as psychologically purgative, for it produces in an audience a purgation (or purification) of the emotions aroused by pity and fear. Thus, an audience comes away from tragedy having felt and even been modified by these emotions. Catharsis, it has been argued, produces a psychologically useful role for tragedy in society.

Character Drama's characters are sometimes divided into two types: *flat* and *round*. Flat characters represent a single trait (for example, a lecherous villain or faithful wife) and are highly predictable. Round characters are more complex, seen as it were from many sides. Like Hamlet, Blanche DuBois, and Troy Maxson, their motives, insights, and behavior, though sometimes unexpected, are credible and provocative. See **Stock character**.

Climax A decisive turning point in the plot where tension is highest. The burning of the orphanage in Henrik Ibsen's *Ghosts* is a good example of climax.

Comic relief Humorous episodes in tragedy that briefly lighten the growing tension and tragic effect. Scenes of comic relief often deepen rather than alleviate the tragic effect. The gravedigger's scene in *Hamlet* is one such example. Despite its jokes and humor, the scene calls attention to the common end of all humanity—death and the grave.

Commedia dell'arte Professional, improvisational companies of actors, including women, that flourished in Italy in the sixteenth century. An average size *commedia* company had ten to twelve members, divided usually into stock characters of two sets of lovers, two old men, and several *zanni* (the array of comic servants, braggarts, buffoons, tricksters, and dupes). Each character had an unvarying name, like Pantalone, costume, mask, and personality traits. *Commedia* actors worked from a basic story outline (posted backstage), improvising dialogue, action, and stage business (called *lazzi*) from that outline. They performed on temporary outdoor stages. The best companies also performed in the halls and palace theatres of dukes and kings.

Since the *commedia dell'arte* was improvisational theatre, and even though we have some 700 or more *scenarios*, or plot outlines, performed by the companies, we are left today with only the bare bones of a theatrical tradition: its characters, events, disguises, *lazzi*, and artists' illustrations of costumes and masks.

Convention An understanding established through custom or usage that certain devices will be accepted or assigned specific meaning or significance by audiences without requiring that they be natural or real. While delivering a soliloquy, the actor speaks to himself or herself so that audiences can "overhear" private thoughts. Since this behavior is accepted as a theatrical convention dating from the English Renaissance, we do not think it odd or unnatural when it occurs.

Criticism *Criticism* (variously called drama or theatre criticism) is critical assessment of a play as a literary text or as a vehicle for performance. *Drama* (or interpretive) criticism is usually associated with scholarly articles, books on theatre, and classroom teaching. The drama critic is concerned with the what and how of the play—with historical, social, and cultural surroundings, dramatic theories, ideas, imagery, themes, genres, audience interactions, and staging. Written by journalists, *theatre* criticism is found largely in newspapers, magazines, and popular journals. The theatre reviewer evaluates productions of new or revived plays and theatrical events. The *New York Times* remains the most important and powerful newspaper in America to review theatre. The daily critic for the *Times* has the power to make reputations and close shows. Outside of New York, critics for dominant newspapers in major urban cities also have gained immense power over theatre in their areas. Critics, such as Elliot Norton of the *Boston Post*, Claudia Cassidy of the *Chicago Tribune*, Sylvie Drake of the *Los Angeles Times*, and Richard Coe of the *Washington Post*, gained widespread recognition because their writings had an influence upon the national theatre of their day.

Cycle plays (Medieval) By the end of the fourteenth century in Europe and England, lengthy religious cycles, spoken in the vernacular, had replaced liturgical or church drama. The cycles were staged outdoors and performed by laymen during spring and summer months but chiefly on the feast of Corpus Christi. Most English cycle plays take their names from four towns where they were chiefly staged: York (48 plays), Chester (24), Wakefield (32, sometimes called the Towneley plays), and the *Ludus Coventriae* or *N_____* town play (42, town unknown). Most English cycles covered Biblical material from the Creation to the Last Judgment and were performed on pageant wagons drawn through the towns.

Dada Following the First World War in Europe, many artists revolted again traditions of realism in painting and theatre. Switzerland, where dada was launched in 1916, was the refuge for many artists and political dissenters. Tristan Tzara, the principal spokesman for dada, published seven manifestoes on the art between 1916 and 1920.

Dada grew out of skepticism about a world that could produce a global war. Convinced that insanity was humanity's true state, the dadaists substituted discord and chaos for logic, reason, and harmony. They composed "sound poems," dances, visual art, and short plays. For a time, the movement thrived in postwar Germany but received its greatest support in Paris. By 1920, interest declined and dada shortly disappeared. The dadaists were one among many forerunners of the Theatre of the Absurd.

***Deus ex machina* ("a god out of the machine")** In Greek plays, a cranelike device (the *mechane*) used to raise or lower "gods" into the playing space. Euripides used the device to solve a problem in a story, usually the ending. Medea escapes from Corinth on a winged chariot, for example. Hence, in drama and literature, the term has come to mean any unexpected or improbable device used to unknot a plot and thus conclude the work. The king's officer who arrests Tartuffe and rewards Orgon in Molière's comedy is one such example.

Dionysus According to myth, Dionysus was the son of Zeus (the greatest of Greek gods) and Semele (a mortal). For this reason, some refer to him as a demigod. Reared by satyrs (woodland deities represented in classical mythology as part human and part goat), Dionysus was killed, dismembered, and resurrected. As a god, he was associated with fertility, wine, and revelry. The events of his life also link him to recurring patterns of birth, maturity, and death among seasonal cycles and human beings. Since his worshippers sought a mystical union with primal creative urges, he is also associated with the *dithyramb*, drama, and art. On a more practical level, his followers sought to promote fertility in order to guarantee the productivity of human beings, their crops, and their harvests.

It is commonly held that Greek tragedy evolved from choral celebrations (dithyrambic odes) in Dionysus' honor. The Greater Dionysia (or City Dionysia) in Athens was a festival held each year in the god's honor, and the popular dramatic contests took place in the theatre named for him—the Theatre of Dionysus.

Double plot, subplot, simultaneous plots Drama's *plot* is the arrangement of incidents or sequences in the story, that is, the order of events. Aristotle not only called plot the "soul of tragedy," but "the whole structure of the incidents." He considered it more important than character or the traits of the story's individuals.

The double or simultaneous plot (sometimes called a subplot or underplot) develops two plots, usually with some sort of connection between them. In the order of things, one will be more important than the other. The secondary plot (the story of Polonius' family in *Hamlet* or the Gloucester plot in *King Lear*) is a variation on the main plot. In *Hamlet*, the main plot and the subplot deal with two families whose children suffer parental loss, grief, and untimely deaths. In repeating themes, problems, and events, the double plot demonstrates the world's complexity by engaging a large number of people, events, and locales.

Dramaturg The dramaturg's profession, which was created in eighteenth-century Germany, has recently been instituted in professional regional theatres in the United States. The dramaturg is a critic in residence who performs a variety of tasks before a play opens. He or she prepares, adapts, and even translates texts of plays for performance; advises directors and actors on questions of the play's history and interpretation; and educates audiences by preparing lectures, program notes, and essays. To accomplish all of this, the dramaturg serves as theatre historian, translator, play adaptor, editor, director's assistant, and resident critic of the work in progress. The term *production dramaturg* describes a full-time member of the production team. Sometimes the work of the dramaturg is confused with the *literary manager* (sometimes the duties are combined into one position). The literary manager is also a staff member in the not-for-profit regional theatres whose essential job is to find and develop new plays.

Ensemble acting (ensemble performance) Acting that stresses the total artistic unity of the performance rather than the individual performance of a specific (or "star") actor. The photos of Stanislavski's productions of *The Three Sisters* and *The Cherry Orchard* show the unity of acting style for which the Moscow Art Theatre was celebrated.

Epilogue Usually, a concluding address following the play's ending. Many epilogues were written to encourage applause or to feature a popular actor one final time.

Existentialism A philosophical viewpoint espoused in France by Jean-Paul Sartre and Albert Camus—novelists, essayists, and playwrights—in the 1940s. Sartre conceived of a universe without God, fixed standards of conduct, or moral codes. In this absence, Sartre argued, the individual must choose his or her own values and live by them regardless of the choices of others, or prevailing ideas. He also believed that people must be politically "engaged" and make choices to determine the direction of events. His plays (*The Flies, No Exit, Dirty Hands*) show characters faced with choices that require them to reassess their beliefs and to forge new personal standards.

Albert Camus' work was of equal importance. He defined the "absurd" as part of the existential outlook. A journalist and editor of a clandestine newspaper during the German occupation of France, his influence on the theatre came in part from his essay

"The Myth of Sisyphus" (1943) in which he supplies the name for the "absurdist" movement that emerged in the early 1950s. Camus argued that the human condition is absurd because of the gap between a person's hopes and an irrational universe into which he or she has been born. The remedy rested in the individual's search for a set of standards that allowed him or her to bring order out of the chaos. Camus rejected Sartre's argument for "engagement" and even denied being an existentialist, although his conclusions about individual choice are similar to Sartre's.

Although Sartre and Camus wrote plays about an irrational universe, they used traditional dramatic forms with a cause-to-effect arrangement of episodes along with discursive language. Their plays were labeled "existentialist drama." The later absurdist playwrights accepted the existentialist's view of the irrationality of human experience but arrived at a dramatic structure that mirrored the chaos of experience and the inadequacy of language to make sense of it all.

Expressionism A term coined in 1901 by the French painter Julien-Auguste Hervé to describe his paintings as "expressing" emotional experiences, rather than giving impressions of the physical world. Expressionism became synonymous with nonrealistic works in art and theatre. The rise of theatrical expressionism occurred in Germany between 1907 and the mid-1920s. The movement was lead by such writers as Reinhard Sorge (*The Beggar*), Georg Kaiser (*From Morn to Midnight*), and Ernst Toller (*Masses and Man*). While the production style was antirealistic employing garish colors, harsh lighting, distorted lines, stairs, treadmills, and bridges, the themes were aimed at a spiritual regeneration of humankind. Often the plays were acts of rebellion against generations, class, sex, and taboo subjects (incest and patricide, for example). Plays were made up of nameless character types, short scenes, telegraphic dialogue, long rhapsodic speeches in an effort to depict the injustices, warmongering, and materialism suffered by society's powerless. The work of Eugene O'Neill and Sophie Treadwell introduced theatrical expression to the United States.

Farce A comedy of situation, *farce* (the word derives from the Latin *farsa*, meaning "stuffing") entertains with seemingly endless and raucous variations on a single situation usually having to do with pursuit of brides, bedroom adventures, and sexual antics. Farce depends upon broad physical humor for its effects, such as mistaken identities, harmless beatings, pies in the face, doors opening onto awkward situations, and general human ineptitude.

Traced from short medieval plays and the Italian *commedia dell'arte,* modern forms of farce include vaudeville sketches, silent films, absurdist plays, and farcical plays by Michael Frayn, Alan Ayckbourn, and Neil Simon. Critic Eric Bentley has written perceptively on farce in *The Life of the Drama* (1964).

Green room A room backstage in the theatre where actors wait for their cues to go onstage, relax, drink coffee, eat snacks, receive instructions from stage management, and meet guests after the show.

***Hamartia* (hybris; hubris)** A Greek word variously translated as "tragic flaw" or "tragic error." Though Aristotle used *hamartia* to refer to those personality traits that lead heroes to make fatal mistakes, the idea of tragic flaw became simplified over the centuries to mean a single vice, frailty, or even a virtue (for example, pride, ambition, arrogance, overconfidence) that brings about the tragic hero's downfall. When applied to Sophocles' and to Shakespeare's great heroes, *hamartia* becomes a very complex concept related to reasons underlying human choice and action.

Hand properties See **Properties.**

Interlude The interlude dates from the Middle Ages where it was a loose term applied to short plays presented indoors as entertainment for rulers, nobles, and rich merchants. They took place within other events or occasions, for example, between courses of a banquet. The interlude had a variety of subjects (religious, moral, farcical) and included singing and dancing as well. Today, an "interlude" is synonymous in the British theatre with an intermission.

Irony *Dramatic irony* (Sophoclean irony or tragic irony) refers to a condition of affairs that is the tragic reverse of what the participants think will happen but what the audience knows at the outset. Thus, it is ironic that Oedipus accuses the blind prophet Teiresias of corruption and lack of understanding. By the play's end, Oedipus learns (as the audience has known from the beginning) that he himself is corrupt, that he has been mentally blind (ignorant), and the prophet has had superior sight (knowledge).

Dramatic irony also occurs when a speech or action is more fully understood by the audience than by the characters. Found in both tragedy and comedy, this sort of irony is usually based on misunderstanding or partial knowledge. It is ironic, for example, that Tartuffe thinks the king's officer has come to arrest Orgon when, in fact, he has come to arrest Tartuffe.

Kabuki Dating from the sixteenth century, Kabuki has become the principal form of indigenous commercial theatre in urban Japan. The word *Kabuki* derives from the adjective *kabuku,* meaning "tilted or off-center," and came to describe a new and unorthodox form of popular theatrical entertainment. In order to appeal to popular audiences, Kabuki performers were always creating new plays and blending acting and musical styles to appeal to changing times. Actors both speak and dance. The heroic figures (*aragoto*) are performed in a bravura acting style dressed in exaggerated costumes with bold red and black facial makeup. Actors of female roles (*onnagata*) display their charm and skill through solo dances. A Kabuki performance originally lasted ten to twelve hours and matched the moods and emotional states of the seasons: love, martial concerns, and lament for the spirits of the dead.

Special theatres were built for Kabuki performances. They are oblong boxes in which stage and audience are physically part of the same space. A ramp way or *hanamichi* (meaning "flower path") extended the stage through the left part of the auditorium and permitted actors to exit or enter through the audience, or deliver a major speech standing among them. Floor-level revolving stages were installed in the mid-eighteenth century, and elaborate painted scenery and other staging devices were part of a Kabuki performance. In the twentieth century, large theatres (three times the size of the traditional theatres) modeled on European opera houses were built to accommodate the commercial appeal of Kabuki. The present Kabuki-za in Tokyo has a ninety-three-foot-wide stage and seats 2,600.

Kathakali A major dance drama from the Kerala state in South India. Dating from the seventeenth century, Kathakali (the word literally means "story play") blends dance, music, and acting in a vigorous masculine style of physical movement, vivid emotionalism, and superhuman characters in stories adapted from the *Ramayana* and *Mahabharata* epics. Kathakali blends various theatre and dance forms from regions rich in cultural traditions and in the creation of an indigenous dance drama. Performances take place almost anywhere—in family homes, large halls, temple compounds, and formal stages—and take about two to three hours to complete. Since actors do not speak, the stories and ideas are conveyed through lyrics sung by two singers, by musicians, and by actors' facial expressions, physical movements, and hand gestures.

Melodrama Derived from eighteenth-century plays having music as background for dialogue, *melodrama* is a popular type of serious play that contrives and oversimplifies experience with characters whose goals and morality are clear-cut and the dangers to the innocent and virtuous spectacular. Characters in melodrama are clearly divided between the virtuous and the villainous, the sympathetic and the unsympathetic. After many complications, the villain's destruction brings about the happy ending. Some modern critics have stressed the social and humanitarian features of the genre in which central figures are crushed by external forces rather than by forces within themselves. Modern examples of melodrama include television cop shows, horror films, suspenseful stage thrillers, and realistic plays whose messages ring out with the triumph of the righteous victim over dark social forces. Many of the world's great tragedies have melodramatic elements, including plays written by William Shakespeare and Eugene O'Neill.

Mise-en-scène The arrangement of all the elements in the stage picture either at a given moment or dynamically throughout the performance. Modern directors give careful attention to the mise-en-scène, or total stage picture, integrating all elements of design, acting, and so forth. The mise-en-scène created by director Andrei Serban and designer Santo Loquasto for the 1977 New York production of *The Cherry Orchard* reflects the director's emphasis on the cherry trees and the dying civilization.

Monologue Usually, a long speech delivered by one character that may be heard but not interrupted by others. Or it may refer to a performance by a single actor, called a "solo performance." The term *monologue* has been applied to the soliloquy, a lengthy aside, and to "direct address" where a character steps out of the world of the play and speaks directly to the audience, like Tom Wingfield, both narrator and character, in Tennessee Williams' *The Glass Menagerie.*

Musical theatre Musical theatre in America dates from the colonial period, when English touring companies presented ballad operas (plays interspersed with songs). As background to today's musical theatre, we find burlesque, spectacles with music and dance, minstrel shows, and comic opera (namely, Gilbert and Sullivan operettas). The *revue*, a musical form featuring songs, dances, comedy sketches, elaborate production numbers, and loosely connected stories and themes, was also highly influential. Florenz Ziegfield produced the *Follies of 1907,* the first of a series of annual revues that featured star comedians and singers such as Fanny Brice, Bert Williams, and Will Rogers. George M. Cohan followed with a series of musical comedies with contemporary characters and settings and patriotic sentiments. Irving Berlin introduced another American idiom, ragtime, onto the musical stage in 1914. Others experimented with modern plots, settings, characters, and fresh musical styles. Among them were Jerome Kern (and librettist Guy Bolton), George and Ira Gershwin, Cole Porter, and Richard Rodgers and Oscar Hammerstein II. *Oklahoma* in 1943 brought other changes to the evolving musical theatre. With *Oklahoma,* Rodgers and Hammerstein introduced a "musical play" with simple American values having broad appeal, a "dream ballet" choreographed by Agnes De Mille, and a storyline (called the "book") that allowed a murder to take place on stage. It became the most influential and imitated musical of its day.

Despite innovations, the two basic threads of musical theatre to continue throughout the 1960s were operetta and musical comedy. The operetta-style musicals of Leonard Bernstein, Arthur Laurents, Stephen Sondheim, Jerome Robbins, Jerry Bock, and Sheldon Harnick produced *West Side Story, She Loves Me,* and *Fiddler on the Roof.* Musical comedy creators provided *Gypsy, Hello, Dolly!,* and *Cabaret.* Beginning in the 1970s composer-lyricist Stephen Sondheim introduced, among the revivals and revues, a unique sound tempered with rock rhythms and bold, cynical lyrics in *Company, Sweeney Todd, Sunday in the Park with George,* and *Into the Woods.* He popularized the "concept musical" in which a creative team of composer, lyricist, director, and choreographer collaborate during the creation of a show. Director-choreographers like Bob Fosse, Michael Bennett, and more recently, Ann Reinking and Susan Stroman dominated the musical theatre with *Pippin, Chicago, A Chorus Line, Dreamgirls, Fosse,* and *Contact.* Also, in the 1980s and 1990s, the London musical connection flourished on Broadway with the restaging of such British successes as *Cats, Miss Saigon, Phantom of the Opera,* and *Les Misèrables.*

With rising production costs and prohibitive ticket prices where a new musical costs as much as $15 million, other solutions are being tried in the regional theatres and Off Off Broadway. Successful creations, like *Rent* and *The Full Monty*, are developed within a regional theatre and then find their way onto Broadway with less initial capitalization and greater certainty in the success of the product. Taken all in all, musical theatre is considered by many to be America's unique contribution to world theatre.

Naturalism Like realistic writers, the nineteenth-century naturalists accepted that reality was discoverable only through the five senses. They departed from the realists in their insistence that art must adopt scientific methods in its examination of human behavior. The two most important factors to observe were *heredity* and *environment*. French playwright and novelist Émile Zola became the early spokesman for the naturalistic movement. He argued that artists should select subjects and analyze them in the detached way of a medical doctor to determine the consequences of birth and background. In practice, naturalists emphasized how behavior is determined by factors (heredity, for example) largely beyond our control. Inevitably, human beings appeared as victims of birth and society and the conclusions for happiness and well-being were pessimistic. In the firm belief that environment was also a determinant of character and choice, naturalists reproduced stage environments as accurate reflections of real locales. The great naturalistic playwrights of the late nineteenth century were Émile Zola, Henrik Ibsen, August Strindberg, Gerhart Hauptmann, and Maxim Gorky.

Neoclassicism The rebirth of classical ideals (called neoclassicism) found expression, first, in Italy in 1570 and spread to the rest of Europe, where it was to dominate writing and criticism from the mid-seventeenth century until the late eighteenth century. Two influential classical works influenced the rebirth of "classicism." They were Aristotle's *Poetics* and Horace's *Art of Poetry*. Aristotle came to be considered the supreme authority on literary (and dramatic) matters. His position was enhanced by three Italian critics: Antonio Minturno, Julius Caesar Scaliger, and Lodovico Castelvetro. They were in agreement on the basic precepts that constituted the neoclassical ideal. These were (1) *verisimilitude*, or the appearance of truth (events that could happen in real life, violence and death held offstage, and a confidant or trusted companion to receive inmost secrets rather than a chorus or by way of a soliloquy); (2) the demand that drama teach a moral lesson enhanced by *poetic justice* where the wicked were punished and the good rewarded; (3) the requirement that all drama be reduced to two types—tragedy or comedy—with no intermingling of comic and serious elements; (4) adherence to *decorum* whereby characters were proper to the subject matter; for example, royal persons in tragedy and lower-class people in comedy; and (5) precise conventions of language. The seventeenth-century French playwright Jean

Racine is considered the finest writer of neoclassical tragedies. In *Phèdre, Britannicus,* and *Bérénice,* he transcended the limitations of the neoclassical "rules" and wrote remorseless psychological tragedies of human beings vacillating between extremes of duty and desire.

Noh A serious Japanese dance drama that evolved in the fourteenth century out of songs, dances, and sketches and was first performed by Buddhist priests. There are about 240 extant plays, or "song books," that contain prose and poetry sections. The majority of the text is in verse and sung by the Doer (*shite*), the Sideman (*waki*), or Chorus (*ji*). The plays are categorized into one of five types according to the *shite* role. The Warrior play is one such category. The dignified and aesthetic conventions of Noh performance were set down by the Japanese actor and playwright Zeami during his years in the Kyoto court under the patronage of Shogun Yoshimitsu. These conventions extend to the locations on stage of role types, stage assistants, chorus, and musicians.

Modern-day Noh is performed on traditional outdoor stages maintained by temples and shrines and in contemporary buildings constructed especially for Noh performances. Among the major stages in modern Japan are the National Noh Theatre in Tokyo, the Kanze and Kongō theatres in Kyoto, and the Yamamoto Theatre in Osaka.

Off Broadway A term that came into theatrical usage in the 1950s. Defined by the Actors' Equity Association minimum basic contract as theatres located in the Borough of Manhattan outside the Broadway area surrounding Times Square. In addition to being outside that area, an Off Broadway theatre has 100 to 299 seats.

Off Broadway playhouses developed as alternatives to Broadway's commercialism. Today, the term refers to professional (Equity) theatres operating on significantly reduced budgets in comparison with Broadway, but under a financial structure prescribed by the Actors' Equity Association and other unions. David Mamet's plays are often performed Off Broadway, and some popular Off Broadway plays and musicals transfer to Broadway. Michael Bennett's *A Chorus Line* and Terrence McNally's *Love! Valour! Compassion!* are two examples.

Off Off Broadway A term that came into use in the 1960s, referring to experimental theatres and converted spaces located between West Houston Street ("Soho"), Greenwich Village, and the Bowery. These theatres are found in lofts, garages, warehouses, studios, churches, and coffee houses where noncommercial and experimental workshops and performances take place. As Broadway's commercialism and Actors' Equity Association encroached on the Off Broadway theatres, adventuresome producers and artists moved elsewhere, looking for solutions to high production costs and union demands. The Open Theatre, The Living Theatre, the Performance Group, the Wooster Group, and La Mama Experimental Theatre Club are in this category.

Open stage See **Stages.**

Performance A word used, especially in modern theatre criticism, to describe the whole theatrical event. In environmental theatre, for example, the performance begins as the *first* spectator enters the performing space and ends when the *last* spectator leaves.

Producer In the American theatre the person who puts together the financing and management, publicity and artistic teams to "produce" a show, usually commercial. The producer hires (and even fires) the artistic personnel and in this way may put a kind of stamp on the overall artistic effect. Producers who have significantly affected the Broadway theatre are Roger L. Stevens, David Merrick, Bernard Jacobs and Gerald Schoenfeld (the Shuberts), Alexander H. Cohen, James M. Nederlander, Emanuel Azenberg, Andrew Lloyd Webber, Cameron Mackintosh, Hal Prince, and Rocco Landesman.

Properties There are two categories for properties: *set* and *hand* properties.

Set properties are items of furniture or set pieces; they are placed on stage for design reasons and to accommodate the requirements of the text. The size and structure of set properties, especially furniture, determine the actor's movement in and around them.

Hand properties, such as fans, pistols, swords, or telephones, are required for the actor's use within the play's action. Sometimes the distinction between set and hand props is unclear, but staging is the main function of the set prop; the hand prop first satisfies the needs of the actor using it. The table lamp that Mrs. Alving turns out in the final act of *Ghosts* is a hand prop, one with symbolic significance. As a set prop, the tree in *Waiting for Godot* is part of the playwright's intention and the scenic design. Properties are the initial responsibility of the designer. There is a property head and crew responsible for acquiring or making props, supplying rehearsal props, handing out and storing props during the production, and repairing and returning props to storage at the production's close.

Proscenium theatre See **Stages.**

Protagonist The major character in a play. The Greek word literally means "first" (*protos*), that is, the first contender or chief actor in the performance. For example, Oedipus, Hecuba, Hamlet, Macbeth, and Othello are all protagonists. The Greeks labeled the second role the *deuteragonist,* and the third the *tritagonist.* The character in conflict with the protagonist is the *antagonist.*

Realism Realism developed in Europe about 1860 as a conscious rebellion against Romanticism. The realists set about depicting the world truthfully by what could be verified by direct observation of ordinary people (usually the middle class) and recognizable places. Playwrights and novelists set about emphasizing observed details of contemporary life to present a truthful depiction of the world and in stage language both familiar and appro-

priate. They introduced new subjects (many considered shocking and controversial) dealing with outcomes of poverty, prostitution, industrial conditions, disease, and social and judicial prejudices and injustices. Many held society responsible for human ills and argued indirectly for social reforms. Influential playwrights pioneering realism in the theatre were Henrik Ibsen, August Strindberg, and George Bernard Shaw.

Recognition See **Anagnorisis.**

Regional theatres, resident theatres The terms *regional* and *resident* have been used interchangeably for the past forty years to describe professional not-for-profit theatres. Today, there are more than sixty theatres (members of the League of Resident Theatres) in fifty-one cities with operating budgets ranging from $200,000 to $25 million. They produce more than 600 productions yearly to audiences of over 12 million. Most perform seasons from five to eleven months, generally to subscription audiences. Established in the fifties and sixties, these theatres from Seattle to Boston have been heralded as alternatives to the commercialism of Broadway and to the American theatre's centralization in major urban centers. In a society as diverse and as far-flung as that of the United States, these theatres make up a matrix that many call our *national theatre.* Among the most prestigious of the regional theatres are Guthrie Theatre (Minneapolis), American Repertory Theatre (Cambridge, Mass.), Arena Stage (Washington, D.C.), Mark Taper Forum (Los Angeles), Lincoln Center Theater (New York City), Alley Theatre (Houston), Seattle Repertory Theatre (Wash.), The Globe Theatre (San Diego), Goodman Theatre (Chicago), and Actors Theatre of Louisville (Ky.).

Revenge play The development of revenge plays was influenced in the Renaissance by the work of the Roman author Lucius Annaeus Seneca (4 B.C.–A.D. 65). Seneca's ten extant Roman tragedies, probably written for private readings, were filled with deranged heroes, ghosts, deeds of vengeance and horror, stoical speeches, messengers reporting offstage horrors, and pithy moralisms (called *sententiae*).

The Elizabethans read the Roman writers in their classrooms and transposed revenge conventions to the public stage. *Hamlet* has its ghost; its variety of deaths by sword, poison, trickery; and its revengers (Hamlet, Laertes, Fortinbras). In *King Lear,* Gloucester is blinded on stage, and *Titus Andronicus* is a virtual feast of atrocities. The revenge play had its own excitement in its many variations on patterns and conventions (like today's horror films), but some, like *Hamlet,* achieved greatness in the writing, characters, originality, and universal insights.

Reversal (peripeteia; peripety) A plot reversal occurs when an action produces the opposite effect of what was intended or expected. Reversals occur in tragedy, comedy, and tragicomedy. A complex play may have several reversals before its ending. The reversal that occurs when Tartuffe's true nature is revealed to Orgon in the seduction scene is not at all what the characters anticipate. In fact, this reversal "reverses" their situation in the sense that it only makes it worse. The king's officer brings about the final reversal by restoring Orgon's family to good fortune and by punishing Tartuffe.

Romanticism The roots of Romanticism lie in European philosophical, political, and social movements more so than in artistic ones. In the early days of the nineteenth century, Romantic writers, like political revolutionaries, rejected the rigid neoclassical rules for writing tragedy and comedy. They turned to Shakespeare as a model for avoiding rules and including varieties of experience. Their subjects were inclusive since higher truths were found in nature and the human spirit. They preferred subjects about unspoiled nature, or human beings in rebellion against restraints imposed by despotic societies. The most celebrated Romantic novelist and playwright was Johann Wolfgang von Goethe, whose *Faust, Part I,* represented the indomitable human will engaged in an unquenchable searching for experience.

Satyr play The fourth play in the series of fifth-century B.C. classical Greek tragedies functioned as an afterpiece to the tragic trilogy and always had a happy ending. The satyr play usually burlesqued the serious themes or the major characters of the three earlier plays (the trilogy) by showing persons such as Heracles, Dionysus, or Odysseus in ludicrous situations. The piece had a chorus of lewd satyrs (creatures half-man, the other half either horse or goat) led by Silenus, who was a regular character. Euripides' *The Cyclops* is the only complete satyr play in existence. It travesties the legend of Odysseus' encounter with Polyphemus.

Scenographer A designer with artistic control over all design elements, including set, lighting, and costume. The recent development of theatre technology, particularly the use of film projections and moving scenery, frequently called for unified production with one person integrating the various design elements. Although the scenographer works closely with the director, he or she is responsible for the totality of theatrical expression in time and space. Artistic unity is the goal. The idea that one person must have total control over design is derived from the theatrical concepts of the early-twentieth-century theorists Adolphe Appia and Edward Gordon Craig.

One of the world's most famous scenographers today is Josef Svoboda, the leading designer of the Prague National Theatre in the Czech Republic. He became known in America through the Czech Pavilion at the 1967 Montreal Exposition, where he orchestrated films and stills, cascading images over surfaces and spectators. The result was a visually kinetic assault on the spectators. Svoboda's stage designs feature moving blocks, projections, and mirrors. The basis of his theory is that all scenic elements must appear and disappear, shift and flow, to complement the play's development.

Set properties See **Properties.**

Simultaneous plots See **Double plot.**

Soliloquy A speech delivered by an actor alone on stage, which, by stage convention, is understood by the audience to be the character's internal thoughts, not part of an exchange with another character or even with the audience.

Spine In the Stanislavski method, a character's dominant desire or motivation, which underlies his or her action in the play. For a director, the *spine* is the through-line of a character's action that propels the play forward toward its conclusion. Director Elia Kazan conceived of the spine of Tennessee Williams' character Blanche DuBois in *A Streetcar Named Desire* as the search for refuge from a brutal and hostile world.

Stage business An actor's "business" in a role can be anything from the reading of a newspaper to smoking a cigarette to drinking a cup of coffee while he or she performs the text. Stage business is the actor's "busyness," activities devised by the actor (sometimes at the director's suggestion) to create a sense of character apart from the dialogue.

Stages—proscenium, arena, thrust or open, and black box Throughout theatre history, there have been five types of theatre buildings and basic arrangements of audience seating: (1) the proscenium or picture-frame stage; (2) the arena stage, or theatre in the round; (3) the thrust or open stage; (4) the black box; and (5) created or found space of the kind discussed as environmental theatre in Chapter 3.

The *proscenium* or picture-frame stage is the most familiar. Almost all college campuses have proscenium theatres, and our Broadway theatres are proscenium playhouses. The word *proscenium* comes from the wall with a large center opening that separates the audience from the raised stage. In the past the opening was called an "arch" (the proscenium arch), but it is actually a rectangle. The audience faces in one direction before this

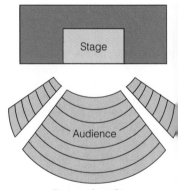

Proscenium Stage

opening, appearing to look through a picture frame into the locale on the other side. The auditorium floor slants downward from the back of the building to provide greater visibility for the audience; usually there is a balcony above the auditorium floor protruding about halfway over the main floor. Frequently, there is a curtain just behind the proscenium opening (along with a safety curtain) that discloses or hides the event on the other side. The idea that a stage is a room with its fourth wall removed comes from this type of stage; the proscenium opening is thought of as an "invisible wall."

The *arena* stage (also called a theatre in the round) breaks away from the formality of the proscenium theatre. It places the

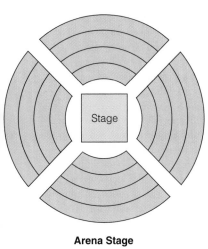

Arena Stage

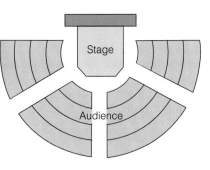

Thrust Stage

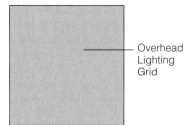

Black Box

Overhead Lighting Grid

stage at the center of a square or circle with seats for the spectators around the circle or on the four sides. This stage offers more intimacy between actor and audience since the playing space usually has no barriers separating them. In addition, productions can usually be produced on low budgets since they require minimal scenery and furniture to indicate scene and place. Margo Jones (1913–1955) pioneered arena theatre design and performance in America, establishing Theatre 47 in Dallas, Texas, in 1947. Today, Arena Stage in Washington, D.C., founded by Zelda Fichandler and Edward Mangum, is one of the most famous.

The *thrust,* or *open* stage, combines features of the proscenium theatre and the arena stage with three-quarter seating for the audience. The basic arrangement has the audience sitting on three sides or in a semicircle around a low platform stage. At the back of the stage is some form of proscenium opening providing for entrances and exits as well as scene changes. The thrust stage combines the best features of the other two stages discussed here: the sense of intimacy for the audience, and a stage setting against a single background that allows for scenic design and visual elements. After the Second World War, a number of thrust stages were built in the United States and Canada, including the Guthrie Theatre in Minneapolis and the Shakespeare Festival Theatre at Stratford, Ontario.

The *black box* is a type of minimal performance space developed in the 1960s for experimental work and new plays. Essentially a large rectangular room (usually painted a flat black to avoid glare from the overhead lighting instruments), the black-box theatre is usually equipped with a complex overhead lighting grid with instruments and movable seating (approximately 90 to 200 seats). The movable seating permits experimentation with the shape and size of the performance space. The Cottesloe The-

atre at the National Theatre, London, is a black-box theatre with two galleries surrounding three sides of the rectangular space. Designed along the lines of an Elizabethan innyard, the galleries are permanent but the risers (with seating) positioned along the floor are movable.

Stock character The stock character is not only a "flat" character but a generic type found throughout drama: jealous husband, clever servant, braggart soldier, hypocrite, pedant, cuckold, miser. Though most common to comedy (Molière has a number of stock characters in *Tartuffe* ranging from hypocrite to clever servant), stock characters are also found in serious plays. In tragedy we find the avenger, the usurper, the tyrant, and so on.

Surrealism In France, *surrealism* followed dada and drew inspiration from the works of Guillaume Apollinaire, Alfred Jarry, and André Breton. The play *The Breasts of Tiresias,* written by Apollinaire and subtitled a *"drame surréaliste,"* influenced the new movement in painting, writing, and theatre. The play concerns Thérèse who, after releasing her breasts (balloons which float away), is transformed into Tiresias. Forced to take over her functions, her husband discovers the meaning of creating children (through sheer willpower) and becomes the parent of 40,000 offspring.

Apollinaire's new form of expression rejected everyday logic and mingled comedy, burlesque, tragedy, fantasy, acrobatics with music, dance, color, and light. The critic André Breton defined the movement in his 1924 manifesto: the subconscious mind in a dreamlike state represented the basis of artistic truth. The crowning achievement of surrealism was the 1938 Paris international exhibition of painting and the theatre of Jean Cocteau (*Parade,* 1917).

Symbolism Between 1850 and 1900 in Europe, the symbolists challenged the realistic and naturalistic outlook in all the arts. To the symbolists, subjectivity, spirituality, and mystery represented a truth higher than mere observance of outward appearance. This deeper truth could only be evoked indirectly through symbols, myths, legends, and moods. The French poet Stephane Mallarmé became the principal spokesman for the symbolist movement. In theatre, the movement was led in the 1890s by director Aurélieu-Marie Lugné-Poe at the Théâtre de L'Oeuvre and by dramatists Maurice Maeterlinck (*The Intruder*) and Alfred Jarry (*Ubu Roi*).

Theatre of cruelty A phrase coined by French actor and director Antonin Artaud, an avant-garde figure in Paris following the First World War. Artaud formulated a theory of theatre (published as *The Theatre and Its Double,* 1938) in which he advocated a theatrical experience that would free people from actions that lead to hatred, violence, and disaster. Theatre, according to Artaud, would operate directly on the senses, not the rational mind, and force audiences to confront themselves. He intended theatre to operate directly on the human nervous system with bombardments of sound, lighting effects, and dissonances of the human voice in nontraditional spaces like factories and airplane hangars. His purpose was to assault the senses, break down the resistances of the conscious mind, and purge it morally and spiritually. The "cruelty" Artaud advocated was not primarily physical but moral and psychological.

Thespis Tradition credits Thespis as winner in 534 B.C. of the first contest for the best tragedy presented at the City Dionysia, Athens. Tradition also credits him with inventing drama as it developed out of improvisations by the chorus leader of dithyrambs. In truth, Thespis was probably in a line of early tragic poets. Some think his innovations were the addition of a prologue and lines (spoken by an actor as a character) to a previously sung narrative work. Almost nothing is known of Thespis. Today, *thespian* refers in general to actors or performers.

Thrust stage See **Stages.**

Tiring-house The backstage space in the Elizabethan public theatre. We know little about this area behind the stage wall used for preparing and maintaining productions. Some reconstructions suggest the space was used for dressing rooms, and for storing costumes, furniture, properties, and other equipment.

Unity A critical term implying a coherence in which the parts of a play work together to contribute to the whole. *Unity* suggests completeness or a recognizable pattern that ties together beginning, middle, and ending. Aristotle thought a tragedy should have a unified action, meaning a completeness without loose ends or the *deus ex machina* abruptly resolving the play.

Italian critics of the late sixteenth century codified Aristotle's comments on unity of action and themselves established "three unities" of time, place, and action. These unities have often mistakenly been passed down to generations as Aristotle's prescription. The unities so revered by sixteenth-century Italian critics and by seventeenth-century French neoclassical writers were (1) the action of a play must not cover more than twenty-four hours; (2) it must occur in a single place or room; and (3) it must be entirely tragic or entirely comic with no mixture of plots or characters from either kind of writing. What is interesting is that most Greek tragedies in some way violate these unities.

Well-made play (pièce bien faite) A well-made play is a commercially successful pattern of play construction. Its techniques were perfected by the nineteenth-century French playwright Eugène Scribe (1791–1861) and his followers. The well-made play uses eight technical elements for success: (1) a plot based on a secret known to the audience but withheld from certain characters until it is revealed at the climax to unmask a fraudulent character and restore the suffering hero, with whom the audience sympathizes, to good fortune; (2) a pattern of increasingly intense action and suspense prepared by exposition, contrived entrances and exits, and devices like unexpected letters; (3) a series of gains and losses in the hero's fortunes, caused by a conflict with a hostile opponent or force; (4) a major crisis in the hero's bad fortune; (5) a revelation scene brought about by the disclosure of a secret that brings a turnabout in the hero's bad fortune and defeats the opponent; (6) a central misunderstanding made obvious to the audience but withheld from the characters; (7) a logical, credible resolution or tying-up of events with appropriate dispensations to good and bad characters; and (8) an overall pattern of action repeated in each act, and act climaxes that increase tension over the play's three or four acts.

The features were not new in Scribe's day, but represented the technical methods of most great writers of comedy and even serious drama. Scribe and his followers turned the techniques into a formula for commercially entertaining plays as well as serious plays dealing with social and psychological subjects. In plays by Henrik Ibsen, George Bernard Shaw, Oscar Wilde, Arthur Miller, and Neil Simon, we can find well-made play elements underpinning the action.

West End, London The commercial theatre district in central London, equivalent to our Broadway, with more than twenty-five theatres located in a small area. Famous West End theatres include the Haymarket, Drury Lane, the Aldwych, and the Lyceum. The musicals *Cats* and *The Phantom of the Opera* and new plays by Tom Stoppard, Michael Frayn, and Alan Ayckbourn were first produced in the West End.

APPENDIX A

SUGGESTED READINGS

Chapter 1 Discovering Theatre

Bennett, Susan. *Theatre Audiences: A Theory of Production and Reception.* 2nd ed. New York: Routledge, 1997.

Blau, Herbert. *The Audience.* Baltimore, MD: Johns Hopkins University Press, 1990.

Brook, Peter. *Between Two Silences: Talking with Peter Brook.* Ed. Dale Moffitt. Dallas, TX: Southern Methodist University Press, 1999.

———. *The Empty Space.* New York: Simon & Schuster, 1995.

———. *Threads of Time: A Memoir.* London: Methuen, 1999.

Carlson, Marvin. *Performance: A Critical Introduction.* New York: Routledge, 1996.

Henderson, Mary C. *The New Amsterdam: The Biography of a Broadway Theatre.* New York: Hyperion, 1997.

Schechner, Richard. *The End of Humanism: Writings on Performance.* New York: Performing Arts Journal Publications, 1982.

Video Library

Hamlet, by William Shakespeare. With Laurence Olivier. (153 min., black & white, video, 1948) Paramount Home Video, distributors.

Henry V, by William Shakespeare. Directed by Kenneth Branagh, with Emma Thompson, Derek Jacobi, and Kenneth Branagh as Henry V. (138 min., color, video, 1989) Fox Video, distributors.

Oedipus Rex, by Sophocles. Directed by Tyrone Guthrie with Douglas Campbell as Oedipus. Stratford (Ontario, Canada) Festival Theatre. (87 min., color, video, 1957) Insight Media, distributors.

Othello, William Shakespeare. With Laurence Fishburne as Othello and Kenneth Branagh as Iago. (125 min., color, 1995). Columbia Tristar Home Video, distributors.

Chapter 2 The Seeing Place

Bradley, David. *From Text to Performance in the Elizabethan Theatre: Preparing the Play for the Stage.* New York: Cambridge University Press, 1992.

Brandon, James R., ed. *Nō and Kyōgen in the Contemporary World.* Honolulu, HI: University of Hawaii Press, 1996.

Brockett, Oscar G. *History of the Theatre.* 8th ed. Boston, MA: Allyn & Bacon, 1999.

Hildy, Franklin J., ed. *New Issues in the Reconstruction of Shakespeare's Theatre.* New York: Peter Lang, 1990.

Hodges, C. Walter. *The Globe Restored.* 2nd ed. London: Oxford University Press, 1968.

Lommel, Andreas. *Shamanism: The Beginnings of Art.* New York: McGraw-Hill Book Company, 1967.

Mullin, Donald C. *The Development of the Playhouse: A Survey of Theatre Architecture from the Renaissance to the Present.* Berkeley, CA: University of California Press, 1970.

Ortolani, Benito. *The Japanese Theatre: From Shamanistic Ritual to Contemporary Pluralism.* Rev. ed. Princeton, NJ: Princeton University Press, 1995.

Schechner, Richard, and Willa Appel. *By Means of Performance: Intercultural Studies of Theatre and Ritual.* New York: Cambridge University Press, 1990.

Turner, Victor. *From Ritual to Theatre: The Human Seriousness of Play.* New York: Performing Arts Journal Publications, 1982.

Wickham, Glynne. *Early English Stages, 1300–1660.* 3 vols. New York: Columbia University Press, 1959–1979.

Video Library

Aspects of Peking Opera. (15 min., color) Insight Media, distributors.

Bunraku Puppet Theater. (35 min., black & white, 1968) Films, Inc., distributors.

Chinese Opera. (27 min., color, 1992) Insight Media, distributors.

Farewell, My Concubine. (157 min., color, 1993) Buena Vista Home Video, distributors.

Kabuki: Classic Theater of Japan. (30 min., color) Modern Talking Picture Services, distributors.

Noh: Classical Theater of Japan. (28 min., color, 1980) Insight Media, distributors.

Shakespeare's Globe Theatre Restored: Much Ado About Something. (30 min., color, 1997) Insight Media, distributors.

The Tradition of Performing Arts in Japan. (35 min., color, 1990) Insight Media, distributors.

Chapter 3 Alternative Theatrical Spaces

Brecht, Stefan. *Peter Schumann's Bread and Puppet Theatre.* 2 vols. New York: Routledge, 1988.

Carrière, Jean-Claude. *The Mahabharata.* Trans. Peter Brook. New York: Harper & Row, 1987.

Grotowski, Jerzy. *Towards a Poor Theatre.* New York: Clarion Books, 1968.

Kiernander, Adrian. *Ariane Mnouchkine and the Théâtre du Soleil.* New York: Cambridge University Press, 1993.

Malina, Judith. *The Diaries of Judith Malina 1947–1957.* New York: Grove Press, 1984.

Schechner, Richard. *Environmental Theatre.* Rev. ed. New York: Applause Theatre Books, 1993.

Tytell, John. *The Living Theatre: Art, Exile, and Outrage.* New York: Grove Press, 1995.

Video Library

Brother Bread, Sister Puppet (The Bread and Puppet Theater). (60 min., color, 1993) Insight Media, distributors.

Brown, Kenneth, with The Living Theatre. *The Brig.* (65 min., color, 1964) Facets Multimedia, distributors.

Gelber, Jack, with The Living Theatre. *The Connection.* (105 min., color, 1961) Facets Multimedia, distributors.

Grotowski, Jerzy, with the Polish Laboratory Theatre. *Akropolis.* (60 min., black & white, 1968). Insight Media, distributors.

Jerzy Grotowski. (55 min., black & white, 1970) Insight Media, distributors.

Mnouchkine, Ariane, with Théâtre du Soleil. *1789.* (35 mm., color, 1974) M. Mnouchkine Films, Paris, distributors.

Schechner, Richard, with The Performance Group. *Dionysus in 69.* (90 min., black & white, 1970) Sigma III, distributors.

Chapter 4 The Playwright

Bigsby, Christopher. *Contemporary American Playwrights.* New York: Cambridge University Press, 1999.

Conversations with Lillian Hellman. Ed. Jackson R. Bryer. Jackson, MS: University Press of Mississippi, 1986.

Conversations with Tennessee Williams. Ed. Albert J. Devlin. Jackson, MS: University Press of Mississippi, 1986.

DiGaetani, John L. *A Search for a Postmodern Theatre: Interviews with Contemporary Playwrights.* Westport, CT: Greenwood Press, 1991.

Dramatists Sourcebook 1999–2000: Complete Opportunities for Playwrights, Translators, Composers, Lyricists and Librettists. New York: Theatre Communications Group, 1999.

Gussow, Mel. *Edward Albee: A Singular Journey.* New York: Simon & Schuster, 1999.

Interviews with Contemporary Playwrights. Eds. Kathleen Betsko and Rachel Koenig. New York: Beech Tree Books, 1987.

Mamet, David. *Writing in Restaurants.* New York: Viking Penguin, Inc., 1987.

Miller, Arthur. *Echoes Down the Corridor: Collected Essays 1944–2000.* Ed. Steven R. Centola. New York: Viking, 2000.

——. *The Theatre Essays of Arthur Miller.* Eds. Robert A. Martin and Steven R. Centota. Rev. ed. New York: Da Capo Press, 1996.

——. *Timebends: A Life.* New York: Grove Press, 1987.

Murphy, Brenda. *Tennessee Williams and Elia Kazan: A Collaboration in the Theatre.* New York: Cambridge University Press, 1992.

The Paris Review Playwrights at Work. Ed. George Plimpton. New York: Modern Library, 2000.

Savran, David, ed. *In Their Own Words. Contemporary American Playwrights: Interviews.* New York: Theatre Communications Group, 1988.

——, ed. *The Playwright's Voice: American Dramatists on Memory, Writing and the Politics of Culture.* New York: Theatre Communications Group, 1999.

Simon, Neil. *The Play Goes On: A Memoir.* New York: Simon & Schuster, 1999.

Speaking on Stage: Interviews with Contemporary American Playwrights. Eds. Philip G. Kolin and Colby H. Kullman. Tuscaloosa, AL: University of Alabama Press, 1996.

The Theater of María Irene Fornés. Ed. Marc Robinson. Baltimore, MD: The Johns Hopkins Press, 1999.

Van Itallie, Jean-Claude. *The Playwright's Workbook.* New York: Applause Theatre Books, 1998.

Women in American Theatre. Eds. Helen Krich Chinoy and Linda Walsh Jenkins. 3rd ed. New York: Theatre Communications Group, 2001.

Women Who Write Plays: Interviews with Contemporary American Dramatists. Ed. Alexis Greene. Lyme, NH: Smith and Kraus, 2000.

Video Library

August Wilson (Interview). (22 min., color, 1992) Insight Media, distributors.

David Mamet: An Interview with the Playwright. (55 min.) Facets Multimedia, distributors.

Death of a Salesman, by Arthur Miller, with Dustin Hoffman. (135 min., color, 1986). Facets Multimedia, distributors.

A Raisin in the Sun, by Lorraine Hansberry, with Sidney Poitier, Claudia McNeil, and Ruby Dee. (128 min., black & white, 1961). RCA/Columbia Pictures Home Video, distributors.

Wendy Wasserstein (Interview). (30 min., color, 1976) Insight Media, distributors.

Chapters 5, 6, and 7 Dramatic Forms, Structures, Conventions, Language

Barranger, Milly S. *Understanding Plays*. 2nd ed. Needham Heights, MA: Allyn & Bacon, 1994.

Beckerman, Bernard. *Dynamics of Drama: Theory and Method of Analysis*. New York: Alfred A. Knopf, 1970.

Bentley, Eric. *The Life of the Drama*. New York: Applause Theatre Books, 1990.

Bigsby, C. W. E. *A Critical Introduction to Twentieth- Century American Drama: Beyond Broadway*. Vol. 3. New York: Cambridge University Press, 1985.

——. *Modern American Drama, 1945–1990*. New York: Cambridge University Press, 1992.

Bloom, Harold. *Shakespeare: The Invention of the Human*. New York: Riverhead Books, 1998.

Brecht, Stefan. *Theatre of Visions: Robert Wilson*. New York: Routledge, Chapman, & Hall, 1984.

Esslin, Martin. *An Anatomy of Drama*. New York: Hill and Wang, 1977.

——. *The Theatre of the Absurd*. 3rd ed. New York: Penguin, 1983.

Fergusson, Francis. *The Idea of a Theater: A Study of Ten Plays. The Art of Drama in Changing Perspective*. Princeton, NJ: Princeton University Press, 1987.

Fuchs, Elinor. *The Death of Character: Perspectives on Theater After Modernism*. Bloomington, IN: Indiana University Press, 1996.

Hirst, David L. *Tragicomedy*. London: Methuen, 1984.

Hoy, Cyrus. *The Hyacinth Room: An Investigation into the Nature of Comedy, Tragedy, and Tragicomedy*. New York: Alfred A. Knopf, 1964.

Ionesco, Eugène. *Notes and Counter Notes: Writings on the Theatre*. Trans. Donald Watson. New York: Grove Press, 1964.

Mamet, David. *Writing in Restaurants*. New York: Viking Penguin, 1986.

Marranca, Bonnie, ed. *Theatre of Images*. New York: Drama Book Specialists, 1977.

Pavis, Patrice. *Languages of the Stage: Essays in the Semiology of Theatre*. New York: Performing Arts Journal Publications, 1982.

Quador, Franco, Franco Bertoni, and Robert Sterns. *Robert Wilson*. New York: Rizzoli, 1999.

Robert Wilson: From a Theater of Images. Ed. Robert Stearns Rev. ed. New York: Harper & Row, 1984.

Styan, J. L. *Drama, Stage and Audience*. New York: Cambridge University Press, 1975.

——. *Modern Drama in Theory and Practice*. 3 vols. New York: Cambridge University Press, 1981.

Willett, John. *The Theatre of Bertolt Brecht: A Study of Eight Aspects*. New York: New Directions, 1959.

Video Library

Beckett, Samuel. *Rockaby*, directed by Alan Schneider. (58 min., color, 1982). Insight Media, distributors.

Gray, Spalding. *Gray's Anatomy*. (80 min., color, 1996) Columbia Tristar Video, distributors.

——. *Monster in a Box*. (96 min., color, 1992) Columbia Tristar Video, distributors.

——. *Swimming to Cambodia*. (85 min., color, 1987) Cinecom, distributors.

——. *Terrors of Pleasure*. (60 min., color, 1988) Columbia Tristar Video, distributors.

Wilson, Robert, with Philip Glass. *Einstein on the Beach*. (58 min., color, 1986) Direct Cinema Ltd., distributors.

Chapter 8 Acting, Voice, Movement

Adler, Stella. *The Technique of Acting*. New York: Bantam, 1990.

Anne Bogart: Viewpoints. Eds. Michael Bigelow Dixon and Joel A. Smith. Lyme, NH: Smith Kraus, 1995,

Barr, Tony. *Acting for the Camera*. Rev. ed. New York: HarperCollins Publishers, 1997.

Berry, Cicely. *The Actor and the Text*. Rev. ed. New York: Applause Theatre Books, 1992.

——. *Voice and the Actor*. London: Virgin, 1993.

Boal, Augusto. *Games for Actors and Non-Actors*. Trans. Adrian Jackson. New York: Routledge, 1992.

Boleslavsky, Richard. *Acting: The First Six Lessons*. New York: Theatre Arts Books, 1933.

Branaugh, Kenneth. *Beginnings*. New York: St. Martin's Press, 1989.

Brown, Jared. *The Fabulous Lunts: A Biography of Alfred Lunt and Lynn Fontanne*. New York: Atheneum, 1986.

Bruder, Melissa, with others. *A Practical Handbook for the Actor*. New York: Vintage Books, 1986.

Caine, Michael. *Acting in Film: An Actor's Take on Movie Making*. Reprint. New York: Applause Theatre Books, 1997.

Chaikin, Joseph. *The Presence of the Actor: Notes on the Open Theatre, Disguises, Acting and Repression*. New York: Atheneum, 1972.

Cohen, Robert. *Acting Professionally: Raw Facts About Careers in Acting*. 4th ed. New York: Harper & Row, 1990.

Cole, Toby, and Helen Krich Chinoy, eds. *Actors on Acting: The Theories, Techniques, and Practices of Great Actors of All Times as Told in Their Own Words*. 4th ed. New York: Crown Publishers, 1995.

Gates, Linda. *Voice for Performance*. New York: Applause Theatre Books, 2000.

Gielgud, John. *Acting Shakespeare*. Reprint. New York: Applause Theatre Books, 1999.

Hagen, Uta. *A Challenge for the Actor.* New York: Charles Scribner's Sons, 1991.

———. *Sources: A Memoir.* New York: Performing Arts Journal Publications, 1984.

———, with Haskel Frankel. *Respect for Acting.* New York: Macmillan, 1973.

Hare, David. *Acting Up.* London: Faber & Faber, 1999.

Hill, Holly. *Actors' Lives on and off the American Stage: Interviews.* New York: Theatre Communications Group, 1993.

Hirsch, Foster. *A Method to Their Madness: The History of the Actors Studio.* New York: W. W. Norton, 1984.

Lewis, Robert. *Advice to the Players.* New York: Theatre Communications Group, 1989

———. *Slings and Arrows: Theater in My Life.* Reprint. New York: Applause Theatre Books, 1997.

Linklater, Kristin. *Freeing the Natural Voice.* New York: Drama Book Specialists Publications, 1976.

Mamet, David. *True and False: Heresy and Common Sense for the Actor.* New York: Vintage Books, 1997.

McIntyre, Ian. *Garrick.* London: Allen Lane, 1999.

Mekler, Eva. *Masters of the Stage: Twenty-Seven British Acting Teachers Talk About Their Craft.* New York: Grove Press, 1989.

Olivier, Laurence. *Confessions of an Actor: An Autobiography.* New York: Simon & Schuster, 1982.

———. *On Acting.* New York: Simon & Schuster, 1986.

Peters, Margot. *The House of Barrymore.* New York: Alfred A. Knopf, 1990.

Saint-Denis, Michel. *Training for the Theatre: Premises and Promises.* Ed. Suria Saint-Denis. New York: Theatre Arts Books, 1982.

Skinner, Edith. *Speak with Distinction.* 2nd ed. Eds. Timothy Monich and Lilene Mansell. New York: Applause Theatre Book Publishers, 1989.

Stanislavski, Constantin. *An Actor Prepares.* Trans. Elizabeth Reynolds Hapgood. Reprint. New York: Theatre Arts Books, 1948.

———. *Building a Character.* Trans. Elizabeth Reynolds Hapgood. Reprint. New York: Theatre Arts Books, 1977.

———. *Creating a Role.* Trans. Elizabeth Reynolds Hapgood. New York: Theatre Arts Books, 1961.

———. *My Life in Art.* Trans. J. J. Robbins. Reprint. New York: Theatre Arts Books, 1952.

Strasberg, Lee. *A Dream of Passion: The Development of the Method.* Ed. Evangelina Morphos. Boston, MA: Little, Brown, 1987.

Suzuki, Tadashi. *The Way of Acting: The Theatre Writings of Tadashi Suzuki.* Trans. J. Thomas Rimer. New York: Theatre Communications Group, 1986.

The Vocal Vision: Views on Voice by Twenty-Four Leading Teachers, Coaches, and Directors. Eds. Marion Hampton and Barbara Acker. New York: Applause Theatre Books, 1998.

Video Library

Berry, Cicely, and Andrew Wade. *The Working Shakespeare.* 5 videos. New York: Applause Video Library, 2000.

Caine, Michael. *Acting in Film: An Actor's Take on Movie Making.* New York: Applause Video Library, 1997.

Chekhov, Michael. *Michael Chekhov on Theatre and the Art of Acting. The Six Hour Master Class.* 4 audio tapes. New York: Applause Theatre Books, 1999.

Craig, David. *On Singing Onstage: Six Master Classes.* 6 videos. New York: Applause Video Library, 2000.

Rodenburg, Patsy. *A Voice of Your Own.* New York: Applause Video Library, 1999.

Sanford Meisner: The Theater's Best Kept Secret. (56 min., 1985) Films for the Humanities and Sciences, distributors.

The Stage Fight Director (with David Boushey). (33 min., color, 1990) Insight Media, distributors.

Stella Adler: Awake and Dream. (57 min., color, 1989) Insight Media, distributors.

Strasberg on Acting (Interview with Margaret Croyden). (30 min., color, 1975) Insight Media, distributors.

Chapter 9 Directing

Anne Bogart: Viewpoints. See Chapter 8.

Antoine, André. *Memories of the Théâtre Libre.* Trans. Marvin Carlson. Coral Gables, FL: University of Miami Press, 1964.

Bartow, Arthur. *The Director's Voice: Twenty-One Interviews.* New York: Theatre Communications Group, 1989.

Berry, Ralph. *On Directing.* New York: Hamish Hamilton/Viking, 1991.

Brecht, Stefan. *The Theatre of Visions: Robert Wilson.* New York: Routledge, 1988.

Brook, Peter. *The Open Door: Thoughts on Acting and Theatre.* New York: Pantheon Books, 1993.

———. *The Shifting Point: Theatre, Film, Opera 1946–1987.* New York: Harper & Row, 1987.

Chekhov, Michael. *To the Director and Playwright.* Compiled by Charles Leonard. New York: Limelight Editions, 1984.

Cole, Toby, and Helen Krich Chinoy, eds. *Directors on Directing.* Rev. ed. New York: Macmillan, 1976.

Guthrie, Tyrone. *A Life in the Theatre.* London: Harrap Ltd., 1987.

Hall, Peter. *Peter Hall's Diaries: The Story of a Dramatic Battle.* Ed. John Goodwin. London: Hamish Hamilton, 1983.

Kazan, Elia. *A Life.* New York: Alfred A. Knopf, 1988.

Koller, Ann Marie. *The Theatre Duke: Georg II of Saxe-Meiningen and the German Stage.* Stanford, CA: Stanford University Press, 1984.

Leiter, Samuel C. *The Great Stage Directors: 100 Distinguished Careers of the Theatre*. New York: Facts on File, Inc., 1994.

Murphy, Brenda. *Tennessee Williams and Elia Kazan: A Collaboration in the Theatre*. New York: Routledge, 1992.

No Author Better Served: The Correspondence of Samuel Beckett and Alan Schneider. Ed. Maurice Harmon. Cambridge, MA: Harvard University Press, 1999.

O'Connor, Garry. *The Mahabharata: Peter Brook's Epic in the Making*. San Francisco, CA: Mercury House, Inc., 1990.

Schneider, Alan. *Entrances: An American Director's Journey*. New York: Viking Penguin, Inc., 1986.

Shyer, Laurence. *Robert Wilson and His Collaborators*. New York: Theatre Communications Group, 1989.

Stage Directors Handbook: Opportunities for Directors and Choreographers. Eds. David Diamond and Terry Berlinis. New York: Theatre Communications Group, 1999.

Taymor, Julie, with Alexis Greene. *The Lion King: Pride Rock on Broadway*. New York: Hyperion, 1997.

The Theatre of Images. Ed. Bonnie Marranca. New York: Drama Book Specialists, 1977.

Toporkov, Vasily Osipoval. *Stanislavski in Rehearsal: The Final Years*. London: Routledge, 1997.

Waxman, S. M. *Antoine and the Théâtre Libre*. Cambridge, MA: Harvard University Press, 1926.

Willett, John, ed. and trans. *Brecht on Theatre: The Development of an Aesthetic*. New York: New Directions, 1964.

Video Library

Andrei Serban: Experimental Theater. (27 min., color, 1978) Insight Media, distributors.

Beckett Directs Beckett (Waiting for Godot, Krapp's Last Tape, Endgame). (Visual Press, 1990) Smithsonian Institution, distributors.

Film by Samuel Beckett, directed by Alan Schneider. (20 min., black & white) Applause Theatre Books, distributors.

Marat/Sade, by Peter Weiss, directed by Peter Brook with the Royal Shakespeare Company. (116 min., color, 1966) United Artists, distributors.

One Step in a Journey: Tadashi Suzuki. (54 min., color, 1993) Insight Media, distributors.

Peter Brook (Interview). (27 min., color, 1973) Insight Media, distributors.

Peter Brook: The Empty Space. (60 min., color, 1975) Insight Media, distributors.

A Streetcar Named Desire, by Tennessee Williams, directed by Elia Kazan, with Vivien Leigh and Marlon Brando. (122 min., black & white, 1951). CBS/Fox Video, distributors.

Waiting for Godot by Samuel Beckett, directed by Alan Schneider. (l02 min., black & white, 1976) Insight Media, distributors.

Chapters 10 and 11 Scenery, Costumes, Lighting, Sound, Technology

Anderson, Barbara, and Cletus Anderson. *Costume Design*. New York: Holt, Rinehart and Winston, 1984.

Apperson, Linda. *Stage Managing and Theatre Etiquette*. Chicago, IL: Ivan R. Dee Publisher, 1998.

Arnold, Richard L. *Scene Technology*. 3rd ed. Englewood Cliffs, NJ: Prentice-Hall, 1994.

Aronson, Arnold. *American Set Design*. New York: Theatre Communications Group, 1985.

Bellman, Willard F. *Scenography and Stage Technology: An Introduction*. New York: Thomas Y. Crowell, 1977.

Burris-Meyer, Harold. *Sound in the Theatre*. Rev. ed. New York: Theatre Arts Books, 1979.

——, and Edward C. Cole. *Scenery for the Theatre*. 2nd ed. Boston, MA: Little, Brown, 1972.

Collison, David. *Stage Sound*. New York: Applause Theatre Books, 1990.

Corson, Richard. *Stage Makeup*. 9th ed. Needham Heights, MA: Allyn & Bacon, 2000.

Effects for the Theatre. Ed. Graham Walne. New York: Drama Book Publishers, 1995.

Essig, Linda. *Lighting and the Design Idea*. New York: Harcourt, Brace & Co., 1997.

Fraser, Neil. *Lighting and Sound*. London: Phaidon Press, Ltd., 1998.

Holden, Alys E., and J. Sammler Bronislaw. *Structural Design for the Stage*. Boston, MA: Focal Press, 1999.

Ingham, Rosemary, and Liz Covey. *Technician's Handbook: A Complete Guide for Amateur and Professional Costume Technicians*. (Rev. ed. of *The Costumer's Handbook*.) Portsmouth, NH: Heinemann Educational Books, Inc., 1992.

Izenour, George C. *Theatre Design*. 2nd ed. New Haven, CT: Yale University Press, 1996.

James, Thurston. *The Theater Props Handbook: A Comprehensive Guide to Theater Properties, Materials and Construction*. Crozet, VA: Betterway Publications, 1989.

Jones, Robert Edmond. *The Dramatic Imagination: Reflections and Speculations on the Art of the Theatre*. New York: Methuen, 1987.

Leacroft, Richard, and Helen Leacroft. *Theatre and Playhouse: An Illustrated Development of Theatre Building from Ancient Greece to the Present Day*. New York: Methuen, 1984.

Motley. *Designing and Making Stage Costumes*. London: Herbert Press, 1992.

Owen, Bobbi. *Costume Design on Broadway: Designers and Their Credits, 1915–1985*. Westport, CT: Greenwood Press, 1987.

———. *Lighting Design on Broadway: Designers and Their Credits, 1915–1990*. Westport, CT: Greenwood Press, 1991.

———. *Scene Design on Broadway: Designers and Their Credits, 1915–1990*. Westport, CT: Greenwood Press, 1991.

Palmer, Richard H. *The Lighting Art: The Aesthetics of Stage Lighting Design*. 2nd ed. Englewood Cliffs, NJ: Prentice-Hall, 1994.

Parker, W. Oren, and R. Craig Wolf. *Scene Design and Stage Lighting*. 7th ed. New York: Harcourt Brace & Company, 1996.

Pectal, Lynn. *Costume Design: Techniques of Modern Masters*. New York: Back Stage Books, 1993.

———. *Designing and Drawing for the Theatre*. New York: McGraw-Hill, 1995.

Pilbrow, Richard. *Stage Lighting Design: The Art, the Craft, and the Life*. New York: Design Press, 1999.

Reid, Francis. *The Stage Lighting Handbook*. 5th ed. New York: Routledge, 1996.

Rosenthal, Jean, and Lael Wertenbaker. *The Magic of Light*. Boston, MA: Little Brown, 1972.

Russell, Douglas A. *Costume History and Style*. Englewood Cliffs, NJ: Prentice-Hall, 1983.

———. *Stage Costume Design: Theory, Technique and Style*. 2nd ed. Englewood Cliffs, NJ: Prentice-Hall, 1985.

Svoboda, Josef. *The Secret of Theatrical Space*. Ed. and trans. Jarka M. Burian. New York: Applause Theatre Books, 1993.

Taymor, Julie, and Eileen Blumenthal. *Playing with Fire*. New York: Harry N. Abrams Publishers, 1995.

Thudium, Laua. *Stage Makeup*. New York: Back Stage Books, 1999.

Warfel, William B., and Walter R. Klappert. *The New Handbook of Stage Lighting Graphics*. Rev. ed. New York: Drama Book Publishers, 1990.

Video Library

Fool's Fire, directed and designed by Julie Taymor. (**000** min., color, 1992) PBS Video, distributors.

Fundamentals of Scenic Painting, with Ron Ranson Jr. (81 min., color, 1989) Theatre Arts Video Library, distributors.

Laurie Anderson: Home of the Brave, performed and directed by Laurie Anderson. (90 min., color, 1986) Music Video, distributors.

Play It Safe: Introduction to Theater Safety. (82 min., color, 1994) Insight Media, distributors.

Chapter 12 Producers and Managers

Alexander, Jane. *Command Performance: An Actress in the Theater of Politics.* New York: Public Affairs, 2000.

Botto, Louis. *At This Theatre: Playbill Magazine's Informal History of Broadway Theatres.* New York: Dodd, Mead, 1984.

Crawford, Cheryl. *One Naked Individual: My Fifty Years in the Theatre.* Indianapolis, IN: Bobbs-Merrill, 1977.

Farber, Donald C. *From Option to Opening: A Guide to Producing Plays Off-Broadway.* 4th ed. New York: Limelight Editions, 1997.

———. *Producing Theatre: A Comprehensive Legal and Business Guide.* 2nd ed. New York: Limelight Editions, 1997.

Goldman, William. *The Season: A Candid Look at Broadway.* Rev. ed. New York: Limelight Editions, 1998.

Hirsh, Foster. *The Boys from Syracuse: The Shuberts' Theatrical Empire.* Carbondale, IL: Southern Illinois University Press, 1998.

———. *Harold Prince and the American Musical Theatre.* New York: Cambridge University Press, 1990.

It Happened on Broadway: An Oral History of the Great White Way. Eds. Myrna Katz Frommer and Harvey Frommer. New York: Harcourt Brace & Co., 1998.

Kessel, Howard. *David Merrick: The Abominable Showman.* New York: Applause Theatre Books, 1993.

Langley, Stephen. *Theatre Management in America, Principles and Practices: Producing for Commercial, Stock, Resident, College and Community Theatre.* 2nd ed. New York: Drama Book Publishers, 1990.

Ostrow, Stuart. *A Producer's Broadway Journey.* Westport, CT: Praeger Publishers, 1999.

Schneider, Richard E., and Mary Jo Fred. *The Theater Management Handbook.* Cincinnati, OH: Betterway Books, 1999.

Theatre Profiles 12: The Illustrated Guide to America's Nonprofit Professional Theatre. New York: Theatre Communications Group, 1996.

Video Library

Hey, Mr. Producer! The Musical World of Cameron Mackintosh. (164 min., color, 1998) Insight Media, distributors.

The Producers, directed by Mel Brooks, with Zero Mostel and Gene Wilder. (88 min., color, 1968) Hi Fi Video, distributors.

Chapter 13 Theatrical Diversity

Bogosian, Eric. *The Essential Bogosian.* New York: Theatre Communications Group, 1994.

Brook, Peter. *Peter Brook: A Theatrical Casebook.* Compiled by David Williams. New York: Methuen, 1988.

———. *The Shifting Point: Theatre, Film, Opera 1946–1987.* See Chapter 9.

Brustein, Robert. *Cultural Calisthenics: Writings on Race, Politics and Theatre.* Chicago, IL: Ivan R. Dee Publisher, 1999.

Carrière, Jean C. *The Mahabharata*. Trans. Peter Brook. New York: Harper & Row, 1987.

Extreme Exposure: An Anthology of Solo Performance Texts from the Twentieth Century. Ed. Jo Bonney. New York: Theatre Communications Group, 2000.

Gómez-Peña, Guillermo. *Dangerous Border Crossers: The Artist Talks Back*. New York: Routledge, 2000.

Huerta, Jorge. *Chicano Theatre: Themes and Forms*. Ypsilanti, MI: Bilingual Press, 1982.

The Intercultural Performance Reader. Ed. Patrice Pavis. London: Routledge, 1996.

Interculturalism and Performance. Eds. Bonnie Marranca and Gautam Dasgupta. Baltimore, MD: Johns Hopkins University Press, 1991.

Kanellos, Nicolas. *A History of Hispanic Theatre in the United States: Origins to 1940*. Austin, TX: University of Texas Press, 1990.

Kiernander, Adrian. *Ariane Mnouchkine and the Théâtre du Soleil*. New York: Cambridge University Press, 1993.

Out from Under: Texts by Women Performance Artists. Ed. Lenora Champagne. New York: Theatre Communications Group, 1990.

Pavis, Patrice. *Theatre at the Crossroads of Culture*. Trans. Loren Kruger. New York: Routledge, 1991.

Pottlitzer, Joanne. *Hispanic Theatre in the United States and Puerto Rico*. New York: Ford Foundation, 1988.

Schechner, Richard, and Willa Appel, eds. *By Means of Performance: Intercultural Studies of Theatre and Ritual*. New York: Cambridge University Press, 1990.

Smith, Anna Deavere. *Fires in the Mirror: Crown Heights, Brooklyn and Other Identities*. New York: Doubleday Anchor Books, 1993.

——. *Talk to Me: Listening Between the Lines*. New York: Random House, 2000.

Video Library

Anna Deavere Smith: In Her Own Words. The solo artist talks about her observations on racism and her creative process. (60 min., audio tape, 1993) WGBH Radio, Boston, MA, distributors.

Fires in the Mirror: Crown Heights, Brooklyn and Other Identities, written and performed by Anna Deavere Smith, directed by George C. Wolfe. (60 min., color, 1993) PBS Video, distributors.

Twilight: Los Angeles, written and performed by Anna Deavere Smith. (85 min., color, 2000) Offline Releasing, distributors.

George C. Wolfe (Playwright and Director). (60 min., color, 1995) Insight Media, distributors.

The Mahabharata, directed by Peter Brook with the International Centre for Theatre Research (360 min., color, 1989) Parade Video, distributors.

SubUrbia, written and performed by Eric Bogosian. (118 min., color, 1996) Castlerock Entertainment, distributors.

Chapter 14 Theatre Criticism

Atkinson, Brooks. *Broadway*. New York: Macmillan, 1970.

Brustein, Robert. *Reimagining American Theatre*. New York: Hill and Wang, 1991.

Clurman, Harold. *The Collected Works of Harold Clurman: Six Decades of Commentary on Theatre, Dance, Music, Film, Arts, Letters and Politics*. Eds. Marjorie Loggia and Glenn Young. New York: Applause Theatre Books, 1993.

Gussow, Mel. *Theatre on the Edge: New Visions, New Voices*. New York: Applause Theatre Books, 1998.

Kauffmann, Stanley. *Persons of the Drama: Theater Criticism and Comment*. New York: Harper & Row, 1976.

——. *Theatre Criticisms*. New York: Performing Arts Journal Publications, 1984.

Rich, Frank. *Ghost Light: A Memoir*. New York: Random House, 2000.

——. *Hot Seat: Theatre Criticism for the New York Times, 1980–1995*. New York: Random House, 1998.

Rigg, Diana. *No Turn Unstoned: The Worst Ever Theatrical Reviews*. New York: Silman James Press, 1991.

Sontag, Susan. *Against Interpretation and Other Essays*. New York: Doubleday, 1966.

Tynan, Kenneth. *Curtains: Selections from the Drama Criticism and Related Writings*. New York: Atheneum, 1971.

Wilson, August. *The Ground on Which I Stand*. New York: Theatre Communications Group, 2001.

The World of George Jean Nathan: Essays, Reviews & Commentary. Ed. Charles S. Angoff. New York: Applause Theatre Books, 1998.

Video Library

American Buffalo, by David Mamet. Screen adaptation by Mamet, with Dustin Hoffman and Dennis Franz. (88 min., color, 1995) Evergreen Entertainment, distributors.

The Glass Menagerie, by Tennessee Williams. Directed by Paul Newman, with Joanne Woodward and John Malkovich. (134 min., color, 1987) HBO Video, distributors.

Look Back in Anger, by John Osborne. Directed by David Jones, with Kenneth Branagh and Emma Thompson. (114 min., color, 1989). HBO Video, distributors.

A Streetcar Named Desire, by Tennessee Williams. See Chapter 9.

REFERENCE BOOKS

Brockett, Oscar G. *History of Theatre*. See Chapter 2.

———, and Robert R. Findlay. *Century of Innovation: A History of European and American Theatre and Drama Since 1870*. 2nd ed. Boston, MA: Allyn & Bacon, 1991.

The Cambridge Companion to American Women Playwrights. Ed. Brenda Murphy. New York: Cambridge University Press, 1990.

The Cambridge Companion to Modern British Woman Playwrights. Eds. Elaine Aston and Janelle Reinelt. New York: Cambridge University Press, 1997.

The Cambridge Guide to American Theatre. Eds. Don B. Wilmeth and Tice L. Miller. New York: Cambridge University Press, 1993.

The Cambridge Guide to Asian Theatre. Eds. James R. Brandon and Martin Banham. New York: Cambridge University Press, 1993.

The Cambridge Guide to Theatre. Ed. Martin Banham. Cambridge, UK: Cambridge University Press, 1995.

The Cambridge Illustrated History of British Theatre. Ed. Simon Trussler. London: Cambridge University Press, 1994.

Carlson, Marvin. *Theories of the Theatre: A Historical and Critical Survey, from the Greeks to the Present*. Rev. ed. Ithaca, NY: Cornell University Press, 1994.

The Concise Oxford Companion to the Theatre. Eds. Phyllis Hartnoll and Peter Found. New York: Oxford University Press, 1992.

Gerould, Daniel. *Theatre Theory Theatre: The Major Critical Texts*. New York: Applause Theatre Books, 1998.

International Dictionary of Theatre. Vol. 1, Plays; Vol. 2, Playwrights; Vol. 3, Actors, Directors, Designers. Eds. David Pickering and Judith M. Kass. New York: St. James Press, 1996.

Londré, Felicia, and Daniel J. Watermeier. *The History of North American Theater: The United States, Canada, and Mexico: From Pre-Columbian Times to the Present*. New York: Continuum, 1998.

Notable Women in the American Theatre: A Biographical Dictionary. Eds. Vera Mowry Roberts, Alice Robinson, and Milly S. Barranger. Westport, CT: Greenwood Press, 1989.

The Oxford Companion to Women's Writing in the United States. Eds. Cathy N. Davidson and Linda Wagner-Martin. New York: Oxford University Press, 1995.

Wickham, Glynne. *A History of the Theatre*. 2nd ed. London: Phaidon Press, Ltd., 1992.

World Encyclopedia of Contemporary Theatre. Vol. 1. New York: Routledge, 1994.

———: *The Americas*. Vol. 2. New York: Routledge, 1996.

TRADE PUBLICATIONS

Backstage (weekly). New York: BPI Communications, Inc.

Entertainment Design: The Art and Technology of Show Business (monthly). New York: Intertec Publishing Corp.

Lighting Dimensions: The Magazine for the Lighting Professional (monthly). New York: Primedia, Inc.

Ross Reports: Television & Film. Agents. Casting Directors (monthly). New York: BPI Communications, Inc.

TCG Theatre Directory 2000–2001 (annual). New York: Theatre Communications Group, 2000.

TD&T: Theatre Design and Technology: The Journal for Design, Production & Technology for Professionals in the Performing Arts and Entertainment Industry (monthly). Louisville, KY: USITT.

Variety (daily and weekly). New York: The Variety Group.

APPENDIX B

NOTES

Chapter 1

1. Peter Brook, *The Empty Space* (New York: Atheneum, 1968): 3. Copyright © 1968 by Peter Brook. Reprinted with permission of Atheneum Publishers, New York, and Granada Publishing Ltd., England.

Chapter 2

1. Excerpt from *The Sacred and Profane: The Nature of Religion* by Mircea Eliade, copyright © 1957 by Rowohlt Taschenbuch Verlag GmbH, English translation by Willard R. Trask. Copyright ©1959 and renewed 1987 by Harcourt, Inc., reprinted by permission of Harcourt, Inc.

Chapter 3

1. Jerzy Grotowski, *Towards a Poor Theatre* (New York: Clarion Press, 1968): 19–20. Reprinted by permission of H. M. Berg, Odin Teatret, Denmark.
2. Richard Schechner, *Environmental Theater* (New York: Hawthorn, 1973): 25. Copyright © 1973 by Richard Schechner. All rights reserved. Reprinted by permission of Hawthorn Books, Inc.
3. Grotowski: 19–20. Reprinted by permission.
4. Grotowski: 19–20. Reprinted by permission.
5. Grotowski: 75. Reprinted by permission.
6. Pierre Biner, *The Living Theatre: A History Without Myths* (New York: Avon Books, 1972): 72.
7. Mel Gussow, "The Living Theater Returns to Its Birthplace," *New York Times* (15 January 1984): II, 6.
8. David Williams, ed., *Collaborative Theatre: The Théâtre du Soleil Sourcebook* (New York: Routledge, 1999): x.
9. Peter Schumann, "The Radicality of the Puppet Theatre," *The Drama Review*, 35, No. 4 (Winter 1991): 75. See also Peter Schumann, "The Bread and Puppet Theatre (Interview)," *The Drama Review*, 12, No. 2 (Winter 1968): 62–73.

Chapter 4

1. Tennessee Williams, Afterword to *Camino Real* (New York: New Directions, 1953): xii. Copyright © 1948, 1953 by Tennessee Williams. Reprinted by permission of New Directions Publishing Corporation.
2. David Savran, *The Playwright's Voice: American Dramatists on Memory, Writing and the Politics of Culture* (New York: Theatre Communications Group, 1999): 6.
3. Mel Gussow, "Women Playwrights: New Voices in the Theater," *New York Times Magazine* (1 May 1983): 6, 26. Copyright © 1983 by The New York Times Company. Reprinted by permission.
4. Lillian Hellman, *Pentimento: A Book of Portraits* (Boston, MA: Little, Brown & Company, 1973): 151–152.
5. Lorraine Hansberry, *To Be Young, Gifted and Black*, adapted by Robert Nemiroff (Englewood Cliffs, NJ: Prentice-Hall, 1969): 133–134. Copyright © 1969 by Prentice-Hall, Inc. Reprinted by permission.
6. María Irene Fornés, "The 'Woman' Playwright Issue," *Performing Arts Journal*, 7, No. 3 (1983): 91. Reprinted by permission.
7. "Tina Howe," *American Theatre*, 2, No. 5 (September 1985): 14. Reprinted by permission of the Theatre Communications Group Inc.
8. Carol Lawson, "Caryl Churchill Wins Blackburn Drama Prize," *New York Times* (25 February 1984): 1, 16:5. Copyright © 1984 by The New York Times Company. Reprinted by permission.
9. "Wendy Wasserstein," *Contemporary Authors*, Vol. 129 (Detroit, MI: Gale Research Inc., 1990): 452–457.
10. Kathy Sova, *American Theatre*, 14, No. 2 (February 1997): 24. Reprinted by permission of the Theatre Communications Group Inc.
11. Suzan-Lori Parks, "Elements of Style," in *The America Play and Other Works* (New York: Theatre Communications Group, 1995): 6, 8. Reprinted by permission of the Theatre Communications Group, Inc.
12. John Lion, "Rock 'n' Roll Jesus with Cowboy Mouth," *American Theatre*, 1, No. 1 (April 1984): 8. Reprinted by permission of the Theatre Communications Group Inc.

13. Amy Lippman, "Rhythm & Truths: An Interview with Sam Shepard," *American Theatre*, 1, No. 1 (April 1984): 12. Reprinted by permission of the Theatre Communications Group Inc.

14. Lippman: 9. Reprinted by permission of the Theatre Communications Group Inc.

15. "David Mamet," *Contemporary Authors*, Vol. 15, New Revision Series (Chicago, IL: Gale Research Company, 1985): 300.

16. R. C. Lewis, "A Playwright Named Tennessee," *New York Times Magazine* (7 December 1947): 19. Copyright © 1947 by The New York Times Company. Reprinted by permission.

17. August Wilson, *Fences* (New York: NAL Penguin, 1986): 69.

18. David Henry Hwang, *Contemporary American Dramatists*, ed. K. A. Berney (1994): 285. Reprinted by permission of the Gale Group.

19. Jennifer Tanaka, "Only Connect: An Interview with the Playwright," *American Theatre*, 16, No. 6 (July/August 1999): 27. Reprinted by permission of the Theatre Communications Group Inc.

Chapter 5

1. Bertolt Brecht, "A Short Organon for the Theatre," *Brecht on Theatre: The Development of an Aesthetic*, trans. and ed. John Willett (New York: Hill and Wang, 1964): 204.

2. Peter Brook, *The Empty Space* (New York: Atheneum, 1968): 15.

3. Lane Cooper, *Aristotle on the Art of Poetry* (Ithaca, NY: Cornell University Press, 1947): 17.

4. "Lillian Hellman, Playwright, Author and Rebel, Dies at 79," *New York Times* (1 July 1984): 20. Copyright © 1984 by the New York Times Co. Reprinted by permission.

5. Eric Bentley, "The Psychology of Farce," in *Let's Get a Divorce! and Other Plays* (New York: Hill and Wang, 1958): vii–xx.

6. Danielle Sallenave, "Entretien avec Antoine Vitez: Faire théâtre de tout," *Digraphe* (April 1976): 117.

7. Excerpt from *Brecht on Theatre* edited and translated by John Willett. Translation copyright © 1964, renewed © 1992 by John Willett. Reprinted by permission of Hill and Wang, a division of Farrar, Strauss and Giroux, LLC.

8. Willett: 121. Reprinted by permission.

9. Albert Camus, *The Myth of Sisyphus and Other Essays* (New York: Alfred A. Knopf, 1955): 5. Reprinted by permission.

10. Eugène Ionesco, *Notes and Counter Notes: Writings on the Theatre*, trans. Donald Watson (New York: Grove Press, 1964): 257. Copyright © 1964 by Grove Press, Inc. Reprinted with permission.

Chapter 6

1. David Mamet, *Writing in Restaurants* (New York: Viking Penguin, 1986): 8.

2. Laurence Olivier, *On Acting* (London: George Weidenfeld & Nicolson Limited, 1986): 192. Reprinted by permission.

3. Francis Fergusson, *The Idea of a Theatre* (Princeton, NJ: University Press, 1949): 36.

4. For my understanding of climactic and episodic drama I am indebted to material from Bernard Beckerman, *Dynamics of Drama: Theory and Method of Analysis* (New York: Alfred A. Knopf, 1970).

5. Eugène Ionesco, *The Bald Soprano*, trans. Donald Watson (New York: Grove Press, 1958): 11–13. Copyright © 1958 by Grove Press, Inc. Reprinted by permission.

6. From *Monster in a Box* by Spalding Gray (New York: Vintage Books, 1992): 63–64. Reprinted by permission.

7. Samuel Beckett, *Rockaby* (New York: Grove Press, 1980). Reprinted by permission of Grove Press, Inc.

8. Robert Wilson, *the CIVIL warS*, ed. Jan Graham Geidt (Cambridge, MA: American Repertory Theatre, 1985): 16. Reprinted by permission.

9. Robert Wilson and David Byrne, *The Forest* (West Berlin: Theater der Freien Volksbühne, 1988): 29–32.

Chapter 7

1. From *Naked Masks: Five Plays* by Luigi Pirandello, ed. Eric Bentley, p. 372. Trnsl. copyright 1922 by E. P. Dutton. Renewed 1950 in the names of Stefano, Fausto, and Lietta Pirandello. Used by permission of Dutton Signet, a division of Penguin Books USA, Inc.

2. Tennessee Williams, *A Streetcar Named Desire*. Reprinted by permission of New Directions, Inc.

3. From *Six Characters in Search of an Author* by Luigi Pirandello. Reprinted by permission of Dutton Signet, a Division of Penguin Books USA, Inc.

4. Eugène Ionesco, *Notes and Counter Notes: Writings on the Theatre*, trans. Donald Watson (New York: Grove Press, 1964): 27. Reprinted with permission.

5. Peter Brook, *The Empty Space* (New York: Atheneum, 1968): 12.

6. George Steiner, *The Death of Tragedy*. Copyright © 1963, renewed 1989 by George Steiner. Reprinted by permission of the author's agent, George Borchardt, Inc.

7. From *The Cherry Orchard* by Anton Chekhov, from *Plays*, trans. Elisaveta Fen (Penguin Classics, 1954), copyright © Elisaveta Fen, 1951, 1954. Reprinted by permission of Penguin Books, Ltd.

8. Excerpt from "On Gestic Music" from *Brecht on Theatre*, edited and translated by John Willett. Translation copyright © 1964, renewed © 1992 by John Willett. Reprinted by permission of Hill and Wang, a division of Farrar, Straus, and Giroux, LLC.

9. Bertolt Brecht, *The Caucasian Chalk Circle*, trans. Ralph Manheim, in *Collected Plays*, Volume 7, ed. Ralph Manheim and John Willett (New York: Random House, Inc., 1975).

10. David Mamet, *Glengarry Glen Ross* (New York: Grove Press, 1984). Reprinted by permission.

Chapter 8

1. Laurence Olivier, *On Acting* (New York: Simon & Schuster, 1986): 192.

2. Uta Hagen, *A Challenge for the Actor* (New York: Charles Scribner's Sons, 1991): 50.

3. Lionel Gracey-Whitman, "Return by Popular Demand," *Plays and Players*, No. 367 (April 1984): 21–25. Reprinted by permission.

4. Toby Cole and Helen Krich Chinoy, eds., *Actors on Acting: The Theories, Techniques, and Practices of the Great Actors of All Times as Told in Their Own Words* (New York: Crown, 1959): 132. Reprinted by permission.

5. See Laurence Olivier, *On Acting* (New York: Simon & Schuster, 1986), 21–34.

6. Lewis Funke and John E. Booth, eds., *Actors Talk About Acting* (New York: Random House, 1961): 14. Reprinted by permission.

7. Hagen: 70. See also Jared Brown, *The Fabulous Lunts: A Biography of Alfred Lunt and Lynn Fontanne* (New York: Atheneum, 1986).

8. Konstantin Stanislavski, *An Actor Prepares*, trans. Elizabeth Reynolds Hapgood (New York: Routledge, 1989): 14.

9. Konstantin Stanislavsk1, *An Actor's Handbook*, ed. and trans. Elizabeth Reynolds Hapgood (New York: Theatre Arts, 1963): 100.

10. Robert Hethmon, *Strasberg at the Actors Studio* (New York: Viking Press, 1965): 78.

11. Sanford Meisner and Dennis Longwell, *Sanford Meisner on Acting* (New York: Vintage Books, 1987): 37.

12. Melissa Bruder and others, *A Practical Handbook for the Actor* (New York: Vintage Books, 1986): 5.

13. *New York Times* (7 November 1999): II, 8.

14. Jon Jory, "Foreword", in *Anne Bogart Viewpoints*, eds. Michael Bigelow Dixon and Joel A. Smith (Lyme, NH: Smith and Kraus, Inc., 1995): xv.

15. Cicely Berry, *The Actor and the Voice* (New York: Macmillan, 1973): 121. Reprinted by permission.

16. Richard Eder, "The World According to Brook," *American Theatre*, 1, No. 2 (May 1984): 38. Reprinted by permission of the Theatre Communications Group Inc.

17. Michael Caine, *Acting in Film: An Actor's Take on Movie Making*, rev. ed. (New York: Applause Theatre Book Publishers, 1997): 4. Reprinted by permission.

Chapter 9

1. Alan Schneider, "Things to Come: Crystal-Gazing at the Near and Distant Future of a Durable Art," *American Theatre*, 1, No. 1 (April 1984): 17. Reprinted by permission of the Theatre Communications Group Inc.

2. Elia Kazan, "Notebook for *A Streetcar Named Desire*," in *Directing the Play: A Source Book of Stagecraft*, eds. Toby Cole and Helen Krich Chinoy (Indianapolis, IN: The Bobbs-Merrill Company, 1953): 296.

3. Hubert Witt, ed., *Brecht: As They Knew Him* (New York: International Publishers, 1974): 126. Reprinted by permission.

4. Peter Brook, *Threads of Time: A Memoir* (London: Methuen Publishing, Ltd., 1999): 149–150. Reprinted by permission.

5. Toby Dole and Helen Krich Chinoy, eds., *Directors on Directing*, 2nd rev. ed. (Indianapolis, IN: The Bobbs-Merrill Company, 1977): 364–366.

6. Arthur Bartow, "'Images from the Id': An Interview," *American Theatre*, 5, No. 3 (June 1988): 56–57. Courtesy of the Theatre Communications Group Inc.

7. Bartow: 17.

8. Robert Wilson and David Byrne, *The Forest* (West Berlin: Theater der Freien Volksbühne, 1988): 29–32.

9. Wilson and Byrne: 36.

Chapter 10

1. Robert Edmond Jones, *The Dramatic Imagination: Reflections and Speculations on the Art of the Theatre* (New York: Methuen Theatre Arts Books, 1987): 26.

2. Josef Svoboda, *The Secret of Theatrical Space*, ed. and trans. J. M. Burian (New York: Applause Theatre Books, 1993): 8.

3. Lynn Pecktal, "A Conversation with Ming Cho Lee," in *Designing and Painting for the Theatre* (New York: Holt, Rinehart, & Winston, 1975): 242. Reprinted by permission.

4. Lynn Pecktal, "A Conversation with John Lee Beatty, in *Designing and Painting for the Theatre* (New York: McGraw-Hill, Inc., 1995): 544–545.

5. Pecktal: 51. Reprinted by permission.

6. Jarka Burian, *The Scenography of Josef Svoboda* (Middletown, CT: Wesleyan University Press, 1971): 31. Copyright © 1971 by Jarka Burian. From a speech by Josef Svoboda, the text of which was printed in *Zprávy Divadelního Ustavu*, no. 8 (1967): 28–29. Reprinted by permission of Wesleyan University Press.
7. John Gruen, "She Is One of Broadway's Most Designing Women," *New York Times* (8 April 1984): II, 5, 14. Copyright © 1984 by The New York Times Company. Reprinted by permission.
8. Patricia Zipprodt, "Designing Costumes," in *Contemporary Stage Design U.S.A.* (Middletown, CT: Wesleyan University Press, 1974): 29.
9. Ronn Smith, "Paul Huntley: Big on Wigs," *Theatre Crafts* (February 1983): 23.

Chapter 11

1. *New York Times* (11 January 1995). See also *Current Biography*, 58, No. 7 (July 1997): 52–54.
2. Elizabeth Stone, "Jennifer Tipton Interview," *New York Times* (14 April 1991).
3. "Abe Jacob Profile," *Entertainment Design* (January 2000): 20.

Chapter 12

1. Cheryl Crawford, *One Naked Individual: My Fifty Years in the Theatre* (Indianapolis, IN: Bobbs-Merrill, 1977): 4.
2. Alexander H. Cohen, "Broadway Theatre," in *Producers on Producing*, ed. Stephen Langley (New York: Drama Book Specialists, 1976): 15.
3. Audrey Wood with Max Wilk, *Represented by Audrey Wood* (Garden City, NY: Doubleday and Company, 1981): 7.
4. Robin Pogrebin, "Off Broadway's Mom and Angel," *New York Times* (26 July 1999): 1B.
5. *Producers on Producing*: 78.

Chapter 13

1. Bree Burns, "Breaking the Mold: Julie Taymor," *Theatre Crafts*, 22, No. 3 (March 1988): 51.
2. Susan Bennett, *Theatre Audiences: A Theory of Production and Reception*, 2nd ed. (New York: Routledge, 1997): 171.
3. Richard Schechner, "An Intercultural Primer," *American Theatre*, 8, No. 7 (October 1991): 28–31, 135.

4. Peter Brook, *Threads of Time: A Memoir* (London: Methuen Publishers, 1999): 141. Reprinted by permission.
5. Margaret Croyden, "*The Mahabharata*: A Review," *New York Times* (25 August 1985): 11, 20.
6. Miriam Horn, "A Director Who Can Conjure Up Magic Onstage," *Smithsonian* (February 1993): 72.
7. Burns: 49.
8. Horn: 66.
9. *Juan Darién: A Carnival Mass, Theater*, 20, No. 2, (Spring, 1989): 52.
10. Horn: 66.
11. Rosette C. Lamont, "Ariane Mnouchkine's Theater of History," *TheaterWeek* (October 5–11, 1992): 19.
12. Lamont: 18.
13. Guillermo Goméz-Peñez, "A Binational Performance Pilgrimage," *The Drama Review*, 35, No. 3 (1991): 22–46.
14. Jo Bonney, "Fragments from the Age of the Self: Nine Artists Span the Century of the Soloist," *American Theatre*, 16, No. 10 (December 1999): 32.
15. John Lahr, "Under the Skin," *The New Yorker* (June 28, 1993): 90.
16. Simi Horwitz, "About Face," *TheaterWeek* (June 22, 1992): 25.
17. Cathy Madison, "Hearing Voices: Portraits of America at the Public," *Village Voice* (December 10, 1991): 106.
18. Zelda Fichandler, "Beyond Black & White 'On Cultural Power': 13 Commentaries," *American Theatre*, 14, No. 5 (May/June 1997): 14. Reprinted by permission of Theatre Communications Group Inc.

Chapter 14

1. Samuel Beckett, *Waiting for Godot*. Reprinted by permission of Grove Press, Inc.
2. Frank Rich, "A Critic's Summit: Robert Brustein and Frank Rich Talk About Criticism," *American Theatre*, 16, No. 5 (May/June 1999): 18. Reprinted by permission of Theatre Communications Group Inc.
3. Arthur Miller, *Death of a Salesman*. Copyright 1949, renewed © 1977 by Arthur Miller. Reprinted by permission of Viking Putnam, a division of Penguin Putnam, Inc.
4. Tony Kushner, *Angels in America. Part Two: Perestroika*. Reprinted by permission of Theatre Communications Group Inc.
5. Tennessee Williams, *The Glass Menagerie*. Reprinted by permission of Random House, Inc.
6. Stanley Kauffmann, *Persons of the Drama: Theater Criticism and Comment* (New York: Harper & Row, 1976): 369–380.
7. George Jean Nathan, *The Critic and the Drama* (New York: Alfred A. Knopf, 1922): 133.

8. J. L. Styan, *Drama, Stage and Audience* (New York: Cambridge University Press, 1975): 33.

9. Copyright © 2000 The New York Times Company. Reprinted by permission.

10. Frank Rich, "Stage: Billie Whitelaw in Three Beckett Works," *New York Times* (17 February 1984): III, 3. Copyright © 1984 by The New York Times Company. Reprinted by permission.

11. Brooks Atkinson, "'Streetcar' Tragedy, Mr. Williams' Report on Life in New Orleans," *New York Times* (14 December 1947): II, 3. Copyright © 1947 by The New York Times Company. Reprinted by permission.

12. Kenneth Tynan, *"Look Back in Anger,* by John Osborne, at the Royal Court," in *Curtains: Selections from the Drama Criticism and Related Writings* (New York: Atheneum, 1971): 130–132. Used by permission of the Tynan Estate.

13. Edith Oliver, "Off Broadway," *The New Yorker* (February 9, 1976): 81. Reprinted by permission.

ACKNOWLEDGMENTS

2 © Richard Termine; p. 6 The Museum of Modern Art/Film Stills Archive; p. 7 Eileen Darby/Billy Rose Theatre Collection, The New York Public Library for the Performing Arts, Astor, Lenox and Tilden Foundations; p. 8 top © Mike Smallcombe/Courtesy Royal National Theatre; p. 8 bottom © Mike Smallcombe/Courtesy Royal National Theatre; p. 9 top Courtesy Guthrie Theatre; p. 9 bottom Photo by Jennifer Donahoe/Courtesy Oregon Shakespeare Theatre; p. 10 top Courtesy Arena Stage; p. 10 bottom © Carol Pratt; p. 11 top © Z. Jedrus ; p. 11 bottom © Whitney Cox; p. 12 Courtesy of Williamstown Theatre Festival/Richard Feldman; p. 15 bottom The Museum of Modern Art/Film Stills Archive; p. 16 bottom The Everett Collection; p. 17 top The Museum of Modern Art/Film Stills Archive; p. 17 btm left The Everett Collection; p. 17 bottom right TITUS ©1999 Fox Searchlight Pictures, Inc. All rights reserved; p. 20 © Robbie Jack/CORBIS; p. 21 Courtesy Shakespeare Centre Library, Stratford-Upon-Avon; p. 22 © Eric Y. Exit/The Goodman Theatre (pictured are: Kevin Anderson, Brian Dennehy & Ted Koch.) ; p. 24 © Martine Franck/Magnum Photos, Inc.; p. 26 © Charles & Josette Lenars/CORBIS; p. 28 top © CORBIS; p. 28 bottom © Sandro Vannini/CORBIS; p. 29 © Araldo de Luca/CORBIS; p. 31 © Giraudon/Art Resource, NY; p. 32 top Courtesy Columbia University Press; p. 32 bottom Glynne Wickham, Early English Stages; p. 33 By permission of the Folger Shakespeare Library; p. 34 Courtesy Shakespeare Centre Library, Stratford-Upon-Avon; p. 35 top right Reprinted by permission of Oxford Univerity Press; p. 35 btm left Reprinted by permission of Oxford Univerity Press; p. 35 btm right Reprinted by permission of Oxford Univerity Press; p. 36 Photo by Jennifer Donahoe/Courtesy Oregon Shakespeare Theatre; p. 37 top © Churchill & Klehr; p. 38 bottom Courtesy John F. Kennedy Center for the Performing Arts; p. 39 top Billy Rose Theatre Collection, The New York Public Library for the Performing Arts, Astor, Lenox and Tilden Foundations; p. 39 bottom Auditorium and stage of the Stratford Festival of Canada. Photo by Terry Manzo/Courtesy of Stratford Festival of Canada. p. 41 From The Chinese in Modern Times (1975), Colin Mackerras; p. 42 top © Liu Liquin/China Stock; p. 42 bottom © Stephanie Berger Photography; p. 43 © Liu Liqun/ChinaStock; p. 44 © ChinaStock; p. 45 top Courtesy of Berliner Ensemble ; p. 45 bottom Martha Swope/TimePix; p. 46 top © Martine Franck/Magnum Photos, Inc.; p. 46 bottom © Richard Feldman; p. 47 top Martha Swope/TimePix; p. 47 bottom © Martine Franck/Magnum Photos, Inc.; p. 48 Courtesy Japan National Tourist Organization, NY; p. 49 Courtesy Japan National Tourist Organization, NY; p. 50 top Courtesy Japan National Tourist Organization, NY; p. 50 bottom © Martine Franck/Magnum Photos, Inc.; p. 51 from Naniwa Miyage (souvenir from Naniwa, 1738.); p. 52 Courtesy Japan National Tourist Organization, NY; p. 54 © Martine Franck/Magnum Photos, Inc.; p. 57 © Max Waldman; p. 58 all 4 images Towards a Poor Theatre by Jerzy Grotowski. © 1968 Jerzy Grotowski and Odin Teatrets Forlag; 59 top Towards a Poor Theatre by Jerzy Grotowski and Odin Teatrets Forlag; p. 59 top and bottom Towards a Poor Theatre by Jerzy Grotowski, © 1968 Jerzy Grotowski and Odin Teatrets Forlag; p. 61 left © Fred W. McDarrah; p. 61 right © Fred W. McDarrah; p. 62 © Fred W. McDarrah; p. 63 © Martine Franck/Magnum Photos, Inc.; p. 64 left © Martine Franck/Magnum Photos, Inc.; p. 64 right © Martine Franck/Magnum Photos, Inc.; p. 66 top Towards a Poor Theatre by Jerzy Grotowski. © 1968 Jerzy Grotowski and Odin Teatrets Forlag; p. 66 bottom © Max Waldman; p. 67 top © Max Waldman; p. 67 bottom © Martine Franck/Magnum Photos, Inc.; p. 68 left © Fred W. McDarrah; p. 68 right Dan Charlson/Durham Herald-Sun; p. 72 © Richard Feldman, 1998; p. 74 © T. Charles Erickson/Hartford Stage; p. 75 left Courtesy of Edward Albee/William Morris Agency; p. 75 right © Bruce Bennett /Alley Theatre; p. 77 left © 1996 Susan Johann; p. 77 right Cristofer Gross/SCR; p. 78 National Archives; p. 79 top AP/Wide World Photos; p. 79 bottom © Fred W. McDarrah; p. 80 top © Cori Wells Braun/Courtesy of Tina Howe; p. 80 bottom Courtesy Subuskey & Associates; p. 81 top Courtesy of Paula Vogel/William Morris Agency; p. 81 bottom © 2001 Susan Johann ; p. 82 left AP/Wide World Photos; p. 82 right Allen Nomura; p. 83 © T. Charles Erickson/Hartford Stage; p. 84 left Brigitte Lacombe; p. 84 right Courtesy Brigitte Lacombe/Billy Rose Theatre Collection, The New York Public Library for the Performing Arts, Astor, Lenox and Tilden Foundations; p. 85 © T. Charles Erickson; p. 86 William B. Carter; p. 87 left William B. Carter; p. 87 right © Jim Caldwell/The Alley Theatre; p. 88 © Suellen Fitzsimmons/Courtesy of the Pittsburgh Public Theatre; p. 89 right Eileen Darby/Billy Rose Theatre Collection, The New York Public Library for the Performing Arts, Astor, Lenox and Tilden Foundations; p. 89 left Martha Swope/TimePix; p. 90 left Inge Morath/Magnum Photos, Inc.; p. 90 right © Jim Caldwell/Alley Theatre; p. 91 top © Carol Rosegg; p. 91 bottom Martha Swope/TimePix; p. 92 top Dan McNeil/Courtesy of Denver Center Theatre Company; p. 92 bottom © T. Charles Erickson/Hartford Stage; p. 93 top © Chris Bennion/Courtesy of Seattle Repertory Theatre; p. 93 bottom Cristofer Gross/Courtesy of Goodman Theatre; p. 94 top Barry Forbus/Courtesy of Goodman Theatre; p. 94 middle Courtesy of Goodman Theatre; p. 94 bottom © Carol Rosegg; p. 95 top Courtesy of David Henry Hwang; p. 95 middle Gary Bonasorte/Courtesy of William Morris Agency; p. 95 bottom © Jonathan Cramer; p. 96 top © Lia Chang Gallery Collection; p. 96 middle © Joan Marcus; p. 96 bottom AP/Wide World Photos; p. 98 © Richard Feldman; p. 102 left © Gianni Dagli Orti/CORBIS; p. 104 right © Joan Marcus; p. 104 left Courtesy French Press and Information Office; p. 104 right © Jim Caldwell; p. 106 © Martha Holmes; p. 108 left Courtesy of French Embassy; p. 108 right © Robbie Jack/CORBIS; p. 110 Billy Rose Theatre Collection, The New York Public Library for the Performing Arts, Astor, Lenox and Tilden Foundations; p. 112 Martha Swope/TimePix; p. 113 Martha Swope/TimePix; p. 114 M. Agins/NYT Pictures; p. 115 top M. Agins/NYT Pictures; p. 115 bottom M. Agins/NYT Pictures; p. 116 left © T. Charles Erickson; p. 116 right © Barry Slobin/PlayMakers Repertory Company; p. 117 top © Joan Marcus; p. 117 bottom Jamie Horton, Denver Center Theatre Company photo by Terry Shapiro; p. 118 left Courtesy German Information Center; p. 118 right © Richard Feldman; p. 121 © Ken Friedman/Berkeley Repertory Theatre; p. 122 Courtesy Berliner Ensemble; p. 123 Courtesy French Press and Information Office; p. 124 © Joan Marcus; p. 125 Courtesy French Press and Information Office; p. 126 © Bruce Bennett/Alley Theatre; p. 128 © Richard Feldman 1996; p. 132 Culver Pictures, Inc.; p. 136 © Joan Marcus; p. 138 Courtesy Guthrie Theatre; p. 140 Courtesy French Press and Information Office; p. 142 © Paula Court; p. 143 © Paula Court; p. 144 © Irene Haupt; p. 150 © Richard Termine; p. 151 © Richard Feldman; p. 152 left Ralph Brinkoff/Courtesy Byrd Hoffman Foundation; p. 152 right © Haremann & Clarchen Baus; p. 153 top © Paula Court; p. 153 bottom © Gerhard Kassner; p. 154 top Tom Caravaglia; p. 154 middle Winnie Klotz/Courtesy Metropolitan Opera, Lincoln Center, New York; p. 154 bottom © Stephanie Berger Photography; p. 156 Suellen Fitzsimmons/Pittsburgh Public Theater; p. 158 Eileen Darby/Billy Rose Theatre Collection, The New York Public Library for the Performing Arts, Astor, Lenox and Tilden Foundations; p. 159 © Vandamm Collection/Billy Rose Theatre Collection, The New York Public Library for the Performing Arts, Astor, Lenox and Tilden Foundations; p. 162 © Donald Cooper/Photostage Ltd.; p. 163 © Donald Cooper/Photostage Ltd.; p. 164 George E.

Joseph; p. 166 Anthony Crickmay/V&A Picture Library; p. 167 © Bettmann/CORBIS; p. 168 © Joan Marcus; p. 170 Culver Pictures, Inc.; p. 171 top Billy Rose Theatre Collection, The New York Public Library for the Performing Arts, Astor, Lenox and Tilden Foundations; p. 171 bottom Eileen Darby/Billy Rose Theatre Collection, The New York Public Library for the Performing Arts, Astor, Lenox and Tilden Foundations; p. 172 bottom © Bruce Bennett; p. 173 © Richard Feldman; p. 175 Martha Swope/TimePix; p. 176 George E. Joseph; p. 177 top Anthony Crickmay/V&A Picture Library; p. 177 bottom George E. Joseph; p. 178 left © Michal Daniel; p. 178 right © Michal Daniel; p. 179 © Michal Daniel; p. 181 Ruth Walz; p. 182 left © Bettmann/CORBIS; p. 182 right © Richard Feldman; p. 183 Courtesy Vikki Benner/Perseverance Theatre; p. 184 Courtesy Brigitte Lacombe /Billy Rose Theatre Collection, The New York Public Library for the Performing Arts, Astor, Lenox and Tilden Foundations; p. 186 © Gerry Goodstein ; p. 188 © Joan Marcus; p. 190 Billy Rose Theatre Collection, The New York Public Library for the Performing Arts, Astor, Lenox and Tilden Foundations; p. 191 George E. Joseph; p. 192 David Garrick as MacBeth/Courtesy Theatre Museum/Victoria and Albert Museum; p. 193 © T. Charles Erickson; p. 194 Billy Rose Theatre Collection, The New York Public Library for the Performing Arts, Astor, Lenox and Tilden Foundations; p. 195 George E. Joseph; p. 196 Courtesy Lee Strasberg Theatre Institute; p. 197 © Vandamm Collection/Billy Rose Theatre Collection, The New York Public Library for the Performing Arts, Astor, Lenox and Tilden Foundations; p. 198 left Jack Mitchell/ Courtesy of Barbara Hogenson Agency; p. 198 right Richard Tucker/ Billy Rose Theatre Collection, The New York Public Library for the Performing Arts, Astor, Lenox and Tilden Foundations; p. 201 © Joan Marcus; p. 202 Brennan Cavanaugh; p. 203 Provided by Cicely Berry/RSC; p. 204 © Barry Slobin/PlayMakers Repertory Company; p. 206 Billy Rose Theatre Collection, The New York Public Library for the Performing Arts, Astor, Lenox and Tilden Foundations; p. 207 Billy Rose Theatre Collection, The New York Public Library for the Performing Arts, Astor, Lenox and Tilden Foundations; p. 208 left William B. Carter; p. 208 right © Joan Marcus; p. 209 left © T. Charles Erickson; p. 209 right © Joan Marcus; p. 210 © The Everett Collection, Inc.; p. 212 © T. Charles Erickson; p. 214 © Barry Slobin/PlayMakers Repertory Company; p. 215 Billy Rose Theatre Collection, The New York Public Library for the Performing Arts, Astor, Lenox and Tilden Foundations; p. 216 Billy Rose Theatre Collection, The New York Public Library for the Performing Arts, Astor, Lenox and Tilden Foundations; p. 217 left Culver Pictures, Inc.; p. 218 left © Elisabetta Catalano; p. 218 right Martha Swope/Time Pix; p. 219 © T. Charles Erickson/Alley Theatre ; p. 222 © T. Charles Erickson/Alley Theatre; p. 224 top left© Richard Feldman; p. 224 right © Richard Feldman; p. 224 bottom © Joan Marcus; p. 225 top Martha Swope/TimePix; p. 225 bottom Martha Swope/TimePix; p. 226 top © Hermann und Clarchen Baus; p. 226 bottom © Hermann und Clarchen Baus; p. 227 top © Richard Feldman; p. 227 middle Martine Franck/Magnum; p. 227 bottom © Michele Laurant/The Liaison Agency; p. 228 Max Waldman Archives; p. 229 left Billy Rose Theatre Collection, The New York Public Library for the Performing Arts, Astor, Lenox and Tilden Foundations; p. 229 right Billy Rose Theatre Collection, The New York Public Library for the Performing Arts, Astor, Lenox and Tilden Foundations; p. 230 Martha Swope/TimePix; p. 232 left © 1984 Newsday, Inc. Reprinted with permission.; p. 232 right Billy Rose Theatre Collection, The New York Public Library for the Performing Arts, Astor, Lenox, and Tilden Foundations; p. 233 top Courtesy of Martha Clarke; p. 233 middle © Gert Weigelt; p. 233 bottom © Gert Weigelt; p. 234 top © Richard Feldman; p. 234 bottom © Jim Caldwell; p. 236 © Richard Feldman; p. 238 Edward Gordon Craig/Courtesy The Victoria & Albert Museum; p. 239 top Billy Rose Theatre Collection, The New York Public Library for the

Performing Arts, Astor, Lenox and Tilden Foundations; p. 239 bottom Billy Rose Theatre Collection, The New York Public Library for the Performing Arts, Astor, Lenox and Tilden Foundations; p. 240 Billy Rose Theatre Collection, The New York Public Library for the Performing Arts, Astor, Lenox and Tilden Foundations; p. 241 top Hsu Ping, Taipei/Courtesy of Ming Cho Lee; p. 241 bottom Courtesy of John Lee Beatty; p. 243 Joan Marcus/Courtesy Arena Stage; p. 244 top Eileen Darby /Billy Rose Theatre Collection, The New York Public Library for the Performing Arts, Astor, Lenox and Tilden Foundations; p. 244 bottom Billy Rose Theatre Collection, The New York Public Library for the Performing Arts, Astor, Lenox and Tilden Foundations; p. 245 top KaiDib Films International; p. 246 top Courtesy KaiDib Films International, Glendale, CA; p. 246 bottom © T. Charles Erickson; p. 247 Billy Rose Theatre Collection, The New York Public Library for the Performing Arts, Astor, Lenox and Tilden Foundations; p. 248 top Courtesy of Constance Zipprodt-Zonka; p. 248 bottom Bruce Goldstein/Courtesy Guthrie Theatre; p. 249 top © Joan Marcus; p. 249 bottom © Joan Marcus; p. 250 top © Joan Marcus; p. 250 bottom © Joan Marcus; p. 251 top Martha Swope/TimePix; p. 251 middle © Joan Marcus; p. 251 bottom © Joan Marcus; p. 252 left Courtesy Theoni V. Aldredge; p. 252 right Martha Swope/TimePix; p. 253 top Courtesy of Jane Greenwood; p. 253 bottom Jayne Wexler/Courtesy of William Ivey Long; p. 254 Courtesy of Judy Adamson; p. 255 © John-Francis Bourke; p. 256 Martha Swope/TimePix; p. 258 top © Michele Laurant/The Liaison Agency; p. 258 bottom Illustration of Pantalone from Jacques Callot's etchings, c. 1622, of comedia actor ; p. 259 top © Joan Marcus ; p. 259 bottom © Martine Franck/Magnum Photos, Inc.; p. 260 left Courtesy Paul Huntley Enterprise; p. 260 right Martha Swope/TimePix; p. 262 © T. Charles Erickson/Hartford Stage ; p. 264 left Courtesy of Jennifer Tipton; p. 264 right George E. Joseph; p. 266 © Richard Feldman; p. 267 Courtesy Bill Clarke Designs; p. 268 Courtesy Will Owens/PlayMakers Repertory Company; p. 269 top © Peter Simon; p. 269 bottom Courtesy of Tharon Musser, Lighting Designer; p. 270 all four images Courtesy of Altman Lighting, Inc.; p. 271 top left Courtesy of High End Systems; p. 271 top right Courtesy of High End Systems; p. 271 bottom left Courtesy of Leviton, NSI - Colortran Division; p. 271 middle right Courtesy of Leviton, NSI - Colortran Division; p. 271 bottom right Courtesy of High End Systems; p. 272 © Joan Marcus; p. 273 © Carol Rosegg; p. 276 left Courtesy Jonathan Deans; p. 276 right Courtesy of Milly S. Barranger; p. 277 © Frank Micelotta/Image Direct; p. 280 top Courtesy of High End Systems; p. 280 middle Courtesy of High End Systems; p. 280 bottom © 2001, Vari-Lite Inc. Photo by Lewis Lee; p. 281 top Courtesy of Clear Com; p. 281 middle Courtesy of Sennheiser Electronic Corporation; p. 281 bottom Courtesy of Sennheiser Electronic Corporation; 286 © T. Charles Erickson; 288 top Courtesy of Milly S. Barranger; 288 bottom Courtesy of Milly S. Barranger; 289 Martha Swope/ TimePix; 290 top © Joan Marcus; 290 middle © Joan Marcus; 290 bottom © Joan Marcus; 291 top © Carol Rosegg ; 291 middle © Peter Cunningham; 291 bottom © Joan Marcus; 292 left Michael Le Poer Trench/Courtesy Cameron Mackintosh, Ltd.; 292 right Martha Swope/ TimePix; 293 Courtesy of Milly S. Barranger; 294 top © Joan Marcus; 294 bottom © Carol Rosegg; 296 NYT Pictures; 297 Courtesy of Milly S. Barranger; 298 Martha Swope/ TimePix; 299 bottom Cristofer Gross/ SCR; 299 top Daryl Roth; 300 © Joan Marcus; 301 © Liz Lauren/ Goodman Theatre (pictured are: Mary Beth Fisher & Ian Lithgow); 304 © T. Charles Erickson; 306 © Eric Y. Exit/ The Goodman Theatre (pictured are Gabriel Byrne & Cherry Jones; 307 Annalisa Kraft/ Courtesy Arena Stage; 308 left Courtesy of Alley Theatre; 308 right © T. Charles Erickson/ Alley Theatre ; 310 San Francisco Chronicle; 314 Martha Swope/ TimePix; 316 left © Elisabetta Catalano; 316 right © Joan Marcus; 317 © Joan Marcus; 318 © Richard Feldman; 319 Martine Franck/Magnum; 320 Martine Franck/Magnum; 321 left Martine Franck/Magnum; 321 right Martine Franck/Magnum; 321 bottom Martha Swope/ TimePix; 322 top © Richard Feldman; 322 middle © Richard Feldman; 322 bottom © Joan Marcus; 323 top San Francisco Chronicle; 323 bottom © Joan Marcus; 324 top Photo by Ivan Kyncl/ Courtesy of Eric Bogosian; 324 middle © 1997 Susan Johann; 324 bottom © Timothy Greenfield-Sanders; 325 top Photo by Eugenio Castro/ LA POCHA NOSTRA; 325 middle Kelly Campbell/ Courtesy of Holly Hughes; 325 bottom The Everett Collection; 326 San Francisco Chronicle; 327 San Francisco Chronicle; 328 top San Francisco Chronicle; 328 bottom © Michal Daniel; 330 Maurice Meredith/ Courtesy of St. Louis Black Repertory Company; Scene: The Ladies who sing with the band. J. Samuel Davis, (actors equity - as Ken) and Eddie Webb, (Andre); 331 top © Lia Chang; 331 bottom Photo by Michael Lamont/ East West Players production of GOLDEN CHILD by David Henry Hwang 1/26-2/20, 2000. Left to Right: Kerri Higuchi*, Connie Kim, Annette Lee, Amy Hill*, Daniel Dae Kim*, Melody Butiu*, Ming Lo, Emily Kuroda* * Members of Actors Equity Association; 333 Courtesy El Teatro Campesino; 334 top Margarita Galban/ Courtesy Bilingual Foundation of the Arts; 334 bottom Martha Swope Associates/ William Gibson; 336 © 2001 Susan Johann; 338 Craig Schwartz Photography © 2000; 340 George E. Joseph; 341 © Peter Cunningham; 342 Courtesy PlayMakers Repertory Company; 343 © Joan Marcus; 345 © T. Charles Erickson; 346 © Ken Friedman/ American Conservatory Theatre; 347 © Jasper Johns/Licensed by VAGA, New York, NY; 349 Patrick Bennett/ Courtesy Seattle Repertory Theatre; 350 left © CORBIS; 350 right Courtesy The Chicago Tribune; 351 top Courtesy of The New York Times Company; 351 middle Courtesy of The New York Times Company; 351 bottom Photo by Bill Aller, The New York Times; 352 Courtesy of Milly S. Barranger; 353 top Eileen Darby/Billy Rose Theatre Collection, The New York Public Library for the Performing Arts, Astor, Lenox and Tilden Foundations; 353 bottom Martha Swope/ TimePix; 354 top © Joan Marcus; 354 bottom © Joan Marcus; 355 © Eric Y. Exit/The Goodman Theatre; 356 © Irene Haupt; 361 AP/ Wide World Photos; 362 © Sara Krulwich/ NYT Pictures

INDEX

Melodrama
    definition of, 109
    as mixed form, 109
    view of life in, 109
Merritt, Theresa, in *Ma Rainey's Black
        Bottom*, 87
Metaphor, conventions of, 167–173
Method, of Stanislavski, 194–197
Meyerhold, Vsevolod, 56
    in *The Three Sisters*, 107
Microphones, 274, 281
A Midsummer Night's Dream
    (Shakespeare), Brook's
    adaptation of, 21, 222–223, 228
Mielziner, Jo, 239
    Death of a Salesman designed
        by, 244
    selective realism of, 229, 244
    A Streetcar Named Desire designed
        by, 158, 244
    Sweet Bird of Youth designed by, 85
Miguel, Gloria, 335
Miguel, Muriel, 335
Miller, Arthur
    All My Sons, 90
    biography of, 90
    Death of a Salesman, 22, 244,
        268, 342
    A View from the Bridge, 90
Millman, Howard J., 302
Milwaukee Repertory Theatre
    (Milwaukee, WI), 303
Mimesis, 130
Mimical behavior, 191
Ming Dynasty, drama during, 40–41
Mirror, stage as, 7–13
Missouri Repertory Theatre (Kansas
    City, MO), 303
Miss Saigon (musical), casting for, 294
Mitchell, Brian, in *Kiss of the Spider
    Woman*, 91

Mnouchkine, Ariane
    alternative spaces of, 55
    biography of, 64–65
    Drums on the Dike staged by, 47
    Les Atrides produced by, 258,
        318–320, 321
    Richard II directed by, 46, 227
    Thèâtre du Soleil, 63–65
    transculturalism in works of,
        318–320
Model, of scene design, 243
*The Modern Theatre Is the Epic
    Theatre* (Brecht), 120
Molière
    biography of, 104–105
    Don Juan, 248
    Tartuffe, 5, 103, 104, 105
Monodrama, 145–149
Monster in a Box (Gray), 143
    excerpt from, 143
Montresor, Beni, *The Three Sisters*
    designed by, 182
Morey, Charles, 303
Morse, David, in *How I Learned to
    Drive*, 91
Morton, Carlos, 93
Morton, Jelly Roll, *Jelly's Last Jam*
    music by, 289
Moscow Art Theatre (Russia), 217
Moses, Gilbert, 329
Mosher, Gregory
    Glengarry Glen Ross directed
        by, 184
    Speed the Plow directed by, 85
Moss, Bob, 303
Mother Courage and Her Children
    (Brecht), 245
Movable stages, in medieval theatre,
    32–33
Movement coaches, 219
Movement training, 200–201

Much Ado About Nothing
    (Shakespeare), film of, 13
Müller, Heiner
    the CIVIL warS, 150
    Hamletmachine, 150
Multiculturalism, 312
Music, in theatre, purposes of, 274
Music and Stage Setting (Appia), 238,
    239, 265
Music videos, 4
Musicals
    about black experience, 92–93
    Broadway, 290–291
Musser, Tharon
    biography of, 269
    The Secret Garden lighting by, 249
The Myth of Sisyphus (Camus), 122

N

Nagaswaram, 313
Napier, John
    Sunset Boulevard designed by, 249
    The Trojan Women designed
        by, 162
Narrative plays, 118–119
Nathan, George Jean
    biography of, 350
    on criticism, 352
National touring companies, 298
Native American theatre companies,
    334–335
Native American Theatre
    Ensemble, 335
Naturalism, 150
Neals, Lawrence, Jr., in *Juan Darién*,
    322
Negro Ensemble Company (NEC)
    (New York City), 329

406   Index

Your Guide to the "Seeing Place"

The Greeks called it a theatron—or "seeing place." It is in that special place where, for a brief time, actors and audiences are engaged together in the remarkable experience of theatre.

In *Theatre: A Way of Seeing*, Fifth Edition, Milly S. Barranger introduces you to the "seeing place." You'll experience theatre as a multifaceted, living art. With clarity and enthusiasm, Barranger guides you through all aspects of theatre—from the individuals who contribute to this collective performing art to the plays that have shaped its history. Through the book's vivid design and insightful narrative, you'll become immersed in the passion, wisdom, and excitement that the theatre brings to participants and audiences alike.

Available from Wadsworth to accompany *Theatre: A Way of Seeing*, Fifth Edition

Theatregoer's Guide

This brief introduction to attending and critiquing drama enhances the first-time theatregoer's experience and appreciation of theatre as a living art. 0-534-51495-2

FREE with every new copy of this text! InfoTrac® College Edition

An online library at your fingertips! Turn to InfoTrac College Edition for the latest news and research articles online—updated daily and spanning four years. *Theatre: A Way of Seeing* includes four months of FREE access to InfoTrac College Edition's easy-to-use, online database of reliable, full-length articles (not abstracts) from hundreds of top academic journals and popular sources. Among the journals available 24 hours a day, seven days a week are *American Theatre*, *Arts Education Policy Review*, *New York Times Upfront*, *Variety*, and *Performing Arts and Entertainment in Canada*.

Available only to North American college and university students. Journals subject to change.

Communication Café: Wadsworth Communication Resource Center

http://communication.wadsworth.com

Expand your learning opportunities to the Web with Wadsworth's Communication Café. The resource center includes timely news, interactive activities in communications, discussion forums, links, and more. Plus, every chapter of *Theatre: A Way of Seeing* includes Web sites for research and entertainment.

The Wadsworth Group is the publisher of the following imprints:
Brooks/Cole, Duxbury, Heinle & Heinle, Schirmer, Wadsworth, and West.

WADSWORTH

THOMSON LEARNING

Visit Wadsworth online
www.wadsworth.com

For your lifelong learning
www.thomsonlearning.